D0709570

Elizabeth Palmer Peabody

Elizabeth Palmer Peabody

A REFORMER ON HER OWN TERMS

BRUCE A. RONDA

HARVARD UNIVERSITY PRESS

Cambridge, Massachusetts
London, England   1999

Copyright © 1999 by the President and Fellows of Harvard College
All rights reserved
Printed in the United States of America

Library of Congress Cataloging-in-Publication Data
Ronda, Bruce A.
Elizabeth Palmer Peabody: A Reformer On Her Own Terms /
Bruce A. Ronda.
p.   cm.
Includes bibliographical references (p.   ) and index.
ISBN 0-674-24695-0 (cloth: alk. paper)
1. Peabody, Elizabeth Palmer, 1804–1894.
2. Women educators—Massachusetts—Biography.
3. Women reformers—Massachusetts—Biography.
4. Women intellectuals—Massachusetts—Biography.
5. United States—Intellectual life—1783–1865.
6. Massachusetts—Biography. I. Title.
CT275.P484R66   1999
974.4'03'092
[b]—DC21   98-33902

For Chris

Preface

CREATIVE WORK OF ANY KIND goes on in the midst of a paradox, the solitude of thought and expression coexisting with the community of fellow workers, audience, and well-wishers. I have shared joyfully in both sides of that paradox, in the long hours of library research and silent writing, and in the vigorous conversation with many who share my fascination with nineteenth-century America and with the lure of biography.

I want to acknowledge here those whose ideas, insights, friendship, efforts, and hospitality made this study possible.

This is the first full-length scholarly and interpretive biography of Elizabeth Peabody. It is not by any means the first writing on Peabody, nor the first biographical study. Louise Hall Tharp's *The Peabody Sisters of Salem*, which preceded this book by nearly fifty years, served to link reminiscences of Peabody and her circle from the late nineteenth and early twentieth centuries with the more interpretive works of our own time. Because Tharp's book lacks scholarly apparatus and appears in some places to substitute invention for documentation, I have not made use of it here, although I do want to acknowledge her work. Other writers from midcentury whose work I did rely on include Ruth Baylor, whose *Elizabeth Peabody, Kindergarten Pioneer* is reliable and informative, and John Wilson, whose essays in the *Historian* and *The New England Quarterly* helped to pique my interest in Peabody back in the early 1970s.[1]

The side of the paradox mentioned before that deals with a writer's indebtedness to communities of readers and writers is amply evident for those who deal with the "American Renaissance." Try as we might to find a new angle of vision or body of material, we are always aware of the "cloud of witnesses" whose work has preceded ours. Although some might suffer from an anxiety of influence about such an overcrowded field, I choose to express not anxiety but gratitude for those whose writing has so shaped mine.

Every age thinks of itself as transitional, and so it is, and so was mine. I was a graduate student in the Yale University American Studies Program in the early 1970s, and among my mentors there were some of the dominant figures of the postwar American studies movement: R. W. B. Lewis, Charles Feidelson, Sydney Ahlstrom, Alan Trachtenberg, Kai Erikson, among others. These men (and at that point they were all men) practiced forms of interdisciplinary scholarship, looking for the interplay of ideas and culture, personal life and social context. My work on Elizabeth Peabody began under the tutelage of R. W. B. Lewis, who encouraged me to include her in my dissertation study of Transcendentalist understandings of the child and who prompted me to work on an edition of her letters as my first project after graduate school.

Much has changed since the early 1970s. The focus in literary scholarship has shifted to works by previously marginalized or unrepresented writers. Some scholarship is heavily indebted to various theoretical stances that challenge assumptions about universals like national character or regional identities. Occasionally the scholarship of the 1980s and 1990s asserted its identity through the familiar move of belittling the works of its predecessors. From another perspective, however, all scholarship builds on and reinterprets earlier work, challenging some claims, enlarging others.

Two works have been most influential in my efforts to understand the career of Elizabeth Peabody. They are Perry Miller's introduction to his 1950 anthology, *The Transcendentalists*, and Anne C. Rose's *Transcendentalism as a Social Movement*, published in 1981. Miller assembled a brilliant collection of documents from a wide variety of sources to substantiate a "myth" of the Transcendentalists. For him, the writers and reformers of the second quarter of the nineteenth century constituted a generational revolt against the stodgy conformism of their Unitarian parents. Miller's Transcendentalists were religious revolutionaries, championing individual intuition and the primacy of feeling.[2]

More than thirty years later, Anne Rose sought to challenge and complicate Miller's myth. For her, the line between Unitarians and Transcendentalists was much less distinct and the generational boundaries less obvious. Even more, Rose argued that the Transcendentalist movement had a powerful social component and was not only, as Miller seemed to suggest, an epoch in intellectual history. Transcendentalists sought to embody their insights about human nature and social life in reformed institutions, including schools, communities, churches, and the family itself.[3]

My early interest in Elizabeth Peabody resulted in a dissertation, some journal articles, and a one-volume edition of her letters that was published in 1984. That book was the first effort to collect and annotate in book form any of Peabody's unpublished writing. As students of the New England Renaissance know, the Peabody manuscripts are staggering in number and often confusing in their dating and handwriting. As an early effort, *Letters of Elizabeth Palmer Peabody, American Renaissance Woman* made available a number of her important letters, but it also left out many others, equally valuable, and contains some errors of date and attribution. Careful readers of this volume will see here my efforts at correction. By 1984, nearly ten years after I had first heard of her, I was thoroughly sick of Peabody and had moved on to other subjects and other issues in my life.

In 1990 I served as faculty for an NEH-sponsored "New England Renaissance Institute" for Colorado high school and junior high school teachers, offering them a seminar on New England cultural history at Colorado State University, followed by on-site visits to important locations in Massachusetts. This highly successful program, repeated in 1992 and 1994, was directed by my CSU English Department colleague Ed Schamberger and Poudre School District curriculum specialist Carol Anne Hixon. Accompanying the groups out to New England, I was startled to realize that the *Letters* volume had created for me a modest reputation among scholars and curators, who encouraged me, as did the Institute leaders and participants, to write Peabody's biography.

As I worked on this biography, I renewed old acquaintances and made new friends in and outside of academia. I want to name some to

whom I am particularly indebted: Joel Myerson, Margaret Neussendor-
fer, Nina Baym, David Van Leer, Philip Gura, Phyllis Cole, Jayne Gor-
don, William Wheeler III, and Robert Richardson. I owe an immense
debt of thanks to librarians and staff at many institutions: Nina Myatt at
Olive Kettering Library of Antioch College; Marcia Moss and Leslie
Perrin Wilson of the Concord Free Public Library; and the staffs at
Massachusetts Historical Society, American Antiquarian Society, Smith
College, the Henry W. and Albert A. Berg Collection of the New
York Public Library, the Boston Public Library, the Houghton Library
of Harvard University, and the Schlesinger Library at Radcliffe Col-
lege.

Unpublished manuscript material is herein quoted by permission of
the American Antiquarian Society; Royall Tyler Collection, Gift of
Helen Tyler Brown, Vermont Historical Society; the Peabody Essex
Museum; Sophia Smith Collection, Smith College Library; Henry W.
and Albert A. Berg Collection, the New York Public Library, Astor,
Lenox and Tilden Foundations; Duyckinck Family Papers, Manu-
scripts and Archives Division, the New York Public Library, Astor,
Lenox and Tilden Foundations; Bryant-Godwin Papers, Manuscripts
and Archives Division, the New York Public Library, Astor, Lenox and
Tilden Foundations; The Historical Society of Pennsylvania; Massa-
chusetts Historical Society; Dr. Leslie Perrin Wilson, Concord Free
Public Library; Missouri Historical Society; The Bancroft Library,
University of California, Berkeley; Yale University Library; Robert
Straker Collection, Antiochiana, Olive Kettering Library, Antioch Col-
lege; The Library of Congress; Schlesinger Library, Radcliffe College;
Allyn Kellogg Ford Collection of Historical Manuscripts, Minnesota
History Society; Houghton Library, Harvard University; Wesleyan
University Press; University of Notre Dame Archives; and by courtesy
of the Trustees of the Boston Public Library.

Citations for Massachusetts Historical Society and Antioch College
deserve special notes. At the former is deposited a set of typescripts in
the Ruth M. Baylor Collection, copies of notes assembled by Nathaniel
Cranch Peabody on his family history. This material provides rich anecdotes for the early history of the Palmer and Peabody families, but
the whereabouts of the originals of these typescripts is unknown. Readers may want to treat the conclusions based on this resource as speculative. The Robert Straker Collection at Antioch College is a treasure of

material for research on the Peabody and Mann families, but is also somewhat problematic. Some of the letters in the many black binders in the Antiochiana Collection are backed up by originals in the Olive Kettering Library; I have noted those as "Antioch" in my notes. Others, however, are typescripts of letters not held at the library, and they are noted as "ts copy." Most of these typescripts bear annotations that indicate the deposit of the originals at the Massachusetts Historical Society or, in a few cases, at the Houghton Library of Harvard University. In most cases, however, those libraries do not have these originals, and so we are left with plausible but unverifiable typescripts.

~ MANY THANKS go to assistants Kathleen Dery and Maxine Garcia, to the Colorado State University American Studies Reading Group for comments on early drafts, and to CSU colleagues Ruth Alexander, Pattie Cowell, and Rosemary Whitaker for their insights and encouragement. Other venues for presentation of my thoughts on Peabody included a presentation at "Art and Education in the Nineteenth Century: Romantic Theory, Romantic Practice," a conference sponsored by the Concord Museum in July 1993; a CSU English Department colloquium on literary biography in October 1996; a panel on feminist biography at the American Studies Association Annual Meeting in November 1996; and an Emerson Society panel on Transcendentalist women and biography in July 1997. Some of this material was also presented informally to classes conducted by Martin Bickman and Mary Ann Shea at the University of Colorado, Boulder, for whose support I am most grateful. Thanks also to Frances and David Hawkins, ardent teachers of the young for many decades, for their interest in Elizabeth Peabody.

I owe a debt of thanks to the editorial staff of Harvard University Press. Aida Donald has shown unwavering support of this project, as has Elizabeth Suttell. Carolyn Ingalls copyedited the manuscript with care and forethought, improving its style and clarity with each question and correction.

None of these friends, colleagues, and contributors can save a book from its inevitable errors and oversights, for which I assume responsibility.

This work was supported by a National Endowment for the Humanities Fellowship for College Teachers and Independent Scholars in

1993–94 and by several CSU College of Liberal Arts Professional Development Fund grants. I am grateful to Dean Loren Crabtree and Associate Deans Robert Hoffert and Robert Keller for their support.

My thanks also to Henry and Phyllis Nelson for the use of their cottage on Lake Michigan, and my acknowledgments to the patience of many friends who had to endure the endlessly repeated news updates on the biography in annual Christmas letters.

I owe an outstanding debt of gratitude and love to my daughter Meg, who grew up with this and the previous book, and whose love of literature is moving and inspiring. My largest debt is recorded elsewhere.

Contents

Illustrations follow p. 142

Elizabeth Palmer Peabody

Introduction

و

In 1839 Margaret Fuller moved to Boston and prepared to offer the first of her Conversations. Living near her in the Jamaica Plain neighborhood was Theodore Parker, who found her a prodigous reader and critic but "not a good analyst, not a philosopher." In contrast, Parker thought Elizabeth Palmer Peabody, at whose bookshop Fuller's Conversations would convene, was "a woman of most astonishing powers; has a many-sidedness and a largeness of soul quite unusual; rare qualities of head and heart. I never before knew just with what class to place her; now I see she is a Boswell. Her office is to inquire and answer, 'What did they say?' 'What are the facts?' A good analyst of character, a free spirit, kind, generous, noble. She has an artistic gift also. She may well be called the 'narrative Miss Peabody.'"[1]

Despite Parker's high praise for Peabody, it has been Margaret Fuller's destiny to receive the greater critical and biographical attention. Fuller's brilliant Conversations, her feminist challenge to assumptions about gender and social institutions, her career as critic and journalist, the dramatic end to her Italian adventure—all these have fascinated readers and commentators since her death in 1850. In contrast, Peabody appears in a variety of supporting and secondary roles in New England reform and literary culture throughout much of the nineteenth century. Many of her contemporaries, like Parker, found her learned and perceptive, and respected her grasp of history and languages. But even her greatest admirers could not help mixing praise

1

with amusement and condescension. Ralph Waldo Emerson described her as possessing "a wonderful literary head, with extraordinary rapidity of association, and a methodising faculty which enabled her to weave surprising theories very fast & very finely, from slight materials. Of another sex, she would have been a first-rate academician; and, as it was, she had the ease & scope & authority of a learned professor or high literary celebrity in her talk. I told her I thought she ought to live a thousand years, her schemes of study & the necessities of reading which her inquiries implied, required so much." In this same passage, Emerson observed that Peabody was "superior, & really amiable, but took no pains to make herself personally agreeable, & was not neat—& offended."[2]

Comments like this multiplied as Peabody grew older. She seemed to generate respect and anecdotes in equal measure. Her absent-mindedness prompted several versions of her bruising encounter with a tree limb on Boston Common, which she professed to "see, but not realize." Her increasing girth caused concern on the part of her sisters as well as a famous anecdote from her nephew Julian Hawthorne, who reported that his aunt once sat down in a comfortable chair without looking first, and only after observing the persistent crying and pawing of a mother cat did Aunt Lizzie realize that she had sat on a family of kittens, suffocating them all. Perhaps the most famous set of anecdotes sprang from the James family, at whose dinner table its members once ridiculed Elizabeth Peabody's disjointed and careless appearance. Henry James denied caricaturing Peabody in the portrayal of Miss Birdseye in his 1886 novel *The Bostonians*. But it is is hard to miss the remarkable similarities in all but relative body size between the scattered, garrulous, good-natured, eternally optimistic fictional Miss Birdseye and the real-life Miss Peabody.

Peabody has thus descended to the modern reader through a haze of stories by which her contemporaries sought to comprehend and categorize her as the fuzzy do-gooder, the bluestockinged busybody. In our own time, which has generated an ocean of scholarship about New England literary and reformist culture, Peabody has been treated more respectfully, as a source of information and insight about the many others whose lives she intersected and informed—Emerson, Fuller, William Ellery Channing, Bronson Alcott, Jones Very, Horace Mann, Nathaniel Hawthorne. Even so, the focus of attention has been away from Peabody and toward the other already brightly lit figures about whom she had so much to say. Peabody herself has received only two biographical treatments, one a highly fictionalized volume published in 1950, the other a reliable text that narrowly studies her involvement in the kindergarten movement.[3]

It is just our lack of familiarity and our unfocused and derivative understanding of her, filtered through her contemporaries' amusement and our current preoccupations, that make a biography of Elizabeth Peabody so needed. She was, after all, a woman of extraordinary achievements: she was teacher, editor, publisher, translator, historian, bookseller, correspondent, essayist; and was gifted in linguistics, literature, history, theology, philosophy, geography. Julian Hawthorne thought that his aunt daily spoke Greek, Latin, Hebrew, and Sanskrit—doubtless an exaggeration, but reflecting Peabody's reading knowledge of ten languages.[4] Best known as the champion of the kindergarten in the 1870s, Peabody had by that time taught in several of her own private schools and had assisted in Bronson Alcott's Temple School in the 1830s, had opened a remarkable book store in Boston, had published the *Dial* and many other titles under her own imprint, had championed textbook reform in history education, and had advocated for anti-slavery, European liberal revolutions, and Spiritualism. Still ahead of her were nearly two decades of memoir and reminiscence as well as a final burst of social activism on behalf of the Paiute Indians and their spokeswoman, Sarah Winnemucca. And this list does not touch on her many essays, translations, and editions, nor on her tangled personal relationships with her sisters Mary and Sophia and their husbands Horace Mann and Nathaniel Hawthorne.

We can enumerate to exhaustion Elizabeth Peabody's accomplishments and still fail to grasp the significance of her life. What has made Peabody so invisible or so easily caricatured was the way her life and career blended avant-garde ideas and conventional beliefs, her ability to mediate between advanced thinking and cultural commonplaces. Teaching, writing, bookselling, publishing, social reform—in all these activities and more, Peabody created texts and situations in which, she hoped, a larger public could absorb insights from a smaller group of thinkers. This is not to say that she was without original thoughts or distinctive contributions. She certainly made important contributions in defense of Brook Farm and built unique institutions in the West

Street Bookshop and the kindergarten movement. But much as recent work in reader-response literary theory reminds us that texts require the active involvement of readers to come most fully alive, so ideas about human will and intuition, history, education, and social change achieve larger effectiveness as they pass out of the realm of theory into the space of action.[5]

For all her reputation as a fuzzy thinker and an impractical activist, Elizabeth Peabody is best understood, I think, as a practical intellectual. She was fascinated with theory, particularly notions of cosmic connectedness and human unity. But her speculative essays, like "Primeval Man," are often murky and unconvincing. In striking contrast are her essays on reforms like Brook Farm or kindergartens, and on the particular schools and other institutions she designed or conducted. To claim that Peabody was secondary in the ranks of New England and American intellectuals because she was not an original thinker misses the point: at her best, Peabody's life of action and her times of reflection were mutually reinforcing, and they are an example of what Aristotle and many other theorists call praxis. "For Aristotle," Thomas Groome has written, "*praxis* means a purposeful and reflective action by which knowing arises through engagement in a social situation." In a praxis way of knowing, knowledge does not arise from detached speculation but from reflective engagement, in which thought and action are not separated. In the twentieth century, the Brazilian educator Paulo Freire would devote his life to education as liberating praxis; in a sense he followed in the steps of Elizabeth Peabody, for the act of teaching necessarily requires some reflection on the theory and implications of teaching, which in turn informs the daily classroom work.[6] In many other ways as well, Peabody needs to be understood as a practical intellectual, reviewing and interpreting the work of Emerson, championing (and critiquing) the pedagogy of Alcott, making texts available in her bookshop and lending library, trying in practical ways to improve the lives of marginalized groups whose causes she advocated. As synthesist and mediator, Peabody sometimes misunderstood the ideas of others; sometimes missed causes that would later assume monumental importance, like the antebellum women's movement; and sometimes proposed means that were cumbersome or impossible, like her efforts on behalf of Josef Bem's chronological charts to teach world history. Even her failures or missteps illlustrate her continual effort to work out, in the modernizing, market-driven United States, the practical implications of the ideas and causes to which she was committed.

Seeing Elizabeth Peabody as a practitioner of praxis in her long career as educator and reformer goes some distance toward rescuing her from the prisonhouse of anecdotes. But there is a danger in overtheorizing Peabody, in making her appear too contemporary, too familiar. A deeper understanding of this complex woman requires some awareness of the intellectual and social world, now lost or substantially altered, in which she matured. Several of the early chapters in this biography describe that world, and here I suggest some of the themes pursued later.

When Elizabeth Peabody was born in 1804, Americans had begun to reshape their new nation from a collection of isolated, tradition-bound localities into an interconnected society where innovation and ingenuity rather than custom prevailed. This process of modernization, the dimensions of which were only beginning to emerge in the early nineteenth century, had its parallel in religious belief and practice. Since the mid-eighteenth century, groups of "liberal Christians," as they liked to be called, in British North America, as in England, had been challenging the Calvinist interpretation of Christian belief, using the tools of modern science and the power of human reason as their weapons. In effect, as Sydney Ahlstrom and Jonathan Carey point out, the liberals were trying to accommodate Renaissance and Enlightenment rationalism with Biblical Christianity, to find some reconciliation between the Hebrew and the Hellenic.[7]

By the early nineteenth century in New England, where liberal thought had gained the most adherents, battle lines had been drawn between those who insisted on Calvinist orthodoxy and those for whom the beliefs in a triune God of wrath and judgment and an inherently sinful humanity were gloomy and superstitious. For these Christians, as they felt they still were, God was to be understood as a loving Parent, revealed both through scriptural revelation and by the powers of human reason, creator of an orderly universe and a humanity who can aspire to perfection through the development of its faculties and powers.

Like her mother, Elizabeth Peabody wholeheartedly embraced the liberal perspective, which would eventually be called Unitarian, accepting its pivotal interpretations of the Christian faith. She deeply believed in an orderly world, learning that God is revealed in the intricacy of the natural world from such books as William Paley's *Natural Theology* and *Evidences of Christianity*, which she probably read in the early 1820s. Interested as they were in the law-filled natural world, Unitarians were just as interested in describing and nurturing the orderly self. Profoundly influenced by Scots moral philosophers like Thomas Reid, Adam Ferguson, and Dugald Stewart, American liberals adopted a "faculty psychology" understanding of the human constitution. In this view, the powers of the human being are arranged in a hierarchy, with the moral sense at the top and mechanical, nonrational drives at the bottom. Education consisted in balancing the faculties, allowing each its place, and permitting the moral sense to grow and govern the whole.

Although Peabody does not mention the faculties anywhere in her personal or published writing, it is clear that she understood this philosophy. In the 1820s she was horrified by the religious revivalism that she witnessed in rural Maine and told William Ellery Channing that "people were united to the church in trances of excitement that seemed to me to reduce men from rational free agents . . . to mere victims of nervous passion."[8] Even though she would encounter situations where passion, not reason, ruled, Peabody never abandoned her early conviction that all life is inherently patterned and organized.

In the 1830s and 1840s, Peabody's belief in cosmic connectedness gained a more Romantic edge. Her mentor Channing had taught her that one's own experience, rightly understood, might be a guide to divine truths and universal patterns, although Channing would never elevate the authority of intuition above the authority of reason, as Emerson sometimes did. Still, Peabody was attracted to the new view, which proposed that the universe is a vast sign system interpreted not just through rationality but through Reason, Coleridge's term for intuition. In that spirit she counseled a grieving Horace Mann to find within himself the divine gift of consolation for the loss of his first wife, Charlotte; in that mood she agreed with Bronson Alcott that children already possess the spark of imaginative insight that requires only the sensitive "leading out" of inspired educators; and in that sense she might have agreed with Thoreau's *Walden* that life is best understood as a vast throbbing organism, moving and growing according to its own internal principles.

To describe the universe not as dichotomous or separated or alienated, but as interconnected, Emerson preferred the word *correspondence*. The belief that the natural world, the social order, the spiritual realm, and the mental frame, are all linked through vast and intricate analogies is an ancient idea, dating back to Egyptian and Babylonian civilizations. Emerson most likely learned about this belief's most articulate modern advocate, the eighteenth-century Swedish theologian Emmanual Swedenborg, from J. J. Garth Wilkinson's English translation of Swedenborg's *Economy of the Animal Kingdom* and from Sampson Reed's *The Growth of the Mind*. Swedenborg imagined a system in which spiritual and material realities were linked in fixed and static analogies, but Emerson grasped the doctrine of correspondence as a way to spiritualize nature, to heal the separation between subject and object. As Sherman Paul puts it, "correspondence focused the age's discontent . . . the problem of a language of correspondence connecting the material image and the moral sentiment returned once more to the mystery of the Reason and the Imagination."[9]

Through her exposure to Emerson and other members of the Transcendentalist circle, the doctrine of correspondence entered deeply into the iron of Elizabeth Peabody's soul. It was a dominant theme in her one-volume 1849 journal *Aesthetic Papers*, which contained an essay on "Genius" by Sampson Reed and another on "Correspondence" by Garth Wilkinson. In the 1840s as well, she championed the work of Charles Kraitsir, a philosopher of language who argued that all language is rooted in the same physical sounds produced in reaction to stimulus or emotion, suggesting the essential oneness of humanity.

Emerson believed, as Catherine Albanese has pointed out, that one perceives the correspondence of all life through intuition rather than through rationality.[10] Peabody, ever the practical intellectual, believed that education was key to proper vision. From her first school at age sixteen to her septagenarian championing of the kindergarten, education was her great calling and her grand passion. Much of that calling had to do with the enormous influence of her mother, also named Elizabeth Palmer Peabody. Raised in the refined New England home of her paternal grandparents, Eliza Palmer read Shakespeare in her grandfather's study and wrote poetry as a young adult. Her intellectual gifts were at odds with her work as a domestic in the home of the Reverend Stephen Peabody, who was principal of a boys' academy in Atkinson, New Hampshire. It was there that Eliza met Nathaniel Peabody, who was distantly related to the Atkinson Peabodys and a tutor in the academy, and together they went to North Andover, Massachusetts, to become tutors at an academy there. Thus the subject of this volume could say with justification and pride that she was "pre-natally educated for the profession which has been the passionate pursuit of my life."[11]

For Elizabeth Peabody, education was there at the beginning, "pre-natally," and there near the end, as she labored in her eighties to support Sarah Winnemucca's Peabody Indian School in Nevada. It was, directly or indirectly, the center of all her intellectual work and the centerpiece of her reform activities. Education, she believed, brought together self and society, history and the future, into one activity. Education has to do with the intimate nurture of selves, and she practiced such nurture intensively in the 1820s and 1830s. To each of her pupils at her private school in Brookline in the late 1820s, Peabody gave letters describing their character traits and flaws, with tips about personal improvement. At Temple School in the 1830s, she dissented from Bronson Alcott's insistence that students read aloud from their journals, arguing that "the instinctive delicacy with which children veil their deepest thoughts of love and tenderness for relatives, and their reasonable self-gradulations, should not be violated."[12]

On the other hand, education is a social practice. It mostly occurs in the midst of others; it puts students in touch with nature and with the past, worlds beyond their immediate knowledge; it disciplines and structures their interior knowledge. Education is the great mediating activity of life, negotiating the competing claims of self and other. So it is not surprising that Elizabeth Peabody, always the great synthesist and mediator, should be drawn to education as her lifelong career. Nor is it surprising that one of her last great reforms should be to champion the kindergarten. Preschool children were precisely at that decisive moment of balance between the richly imaginative inner life and the richly sensory and relational outward life. Peabody brilliantly wove together her own long experience with the schemes of German reformer Friedrich Froebel to create a system that continues to focus attention not on mastering subject matter but on experiencing through play the shapes and forms of the material and social world.

If the kindergarten was her great synthesis, then training in history was for Elizabeth Peabody the key to understanding the correspondential cosmos. Her earliest school, in 1820, concentrated on history and biography. "I taught history as a chief study," she recalled in 1882, "the History of the United States,—not in text-books, but Miss Hannah Adams's History of New England, and Rollins's Ancient History, and Plutarch's Lives."[13] Nearly every decade from the 1820s on revealed Peabody's historical bent—her courses and textbooks on Hebrew and Greek history, her classes on European and American history. Linked both to Cotton Mather's *Magnalia Christi Americana* in the early eighteenth century and to George Bancroft's *History of the United States* in the nineteenth, Peabody saw history as the linear unfolding of a unified though complex divine intention. One reads the past as a vast code, God's language of chronology. Emerson saw evidence of correspondence in nature, read perceptively through the power of intuition. Peabody read history as correspondence, understood both through powers of intellect and through the eyes of faith.

Peabody's insistence on the importance of history and social life suggests her nuanced relationship with the Transcendentalist movement. Some historians have proposed recently that Peabody was a "Romantic Channingite," as Charles Capper puts it, "not a Transcendentalist at all," according to Nina Baym.[14] What constituted Transcendentalism and who belonged to its circle have been vexed questions at least since Octavius Brooks Frothingham's early effort to define the movement, *Transcendentalism in New England*, published in 1876. Some scholars, like Arthur Ladu and Conrad Wright, agree with Frothingham that the core of Transcendentalism was ideological, a distinct philosophy of intuition and individualism. Others, like Anne Rose, have stressed the social aspects of Transcendentalism, the common institutions and causes that linked its adherents.[15]

If we see Transcendentalism as the lengthened shadow of Emerson or Fuller, then figures like Peabody, with her Channing-like belief in self-culture, her insistence on Christian language, and her eternal optimism, do not belong. But several commentators, like William Hutchison and David Robinson, have pointed out the fluid boundaries between Transcendentalism and its parent Unitarianism. Emerson's own early lectures were indebted to his Unitarian roots; important members of the Transcendental Club like Convers Francis and Frederick Henry Hedge were Unitarian clergy.[16] For one-time ministers like George Ripley, founder of Brook Farm, Transcendentalism was the next obvious step toward a humanitarian religion based not on inherited tradition or ritual but on the infinite possibilities of the human spirit. In that sense of a movement of fluid boundaries deeply influenced by its parent cause, figures like Ripley, Hedge, and Francis were, at a point in their careers, Transcendentalists, as was Elizabeth Peabody. As a practical intellectual, she took the debates of the Transcendental Club into larger arenas, into classrooms and conversations, into the pages of the *Dial* and *Aesthetic Papers*, and into textbooks, essays, and lectures. No unquestioning Emersonian, Peabody was more like Orestes Brownson or Theodore Parker in her interest in social issues, and was convinced, with them, that we belong in and to community. She distrusted those who, like Jones Very, set aside social conventions and advocated direct contact with the divine. This insistence on the boundaries set by history and society put her athwart her peers sometimes, as when Emerson cheekily rejected an essay of hers on the Hebrew Prophets that she had submitted for the *Dial*: "Instead of reverently exploring the annals of Egypt Asia & Greece as the cardinal points of the horizon by wh. we must take our departure, go where we will," he wrote her in 1840, "it is too plain that the modern scholar begins with the fact of his own nature & is only willing to hear any result you can bring him from these old dead men by way of illustration or ornament of his own biography."[17] Uncowed by Emerson's rejection, Peabody would continue to synthesize liberal Christian language, intuitional philosophy, and social/historical interests throughout her long career.

The pieces of Peabody's intellectual life—her Unitarian background, her Transcendentalist involvement, her commitment to education and especially to history teaching—are facets of her belief in interconnected unity. This belief likewise contributed to a sometimes crippling social conservatism. To see the world as a harmonious whole may be comforting, even inspiring. But such a view masks disharmonies and inequities in social and economic relations, portraying as natural and organic what is better understood as social and cultural. Sarah Bagley and the members of the Lowell Female Labor Reform Association struggled against just such an organic justification of speedups and wage cuts at the textile mills of Lowell and Lawrence, Massachusetts. Abolitionist, labor, and women's rights advocates likewise resisted organic arguments about the natural orders of superiority and inferiority from owners, bosses, and defenders of the patriarchy.

Peabody's delight in organic and correspondential metaphors blinded her to these conservative applications, and so she was slow to embrace the women's movement, slow to grasp the significance of antislavery, and virtually ignorant of the labor movement. Raised, as so many others were, to see culture and education as women's work, and business and politics as men's province, Peabody early absorbed a "separate spheres" understanding of gendered relations and never quite abandoned it, even while many of her peers in middle-class and working-class cultures challenged or ignored those distinctions.

Undoubtedly Peabody believed in wholeness and oneness. Her sister Sophia had every reason to say this of her: "As I sit and look on these mountains, so grand and flowing and the illimitable aerial blue, beyond and over, I seem to realize with peculiar force that bountiful, fathomless heart of Elizabeth, forever disappointed, but forever believing; sorely rebuffed, yet never bitter; robbed day by day, yet giving again, from endless store; more sweet, more tender, more serene, as the hours pass over her, though they may drop gall instead of flowers upon this un-guarded heart."[18] Yet it does no injustice to her conviction to ask about the connection between conviction and circumstance, to look at the life that embraced such belief. It seems clear that Peabody's family was anything but harmonious and organic. Her great-grandfather Joseph Palmer may have contributed to the invalidism of his much-loved daughter Polly through a thoughtless macho prank; her grandfather Joseph Pearse Palmer abandoned his family; Royall Tyler brutally pur-sued her aunt Mary, so much younger than he, until she agreed to marry him, and he may have seduced Elizabeth's grandmother Eliza-beth Hunt Palmer while her husband Joseph was away on one of his many unsuccessful quests for employment; Elizabeth's father Nathaniel Peabody was a failure in the eyes of his ambitious and impatient wife; and Elizabeth's brothers Wellington, George, and Nat were equally dismal failures at careers and in life.

Peabody's own emotional life was often in disarray. During her stint as tutor for wealthy families in Hallowell, Maine, she had a romantic fling that scarred her more deeply than she wanted to admit. A few years after her return, she found herself in an intensely emotional trian-gle with her sister Mary and Horace Mann; and thirteen years after that, she was in another triangle, this time with her other sister Sophia and Nathaniel Hawthorne. Elizabeth certainly liked men, enjoyed their

company, and counted among her mentors such figures as William
Ellery Channing and Ralph Waldo Emerson. Yet both the example of
weak or predatory men in her own family and the example of her
mother's career brought to an abrupt end by marriage, must have raised
doubts in Elizabeth's mind about actually living with a man. The men
she did have romantic feelings for were either spoken for, and by her
sisters at that, or were, like Channing, inappropriate partners.[19]

As for women, Peabody had intensely emotional attachments with
several, including her pupil Lydia Sears Haven and her sister Mary.
Near the end of Mary's life, Elizabeth described their relationship as a
kind of marriage. What Mary thought of this description, recalling how
she felt that she had to fight off both Elizabeth and the brooding presence of Horace Mann's dead first wife Charlotte to have him as her
husband, we do not know. Whether there was any physical intimacy
in these relationships we also do not know, although it seems highly
doubtful. Peabody was obsessively concerned about propriety throughout her life, and sexual expression outside of heterosexual marriage
would, I think, not have occurred to her.

Indeed, the notion of propriety runs through Peabody's life as a major theme. She often sputtered angrily at her sister Mary, who often
accused her of behaving improperly, that she was indeed the very soul
of discretion and propriety. She was sure that Emerson was a closet
Christian who deliberately edited his essays so as not to give offense to
believers. She worried constantly that parents would remove their students from her classrooms if they felt the pedagogy or subject matter
were too outré, and she rightly intuited the storm that descended on
Bronson Alcott in 1836 and 1837 for exactly those reasons. She tried to
call Caroline Dall, a women's rights author and public speaker, to account for her frank talk about biology. To the end of her life, Peabody
supported the most conventional views of monogamy and sexuality,
agonizing over several pages in a letter to her friend Ellen Conway
about whether or not novelist George Eliot lived with George Henry
Lewes as a "pure chaste woman" or as an "adulteress" in the most
"brutal selfindulgence." Most of all, Peabody understood the limits
society placed on single women, knew she was responsible for her own
survival, knew how far to go and when to trim her sails.[20]

Even though she echoed middle-class culture's understanding of propriety as a mainstay of the social organism, Peabody was nonetheless
continually accused of impropriety and indiscretion, associating with

avant-garde thinkers, and embracing some beliefs that would have been appalling to her more conventional Unitarian associates. Her aunt Catherine Putnam thought she had abandoned Christian truth for a kind of fuzzy religious liberalism. Sister Mary thought she was highly indiscreet, talky, emotional. Both sisters, and particularly Sophia, were outraged by Elizabeth's improper interference in the raising of their children. To all that should be added her association with Alcott, Emerson, Very, Fuller, and Parker. No matter how much she insisted that Transcendentalism was an extension of Unitarianism and no threat to true religion, Peabody ran in a circle in the late 1830s and 1840s that signified atheism and anarchy to many shocked observers.

Out of the rich and contradictory mix of correspondential philosophy and an often fragmented and unharmonious personal life came a seventy-year career as teacher, editor, publisher, and memoirist. While her contemporaries found it easy to categorize or to dismiss Elizabeth Peabody with a clever quip or anecdote, it turns out that anecdote and recollection were among her strongest suits. In his criticism of what seemed like a fatal career mistake in championing the kindergarten, Moncure Conway once argued that Elizabeth Peabody "should spend her last years in writing her recollections of literary men and women. She had a larger circle of friends than any other one person, and she should write of 'The Men and Women I Have Known.'"[21] In a sense, as I explain in Chapter 9, the kindergarten was Peabody's great work, her "Song of Myself," her *Walden*. Still, her choice to throw her energy into the kindergarten and then into the cause of the Paiutes meant she never did organize her papers into the systematic memoirs Conway desired. In 1887 she wrote to Horatio Bridge that she was "writing the Reminiscences of My Contemporaries during my lifetime which I shall have for posthumous publication" based, in part, on "my most secret [papers?] wrapt up with the endorsement—'to be burnt—unread—if I do not burn them myself before I die.'"[22] That volume never appeared. What we do have shows what we miss. Where many of her essays on philosophical topics are prolix and diffuse, her recollections of Channing, Hawthorne, Very, Emerson, and Fuller are sharp, vigorous, and detailed. She was indeed a Boswell, to return to Theodore Parker's observation, and could have been a Johnson or a Gibbon had she not turned her attention so usefully and practically elsewhere. Indeed, the "narrative Miss Peabody" had more stories to tell, and her own life is itself a remarkable story.

Prologue:
Nathaniel Cranch Peabody in the 1870s

ॐ

NATHANIEL CRANCH PEABODY WAS, to put it simply, a failure and the heir of failure. Men in the Palmer family on his mother's side had been failing, abandoning, and disappointing since the 1780s. Gentle and good-natured Joseph Pearse Palmer, Nat's maternal grandfather, lost out in several business ventures after the Revolutionary War, as had *his* father Joseph Palmer; and eventually he abandoned his family. Bearing an equally prestigious family name, Nathaniel Peabody, Nat's father, became a doctor and dentist, but never lived up to his wife's hopes for professional success and often relied on his children for the family's support. And now Nat seemed equally inept in the ways of the world, "destitute of all kinds of get-a-long-ity," according to his sister Elizabeth.[1] Clerk, shopkeeper, schoolteacher, druggist—he wandered from job to job, often seriously in debt. His two younger brothers George and Wellington were also, like Nat, bitter disappointments to their parents and embarrassments to their sisters Elizabeth, Mary, and Sophia. At least these two were spared Nat's years of unhappy work and grinding poverty by dying young.

At last, in the 1870s, Nat Peabody found his calling, if not his career. He would become the family historian. Nat corresponded with Palmer, Cranch, and Peabody relatives in England. He pondered the family tradition that the Peabodys were descendants of the legendary

Boadicea, Queen of the Britons, whose offspring bore the name Pe-Boadie, or Men of the Peak.[2] He assembled genealogies of the Palmers and the Peabodys, and wrote accounts of his own family—his parents, now nearly twenty years dead, his sisters Elizabeth and Mary, still living, and Sophia, who had just died in London. Oddly, nearly all Nat's documents, other than the family trees, have to do with the Palmer line, as if in tacit acknowledgment of his father's failure to achieve the prominence of other Peabodys, like Joseph the Salem merchant prince, or George the financier and philanthropist, all descended from the same Francis Peabody.

The other great gap in his archive concerned his mother and her story. Nat recalled that Mrs. Elizabeth Palmer Peabody, who had died in 1853, was "singularly reticent upon these subjects" of her family's history and of her own early years. She evidently found them too "painful to recall." There were other sources, including his aunts Mary Palmer Tyler and Catherine Palmer Putnam, as well as letters that his mother had written to her grand-aunt Mary Cranch in the 1790s. From these fragments Nat was able to piece together the story of his mother's early years. What he found and reconstructed was an extraordinary tale of the disintegration of a prominent New England family, set against the tumult of the Revolutionary and post-Revolutionary years. In that chaotic setting, Eliza Palmer struggled to find her own identity as a writer and teacher in a family riven by bankruptcy, parental abandonment, and sexual scandal. Given the family history that Nat had unearthed, his mother's silence was understandable. "Only on occasions, far apart, did she speak of General Palmer [her grandfather], her Framingham life (but nothing of its peculiar trials), Mr. [Royall] Tyler, and her mother. Since her death, and from her letters, I have learned nearly all that I know of my mother's early life. There was so much that was sad that it may have been painful to recall it, to which repugnance may be added the abhorrence of vice and crime instilled in her heart, as it were, by her early unwilling knowledge of the natural depravity of man."[3]

Having experienced so much hardship and failure himself and having been so often at odds with his own family, Nat doubtless felt a new sympathy for his mother. Whether he caught a glimpse of his own failure as provider in the accounts of his sensitive but unlucky grandfather Joseph Pearse Palmer or of his silent and sad father is uncertain.

Whatever the reason, Nat never wrote more than biographical sketches of his family and never compiled all his notes into a coherent narrative. He left only pithy, sometimes disturbing and ironic, fragments.

Nat's sister Elizabeth was also much interested in history, but of an utterly different version. She was devoted to universal history, to studying the grand patterns and designs revealed in the histories of ancient Israel and Greece and more recently in the seemingly providential history of the new Republic. The past revealed divinely ordained patterns of growth and change, a cosmic story of which each child's development was a microcosm. Life might be full of unhappiness, disruption, and loss, but history provided consolation and compensation. "I cannot understand unhappy people," she wrote at the end of her life. "Those people who say that life is not worth living, find it so because they do not go to work to make it worth living."[4] It is likely that Elizabeth knew the stories that Nat was uncovering, and occasionally, in the 1870s and 1880s, she wrote her own vivid accounts of individuals and their often foolish ways. But such incidents, she liked to believe, were only minute disturbances in the social and spiritual progress of humanity.

Ironically, it is Nat, the failed historian, whose records provide invaluable information for the modern biographer. The further irony is that it is his sister, whose view of the past now seems so distant and quaint, who deserves the biography, rather than Nat, who is once more eclipsed by another's radiance.

1

"A Rightly Educated Woman"

%

In 1746 Joseph Palmer emigrated to Massachusetts with his wife Mary and her brother Richard Cranch. Palmer had been born in Devonshire, England, in 1716, and had learned something of salt processing during a stay near Liverpool. Once in New England, Palmer set about using his technical skills. After a stint making cards for wool-carding, he and Cranch leased land in Braintree (later Quincy) and set up chocolate- and spermaceti-processing mills, glassworks, and salt factories. His endeavors at "Germantown," named after the German laborers employed there, made him wealthy, and Palmer was able to purchase extensive land holdings near Pomfret, Connecticut, and to erect "Friendship Hall" on the coast near Braintree. There, on an estate that contained a fruit garden, tree nursery, poultry yard, and an orchard of several acres stretching beyond the house down toward the bay, Palmer lived like an English country gentleman.[1]

By the early 1770s, the Palmers—Joseph, Mary, and their children Elizabeth, Mary, and Joseph—had become a distinguished family in eastern Massachusetts. Of his children, Palmer seemed particularly proud of Mary, called Polly, whose birth date is uncertain but who was baptized in Boston in 1747. Polly's independence and self-assurance contradicted colonial assumptions about the role of women. In colonial America, even among families of privilege, women were universally thought to be naturally suited for domesticity, destined to be wives and mothers. Considered men's intellectual inferiors, colonial

women worked at tasks judged necessary but trivial, and women themselves denigrated their assignment as "my Narrow sphere" or my
"humble task."[2] Trained in domestic arts and instructed in pleasing
behavior, young women were readied for the marriage condition that
was seen to be their appointed end. Flaunting these prescriptions, Polly
Palmer would take horse and carriage on narrow roads into Boston and
conduct business there on her father's behalf, "and return after dark
frequently, and laugh at her mother's and sister's fears on her account."[3]

Joseph Palmer admired Polly's fearlessness; but he was also responsible for crushing her spirit and rendering her an invalid. After a day of
hunting with Colonel Josiah Quincy, Palmer and Quincy saw Polly
reading outside, just beneath the window where they were standing.
Bragging of Polly's nerves of steel, Palmer said that she could with-
stand any shock. To test her will and that of her father, Quincy fired off
a gun outside the window. Polly "sprung up, but fainted and fell immediately." From that day, she was bedridden and "the slightest noise
alarmed her. . . . Her boasted nervous system was ruined forever."
Whether her nerves were in fact shattered is of course unknown, as is
the exact nature of her medical problem, if that is what it was. What is
clearer, perhaps, is that the independent Polly found a way, much as her
descendant Elizabeth Peabody would find, to evade marriage and maintain her freedom.[4]

Palmer's only son, Joseph Pearse, was born in 1750. Nineteen years
later, a student at Harvard College, he met Elizabeth Hunt, daughter
of John Hunt and Ruth Fessenden Hunt of Watertown. Elizabeth's
father reflected his culture's assumptions about the extent of female
education in his belief "that it was sufficient for a woman to know
enough to make a shirt and a pudding." The Palmers, however, expected more of women. Young Joseph's first question of his new fourteen-year-old acquaintance was "what books have you read?" She replied, "none at all . . . except 'The Spectator.'" Palmer is said to have
replied, "your reading should be more extensive. I have a large library at
college which shall be at your service." Years later Elizabeth Hunt Palmer recalled, "Mr. Palmer used to visit me every week, and bring me
books to read, which I was obliged to do up garret, for my sisters were
much opposed to my reading at all. The first book he brought me was
'Sir Charles Grandison,'" a novel by Samuel Richardson. This secret
tutoring, so contrary to the expectations of the Hunts and of the larger

culture, became the occasion for Joseph and Elizabeth to develop their relationship. In her family history, Mary Palmer Tyler recounted her parents' courtship, relying undoubtedly on her mother's memories. "He gave her regular weekly lessons in writing, arithmetic, and so forth, and she, of course, made rapid improvement under such a teacher, geography, history, and so forth were added . . . the lessons were often oral, and given while the happy pair were taking an afternoon ride or walk; and all teachers will bear witness of the facility with which pupils imbibe wisdom when the will is engaged and the instructor beloved."[5]

Palmer graduated from Harvard in 1771, and the following year, again violating a social norm that called for parents to be involved in the choice of spouses for their children, eloped with Elizabeth in a coach and four. Reflecting her prosperous family background and flaunting social custom, Elizabeth was married in Sandborn's Tavern in Hampton, New Hampshire, wearing her riding habit of silk and satin, trimmed in silver lace.[6]

The young couple's privileged background and the ease with which they maneuvered through social expectations would soon be tested, however, for the Palmers quickly became involved in Revolutionary-era politics and warfare. After their wedding, the young Palmers settled in Boston, where Joseph managed his and his father's warehouses on Long Wharf. Palmer was a leader in the Boston Tea Party in December 1773. His wife recalled opening the parlor door late one night and finding "three stout Indians" standing there. "Don't be frightened, Betsey, it is I," her husband said through his disguise. "We have only been making a little salt water tea." Palmer suffered the destruction of his wares and storehouses at the hands of British troops eager for revenge against the "mob" action. The family fled to the safety of the Hunt homestead in Watertown, where their daughters Mary (1775) and Elizabeth (1778) were born.

In September 1774 the elder Palmer was appointed moderator of a committee of representatives of South Shore communities that met to discuss the crisis with Great Britain, and later he served on the Cambridge Committee of Safety and the Massachusetts Provincial Congress. When hostilities broke out, both Palmer men assumed positions of leadership. In 1776 the elder became a brigadier general in charge of troops drawn from Suffolk County and in the following year assumed command of an expedition sent to attack British troops at Newport.

The young Palmer served as his father's aide and as a Quartermaster General for the Continental Army.[7]

Shortly after Elizabeth was born, mother and children moved to the Palmer mansion at Germantown. During the 1760s and 1770s, many American women found themselves increasingly involved in the public life from which colonial culture had thus far barred them. The pamphlet wars, vigorous political discussions, and mob activities drew colonial women into the fray. Their involvement in public matters became especially prominent during the boycotts of British goods upon the passage of the Townshend Duties in 1767. In the later 1760s, women contributed to political activism by producing homespun cloth rather than purchasing British imports.[8]

In contrast, Germantown and Friendship Hall comprised an island of safety and privilege for the Palmer women, far removed from the turmoil and violence of the Revolution. Mary Palmer Tyler remembered, "I have reason to think that the seven or eight years [actually six] spent about this time in Germantown, notwithstanding the political troubles, was the happiest portion of my mother's life. Quite retired from the noise and strife of war, she devoted her time to the education of her little ones. I remember with great delight her calling us to our daily lessons, reading and writing (for we were mere babies when we began). . . . Here in this pleasant chamber we, Joe, Betsey, and myself, received our first lessons. . . . Betsey and I learnt with comparative ease."[9]

Like so many other eighteenth-century children, the Palmer children learned their first lessons at home. As heirs of a distinguished family, moreover, the education of both sexes went beyond basic skills. They learned English literature and the principles of composition from their parents and grandparents. Elizabeth Peabody, our subject, recalled her mother's "telling me that she never remembered the time when she did *not* read Shakespeare, and I have a vivid picture of her as she described herself lying on her stomach on the floor of her grandfather's study, in Germantown, reading from the old *Folio* aloud to her grandmother when she was four years old."[10]

This idyll was not to last, however. With the war over, Joseph Pearse Palmer moved his family to Boston in 1784, where he opened a store on Cornhill, the family living in a house on the corner of Beacon and School streets. His daughter Mary remembered that her "father was thought to be doing very well," unlike his father, old General Palmer, who had spent over five thousands pounds of his own money for the Revolutionary cause and now found himself seriously in debt to John Hancock.[11] When the General tried to pay off his debt by selling the family land in Pomfret, Hancock refused to take the currency, which had fallen dramatically in value during those inflationary times; he exploded in rage at a dinner party when General Palmer observed that "Congress ought to secure individuals against loss who held a large quantity of Continental money." Hancock, a major lender in those years, swore he would be the ruin of Palmer and his family for such an outrageous opinion. Shortly afterward, Hancock foreclosed, and soon the sheriff and Thomas Daws, Hancock's lawyer, came to take possession of Friendship Hall. Mary remembered seeing "my old and infirm grandmother, who had been for some years cosseted like a pet lamb in her chamber, come down stairs to see Thomas Daws . . . take possession of the premises so long the abode of hospitality and benevolence."[12]

In fact, the younger Palmers were doing no better financially. Joseph Pearse could not pay his debts, lost his Cornhill store, and moved his family to a building owned by a Mrs. Clarke, which they operated as a boardinghouse. This undertaking proved to be no financial improvement, and in the winter of 1784–1785, Palmer traveled to Maine to act as agent for some Boston merchants interested in buying lumber, leaving Elizabeth to tend both the boarders and the family.

Many colonial women, who had been kept in ignorance of their husbands' financial affairs, found themselves suddenly thrust into the public world when they were widowed or otherwise newly on their own, with virtually no training in the management of money or business. Still only twenty-nine, having lived an exceptionally sheltered life in Watertown and Germantown, Elizabeth Hunt Palmer was ill prepared for the tasks of managing a boardinghouse. Her daughter Mary put the problem this way: "My mother, born and brought up in the lap of plenty, and married as a mere child as to care of all kinds, and having a husband who almost worshipped her and devoted himself for the first years of their life to saving her every anxiety, was quite inadequate to providing for such a family as was then left entirely to her care." Mrs. Palmer found herself unable to cover her debts with the boarders' income, and one day "an officer came with a writ, the grocer would wait no longer, and the baker was out of patience, and several other petty demands had agreed to join and send in their claims all at once." Faced

with the real possibility of imprisonment for debt, the family was rescued by the timely arrival of one of the boarders, Royall Tyler, who, it
seems, paid off the family's creditors.[13]

‿ LATER TO BECOME professor of law at the University of Vermont and Chief Justice of the Vermont Supreme Court, poet and play-
wright, author of *The Contrast*, Royall Tyler had first come into the life
of the Palmer family in 1783 or 1784. Mary Palmer, then eight or nine
years old, vividly recounted her first meeting with her future husband,
nearly twenty years her senior. She was dressed in her finest pink calico
frock, waiting at the window for her father, who was to take her to
Boston. Seeing a carriage, Mary ran out, but she turned back in disappointment, for it was not he. A stranger followed her inside and "began
to ask me whom I expected . . . at the same time seating himself and
taking my hand drew me to him, setting me on his knee, repeating his
enquiries. I was astonished; his appearance, his manners, his looks overpowered me."[14]

Mary's father was equally impressed with Tyler, who had come to
Quincy to establish a law practice. Mary described the friendship this
way: "Perhaps few men ever loved each other more devotedly and for a
longer time than did he and my father. They seemed twin souls in
everything that was amiable and estimable. My father loved him like a
son long before he ever suspected he would be one to him."[15] Mary
Palmer's recollection is from late in her life, and she clearly intended to
portray her father and her husband in the best light. Still, it is striking
how quickly Tyler moved in and "overpowered" the young child, sup-
planting her often-absent father as a paternal figure and functioning as
father-provider for the distressed Palmer family, who were facing evic-
tion and debtors' prison.

The friendship of the ambitious and manipulative Tyler and the
sweet but unworldly Palmer may seem an odd one, but the Palmers
were a useful family to know in the immediate postwar years. In the
months before the sudden collapse of General Palmer's fortunes,
Friendship Hall glowed with guests and parties. Among the frequent
visitors was Tyler, who would ride out to the estate with his new fiancée,
Abigail Adams, the nineteen-year-old daughter of John and Abigail
Adams. By October 1783 this connection had been called off, in large
part because the Adamses had heard disagreeable rumors about Tyler's

dissipated behavior. A year later, Tyler was boarding with the Palmers in Boston, first at School and Beacon streets, then at Mrs. Clarke's. He had shown himself to be a true friend to the Palmers, despite the nasty stories about him. Certainly Joseph Pearse Palmer, so often away from home in a vain effort to gain financial footing, was grateful for such support for his bewildered wife and children.[16]

Eighty years later, as Nathaniel Peabody worked his way through the evidence he was gathering for his family history, another version of Tyler emerged. In the early 1790s, Tyler would appear at the family farm in Framingham, aggressively court Mary, secretly marry her, and, insisting that she reveal her new condition to no one, return to Vermont. This misuse would have been enough to rankle any family, much less a family of such accustomed privilege. But apparently, there was even more, a much more damaging accusation.

In November 1833, Elizabeth, the second-born Palmer daughter and mother of Elizabeth Palmer Peabody, anonymously contributed an essay called "Seduction" in the *Christian Examiner*. This essay shocked her son Nathaniel when he realized that his mother was the author. "She refers to that which she witnessed," he wrote. "It has been found impossible to obtain from anyone informed as to the mystery, anything like a clear and plain statement in regard to it, leaving me to form my own theory. And remote from the present time as was the occurrence of this first tragedy in the family history, it is nevertheless of a nature that repels speech."[17]

This is what Elizabeth's and Nathaniel's mother had written:

> We hope we deserve to be called pure, in some good degree; but to us it did not seem pure for a polished man of literary eminence, to enter the sanctuary of sleeping innocence, of absolute childhood, for the basest purpose. We did see it, however, and though more than forty years have since passed by, we recollect with almost incredible vividness the shudder of terror and disgust which then shook our infant frame. We have traced the career of that man. He seduced the woman, whose children he would have corrupted, caused the self-murder of a wife and mother, and afterwards married the daughter of that victim. He is dead, and the horrors of his mind, during a lingering disease, were the dreadful fruits of sin; but not of disgrace, for this man had a *good standing in society*.[18]

If taken as factual, this account proposes that Royall Tyler (who died in 1826 from cancer of the jaw) seduced Elizabeth Hunt Palmer, the "wife and mother," who was his age, sometime in the early 1790s, before he married "the daughter of that victim," that is, Mary, twenty years his junior. Nathaniel refers to this event as the "first tragedy," implying that it occurred before a second scandal, apparently the private marriage between his aunt Mary and Tyler. Regarding these events, Nathaniel noted that Hannah Fifield, whose informant was Mrs. Richard (Mary) Cranch, and Catherine Palmer Putnam, Mary's and Elizabeth's younger sister, both knew the story.

Nat's exploration of this closet of family skeletons did not reveal which child, if any, resulted from Tyler's seduction. Joseph Pearse Palmer's Aunt Mary thought that Sophia, born September 2, 1786, could not claim Palmer lineage. Sophia's birth would put her conception around the time that Joseph Pearse was often absent from home. But the matter was even more complex than that. According to family tradition, Catherine (born March 1, 1791) was not the daughter of Joseph Pearse or Elizabeth Hunt Palmer, although she was accepted as one of their children. Nathaniel wrote that he "endeavored, some years ago, to obtain from Mrs. Putnam an explanation of the 'tragedy' in the family history, but she declined to give it on the ground that the inquiry was 'improper' and the parties concerned dead." Aunt Catherine hinted that there were two distinct tragedies—"their occurrence is not to be doubted"—but cautioned that "the inference drawn from one of them may be the wrong one."[19]

Nathaniel gathered another document that sheds some light on this family secret. He had found an undated and unattributed fictional re-telling of the collapse of the Palmer family. Handwritten in a hardcover notebook, this sketch of a novel is attributed to Eliza Palmer, mother of our subject Elizabeth Peabody and author of the astonishing essay "Seduction." The author retells several family stories, including the seizing of Friendship Hall and the secret engagement of Tyler and Mary Palmer; and the author hints at some connection between the Tyler figure, here named Rudolph Talbot, Mary, named Rose, and Mrs. Palmer, here fictionalized as Mrs. Lawson. The relevant passage is this:

One evening the usual coterie of young and old had assembled in our Library, wishing for our absent ones to return, and whiling away the time with books, work, singing, working and talking, when Rudolph Talbot suddenly appeared among us evidently much agitated. . . . We had long noticed his growing attachment to our lovely Rose, and so thought little of the blushing and trembling. But, when he asked to speak a word in private with Madame Lawson, we looked inquiringly at each other. . . . They were absent some time, and when they returned Mrs. Lawson looked paler than usual, and Rudolph seated himself by Rose, blushing deeper and trembling more than when he left us.

Rudolph tells the group of the treachery of the Hancock persona, and of the imminent foreclosure on the Lawson estate. "Now, dear Rose, began Rudolph, we have no time to lose, no time for ceremony. Be my wife and I will pour a fortune in your lap, to do just as you please with. My Father is impatient to have you at the head of his table."[20]

The facts have been altered: Tyler's father died thirteen years before the collapse of the Palmers; also, Tyler did not bring news of Hancock's insistence on payment, nor was his courtship coincident with the foreclosure. But several features of the narrative have emotional plausibility. Mrs. Lawson's loss of color may reflect her response to Talbot/Tyler's continuing presence in the household and his obsession with her daughter Rose/Mary. Likewise, the account reflects Tyler's uncanny ability to be present at times of financial and familial crisis, misfortunes that he made the most of. While the account is slight and inconclusive, it suggests the fragility of the Palmers, their vulnerability to intrusion and disruption, and the family's imminent collapse. Most fascinating of all is the attribution of this fragment to Eliza Palmer, who later as Mrs. Elizabeth Peabody would accuse her sister's late husband of seduction and abuse.

It is revealing to read Tyler's most famous literary work, *The Contrast*, in light of these allegations. Performed for the first time in 1787, *The Contrast* is celebrated as the first American-authored play to be staged commercially. Based on Richard Sheridan's *The School for Scandal* (1777), which Tyler had seen in 1787, *The Contrast* pits American virtue in the forms of Colonel Manley, the noble Revolutionary War veteran, and Maria Van Rough, who prefers to trust her feelings rather than submit to a society marriage, against the brittle wit and barnyard morals of Billy Dimple and his entourage of beaux and belles.

Clearly the Yankee values of Manley and Maria are meant to prevail over the seductive appeal of luxury and European manners. But this preference bears an ironic relation to the author of the play, for Tyler had by the late 1780s acquired a reputation for being a dashing but dissolute young man. During his years at Harvard, he fathered an illegitimate child and was part of a high-living and arrogant crowd of recent graduates.[21] His reputation for "dissipation" was part of what so alarmed Abigail and John Adams when their daughter Nabby became seriously involved with Tyler. If any part of the rumors about Tyler are true, they stand in ironic "contrast" with his most famous play. In *The Contrast*, Yankee homespun and American virtue prevail. If the Palmer family stories are true, Tyler betrays his friend, seduces his friend's wife, and marries his friend's daughter. Billy Dimple may have had the last laugh after all, not in art, but in life.

◈ LIKE THEIR CHILDREN, the elder Palmers were likewise at the edge of financial collapse. Banished from Germantown, they relocated in Dorchester, where General Palmer pluckily started manufacturing again, setting up a successful saltworks. This promising venture was short-lived, however; the General suffered a stroke and died in December 1788, his creditors quickly repossessing the works in payment of their loans. His ruin dismally paralleled that of his son, who had moved his family from rented house to rented house in Boston, searching for financial stability and cheap lodging.

In 1790 Elizabeth Hunt Palmer's brothers urged the Palmers to move to a farm they had acquired in Framingham, west of Boston. Their genteel urban poverty was sheerest elegance compared with the hard labor of rural life in the late eighteenth century. Kind neighbors taught Mrs. Palmer to make butter and cheese, while the older girls Elizabeth and Mary "assisted in the laborious part, keeping churn, pans, cheese-hoops and strainers nice and sweet." The girls also had to learn to spin and weave, "how to card wool, cotton and tow, and how to hatchel flax."[22]

This sudden shift into the hand economy of the countryside must have been a particular shock for Joseph and Elizabeth, who came from privileged families in which physical labor was performed by servants and workers. But family name was no longer sufficient to command respect in the new nation and its bustling market economy. Increasingly, family wealth, not lineage, was the key to status. Mary Tyler recalled that "my mother had always been accustomed, especially while nursing, to have a bowl of chocolate carried to her while in bed in the morning, and my father was in distress if she was neglected in any way. It took years to wean him from the idea that we must be ladies, although he knew that we must give up all such pretensions; however, we tried as much as possible to have our mother saved every possible privation as much for his sake as for hers."[23]

Apparently Joseph Palmer had no aptitude for farming, for his daughter Mary noted that he offered "to teach a private school for a few boys" in the farmhouse parlor. This endeavor too proved insufficient as income, and Joseph struggled to find some business connection. Eventually he "fell into despondency, and was of little assistance to his family during the few remaining years of his life."[24]

In the early 1790s, Royall Tyler had relocated to Vermont, becoming district attorney for the region near Guilford. In late 1791 or early 1792, Tyler returned to Framingham to pursue his interest in seventeen-year-old Mary, whom he called his "little wife," a phrase Mary found "common but improper."[25] Mary acknowledged her love for him, and the Palmer parents gave assent to their marriage. A year later Tyler returned to help Joseph and his son Hampden organize a trip to Vermont, where Tyler thought there would be teaching or business opportunities for Palmer. Joseph was reluctant to leave his family, but he had found no useful work in Framingham, and so the Hunt brothers had decided to sell the farm. In late 1793 or early 1794, Palmer left Elizabeth and the children and headed north. He was never to return.

With her father gone, the oldest Palmer girl, now usually called Eliza, began to assume more and more responsibility for the family. In one of her few reminiscences of those years, she recalled that "my sister's [Mary's] infirm health rendered her wholly unfit for labor. I was consequently my mother's chief dependence for manual labor . . . with the assistance of my little brother I have frequently and on the approach and often during a severe storm been necessitated to go to a wood lot half a mile distant from the house, bring home wood in my arms, and cut it up myself."[26]

From her earliest years, Eliza had shown a tremendous passion for reading and study, absorbing Shakespeare in her grandfather's study at age four. The departure of the Palmer men forced her to suppress "the almost unconquerable desire I had for literary improvement, and, convinced of its necessity, applied myself to the acquirement of those arts which might soften my mother's fatigue and lessen the family expenses." Eliza was never quite able to give up Shakespeare, however. "Sometimes, the labors of the day accomplished, we would collect in our little parlor, light a cheerful fire, and, banishing all recollections of the past or anticipations of the future, suffer the incomparable imagination of Shakespeare to interest us in real or imaginary scenes of pleasure or distress. To that author and our English poets, which composed the whole of our little library, I am indebted for many tranquil hours."[27]

In May 1794 Tyler returned to Framingham. In visits with his mother, Tyler had discovered that lady's unalterable opposition to the match with Mary Palmer. Tyler begged Mary to consent to a private marriage, threatening to break off the engagement altogether if she refused. This arrangement violated both the communal understanding of marriage as existing within a network of social relations and the Massachusetts "Act for the Orderly Solemnization of Marriages" of 1786, which called for the publication of banns and the issuing of a certificate of marriage from the town clerk. No such certificate survives, suggesting that Tyler was in effect proposing a sexual relation that would eventually be formalized.

This "private marriage" strategem from the eccentric and unpredictable Tyler, intended to circumvent Madame Tyler's opposition, played havoc with Mary's reputation in Framingham. "It is morally impossible to keep an event of this kind secret in a country community," she observed later.[28] Mary was deeply embarrassed that she could not be acknowledged as a wife and, after the birth of their first child in December 1794, as a mother. She was angry as well, at Mrs. Tyler's resistance and at Royall's acquiescence to his mother's whims. Worst of all, she was angry that Tyler had returned to his law practice in Vermont, leaving her to face the country gossips alone. Finally, in 1796, he returned to take her to Vermont, finally ready to claim her publicly as his wife, a good thing since she was once again pregnant.

Eliza Palmer was horrified by this casual misuse of her sister and by the rapid dissolution of her family. In 1798 she wrote to Elizabeth Norton, Richard and Mary Cranch's oldest daughter, about "the sad story of the Framingham life, her broken-spirited father's struggles to

maintain his position and his credit, his frequent failures in these efforts, her mother's griefs, [and] her sister's relations to Mr. Tyler as his
betrothed wife." This summary, written by Eliza's son Nathaniel, provides brief but memorable evidence both of the family's collapse and of
Eliza's role in supporting her mother and the remaining children: "After her sister Mary and Edward, Hampden and Sophia had gone to
Vermont under Mr. Tyler's wing, there remained only her mother, herself, George, and Catherine. Her father had gone in 1794 to Vermont,
and sister Amelia to West Point in 1795. By keeping school she was
enabled to pay her mother's taxes."[29]

In June 1797 Joseph Palmer fell from a bridge under construction in
Vermont and died. Tyler, who had in effect replaced Palmer as father,
husband, provider, and possibly lover, returned to Framingham and
boarded for several months at the Palmers. Mary Tyler makes no mention of her new husband's departure to live with her mother, nor did
Eliza mention her sister's presence when she recounted this story, so it
appears that Tyler traveled to Massachusetts alone. There Tyler added
"teacher" to the list of his complex involvements with the Palmer family. Eliza recalled that Tyler kept school for the remaining children,
"in which he disciplined them almost exclusively by making them write
composition." Elizabeth Peabody recalled that her mother remembered this educational venture fondly as a "year of charming reading of
English literature and writing of verses and tales," a memory quite at
odds with her version of Tyler in "Seduction."[30]

ॐ AFTER JOSEPH'S DEATH, the family broke apart rapidly. His
widow's brothers repossessed the Framingham farm, and the remaining
members moved to Watertown, the Hunt family seat. Eliza was increasingly determined to separate herself from her family and "had made up
her mind to become a teacher in some female academy as soon as
possible," her sister Mary wrote.[31]

This ambition, virtually impossible a generation earlier, reflected a
significant change in the status of women in post-Revolutionary America. The crisis in relations with Great Britain occasioned a crisis in
domestic relations as well, as more and more American women found
themselves drawn into the public events of the 1760s and 1770s. From
the boycotts of British goods and the production of homespun to the

maintenance of households and farms while men were away at war, women played active parts in the events of political and military conflict.

Women's attitudes about their own intellectual capabilities changed as well. Largely thought intellectually unfit for serious political discourse, women seized the unsettled situation as an opportunity to challenge that cultural assumption and inserted themselves vigorously into the public discussion. Not just women of the middling sort or from privileged backgrounds, either; rural women and those of laboring backgrounds also voiced their partisan views, which were usually—from those classes in particular—a commitment to the Revolutionary cause. By war's end, Mary Beth Norton observes, "wartime circumstances had created a generation of women who, like the North Carolinian Elizabeth Steele, describes themselves as 'great politician[s].'"[32] Young women like Eliza Palmer who grew up in the Revolutionary and post-Revolutionary years no longer had to assume that their lives would be confined only to a domestic arena that society both enforced and ridiculed. Norton summarizes these changes in this way: "The war, in other words, dissolved some of the distinctions between masculine and feminine traits. Women who would previously have risked criticism if they abandoned their 'natural' feminine timidity now found themselves praised for doing just that. The line between male and female behavior, once apparently so impenetrable, became less well defined. It by no means disappeared, but requisite adjustments to wartime conditions brought a new recognition of the fact that traditional sex roles did not provide adequate guidelines for conduct under all circumstances."[33]

Perhaps most significant, however, was the new value being placed on domestic life. Although women had proved that they were quite capable of reflecting on and acting on issues of large public import, post-Revolutionary society was virtually unanimous in assuming that women's primary assignment was still the home. What had changed was the social meaning of that assignment. In a new Republic still anxious about its survival, the quality and virtue of citizens assumed new importance, as did the nursery of those citizens, the family.

In placing new and positive emphasis on the role of the family in the shaping of citizens, Revolutionary-era thinkers were in part echoing the views of seventeenth-century New England clergy, who had insisted on the centrality of the family, the "little commonwealth," for the nurture of believers in the Christian faith. What was different in the 1760s and 1770s was the added influence of the English-originated political philosophy of Republicanism. Developed over nearly a century from the Glorious Revolution to the 1760s, Republicanism taught a distrust of authority and conveyed a profound fear that popular liberties were in danger of subversion. Gaining little support in Great Britain, a society more than willing to prosper from the willing cooperation of merchants and rulers, Republicanism found increasingly attentive hearers in the American colonies, especially after the end of the French and Indian War.

"Virtue alone . . . is the basis of a republic," Benjamin Rush argued in 1778, echoing a key tenet of Republicanism. Virtue prevents the corruption of "the people" and confirms them in their native liberties. But what did "virtue" mean? To the Republicans and their American readers, virtue connoted a kind of rugged manliness, a willingness to sacrifice creature comforts for the good of the whole. Women, to be sure, were capable of virtue, but this consisted of private, Christian traits rather than the public one that Republicans championed.[34]

By the 1780s and 1790s, however, paralleling the changes in women's social status and behavior, a new meaning of "virtue" entered public discourse. Increasingly defined as moral behavior, virtue seemed now to derive from sentiment and sympathy rather than only from rationality. Previously derided as weak and emotional, women and their supposedly affective traits now emerged as the chief defenders of the public good. "How should it enflame the desires of the mothers and daughters of our land to be the occasion of so much good to themselves and others!—You will easily see that there is laid the basis of public virtue; of union, peace and happiness in society. . . . Mothers do, in a sense, hold the reins of government and sway the ensigns of national prosperity and glory," preached William Lyman in 1802.[35] Virtue, Ruth Bloch observes, was distinctly shifting its locus from public to private realms, newly centered in the first decades of the nineteenth century in schools, in churches, and, most of all, in the family.[36] The mothers who gave their children their early lessons and shaped their moral choices became, in Linda Kerber's words, "a fourth branch of government, a device that ensured social control in the gentlest possible way."[37]

Opportunities for female education expanded rapidly around the turn of the century. For both boys and girls, the new institutional arrangement was the academy. Postprimary and precollegiate, academies were maintained by a mix of private tuition from parents of students and public support from land grants or local taxes. Enormously popular for a time, academies sprang up everywhere in the United States, with Massachusetts and Connecticut each possessing twenty-one founded in the 1780s and 1790s. As Bernard Bailyn notes, "independent, for the most part denominational, colleges and the great congeries of private-public institutions known as academies were the almost universal forms of American education above the elementary level before the Civil War."[38]

For many educators, like Noah Webster and Benjamin Rush, academies were appropriate settings for female education. Dozens of private academies for girls and young women opened, offering traditional academic subjects such as grammar, history, languages, and philosophy, as well as more gender-defined ones like music, dancing, and needlecraft. Perhaps the most famous of these was Benjamin Rush's Young Ladies' Academy in Philadelphia. But whether obscure or famous, virtually all these academies and their teachers echoed Rush's formula: women's minds were capable of the most rigorous forms of education, but it was ultimately an education for Republican Motherhood, "the duties in life to which she may be destined."[39]

To some, the notion of an educated woman was a contradiction of nature. To aspire to learning beyond the ability, to use John Hunt's words, to make a shirt and a pudding, was to risk being a "female pedant," a masculinized being. And resistance did not come only from men. In Watertown, where the remaining Palmers moved after Joseph's death in 1797 and where Mrs. Palmer opened a dry goods store, Eliza's interest in literature met with hostility and ridicule from her Hunt aunts. Her son Nathaniel wrote that her "devotion to literature, and her poetical tendencies, did not meet with favor from her mother's sisters, and subjected her to the charge of wasting time." Eliza had indeed come to love the literary life by this time, publishing several poems in the *Haverhill Federal Gazette* in 1798–1799, under the pseudonym "Belinda."[40] But much as the Hunt sisters had mocked their fourteen-year-old sister Elizabeth's education by her young fiancé Joseph Pearse Palmer, so they opposed Elizabeth's daughter Eliza's aspirations. "She writes feelingly of her miserable situation, when living with these aunts," her son concluded.[41]

From this situation Eliza was rescued by the intervention of Mary Cranch, her late father's aunt. Eliza's mother sent her to be with Aunt Cranch because, in Nathaniel Peabody's words, "the family influences and the character of the street children were not favourable to the proper education of her children."[42] Much as Royall Tyler had assumed paternal roles in the Palmer family, so Mary Cranch came to assume a maternal one, at least for Eliza. The girl had evidently seen enough of adult weakness, failure, abandonment, and predation to want to find some shelter out of the family home and some means of independent support. Much of this destructive behavior came from men, but Eliza's mother also seemed unable to cope with her new situation and unwilling to stand up for her children. Years later Mrs. Peabody would write this to her son George: "The truth is, dear George, I had no education myself, and if I had not been endowed with an irrepressible desire to know something, I should have been a mere worldling, unconscious for what I was born. I blame no one for this. Misfortunes crowded thick upon my Parents, one of whom sank under their weight, and my dear Mother was too ill brought up herself to guide others."[43]

Mrs. Cranch took Eliza to Quincy and introduced her to polite society. Still, the issue of financial independence was pressing, and with Mrs. Cranch's help, Eliza went to work in May 1798 as a "shopwoman" in the English goods store of Mrs. Hannah Appleton Downs on Ann Street in Boston. In the fall, Eliza left Mrs. Downs and her accomplished daughters Charlotte and Harriet. Nathaniel Peabody thought that Eliza took this step because Mrs. Downs had decided to replace Eliza with a "shopman," but his sister Elizabeth claimed that it had to do with an epidemic of yellow fever. In her version, her mother did not dare go to Quincy or Watertown for a visit for fear of spreading the infection there. Instead she joined her cousin William Hunt in nursing the sick, sometimes in their own houses. Elizabeth Peabody writes, "but Mrs. Judge Cranch learnt what she was doing, and heroically took her carriage and went into the city and found her, and preemptorily took her home with her to Quincy, seeing that she was all worn out and exhausted by her disinterested labors. There she was medicated and found to be ill of the jaundice" but not of yellow fever.[44]

After her recovery, Eliza was placed out again, this time in the home of Mrs. Cranch's sister, Elizabeth Shaw Peabody, wife of the Reverend Stephen Peabody of Atkinson, New Hampshire. These Peabodys wore their social privilege conspicuously; the clergyman had "a commanding presence and dignified bearing, accustomed to receive the reverence of the parish." His wife, sister of Abigail Adams, "being a lady of family and also of superior education, shared with him the people's veneration."[45] Stephen Peabody was also principal benefactor and supervisor of an academy in Atkinson, several of whose students boarded at the Peabody home.

In this situation, Eliza Palmer occupied a tense and difficult position. Mrs. Peabody may have been attracted to the young woman because she had recently lost a daughter, also named Elizabeth.[46] More likely, Mrs. Peabody saw in Eliza a needy but deserving and willing worker, another pair of hands to help in the endless round of household chores. "[I]t is on record by herself that besides assisting the younger pupils in their tasks, she helped in family affairs, even to scrubbing floors and doing other menial work."[47]

Despite, or perhaps because of, her family background, Eliza soon stirred up resentment in the Peabody household. The head domestic, Lydia Springer, resented Eliza's connection to the family, and "was particularly strong in the wish that Miss Palmer would leave." "Neither Mr. nor Mrs. Peabody have ever accused me of neglecting any of my business," Eliza wrote defensively, probably to Mrs. Cranch. "I always assist in preparing the usual meals, take care of the chambers, scour all the floors, excepting the kitchen and a little bedroom adjoining, wash, iron, Lydia assisting, mend and make mostly for all."[48]

There seemed to be trouble, too, with Mrs. Peabody. Given Eliza's literary background and gift with language, it was inevitable that the student boarders would ask her to help them with assignments. She recalled their asking, "'Miss Betsey, do write my piece off, do compose me a poem to speak next Saturday, do write me a letter to carry into school today, do correct my composition, do look over my figures in rhetoric, or make me some, and pray hear me say my lesson in geography.' All these requests I must comply with, or they will think me unkind."[49] Mrs. Peabody thought this connection between students and the hired help improper, and she wrote to her sister Mary Cranch that Eliza's thoughts wandered too far.[50]

Criticized both upstairs and down, Eliza was "determined never to write anything again, excepting letters, and as few of them as possible; never to touch a book, except upon the Sabbath, and to devote every moment to work of some kind. I am convinced that my attempts to write poetry have gained me more ill will than any action of my life. It is a received opinion that a poet is good for nothing else; and a person may throw five hours away at the toilet and yet be loved and admired, when she would be condemned if she spent one hour at the pen."[51] This, of course, was an unlikely vow for the young intellectual to keep.

Among the instructors at Stephen Peabody's academy was Nathaniel Peabody, a distant relation, then a student at Dartmouth College. Nathaniel was the son of Isaac Peabody, a New Hampshire farmer. The Peabodys were descended from John Paybody, who had come to Plymouth as early as 1635. His son Francis settled near Topsfield, New Hampshire, around 1648 and began the line that would include judges, lawyers, clergymen, university professors and presidents, financiers, philanthropists, and poets. Among the Peabodys were also competent but undistinguished farmers who never strayed from the ancestral acres at Topsfield. It was there that Nathaniel was born March 30, 1774.[52]

Nathaniel was attracted to the bright, bookish, and independent Eliza, but the Atkinson Peabodys, suddenly solicitous of their poor relative, found the couple ill-matched. As Sarah Loring Bailey put it years later, "it is a curious illustration of the peculiar pride of birth of the time, that the social position and family rank of this young man were not regarded by Mrs. Rev. Stephen Peabody and Mrs. Judge Cranch as sufficiently high to entitle him to aspire to the hand of their 'poor relation,'" despite the fact that he was like them a Peabody.[53] After all, as his son Nathaniel would later observe of his father, Nathaniel Peabody was "the son of a New Hampshire farmer . . . all unused to society, such as had been that in which her father had moved."[54]

Besides the attraction each felt for the other, there were other considerations that encouraged them to pursue the relationship. Nathaniel, who was the only son to move into the professions, likely saw in Eliza Palmer a suitable wife for a college graduate. In Nathaniel, Eliza hoped to find a partner who might free her from some of the menial drudgery that was wearing down her health. She feared "that she would become a permanent invalid and thus lose the marriage potential," thought Sarah Bailey. Eliza understood that marriage was no light commitment. She wrote to Mary Cranch that "the formation of any new connection in life, though it may open some agreeable prospects to my view, must be attended with many difficulties . . . as I would avoid being criminally improvident, I would be as cautious of being criminally anxious for the future."[55]

Most of all, Eliza insisted that marriage not spell the end of a woman's intellectual growth and aspirations. Writing to Nathaniel after he returned to Dartmouth, she observed that "the necessity of cultivating the female mind, is a subject, upon which I am almost enthusiastic. Though they move in a different sphere of life from the other sex; yet the duties they have to fulfill are not less important. . . In this view, the fate of our country, is, in some degree dependant [sic] on the education of its females. By properly exercising their understandings their minds are buoyed above those little follies, those headstrong passions, and idle whims, which too often form the most striking lines in a female character."[56]

Receiving no reply, Eliza tried again. "In writing again so soon, I may perhaps overleap the bounds, custom has prescribed for our sex. But knowing it possible that my last letter may not have reached you, I am willing (by writing again) to clear myself from all charges of inattention." She turned again to her main theme of woman's intellectual and emotional capabilities:

> To endeavour to pursuade [sic] the generality of mankind, that a woman, can feel the ennobling/passion/of love, in all its purity, without its weakness; that she could love the virtues of the heart, without one thought, of the charms of persons, and could feel all the tenderness such an affection inspires unalloyed by that blind fondness, so derogatory to female dignity. To endeavour to pursuade [sic] the world in general of this, would be to out Quixote Cervantes. Yet I am confident that a rightly educated woman is capable of so much greatness of mind. Are you of my opinion, my friend? Or do you think, with the world at large, that we are "fair defects in Nature," an after-thought of Creation?[57]

Apparently Nathaniel convinced her of their singleness of mind, for two weeks later she wrote, "my heart is unreservedly yours. . . . I glory in the decided preference my heart has given to the man of virtue." Also, she gently urged Nathaniel to be more confident of their match: "Let no such doubting sentences as 'May I say?' again meet the eye of your friend." Given the family disintegration and sexual violations she had witnessed, it must have given Eliza Palmer pause to enter into a marriage herself. Her words to Nathaniel Peabody take on added meaning in the context of her family's history: "May the knot that unites our hearts be fastened by purity, and innocence, and may the olive branch ever flourish near us."[58]

Despite the Atkinson Peabodys' doubts about Eliza's literary aspirations, they had introduced her to the editor of the Haverhill *Federal Gazette*. In 1801, through the good offices of this editor, Eliza was offered the job of preceptress, or instructor of girls, at Franklin Academy, then called North Parish Free School, in Andover, Massachusetts. Perhaps this offer was also a recognition of her budding relationship with Nathaniel Peabody, since he had been offered the position of preceptor at the academy after his graduation from Dartmouth in 1800.

In response to population growth, the school had been built in 1799 and incorporated in 1801, changing its name to Franklin Academy in 1803. The original establishment of the school made provision for the education of girls. "In respect to this educational movement the town of North Andover may claim some distinction, for the Academy was the first incorporated institution in Massachusetts to which young ladies were admitted, and it also made provision for them at the outset."[59]

This burst of civic pride was perhaps excessive, given the kind of schooling provided at the academy. The first preceptress was a Miss Stone, who limited her instruction to needlework. When offered the chance to be Miss Stone's replacement, Eliza Palmer doubted her abilities; perhaps she should just teach sewing too. "I feel too little confidence in my own abilities to wish for that office, should it be offered me. I never had any school education, having attained the little I do know by robbing my brain, and wasting the midnight oil. If it were possible I would now attend school."[60]

She was concerned, too, about her health. "I have a severe cough, and I feel a sinking faintness; only the more common exercise of making beds sets me all in a tremor." Her anxiety about her health continued even after she had accepted the post and moved to Andover: "There is something dreadful in the idea of being poor and sick. I feel almost depressed at the thought of such a fate." Despite her worries and a staggering number of students for a first-time teacher, Palmer found herself enjoying her new career. "I have fifty-one young ladies under my care; I am happy in their love. No school consisting of so large a number could be more orderly. They follow all my directions with promptitude and, I think, with pleasure. I feel very happy in my employment. They are attending to needlework, grammar, geography, arithmetic, reading, writing, and composition."[61]

With both Nathaniel and Eliza living in Andover and working at the same school, their relationship inevitably came under scrutiny and caused some gossip. Nathaniel evidently felt that prompt marriage was the only solution, but Eliza felt differently. Writing from Watertown, where she had gone during a bout of poor health, she rallied her fiancé: "Let it be another summer—another year or years if necessary. I wish to live to make your after years more happy, not to cloud them with anxiety. That I wish to silence the tongue of scandal is true; but not by the sacrifice of your repose, for the observations made respecting my situation at Andover affect me only, as they affect you."[62] In fact, only eight more months passed until Nathaniel and Eliza were married, in November 1802, in Andover. The couple continued to work at the Franklin Academy until 1804, when they moved to Billerica. Their first child, Elizabeth Palmer Peabody, was born there on May 16, 1804.

Eliza had considerable ambition for her husband. Hoping that Nathaniel would aspire to more than the local schoolmaster's post, she encouraged him to study medicine by accompanying the local doctor on his rounds. Meanwhile, Eliza opened a home school, which constituted Elizabeth's first nursery: "There I was born in 1804—being as it were prenatally educated for the profession which has been the passionate pursuit of my life."[63] Two years later the family moved to Cambridgeport, in search of more medical training for Nathaniel, this time with Dr. John Jeffries in nearby Boston. In this town as in the previous one, Eliza opened a school and gave birth, this time to Mary, born November 16, 1806. The following year, the growing family shifted to Lynn, where Dr. Peabody opened a medical practice, and then in 1808 to a house on Summer Street in Salem.[64]

The Peabodys arrived in Salem just at the end of its golden age of economic prosperity. From 1790 to 1807, Salem's command of ocean-going trade was preeminent in the new nation. Taking advantage of the Napoleonic Wars, the city's merchants carried food and supplies to both sides in the conflict. Salem's ships also dominated the Indian and East Asian trade. Goods from China, the Philippines, India, and

Japan, together with merchandise from Africa, Europe, and the West Indies piled onto Salem's more than thirty wharves. By 1807 Salem merchants owned 252 vessels. One such merchant, Joseph Peabody, another one of Francis's many descendents, owned 83 of these vessels, while another, the famous Elias Hasket Derby, was worth one-and-one-half million dollars at his death, the largest fortune then amassed in the United States. Elegant shops offering English and other imported goods lined Essex Street, and Federalist-style mansions, several designed by Samuel McIntire, graced Chestnut Street.

Despite this impressive history, Salem in 1808 was undergoing dramatic change. Divisions along class lines followed, though imperfectly, political allegiances. Most merchants were Federalists, benefiting from the high tariffs that Congress placed on foreign trading ships. Some traders, however, like the Crowninshields, Silsbees, and Stones, were Republicans, as were virtually all the city's artisans and laborers.

Whether Federalists or Republicans, the entire city felt the consequences of the Embargo Act of 1807, which closed American ports to foreign trade in retaliation for British and French seizures of American ships and impressment of American crews. The addition of East and West Indian and Chinese goods to the Act effectively shut Salem down. The embargo exacerbated tensions in Salem, and throughout New England, Federalists pondered the question of secession. James Madison lifted the embargo in 1809 when he took over the presidency from Jefferson, and Salem's economy rebounded, but in 1812 a second war with Great Britain again brought foreign trade to a standstill. Salem would never be the same. Its shallow bay, constantly silting up because of the many wharves, was inferior to the harbors of Boston and New York. New industries like shoe and textile manufacture were drawing investors away from overseas trade. Much of this change lay in the future. But the Peabodys, arriving during the 1807–1809 embargo, entered a Salem where social stability and economic prosperity were facing serious challenges.[65]

The house on Summer Street, like the Peabodys' other rented houses in Salem, soon became crowded and busy. The remaining Peabody children were born in Salem: Sophia, Nathaniel, George, Wellington, and Catherine. Besides these children, there were other family members under the roof: Uncle John Peabody, Uncle George Palmer, and "my grandmother's daughter, Sophia." Nathaniel's odd way of referring to this Palmer aunt suggested, as Aunt Cranch had supposed, that Sophia was not the child of Joseph Pearse and Elizabeth Hunt Palmer. In any event, the Peabodys hosted even more people at Thanksgivings, when relatives would crowd in to celebrate, as they would each year until 1833. Given this noisy and demanding household, Mrs. Peabody's work was considerable, and she soon acquired a cook and washerwoman, Nancy Saunders, an out-of-doors workman, and a nursery helper, Abigail Stacy.[66]

In 1812 the Peabodys moved to Union Street, to a house that backed onto the Hathorne house facing Herbert Street. There Elizabeth, and later Mary, began to attend their mother's home schools. As in her own experience, Eliza gave her children lessons in the fundamental skills. Even more, she exposed them to the history and legends of New England. Reflecting her belief that women were crucial to the education of citizens and the survival of the Republic, Mrs. Peabody would tell her children stories of the ancestors who came to America and established schools so that children could learn to read the Bible. Elizabeth heard "ancestors" as "Ann Sisters" and imagined them to be white-robed women, building schools in the American wilderness. "I still seem to see these holy women kneel down in the snow under the trees of the forest, and thank God for their safety from the perils of the sea," she recalled almost eighty years later; "and then go to work in the sense of his very present help, and gather sticks to make a fire, and build shelters from the weather with the branches of the trees. Among these rude buildings my mother took pains to tell me that they built a schoolhouse where all the children were to be taught to read the Bible."[67]

Mrs. Peabody's school was not just for her own children, however. As in Billerica, Cambridgeport, and Lynn, her private home school was meant for children whose parents could afford the fee. By the end of the eighteenth century, Salem supported a number of public and private schools, including several known as women's schools because they were operated by women. Public schools attracted children of the artisan class, whereas private schools appealed to merchant and professional parents. In the latter, children could receive a combination of liberal arts and practical training. One such private school in 1799 offered a curriculum of reading, writing, arithmetic, English grammar and composition, oratory, geography, bookkeeping, surveying, navigating, Latin, and Greek.[68] Although the training in classical languages and vocational skills was limited to boys, the other subjects were available to both sexes. Mrs. Peabody had to find her niche in a town where dozens of schools offered a considerable variety of education. Nathaniel recalled one of her mother's several schools, in their house on the corner of Essex and Cambridge Streets: on the second or third floor of the house, he remembered on "a raised platform in one corner . . . his mother, seated at her desk."[69]

The image of her mother presiding over a schoolroom, like the image of the Ann Sisters, must have been a riveting one for Elizabeth as well, for she too had vivid memories of her early education in her mother's schools. The youngest students were eight or ten, making Elizabeth, who entered in 1812, among the youngest. The qualification for entrance was the ability to read English intelligibly. Mrs. Peabody's instruction centered on history and literature, extending back to ancient Greece and focusing particularly on English literature. The youngest students were taught to write, do arithmetic, and master geography by using blank maps, a technique Elizabeth would adapt in the 1850s. Echoing her own training from Royall Tyler, Mrs. Peabody taught composition, assigning students the task of writing biographical sketches of famous people. In the afternoons students read Goldsmith's histories and literary classics like the *Iliad*, the *Odyssey*, selections from Tasso's *Jerusalem*, and extracts from her own modernizations of Chaucer and Spenser. She also had them read selections from British journals including the *Spectator*, the *Edinburgh Review*, *Quarterly Review*, and *Monthly Review*.

As this curriculum makes clear, Mrs. Peabody saw no reason to modify her reading list for girls, offering them instead the same rigorous training as boys would receive at a college preparatory academy. Indeed, like other educated women in the early decades of the century, Mrs. Peabody saw national culture as the particular province of women. Elizabeth recalled her mother's giving her an article from the *Portfolio*, which made the case that because men were preoccupied with politics, business, and westward expansion, women were obliged to take over the work of culture. "I think this idea of the paramount importance of woman to American civilization was with her the governing principle, and she wished to impart it to other women." Reflecting on her mother's early and decisive impact on her, Peabody noted that "the idea that women were less capable of the highest education in literature and science, and of authorship on any subjects, truly never entered my mind." Without a doubt, women could be authors: Mrs. Peabody gave her eldest the memoirs of "many very learned women" to read, and she spoke admiringly of the work of Maria Edgeworth, Mrs. Barbauld, and of Madame de Staël "who broke the way of authorship for women."[70]

Still, girls were not trained for college and did not receive the practical education necessary for the business world. Teachers like Eliza Peabody certainly expanded the intellectual horizons of their students, boys and girls, but the economic and social horizons were still drawn by their genders. Mrs. Peabody herself is a good example of the inherent conflict between increased educational opportunities and exclusion of women from public life. Her eldest child, Elizabeth, would face a similar conflict. Educated in literature, languages, history, geography, biography, philosophy, and theology, Elizabeth's primary model of adulthood was a woman whose own massive learning fitted her only to teach in a home school or an academy. Like her mother, Elizabeth would learn to negotiate the sharp opposition between intellectual prowess and gendered constraints.

౨ Meanwhile, the Peabodys were a growing family. Dr. Peabody was establishing his medical practice in Salem, but his real interest now was dentistry. Belonging neither to the old "cod aristocracy" nor to the town's merchant elite, the Peabodys were part of the newly arrived professional class who contributed much of the intellectual and cultural energy of the town. Still, the family was, on Eliza's side, Palmers, heirs of a distinguished New England family, and it must have pleased Eliza as much as it displeased Nathaniel to be considered a cultivated family and to hobnob with the first families of Salem. Daughter Elizabeth wrote later that her family's house was "always much frequented by the cultivated people among whom we lived." Son Nathaniel added that "the regard which was generally felt in the town for my mother drew to her dwelling the most cultivated ladies. . . . Among the families whose members were on terms of greater or less intimacy with her were the Crowninshields, Derbys, Brookses, Foresters . . . Pickerings, Pickmans, and Endicotts."[71]

The locations of the Peabody houses give some indication of their shifting social circumstances. Union and Herbert Streets are in the eastern part of town, inhabited mostly by artisans and laborers, politically given to Republicanism. By 1815, however, the Peabodys were living at Essex and Cambridge Streets in a house owned by Miss Susy Hawthorne. The house itself, as Mary Peabody recalled it, was a "a dark, dismal abode where I came to a sense of many privations & much sorrow."[72] Nonetheless, the location represented a considerable social rise, since that section was favored by more privileged Salemites, who were building mansions along Essex and Chestnuts Streets in the first decades of the new century.

If Elizabeth and subsequently Mary were among Mrs. Peabody's students, then Sophia had the dubious honor of being one of Dr. Peabody's dental patients. According to Sophia's son Julian Hawthorne, Dr. Peabody administered drugs to his daughter during her painful bouts of teething, bringing about the headaches that plagued her until the time of her marriage to Nathaniel Hawthorne in 1843. These headaches Dr. Peabody and other medical men treated with even more drugs, including mercury, arsenic, and opium. Despite this unwitting paternal damage, reminiscent of General Joseph Palmer's part in invaliding his daughter Polly, Sophia remained a "child of frolicsome spirits, inclined to playful mischief, high-strung, quick-witted, and quick-tempered," according to Julian.[73]

Little Sophia turned her mischief and quick wits to good account once in curing Elizabeth of her habit of biting her nails. "It seems that various expedients had been tried to break the young student of this habit; among others, that of obliging her to wear gloves: but her preoccupation was so great that nothing availed with her; and when she could do nothing else, she would roll up bits of paper, or anything else that happened to be within reach, and put them in her mouth." Sophia noticed this, and quietly rolled up a quantity of bittersweet, "which has a most disheartening flavor," substituting these for the paper "upon which her sister was feeding. The result appears to have fulfilled her most sanguine expectations; Lizzie remembered the bitter-sweet, and never again was guilty of the objectionable practice."[74]

Much as this funny story tells us about Sophia's playfulness, it also offers a glimpse into the young Elizabeth. Serious, bookish, and preoccupied, Elizabeth was quickly taking on adult responsibilities and adult interests. When Sophia was twelve, Elizabeth wrote this to her: "It has been my feeling since the time I was as old as you now are, that life was a serious thing—& that character was of little importance unless the groundwork & foundation was seriousness. . . . I cannot think that I was more reflective at twelve years old than you are: at least, I am sure, I was not more capable of it, therefore I write to you not as a child to be advis'd—but as one who like myself, is seriously engag'd in a serious thing." Still, she added quickly, seriousness is not the same as gloom: "You cannot recall in all the circle of your acquaintance, I verily believe, a person more uniformly & truly happy [double underline] than my-self."[75] Elizabeth's touching awkwardness and her unconvincing defense of her happiness help to focus attention on the ways this first-born child did indeed internalize her mother's career and her mother's cares. Like Eliza, Elizabeth early carried adult burdens, and, like Eliza, she was growing up in a family where women, not men, were the dominant intellectual and emotional forces.

Nowhere is Elizabeth's appropriation of parenting responsibilities clearer than in her relationship with Sophia. Throughout the 1820s Elizabeth peppered her youngest sister with letters filled with advice, admonition, reading lists, and lectures. This parenting first took shape around the issue of the conflict between Trinitarian and Unitarian Christianity. In the 1880s Peabody recalled those years for her nephew Julian: "These dreadful doctrines [of Calvinism] and my protest, kept my mind in a great ferment, and when I was ten years old, and very precocious, I took Sophia (with my mother's consent) under my relig-ious guardianship, determined she never should hear of any of the terrible doctrines."[76]

The religious conflicts that divided New England into liberal and orthodox camps divided the Palmer and Peabody families as well. Mrs. Peabody's sisters Amelia, Catherine, and Mary stayed with the Calvinist orthodoxy, as did their mother, whereas Mrs. Peabody and her sister Sophia embraced the Unitarian position. These family divisions were painful. When Mrs. Peabody's mother came to stay with them in Salem in the late 1820s, she brought her Calvinism with her, prompting Mrs. Peabody to write in exasperation to her daughter Mary, then living in Boston: "Here she goes from room to room, with her books & papers—bursting with desire to read and extol, what revolts every feeling of my soul—the recorder is full of low abuse, and the heralds & many of the sermons are replete with a whining cant scarcely less disgusting. Her influence upon the boys, particularly W[ellington] is bad very bad."[77]

More than twenty years later, theology's impact on family relations reappeared when Elizabeth Peabody wrote her aunt Catherine Putnam, observing that she thought relations had cooled between niece and aunt. Putnam responded that she had indeed grown distant from her now-famous niece because Elizabeth had not demonstrated "those fruits of the spirit—those evidences of a *new-creation in Christ Jesus*, which are inseparable from the true work of grace on the heart. Pardon me, dear, if I speak plainly upon such a subject as this, for if *I am mistaken*, it will be a matter of little consequence, compared with a mistake *on your part.*"[78]

In the 1810s when these battle lines were being drawn, the young Elizabeth had instantly enlisted on the side of her mother and Unitarianism. She recalled debating questions of free will and original sin as a precocious eleven-year-old: "With the community at large, as well as with us children, the interesting question was, whether salvation was a moral growth under the universal Father's eye, with a perfected elder brother to show the way; or whether it was an arbitrary gift of sovereignty, in spite of moral disapprobation."[79]

It is in this double context, of her mother's theological liberalism and its softened image of God, and of her mother's intellectual and emotional dominance in the family, that an incident in Elizabeth's young life assumes powerful symbolic importance. In her late adulthood, she remembered being asked at age four by a young woman, possibly a houseguest, "Who made you?" "I remember my pleased surprise at the question, that I feel very sure had never been addressed to my consciousness before. At once a Face arose to my imagination,—only a Face and head,—close to me, and looking upon me with the most benignant smile, in which the kindness rather predominated over the intelligence; but it looked at me as if meaning, 'Yes, I made you, as you know very well.'" Elizabeth confidently replied to the questioner, "A man." This response brought great ridicule, and Elizabeth ran off to her mother for support and confirmation. To her surprise, Mrs. Peabody's answer was somewhat out of character for her liberal leanings, and it evoked "another image of God . . . conveying not half so much of the truth as did that kind Face, close up to mine, and seeming to be so wholly occupied with His creature. The new image was of an old man, sitting away upon the clouds, dressed in a black silk gown and cocked hat, the costume of our old Puritan minister. He was looking down upon the earth, and spying round among the children to see who was doing wrong, in order to punish the offenders by touching them with a long rod he held in his hand, thus exposing them to everybody's censure."[80]

The first image, only a head and face, evoked a feminized God of emotion, "in which the kindness rather predominated"; the second evoked a masculine God with a phallic rod, exposing and shaming errant children. The parallels between family politics and theology are striking. The males in the Palmer/Peabody family had steadily declined in power and prestige, from General Palmer through Dr. Peabody, indeed slipping into scandal, while the women had maintained the families and even attained respectable levels of intellectual achievement. Likewise, the distant disinterested God of the Calvinists had been replaced, for liberal Christians, with a humanized God of affection and kindness, traits that the early nineteenth century associated with women.

That Mrs. Peabody, when pressed, should give out with an image of God so at odds with her theology is not wholly surprising. Until family crises with her sons forced her into a more supplicatory and conventional faith, her religion was largely a matter of civic responsibility. An image of God drawn from New England's cultural history was not utterly inappropriate. Elizabeth recalled that she "had been brought up by a devout, unconventional mother, who had been educated to religion, like the Israelites of old, by the history of her country, from the Pilgrim emigration to the Revolutionary war, during which last she was born and grew up, amidst the sacrifices that her family enthusiastically made of ample fortune, leaving her in proud poverty." Mrs. Peabody's cool rationalism, at least in the early nineteenth century, is reflected in her textbook *Sabbath Lessons; or, An Abstract of Sacred History* (1813), which she dedicated to her students in the hopes that it would "enable you to give a consistent and rational account of the grounds upon which you found your hopes of immortality."[81]

ᴈᴼ Ironically, it was through her mother that Elizabeth first came into contact with the man who would make liberal religion personal, intuitive, and emotional for her. When she was eight or nine, Elizabeth's mother took her to hear William Ellery Channing, who was filling Thomas Barnard's pulpit at Salem's North Church. "It takes genius to reach children," Mrs. Peabody observed, aware of her eldest's keen interest in religion. Elizabeth was overwhelmed by Channing's look and voice, his rapt, mystic appearance. "I was thrilled as never before by the thought of a man's communing with God, face to face; and years after, when I heard him read those words of the Psalmist, laying the same emphasis on the prepositions, I recognized how it had given me a sense of the Eternal."[82] Channing's sense of God's nearness and his childlike simplicity and transparency of belief contrasted with Mrs. Peabody's civil religion and with Dr. Peabody's rote and memorized family devotions.

Five years later, in 1817, Elizabeth had another chance to hear Channing. In Boston with her mother, she attended a conversation about Jesus' baptism with Channing and some women of his Federal Street congregation. Monologue would perhaps be a better description: "Dr. Channing, at this meeting, seemed to take the position of fellow-inquirer, and tried, to the best of his ability, to get the ladies to own sincerely to themselves and each other whatever seemed to them unreal, unlikely, or incredible in the text. But it was difficult; and often, when he had asked a tentative question, the silence was appalling, and he was obliged himself to answer most of the questions that he asked." Raised on beliefs in the loftiness of the clergy and the unquestioned accuracy of Scripture, these women were unprepared for Channing's seminar approach or for the rough equality he assumed with them.[83]

Elizabeth, with more nerve and intellectual curiosity, hungered for a private talk with Channing, and finally got her chance. The shy minister must have been startled by the teenager's gush of affection; Channing reported to his sister that "a child ran into my arms and poured out her whole heart in utter confidence of my sympathy!" He asked for news from Salem; she reported that her father was physician to the almshouse, where she accompanied him on his rounds. Dr. Peabody was also on the school committee, she told Channing, which met in her father's study; Elizabeth would sit in the corner studying Latin and listening to the debates on education.[84]

Mrs. Peabody must have been proud that her daughter was following her lead so obviously but knew from her own experience that precocity has its drawbacks. Elizabeth was evidently becoming argumentative and even haughty in her superior knowledge. In April 1819, on the eve of giving birth to her last child Catherine, who was to live only a month-and-a-half, Mrs. Peabody wrote to Elizabeth:

> You have arrived at the most interesting, most perilous age, a young woman can reach. . . . Begin, even now, more carefully to guard yourself that in conversation you need not wound the pride or sensibility of others. Maintain your own opinion with the modesty of your extreme youth, rather ask information than give it to any older than yourself. . . . Minds cast in a superior mould will command your sympathy and affection; and the low and grovelling you will feel anxious to raise and improve, not by satire, unkind reproaches, or triumphs of self-conceit, but by shewing that intellect, acquired knowledge, and native genius are the parents of good feelings, respect for age, and an interest in all the great family of the Universal Parent.[85]

At fifteen, the serious, bookish Elizabeth was clearly her mother's daughter. But even at this young age, Elizabeth could not fail to see that marriage and the demands of family life had effectively ended her mother's active intellectual life. Although she would have male admirers in the next decade and several displaced infatuations with utterly inappropriate men, Elizabeth could already discern that romance and marriage might result in the same stifled life. The stark choice that custom and culture presented to all women, and particularly to intellectual women, was clearly before her.

꩜ THE PEABODYS' FIRST TENURE in Salem, which brother Nathaniel described as a "golden period," came to an end in 1820. "My father desired to try farming, and for this purpose he purchased a dwelling house and extensive lands with it, in Lancaster," about forty miles northwest of Boston. The Peabodys' Salem friend Dorcas Cleveland had an estate in Lancaster, built on the fortunes of her husband Richard, a sea captain, navigator, and merchant. The Clevelands had hoped to retire there, but Richard's failing investments forced him to sea again from 1806 to 1821. In his absence Dorcas Cleveland opened a private school for boys in Lancaster, hiring Jared Sparks as master. Most likely Dorcas encouraged the Peabodys to move out there, seeing the potential for a girls' school alongside the boys'. Unlike the crowded neighborhood of Union Street or the busy intersection of Essex and Cambridge Streets, the Lancaster setting was quiet and rural. The house was set back fifty feet from the road, making space for a flower garden.

Farther back were orchards, a cranberry bed, a circular pond, and even farther back, the Nashua River.

In an ell extension of the main house, at age sixteen, Elizabeth Peabody opened her first school, of "respectable account as to numbers and quality," her brother recalled. As in her mother's schools, Elizabeth's home school blended domesticity and education, with Sophia, Mary, and Nathaniel among her students. Joining them were daughters of the farmers and traders of Lancaster, as well as the minister's daughter. Apparently, as Mrs. Cleveland had wished, all the students were girls, except for Nat. Given her mother's intense interest in history and biography, it was no accident that Elizabeth's first school should concentrate on these same topics. "I taught history as a chief study—the History of the United States,—not in text-books, but Miss Hannah Adams's History of New England, and Rollins's Ancient History, and Plutarch's Lives." She began her curriculum with ancient history, she said, "because ancient history was more comprehensible by the imagination and moral sense . . . its moral meaning . . . more obvious than the movements of our complicated and international society."

When Elizabeth Peabody encountered Bronson Alcott and helped him organize and conduct Temple School in the mid-1830s, his methods must have reminded her of her own first experience in teaching. In Lancaster she taught through discussion, through experience, and through analogy and symbol. Studious Elizabeth loved to talk with her students about words. What are words? she would ask. Signs of thoughts and feelings, they would eventually answer. Not arbitrary signs, either, she taught, contradicting John Locke's view that the link between sound and sense was convenient but not necessary. In a striking anticipation of Emerson's theory of language in *Nature* and anticipating her own later interest in language theory, Peabody taught that words signified real things and real thoughts, linking us to a real world, and beyond the real material world to a world of spiritual meaning. So, she reasoned, the words of God must be objects of nature, since like spoken words, they symbolize their origins and meanings. "Every work of God was a word, because it was the means of waking up thoughts in us, and our reply to God's words is our perception of them by our senses." Words stand for psychological states; they also substitute for names, connectives, exclamations, emotions, modifications. All this grammatical and linguistic training was conducted, Peabody observed later, "without one technical word of grammatical science which, as I had myself experienced, covered up meaning instead of explaining it." This symbolizing and analogizing cast of mind had its limitations, Peabody realized. She knew very little mathematics or natural science, and as for the latter, "the symbolic meaning of nature was out of all proportion in my mind to an analytic science of it."[86]

In her first attempt at teaching, Peabody drew heavily on her mother's curriculum and teaching methods, even to the extent of not assigning homework. More deeply, she absorbed and reflected her mother's understanding of what teaching meant. It was "the vocation for which I had been educated from childhood: it was not simply teaching a school, but educating children morally and spiritually as well as intellectually from the first; which my mother had taught me was the most sacred of the duties of the children of the Pilgrims, who founded the Republic to bless all the nations of the earth."[87]

Elizabeth's school may have been a considerable success, but Dr. Peabody was no farmer, whatever his rural roots. In 1822 or 1823, he determined to return to Salem. He had been going back there anyway to practice dentistry. For her part, Mrs. Peabody had always been ambivalent about rural life. It may have reminded her of the deprivations and challenges of her earlier life in Framingham, and she certainly must have missed the intellectual and social excitement of Salem.[88] Elizabeth, however, left Lancaster first. In 1822 she moved to Boston to keep school and earn money in order to send her brothers to Harvard. For the next six decades, until her last sibling Mary died in 1887, Elizabeth passed in and out of the fluid boundaries of the family, often supporting her parents, living with her sisters, and assisting her brother Nathaniel. Still, with Elizabeth as with so many young adults, this move away from home was a decisive moment, her first venture beyond the small circle of familiar faces.

2

"Mind Has No Sex"

⤳

WHEN ELIZABETH PEABODY moved to Boston in the spring of 1822, she joined a growing number of migrants, mainly young people from northern New England, who flooded into eastern Massachusetts to work in the textile mills of Lowell and Lawrence and the offices and shops of Boston, drawn into boardinghouse living and wage labor by the promise of postwar economic prosperity. These new arrivals swelled the population of Boston from about 25,000 in 1803 to more than 50,000 by 1825. Democratic in politics, evangelical in religion, and distrustful of the city's cultural and social elites, Boston's artisans, day laborers, clerks, and new capitalists challenged the ideal of a homogenous community of shared values and hastened the fragmentation of its populace into noisily competing factions.[1]

For Peabody, however, coming into Boston did not have the impact that many other urban migrants felt, and still feel—the shock of anonymity, the loss of community, the struggle for economic and psychic survival. Despite her father's unfocused efforts at supporting his family and its consequent financial struggles, the Peabodys mingled easily with the socially prominent families of Salem and Lancaster, and such advantages eased her transition away from the family and into connection with equally privileged families in Boston.

Even before she left Lancaster, Elizabeth was getting to know some of these families through her friendship with Dorcas Cleveland, experiencing the ways that wealth, birth, education, and shared religious outlook shape a cultural elite. During a visit to Boston in May 1821, she wrote to her Salem friend Maria Chase about the city's landscape and architecture. "The trees are just budding—the sun casting his horizontal rays over the slightly undulating plain that forms the Common . . . the beautiful buildings around Colonnade row and the Belle vue . . . the massy pillars and classical front of St. Paul's Church."

Elizabeth then turned her attention to the high intellectual quality of Cambridge society, singling out the wives of Harvard professors for special praise. Thinking perhaps of the contrast to Salem's social butterflies, she observed, "you will not find any ladies there whose business is dress and visiting—all have some serious pursuit [,] . . . The Cambridge people know that life is not given them to trifle away and while they would adorn and beautify it with every thing beautiful in art or literature—they recollect that all these things are subservient to a higher aim."[2] Here were women who combined moral purpose with intellectual interests, exactly the mix her mother had taught her to admire and pursue.

When Elizabeth finally did move to the city, she boarded with the family of Augustus Peabody, yet another distant relative. The matron of this family was a "modest, retiring woman" who nonetheless possessed a "giant intellect" and who introduced her kinswoman to many of Boston's most important people. She also provided Elizabeth a room with a truly spectacular view. The family's house "is near the state house," Elizabeth wrote to Maria Chase, "and has the highest site in Boston except old governer [sic] Hancock's house—but it towers above that, being five stories high—and my chamber is one with an eastern aspect in the fifth story. This room looks out into the garden belonging to the Bowdoin estate which spreads out considerably and then declines the northern side of Beacon Hill almost to Bulfinch Place—The garden is filled with fruit trees in full blossom—till it comes to this decline which is a rich green and uninterrupted by any shrubbery . . . all Boston lies far below me, who overlooking the whole city can have a perfect view of the beautiful harbour."[3]

Perhaps Elizabeth did not intend the delicious irony that her chamber should look down on the house of "old governer Hancock," her family's nemesis, but she surely meant to convey to her Salem friend a sense of having the entire city at her feet. She promptly reacquainted herself with the people she had met earlier through Dorcas Cleveland.

From these families she drew children for her first Boston school, located at the corner of Hancock and Mt. Vernon Streets on Beacon Hill.

Much later, one of these, Anna Q. T. Parsons, recalled that there were no adequate textbooks in history, so Miss Peabody wrote one, which the pupils copied out weekly as part of their writing lesson. As for discipline, Parsons remembered, there was never any confrontation in public; their young teacher relied on little notes to warn her charges of the consequences of their behavior. Anna Parsons's most vivid memory came from examination day; she recalled their "much loved teacher, a slight, lovely young girl of seventeen or eighteen, with an abundance of fair hair, her face all aglow (clad in a brown concan [a kind of crepe fabric], low-necked, after the fashion of the day, with a long blue cashmere mantle over her shoulders)," examining her pupils, with parents and friends as onlookers.[4]

Young misses on Beacon Hill were not Elizabeth's only students, however. She wrote scores of letters back home to Lancaster and Salem, bombarding Sophia with advice, cautions, and warnings. In fact, her letters became something of a family joke. As Mary wrote to Maria Chase about her elder sister, "she sits with a ream of paper at her elbow—it is enough to frighten any body's ideas away—she looks for all the world as if she was going to write up all the thoughts there are about, and leave nothing for her contemporaries or posterity to do."[5]

Possibly Sophia did not find it so humorous, being the target of the barrage: be careful what you do when you are tired from study, Elizabeth advised in 1822, for "then is the dangerous moment when frivolous thoughts not unfrequently accompanied by impurity . . . creep in. . . . When the hours of study have pass'd by—let your recreations be innocent and pure." Try to be more loving toward others: "You have often felt your heart full of wicked feelings toward your fellow creatures; in deprecating the unamiable, you have forgotten to be amiable yourself."[6]

Elizabeth even had comments on Sophia's writing style. Apparently Sophia enjoyed using pseudonyms in her letters, a common practice at the time. But Elizabeth would have none of it, taking the high ground: "I do think your trouble about real names is nonsense. I shall not use assumed names—or disguise what I think. . . . I will quarrel outright with you if you use those Ossian names." Perhaps a year or so later, Elizabeth took up this line again, writing to say that she had a "criticism to make of a literary character upon your letters—& that is that they abound in a sort of peculiar manner of expression which Mary says arises from your adopting the French idiom into our language—that you first began to do in fun—but now have got into a confirmed habit of doing—& which I must confess strikes me as *slang*. . . . English models have been too long out of your reading."[7]

Elizabeth took the most interest, next to trying to shape Sophia's character, in organizing and monitoring Sophia's education, advising her what to read in theology, philosophy, and poetry. Try the nature poets, she commanded, like Thomson or Cowper, but be careful: "I wish you now to read only those poets with whom no one has found fault & which are perfectly moral"—considerably limiting the list—"for to lay the foundation of elevated character the imagination should sport with no images but those consistent with the most elevated morality." This definition ruled out contemporary poets like Moore, who has "an enervating effect if too intimately known," and certainly Byron, who "cannot be relish'd without a mind more fully stor'd than yours is, with classical recollections."[8]

Elizabeth was, in effect, recommending the same reading that she was absorbing herself, "a classical education . . . a course of college studies." Like her mother, whose instructional role she was adopting, even replacing, in these letters, Elizabeth found such learning suitable for women as well as for men because, as she wrote Sophia, "mind has no sex." These letters to Sophia, like the ones to their Salem friend Maria Chase, suggest the depth and range of Peabody's reading in the early 1820s. She was not only studying French and German but also reading Cooper (whom all the Peabodys admired), Scott, and Germaine de Staël, whose *Corinna* she thought "a very highwrought romance but contain[ing] the best account of Italy extant."[9]

There was even more: in 1822 Elizabeth hired a tutor to train her in classical Greek. Just graduated from Harvard and serving as an assistant in a female academy, Ralph Waldo Emerson was at nineteen a year older than Elizabeth. In 1884 she recalled that "we did not get into a chatting acquaintance, but sat opposite each other at the study table, not lifting our eyes from our books." She recited poems from the "Graeca Majora," and he commented. But when Elizabeth was preparing to leave Boston in 1823 and sent for the bill, Emerson came with his cousin George to say that "he had no bill to render, for he found he could teach me nothing."[10]

So much reading on Elizabeth's part led to serious eyestrain. In March 1823 her grandmother Palmer wrote Aunt Mary that "Elizabeth Peabody has just come in—and is going to dine with us and is going to Boston after dinner—she has been afflicted with her eyes—and obliged to give up her school for a week to get better." Still, life in Boston was not all study, teaching, and writing advice to Sophia. She socialized with Harvard mathematics professor John Farrar and his brilliant wife Eliza Rotch Farrar, danced with schoolmaster George Emerson to Mary Buckminster's accompaniment, thrilled to the view of Boston from the Cambridge side of the Charles, as interpreted by her new artist friend Washington Allston, and delighted to hear Harvard professor George Ticknor's lectures on modern language and literature read aloud. Ticknor, she observed to Maria Chase, "is the best *Spaniard* in our country. He speaks of the *treasures* of Spanish literature and is delivering a course of lectures upon the same at Harvard College."[11]

Exciting as it must have been to be in such company, Elizabeth found the practical side of life disappointing. Her plan of earning money with which to send her brothers to Harvard had failed; she simply could not find enough students to pay her own expenses, much less save for Nat and the others. But rather than return home, Elizabeth had another plan. Her father had written in April 1823 that William Vaughan of Hallowell, Maine, had inquired whether Elizabeth would be interested in opening a school for the Vaughan children and those of some neighboring families; he would pay $200 a year plus room and board. Dr. Peabody could not resist giving some advice about living and working in rural Maine: don't expect to find the cultural level of Boston; do offer some instruction in the useful arts: "You must be prepared to instruct Drawing & painting & embroidery & ornamental Needlework &c &c. For most girls in the country think that the *ne plus ultra* of an education."[12] Perhaps Dr. Peabody recalled either his own experiences as a schoolmaster in rural Massachusetts or perhaps his wife's anxieties about following a schoolmistress at Franklin Academy who taught only sewing. Even so, it is a sign of how little Nathaniel Peabody knew of his daughter's intellectual achievements or ambitions that he could seriously suggest she teach ornamental needlework! Elizabeth accepted the invitation nonetheless, and the following month traveled to Hallowell, on the Kennebec River, to take up her duties.

᠍᠍᠍᠍᠍᠍ ALTHOUGH NOT ONE of the original white proprietors of the land along Maine's Kennebec River, the Vaughans had established themselves as a leading family in Hallowell.[13] From Benjamin Vaughan's arrival in Maine in 1797 to his death in 1836, the home of Benjamin and Sarah Manning Vaughan was a hub around which the literary, cultural, scientific, and social life of Hallowell orbited. A Hallowell native recalled that Vaughan was "the Genius Loci, the spirit of the spot. It was eminently so in Hallowell during Dr. Vaughan's life. In religion, education, gardening, agriculture, and love of reading, he gave a healthy tone to society."[14] Elizabeth Peabody had been recruited by Benjamin's equally talented son William. A merchant and farmer, this Vaughan was also a noted military figure, serving as commander of a militia regiment during the War of 1812. William and his wife Harriet had nine children, six of whom died in early life, and William himself was only forty-two when he died in 1825.

Despite Dr. Peabody's concerns, Elizabeth found the cultural tone of Hallowell quite up to her Boston standards. She had twenty-two students, teaching them history, grammar, Latin, and literature. She kept up with her own reading and language study, reading Livy and Homer in their original languages and working her way through a Greek New Testament.[15]

Politically, Elizabeth agreed with the Whiggish views of her hosts. With them, she celebrated the election of John Quincy Adams over the dangerous Democrat Andrew Jackson in 1824: "The news of Mr. Adams' Election arrived here at twelve o clock to day—& the church bell has been ringing & the cannons firing at intervals ever since," she wrote to Sophia. "The whole town is in an uproar of joy. I am glad Jackson is not elected—and I hope Mr. Adams will 'cut a shine' or make us cut one among the nations of this terraqueous ball."[16]

Despite all this excitement and the demands of her teaching, Elizabeth even had time to socialize, not surprising since the Vaughans and their friends kept up a vigorous round of visits, discussions, parties, and dances. She was quickly drawn into a reading group but found by late 1823 that she was so busy with other activities, including a "metaphysical class," that she had to give it up. This decision caused a bit of a stir, she reported to Sophia: "As I have been accused of indifference to the society of Hallowell," she went out of her way to dress up for the last meeting she would attend, at which she would recite Homer, wearing her best black bombazine dress with crimson and black merino trim.[17]

Leaving the reading group did not after all make Elizabeth less welcome in Hallowell's social circles; the day after writing her letter to Sophia, she attended a Christmas party for fifty at the home of Robert Hallowell Gardiner. Gardiner, another Kennebec landowner and pillar of the local Episcopal church, was so impressed with Elizabeth's teaching abilities that he invited her to move to his estate "Oaklands" and tutor his and neighboring children there. In April 1824, with Mary Peabody's arrival to take over her job at the Vaughans, Elizabeth moved north to the Gardiner house. There she found receptive students and a stimulating environment, much as she had at the Vaughans' home. She wrote to Sophia while visiting back at the Vaughans, "my scholars are perfectly delightful—and every one of them (which is a remarkable fact) is of uncommon talent—and there is a great deal of striking originality in their minds . . . my life is quiet—but fully occupied in walking—riding—drawing—reading—studying—teaching—all delightful employments." Delia Gardiner reported that school with "Miss Peabody" consisted of readings from Robertson's history of America, arithmetic, composition, Latin, Italian, music, and drawing.[18]

Over the "season" of 1823–24, Peabody circulated easily among the brilliantly lit and festively decorated mansions of Hallowell's cultured and wealthy residents. Sometime during her residence there, Elizabeth wrote a poem called "The Blue Stocking Club." In these lines, imitating a then-popular poem called "Mrs. Adams' Ball," Peabody honored a frequent host of these gatherings, Dr. Benjamin Page, who died in January 1824. The first two stanzas are as follows:

> Wend you with the Blues to-night?
> Grave and gay, engaged and free,
> All that kneel to beauty bright,
> All that worship mirth and glee;
> Some the learned page to scan,
> Some perchance to listen too,
> Some for conquering hearts to plan,
> Some the pincushions to sew;

Youths and Misses divers ages,
Are going—gone to Dr. Page's.

Wend you with the Blues to-night?
A gay assemblage will be there;
Vaughan with glowing beauty bright,
Happy heart and joyous air.
The elder Merrick gently grave,
And Mary, silent, full of feeling;
And Gillet skilled on love to rave
Every rising thought revealing;
Youth and Misses divers ages
Going—gone to Dr. Page's.

When Emma Nason showed these verses to Elizabeth Peabody in the 1880s, she "had forgotten their existence, but . . . well remembered the brilliant circle of young people that formed the *Blue Stocking Club.*"[19]

Elizabeth had time even for romance. In her letters to Sophia and to Maria Chase, she tossed off comments on her beaux as if they all meant very little to her. At the Gardiners' dinner in December 1823, a specially invited company included "Mr. Bridge, my steamboat beau," and "the interesting Mr. Crosby."[20] In particular, she confessed to Maria, she was attracted to Sylvanus Robinson. She described him in a wickedly amusing letter, in which making fun of the poor fellow is mixed with some obvious attraction. His mouth is very beautiful "when shut," his complexion is "not perfectly clear," he blushes too much, he seldom talks or writes. Still, she likes his opinions when he has the courage to express them. But it all matters very little since Robinson is engaged to "a fair methodist enthusiast of Bath." Whatever feelings she might have had for him have been put under tight wraps by the following spring, when she writes, "'Sylvester' as you *mis*call the hero of Kennebec continueth to be very interesting. He is one of the finest fellows in the *whole world*—and a particular friend of mine. I have accomplished an acquaintance with the lady in Bath to whom he is engaged. I *actually correspond* with her. Is not that *like me?*"[21]

Still, Elizabeth was stirred by something more than summertime romance at least once during her stay on the Kennebec. When Sophia engaged in some indiscreet flirtations in Cuba in 1834, Elizabeth wrote

Mary several letters critical of her oversight of their younger sister and suggesting that she had had some experience in matters of the heart: "I *know* what the feeling of *love* is, for I have been sought and all but *won*." Four years later, Elizabeth's brother Nathaniel, stung by criticism that he had not been sufficiently self-sacrificing or self-disciplined, wrote Elizabeth sarcastically, "perhaps if you had been married when you had the opportunity, the fortunes of your own and our family would have been different, perhaps prosperous, and I believe it was as much your duty to have been married when you could, as to have toiled for your own and other's subsistence by your personal labors in a single state, unless indeed you preferred a single state."[22]

Other than these brief references to more serious attractions that did not, after all, result in any permanent connection, the impression of Elizabeth as a nineteen- and twenty-year-old is of a young woman intensely serious about her studies and her teaching, enjoying the company of cultivated and sophisticated people, and rather frightened of expressions of strong feeling. Ironically, within a few years her sister Mary and others would be criticizing Elizabeth for her indiscreet and tactless expressions of feeling. Perhaps Peabody felt the strength of her own emotions and preferred to keep them under tight control, only to find that repression usually resulted in inappropriate expression of those feelings. Perhaps, as well, Elizabeth knew the devastation that expression of strong feeling, particularly sexual feeling, had wreaked in her own family, and recoiled from such intimacy as unpredictable and dangerous.

In the Kennebec years, Elizabeth Peabody witnessed the strongest outbursts of emotion not in romance but in the religious revival meetings held in the region. Hallowell had been the site of religious excitement a few decades earlier. The newly formed Congregational church had called Isaac Foster to its pulpit in 1786, but even before his ordination, some parishioners, including town clerk Henry Sewall, found Foster too liberal in his theology, too given to Arminian doctrines of free will and human agency. Sewall and others preferred to worship privately rather than to expose themselves to Foster's liberalism.[23]

About four decades later, Peabody found herself among people who would have been Foster's most vigorous defenders. The families from whom her students came were all liberal in their religious outlook. The Gardiners were influential in the forming of "Old South" Episcopal

Church in Hallowell. The Vaughans, who had come from an English Unitarian background, were followers of Joseph Priestley and Thomas Belsham in their denial of Christ's divinity. In fact, the area's Unitarians had grown sufficiently in numbers that they planned to organize a church and to call a minister. Horrified by this development and feeling partly responsible, the local Congregational clergyman abruptly left Hallowell and turned his pulpit over to a revival preacher named Dantworth.

Watching these developments from her perch at the Vaughan and Gardiner estates, Peabody was both shocked and fascinated by Dantworth's theatrics. Holding revival services night and day for a week, Dantworth wound up the emotions of the townspeople to an intense pitch, working on them until they broke down and declared themselves converted. Professors from a neighboring divinity school and lay preachers from all over southern Maine flocked to Hallowell to see the master at work. Finally, the emotional Dantworth outdid himself, Elizabeth reported to William Ellery Channing. Striding into a room lit only by a few candles, with seats divided by a center aisle, Dantworth saw that all the attendees were sitting on one side. After singing "an exciting solo in the clear, loud voice of a Venetian gondolier," he commanded those who had "obtained a hope" of their salvation to sit on the other side. About half did, to which the revivalist said, "so you will be divided on the day of judgment!" After a moment of silence, a man on the unconverted side was heard to say, "sir, we have often heard you say that you were to be a *witness* on the day of judgment; but this is the first time we learn that you are to be the judge!" whereupon the entire assembly got up and left. Dantworth left the Kennebec area the next morning.[24]

Dantworth's departure was obviously satisfying to Elizabeth, but she was still deeply disturbed by the issue of emotion in religion. She was dismayed to find that some of the Unitarians in Hallowell thought Unitarianism ill-suited to the frontier, that it "smelled too much of the lamp." Yet what was the alternative? In the Maine revivals, "people were united to the church in trances of excitement that seemed to me to reduce men from rational free agents, capable of 'judging of their own self what is right,' to mere victims of nervous passion." Revivals created "a tremendous force of life always ready to press upward through all the surface quiet of every day," but revivalists took that life energy and channeled it by threats of damnation "into the madness of a selfishness forgetful of every being but the individual and narrow self."[25]

In its challenge to a purely private faith and its exposure of sin to public view, revivalism confronted the self-image as well as the religious beliefs of its hearers. Perhaps Elizabeth felt especially violated by the power of the revival during the very months that she was stressing self-control and avoiding emotional attachments. Her descriptions of the orgasmic power of the revival—"a tremendous force of life always ready to press upward"—suggests erotic feeling displaced onto religion. The revival in Maine, combined with whatever romantic adventures she may have had, shook the young woman, exposing her to a realm of passion and intensity far beyond the quiet confines of her Unitarian upbringing, but eerily reminiscent of earlier family traumas.

In any event, Elizabeth poured out her feelings about revivals in an eleven-page letter to Channing and in subsequent conversations. Perhaps, she wrote, the distorted emotionalism of the revivals in New England had something to do with the Calvinist insistence on preaching the sovereignty of God, stimulating a "hard, cold wilfulness, contemptuous of Nature's beauty, and destructive to all play of the gentle natural affections. . . . Even when there is no special revival preaching, throwing the nerves into a state of insanity by the dread of instant and everlasting damnation, the grim fact is assumed in the doctrine of total depravity." Perhaps this situation would be an opportunity for young Unitarian clergy to go into revival-swept areas and preach an alternative gospel of human dignity and religious duty. Certainly when James Walker came to preach C. C. Everett's ordination sermon for Hallowell's first Unitarian congregation, he had a powerful and healing effect "on the wide-awake young men who had been excited, shocked, and disgusted with Dantworth's violation of human dignity in his public and private tirades."

Channing responded warmly to Peabody's idea—"it would unquestionably do good to our young preachers to go upon our frontiers and identify the spirit of American enterprise with this noble idea [of human dignity rather than natural depravity], and give a Christian significance to the motto of our nationality—E pluribus unum."[26] In fact, Unitarianism made very little headway on the frontier, for it did indeed "smell like the lamp." Revivalists like the "Methodist bulldog" Peter Cartwright had nothing but contempt for young Harvard Divinity School graduates whose written prayers and prepared sermons had little relevance to the raw immediacy of life in the Ohio Valley. Commanded to exhort those in the throes of a conversion experience, one such Eastern minister could only say, "be composed, be composed," while Cartwright bellowed, "pray on brothers; there's no compromise in [sic] hell or damnation!"[27]

ELIZABETH PEABODY encountered revivalism in Maine at a moment in her life when she was immersing herself in the literature of the Unitarian-Trinitarian controversy, and so the conflicting notions of human rationality and emotion had particular force for her. Already shaped by her mother's choice of the liberal party and determined to spare Sophia the horrors of Calvinism, Peabody had begun to read deeply in theology as early as 1820. As her family prepared to move from Salem to Lancaster, she encountered Channing again, this time in Salem, and read his essays in the *Christian Disciple*. After her move to Boston in 1822, she wrote a series of letters to Sophia, not just about literary style and good reading but also about religion. She described religion as the combination of "habits of pious meditation, charitable judgement, benevolent feeling and severe self-examination," a most bookish definition. Recommending a set of readings to her youngest sister, Peabody in effect listed the books that were influential on her: William Paley's *Natural Theology* (1802) and *Evidences of Christianity* (1794), both classic arguments for religion based on the evidence of nature; Joseph Priestley's *Institutes of Natural and Revealed Religion* (1774); tract exchanges like that between Calvinist Leonard Woods and liberal Henry Ware; and the writings of Scottish Common Sense theorist Thomas Brown. Undoubtedly Elizabeth was correct in observing, later, that she had become something of a "Unitarian doctrinaire."[28]

Peabody's devotion to liberal Christianity was a story repeated thousands of times in New England in the early nineteenth century, as former believers in orthodox Calvinism began to question the rationality and psychological health of their faith. The liberal party had begun to emerge in the late eighteenth century, when King's Chapel in Boston, once an Anglican church, ordained the liberal James Freeman as its minister in 1787. The decisive moment came in 1805 when Henry Ware was elected Hollis Professor of Divinity at Harvard, followed by the election of John Thornton Kirkland as Harvard's president in 1810.

Both liberal Christians, their rise signaled to the orthodox that the region's most prestigious educational institution was now firmly in liberal hands. What followed was an increasingly bitter argument between orthodox and liberal spokespeople, with the former upholding the Calvinist views of human nature, divine sovereignty, and predestination, the latter defending an expanded and optimistic view of humanity as the creation of a loving God who intends salvation for many rather than for the few.[29]

There was, to be sure, a liberal party in religion in England that also sought to distinguish itself from orthodoxy. But there the stress was on attacking the doctrine of the Trinity, whereas in New England the emphasis was elsewhere. Liberals in America preferred to stress the lawful nature of the cosmos, predictable, orderly, and understandable to human rationality, the product of a loving God. Although nature provides a coherent revelation of the existence of God, they argued, it must be supplemented by the supernatural revelation of Scripture. This position led the liberals to insist on the historicity of miracles as the believable testimony of believable witnesses, and would eventually be one of the points of contention between Unitarians and their more radical Transcendentalist offspring.

The liberal revolt in New England threw up many articulate defenders, but no one seemed to focus the movement so clearly for so many as the minister of the Federal Street Church in Boston, William Ellery Channing. In 1819 Channing preached the ordination sermon for Jared Sparks in Baltimore. "Unitarian Christianity" quickly became a centerpiece of the now increasingly named Unitarian position. In it, Channing argued strenuously for human ability and dignity. Scripture is available to human reason, which can draw out of Holy Writ principles of behavior most akin to common sense. The God whom we discern in Scripture, Channing went on, is understandable and loving, not whimsical and vengeful. Ultimately an ethical faith, liberal Christianity in Channing's view linked human capacity for good behavior with a view of God as ultimate source of morality.[30]

As we have seen, Elizabeth Peabody fell early under Channing's influence, meeting him as a child and reading his essays. Even before leaving Boston for Maine in 1823, Elizabeth was entranced by the shy, self-effacing minister. Pallid and stooped, he was certainly nothing to look at, she confided in her friend Maria Chase. His manner and appearance were ungraceful, even cold. But when he began to speak in "a remarkably sweet" voice, he seemed to address the soul itself, like a "strain of soft but irresistably persuasive music which even before you are aware it affects you has carried captive all your feelings."[31]

But Elizabeth was not simply learning doctrine from Channing. She was capable of doing that on her own, as her reading list to Sophia suggested. At a crucial moment in her young adulthood, Channing gave Peabody an understanding of the emotional life for which she hungered. She had rushed into adulthood, becoming a third parent to her siblings and opening a school at sixteen. She had devised a definition of religion in which emotional response was at best "benevolent feeling." Not surprisingly, she was horrified, but also fascinated, by the passionate revivalism she witnessed in Maine.

Channing would be just the right person to help Peabody find a place for feeling without abandoning liberal principles. "Some preachers," Channing once argued, "from observing the pernicious effects of violent and exclusive appeals to the passions, have fallen into an opposite error. They have addressed men as mere creatures of the intellect; they have forgotten that affection is as essential to our nature as thought [and] that the union of reason and sensibility is the health of the soul."[32] Although drawn into the emerging struggle between liberal and orthodox, Channing much preferred the company of children, to whom a ministry of gentle feeling was more appropriate than the clash of ideologies. "He treats children with the greatest consideration," she wrote in her journal in 1825, "and evidently enjoys their conversation, and studies it to see what it indicates of the yet unfallen nature."[33] Elizabeth's sister Mary was also struck by Channing's opennness to children, and she recounted a time when Channing stopped midway down a church aisle and stooped to pick up a child's glove dropped there; Mary was impressed by the humanity of the gesture and by how different Channing's behavior was from other, older clergy. "Though Mr. Channing seems formal and strikes awe into people frequently I suppose there never was a person more desirous of breaking down all barriers of reserve and formality that would interrupt free and open communication between mind and mind."[34]

Channing's general influence on Peabody was to help her integrate emotion in a coherent understanding of herself, but the particular way he did this in the early and mid-1820s was to wean her from too great a fascination with the work of Scottish Common Sense philosopher Thomas Brown. Brown, whose *Philosophy of the Human Mind* attempted to arrange the powers of the mind in fixed categories and to assign strict rules of causation, appealed to a young person who wanted the world to be logical. "I contend that every person who has talents, time, and opportunity, should not rest contentedly with any creed however simple till they have fully discuss'd every article of it in their dependencies and relations," Elizabeth wrote loftily in 1821, completely under the spell of Brown.[35] Three years later, her enthusiasm was undiminished. "I read nothing but the divine Brown—oh Maria—what a treasure is that book! I think I take more pleasure in the exercise of my most common faculties—now that I have better defined the proper objects of investigation and inquiry—and Brown certainly shows us plainly enough what we ought not to speculate upon—or what it is useless to attempt."[36]

Despite its appeal to the Peabodys, Brown's system was too material-ist for other readers, including Channing, with too little respect for divine initiative or for the proper place of human feelings. This was exactly where Channing leveled his attack on Brown, the next time that Elizabeth praised him. The difficulty with his philosophy, Channing charged, was that he left no room for religious sensibility as a route to truth. In fact, Channing believed, we are led into the good life as much by the promptings of the properly trained and disciplined feelings as by the powers of mind.[37]

Peabody felt that Channing's correction of Brown was life-giving for her. As she recalled in 1880, "these first conversations with him made an era in my life; for the three previous years had been so filled with painful moral experience that I had become depressed in hope. But Dr. Channing gave me back my childhood faith. . ." These words should startle us a bit, since externally she had had a successful time in Maine, gained some social poise, earned money, and was now ready to recon-quer Boston. But it seems that this shell of success concealed a deeper unhappiness, a wrestling with questions of identity and belief. "I thought I believed in Brown's metaphysics during the dark night of my Gardiner life, and I clung to it as if it were my last link with light and goodness, and never was Christianity so *inoperative*," she wrote to her future brother-in-law Horace Mann in 1835. Much later, in her *Remi-niscences*, she returned to this theme of spiritual aridity and darkness.

"Intellectually, I continued to deny the doctrine of total depravity [but] felt 'dry as summer dust.'"[38]

In place of Brown's logic or the salvos of theological warfare, Channing found poetry and philosophy increasingly more appealing, especially after his European trip in 1823. He returned with a new appreciation for the moral and psychological insights of the Lake Country poets, which he passed along to his receptive young disciple. Reading aloud parts of Wordsworth's "Intimations Ode," Channing urged Elizabeth to identify and dispell a sense of being constantly judged and exposed, shown up to the world as being "worse even than I was." The moral life, Channing observed, was one of growth and development rather than of living up to a set of impossible standards. This was the lesson of the poets, he thought, finding in them "a theology more spiritual than in the controversial writings of either Unitarians or Trinitarians," for they spoke of the love of God as one of parent for child.[39]

Peabody found it difficult to accept Channing's advice to brush aside unjust or thoughtless criticism, but she eagerly accepted his recommendation of Wordsworth. As Mary Peabody observed to Maria Chase, "we have been feasting upon Wordsworth—E[lizabeth] procured the four volumes in Boston, and they improve upon acquaintance." A few months later, Mary made a similar observation: "She [Elizabeth] has been living this winter upon Coleridge, Wordsworth, and Dr. Channing, and is more than usually sublimated as you may infer from these facts. She enacts every degree of madness as of old."[40]

As Channing helped Peabody find a place for feeling in the Unitarian system, he likewise exposed her to one of the central themes of his ministry, that of self-culture. For Channing, as Daniel Howe has pointed out, the religious life was one of constant education, development, and growth. In his address "Self-Culture" in 1838, Channing called for his listeners to identify their own powers and abilities and to seek to improve them, not so much for any material gain but rather for the sake of releasing the divine impulse toward perfection. Reflecting his love of the faculty psychology, in which the "lower" elements of passion and impulse need to be tempered, but not crushed, by the higher power of the moral sense, Channing argued that "all the great agents of nature, attraction, heat, and the principle of life, are refined, spiritual, invisible, acting gently, silently, imperceptibly. . . . Much less can I believe, that in the moral world, noise, menace, and violent appeals to gross passions, to fear and selfishness, are God's chosen means to calling forth spiritual life, beauty, and greatness."[41] Therefore, emotion is a crucial part of being human but needs to be part of a balanced, harmonious, integrated whole.

In May 1825 Mary and Elizabeth returned from Maine, according to one report, because the Gardiner children were making insufficient progress, but more likely because the sisters were simply homesick for Boston. A month later they attended the dedication of the monument on Bunker Hill.[42] Elizabeth was surprised at the depth of her feeling at seeing the Marquis de Lafayette, who had come to the United States for this event and for a kind of grand tour. She was equally affected by the presence of two hundred veterans of the Revolution, who were given places of honor at the ceremony. "It was a most interesting sight—most of them looked poor and infirm—many were maimed—but all deeply affected with pleasure and pain." The invocation and singing of a hymn to the tune of "Old Hundred" led one veteran to exclaim, "Good God! this is too much for mortal man to bear!"

"Then rose Webster!" Daniel Webster's reputation and oratory mesmerized, perhaps even frightened, the young teacher. "You will read his oration—but the manner—the energy—the enthusiasm—the feeling displayed—you can never read—nor I describe." Webster seemed to stand "*on air*—pouring out the whole soul of feeling and poetry into the close of his address." Oddly, Webster's praise seemed only to oppress Lafayette, who stood through much of the speech with his head down and his mouth half open.

Elizabeth had a second chance to see the French hero and amend her view. The next day, she heard that his carriage would pass near where she was staying in Brookline, and she "determined to wait till he came." A political hero and media celebrity, Lafayette stimulated a kind of infatuation in Elizabeth, quite out of keeping with her earlier rationalism but now more congruent with her rediscovery of feeling. "All my enthusiasm that I have thought was quenched forever by reason and experience came back again for the time. It was such a delight to me to think of seeing La Fayette again, with a happier or less oppressed expression of countenance than when I saw him last—that I suppose that I appeared half demented."

Then, Lafayette's coach did appear, and Elizabeth and the others rushed toward it. "I felt precisely as if I was dipped in liquid fire when La Fayette's face, glowing with delight—flashed from the carriage." She caught his hand and placed a kiss there, "which had my whole soul in it. I must have jumped three feet from the ground." Lafayette kissed her hand in return, saying "thank you, thank you." Everyone showered him with praise and affection, she wrote. "When he was gone we were all trembling and shaking—like the sea after a storm—and every body congratulated *me* who had 'kicked up the row' as Mary elegantly expresses it."

When the sisters moved to Brookline from Maine in 1825, Elizabeth had much more chance to spend time with Channing, who had an estate there called Oakwood. The following year when the sisters opened a private school in Boston that included the Channings' daughter Mary, Elizabeth visited their city home nearly every evening. One day she appeared at Channing's study and offered to copy one of his sermons that had aroused some interest and controversy. In response to Channing's concern that she had better things to do than copy his sermons, she replied, "it is so easy for me to copy that I can do it while listening to an interesting book read aloud." "I will test that at once," Channing returned, and gave her the manuscript and copying paper, took down Cousin's French translation of Plato's *Timaeus,* and began to read in English.

"This was indeed a severe test," she recalled, "for when he read to any one what interested him, he kept raising his large, devouring eyes to see if it was taken in; and now he frequently stopped to get my assent or dissent to the thoughts expressed," a difficult task since the manuscript Elizabeth was copying was filled with Channing's abbreviations. But she persevered, and "made a great effort to convince him that I heard and in a measure comprehended this most difficult of the Dialogues." What was more, Channing approved of her copy of his sermon. After this, she copied about fifty of his sermons and transcribed his translations of Cousin's Plato and of DeGerando's "Du Perfectionnement Morale," "of which I afterwards published a translation under the name of 'Self-Education.'"[43]

∼ AT THE SCHOOL assembled for Mary and Elizabeth in Brookline, a fashionable suburb of Boston, Elizabeth put into effect Channing's belief that in the work of education, "the soul begins to realize its relations and connections with the invisible world eternally present; when it begins to measure the difference between the material and spiritual ends of life." In this school and one gathered a year later in Boston, Peabody combined her mother's emphasis on rigorous curriculum with stress on character building that was derived in large part from Channing. Most methods of education "ignored the child's consciousness, instead of drawing it out and making it understand itself, to the end of giving it the clew of self-direction," she remembered Channing saying. Education so understood would be the basis of Christian culture.[44]

In August 1825, after only three months of class and just before the late summer recess, Peabody wrote letters to each of her students, informing them of their character flaws. "I told some they were unfeminine and indelicate—some that they acted without principle—some that they were vain—some that they were wickedly passionate—in short I did the work thoroughly." She trembled at doing this, she told Sophia, fearful of their responses. But it turned out that her students appreciated her correction of their faults, even one who was inclined to defend herself. Repeating her feeling that the girl's behavior was "indelicate," "I put my arm round her—for she seemed full of emotions—& she immediately burst into tears—& said, 'I am very much obliged to you'—This girl my predecessor thought had no feeling—& was incorrigible."[45]

All this emphasis on self-culture and self-improvement could be risky, of course, since these were private schools where relations between teacher and pupil were intense, almost familial. Shortly after the Brookline school opened, Elizabeth was spending nearly every evening at the homes of the Sullivans and Guilds, wealthy people whose children were in her school. Mary described young Richard Sullivan as being a delight to teach, "for he understands language very well and takes great interest in stories of all kinds. He is the very pink of beauty and good behaviour and loves me dearly, I know." Their other star pupil, Lucy Gardiner, is "full of conscience and reflexion and disinterestedness and every noble feeling."[46]

In June 1826 Mary wrote that the school had opened its summer term "with twenty-nine scholars. . . . I dont think you ever saw so pretty a school in your life—or so many sweet children together. I have lost the pride of my heart, however—little Richard has gone to a school

kept purposely for children of his age. He came down to the schoolroom to see me this morning little cherub that he is—but I must not
rave."[47] Elizabeth shared this intensity of feeling about their students.
But within a few years of this letter, she would find that this intensity of
feeling and closeness would lead her to some unwanted involvement in
the lives of her students and to the loss of some of her most desirable
patrons, including, for a time, the Sullivans. Neither for the first nor the
last time in her life, Peabody encountered the struggle between strong
personal feeling and the socially accepted norms of behavior.

At her Brookline school, as in Lancaster and probably in Maine as
well, Peabody taught English grammar by presenting the meaning and
relation of words rather than abstract labels and categories. Years later
she recalled that a father of one of her pupils came "to remonstrate with
me for 'not teaching English grammar.'" She invited him to return the
next day to witness her students' parsing a passage from Thomson's
Seasons: "Every grammatical distinction and classification was stated by
the children in plain English, without a technical term . . . after the
lesson was over, the gentleman said I had conquered his doubts and
fears; that he had never passed a more intellectual hour, or received a
more thorough lesson in grammatical analysis."[48]

In the fall of 1826, Elizabeth and Mary moved their school to Boston,
encouraged by their friend Eliza Lee Cabot, who wanted instruction for
her young niece. Elizabeth was moving back to a city where she had had
formative experiences and had developed an influential circle of friends.
The social changes she had witnessed four years earlier had accelerated,
and the efforts of Unitarian families to shape the cultural and political
life of the city now seemed doomed to failure. The population of Boston had passed the 50,000 mark the previous year, and this demographic change was altering Boston's physical appearance. By 1824 Beacon Hill had been leveled down to its present height; the Mill Pond to
the east of Beacon Hill and the marshes on either side of the narrow
neck of the Boston peninsula were being filled in; new streets appeared
on the reclaimed land; and new bridges connected the city to communities north, south, and west. The swelling of the city's population and its
physical size sealed its move to faction-based politics, and increasingly
left the Unitarian Whigs an embattled minority rather than the pace-
setters in a homogenous community.[49]

It was, nonetheless, among these privileged people that Mary and

Elizabeth continued to move. Elizabeth began spending nearly every evening at the Channings, conversing and reading aloud, and working as Channing's unpaid secretary. She began attending his Federal Street Church Sunday morning and afternoon, where, she confided to her mother, she wore her glasses and discovered to her shock that Channing looked rather different than she had seen him before, although, she added hastily, "he looks extremely interesting and his eyes are very fine."[50]

The Channing house and the Federal Street Church seemed fixed points in the Peabody universe, but Mary and Elizabeth's school had no such fixed location, nor indeed did their own rooms. Where they first lived when they moved to Boston is unclear, but by early 1827 the sisters were conducting their school at 17 Franklin Square and living at Mrs. Prescott's on Chestnut Street, where the artist Chester Harding was also a boarder. By September they were moving again, this time to a house on the corner of Bedford and Lincoln, which they shared with the family of William Russell. "You know probably that we are at Mr. Russell's," Mary wrote Maria Chase, probably in October. "And I wish you could come and see how pleasantly we live. We have a paradise of a schoolroom." In 1828 the elder Peabodys moved to Boston, and Elizabeth and Mary likely lived with them for a year at 18 Fayette Place, and then from 1829 to 1831 at 7 Tremont Street.[51]

Besides this variable location, the sisters' school had another distinctive feature in the later 1820s, the presence of William Russell. A native of Glasgow, Russell came to the United States in 1817. He was dedicated to educational reform and to the teaching of elocution, and found Boston, where he moved in 1826, congenial to both efforts. To editing the *American Journal of Education*, lecturing on educational topics, and giving lessons in public speaking, Russell added the Peabody sisters' school to his list of activities. In May 1827 Mary wrote Rawlins Pickman that "Mr. Russell cheers us with his presence twice a week, and our schoolroom is so convenient that we are subjected to none of the disagreeables that annoyed us before."[52] During these visits Russell taught reading, composition, spelling, and definitions, subjects that the sisters could readily teach themselves. But his presence gave their school a boost of recognition in a crowded educational market.

Russell had in fact been making quite a splash in Boston with his elocution lessons. Mary and Elizabeth attended a reading party in November 1826 at which Russell commented on the guests' speaking abilities, a kind of elocutionary master class. Mary described the scene this way: "Elizabeth had the courage to begin to read—but first Mr. Russell made a few remarks upon *utterance*—pitching the voice. She was soon followed by Dr. C[hanning] and I suspect everybody had a queer kind of feeling while Mr. Russell was *criticizing* him with the utmost coolness! He told him his voice was pitched much too low.—I thought he did it admirably—I was afraid he would pass over him without making any remarks, which would have made it very unpleasant to the Dr. He hardly knew how to take the criticism, though he wished to with all meekness—but it was probably the first time."[53]

Mary was a bit put off by Russell's forwardness with their family hero Channing, but Sophia Peabody felt no such hesitation toward Russell. She was quite taken by his gallantry and flirted with him despite the presence of Mrs. Russell, whom Mary described dismissively as "a pretty Scotch lassie with yellow hair and full of animation and simplicity." Sophia simply basked in his attention: "Maria—Maria! my spirit has been reveling to night in the supernatural light of Mr. Russell's eye, as it was raised *without sight* while he recited Scotch airs and suddenly he laid it down and said with one of his beneficent smiles—'I will recite Milton's Invocation for you, Sophia!' My heart leaped, as you may suppose, and 'I was all ears'—Every evening he makes it a practice to recite, and so you see I am experiencing continual and high enjoyment. I *was* born under the most fortunate star that ever twinkled into being." That was not all. Russell's recitation of Robert Bruce's address sent her blood galloping through her veins "like a war horse," she wrote her Salem friend. During that same month, at an evening exhibition of Chester Harding's paintings, Sophia had, as she breathlessly put it, "the felicity of Mr. Russell's arm the whole evening upstairs, and so was the exulting recipient of his striking and exquisite reflections upon what he saw."[54]

Russell's attentions to their younger sister may have caused Elizabeth and Mary some concern, particularly since they considered Russell their partner and would worry about the perennial issue of reputation, his and theirs. In fact, Russell was far too busy in Boston's educational reform circles to consider the Peabodys' school very important. A considerable part of his activities in the late 1820s involved Amos Bronson Alcott, the Connecticut teacher and reformer who had come to Boston in 1828 to seek a larger audience for his ideas. Alcott's beliefs in innate human goodness and his disinclination to use memorization and corporal punishment allied him with Russell, as they would later with Elizabeth Peabody.

Through Russell, Alcott met some wealthy Boston women who had organized themselves as the "Infant School Society of Boston" and agreed to superintend a school for young children of working-class mothers. From June to October 1828, Alcott conducted this school along the lines of his earlier schools in Connecticut, stressing self-development and experiential learning. In October, unhappy with the increasing interference of his wealthy patrons, Alcott opened his own school, the Common Street School, with Russell's own son among the pupils.[55]

All these activities put Alcott in close proximity with Elizabeth Peabody, who definitely did not impress him at first meeting. She "may aim perhaps at being 'original' and fail in her attempt, by becoming offensively assertive. On the whole there is, we think, too much of the *man*, and too little of the *woman*, in her familiarity and freedom, her affected indifference of manner. Yet . . . she is interesting." Alcott's sexist comment indicates both the limits of his appreciation for independent women and probably an uncomfortable feeling that Peabody posed some competition for students. After Peabody wrote a glowing article in the *American Journal of Education* praising his Common Street School, Alcott found himself changing his mind about the brilliant young woman. In February 1829 he described her as having "a mind of superiour order. In its range of thought, in the philosophical discrimination, and originality of its character, I have seldom, if ever, found a female mind to equal it. Her notions of character, the nicety of her analysis, her accurate knowledge of the human mind, are remarkably original and just."[56]

While all this educational reform swirled around them, Elizabeth and Mary Peabody continued to conduct their own school, with pretty much the same students, although at varying locations. There was even some continuity from their previous school in Brookline; five girls from the suburbs now attended the Boston school. "You can hardly imagine the difference between town and country girls," Mary observed to Rawlins Pickman. "They are in effect much less wild and giddy. . . . Dr. Shattuck says children in the country see something of the order of nature which children in town have no opportunity of seeing—here fashions are continually changing, and where fashion has the sway, the order of nature is interrupted."[57]

One of these fashionable city girls was Fanny Appleton, daughter of Nathan Appleton, one of the "Boston Associates" who founded Lowell and the Lowell mill system. In the fall of 1827, Appleton wrote Elizabeth, asking of her intentions regarding his daughter. Peabody's response gives a clear picture of the kind of education she and Mary were offering to the children of such privileged families as the Appletons.

Apparently Fanny, later the wife of Henry Wadsworth Longfellow, was not a prize student. She was often tardy, absent from school during the summer, "exceedingly careless and rather indolent," and "indifferent" in Latin grammar and comparative languages, and "very averse" to the study of arithmetic. Indeed, "what taxes her memory without attracting her taste passes away from her mind as rapidly as it goes into it." This state of affairs was not all Fanny's fault. She was struggling with a rigorous curriculum that included Latin, French, and English grammar and vocabulary, and translations of the foreign languages, arithmetic, geography, and history. Despite her generally poor start, Fanny did show "great interest in this exercise" of history, Peabody observed, and no wonder, since history was her teacher's specialty.

Whether Fanny Appleton stayed in the Peabodys' school is unknown. Elizabeth, who took education with utmost seriousness, might have offended the powerful industrialist with her blunt talk about his daughter's limitations: "You must decide whether Fanny receives advantage from the plan. She has natural talent in abundance. She reads the best in her class. . . . But she dislikes hard study—is too willing to be assisted, and often when *we* would throw her upon her own resources, she obtains assistance from her schoolfellows." Besides, Peabody observed boldly, the school's requirement that students study at home as punishment for "neglect and carelessness" at school cannot be enforced on Fanny since she "has the privilege from home—of never studying at home," a bit of parental indulgence that Peabody doubtless found intolerable.[58]

In these last years of the 1820s, Elizabeth Peabody was groping toward her own distinctive intellectual position, combining the many influences at work on her mind. From her Unitarian family and culture she drew a sense of the orderliness of the cosmos and a belief in universal truth. From her mother she learned that education is a patriotic duty that recognized no barriers of gender. William Ellery Channing expanded Peabody's intellectual range beyond her mother's religious rationalism, showing her how emotion can have a place in liberal religion.

In 1826, "the first year of my intellectual life properly speaking," Peabody wrote several essays that demonstrate precisely that mix of rationalism and idealism. Collectively called "Spirit of the Hebrew Scriptures," these six essays (of which only three were published, and then not until 1833) sprang from "the bosom of Unitarianism" and yet reflected advanced thinking about "the *socialism* of true Religion & the divinity of Christ," Peabody wrote later to Orestes Brownson.[59]

The essays were written under unusual circumstances: a woman who was living in the same boardinghouse with Elizabeth was dying, and she exhorted her children to read the Bible. The children in turn came to Elizabeth and asked for help. Under this impulse, she recalled, she wrote a series of essays on the Hebrew scriptures. If Peabody's story of the essays' origins is accurate, then the children for whom they were intended must have been paragons of intellect and masters of patience. These essays are large, indigestible lumps of prose, distinguished only by flashes of wit or originality. When they were published seven years later, they confirmed the views of many that Peabody was incapable of sustained thought and clear presentation. Still, they help reveal her intellectual development and show the way she was synthesizing her diverse influences.[60]

From her considerable reading, Peabody understood that the Bible's history, status, and authority were among the cluster of issues that separated liberal Unitarians from orthodox Protestants in the early nineteenth century. As children of the Enlightenment, liberals believed that the Bible could be approached with the tools of reason, common sense, historical knowledge, and linguistic training. The liberals were confident that its essential message would remain unscathed after such examination. Like John Locke, American Unitarians believed in successive revelations. That is, the messages of the Bible became more normative as one moved from Old to New Testaments, the teachings of Jesus and his disciples being the most normative. All these insights were based on a belief that the Bible, while divinely inspired, was a book like other books, the product of history and human consciousness, written in language and thus open to critical and comparative judgments. This perception was of course anathema to more conservative believers, for whom the Bible was verbally inspired throughout and occupied a status unlike that of any other book.

German theologians in the late eighteenth and early nineteenth centuries took the lead in developing this new Biblical criticism. Men like Johann Griesbach and Johann Eichhorn worked to free Biblical study from theological assumptions and used their knowledge of ancient languages and history to discern the origins and contexts of the Biblical texts. Some American intellectuals, including Joseph Buckminster, Edward Everett, George Bancroft, and Theodore Parker, worked to keep up with the new ideas, whereas others, like Andrews Norton, Dexter Professor of Sacred Literature at Harvard, were suspicious of these new trends and their relativistic implications. Still others, including Princeton's Charles Hodge and Andover's Moses Stuart, rejected the new scholarship altogether as impious and atheistic.

Because of his position and prestige, Andrews Norton exerted enormous influence on the subject of the Bible. For him the Bible was first a historical document, recording God's dealings with people in their own time and language. One needs to read down through the accretions of language to find the nugget of truth that lies there. The message of the Bible thus lay in its concepts, not in its language. Like Norton and her mentor Channing, Elizabeth Peabody drew moral lessons from the narratives in Genesis. God's command that Adam and Eve should have dominion over the rest of nature meant that they, and we, should exert self-control; to be made perfect in a garden means that each person is born a morally free and responsible agent; sin represents a failure to live up to our own moral potential.[61]

This approach in her essays was combined with its opposite, a much more linguistically and aesthetically sensitive one. In 1826, the same year as Elizabeth's composition of "Spirit of the Hebrew Scriptures," James Marsh published a translation of Herder's "Spirit of Hebrew Poetry" in the journal *Biblical Repertory*. In this work Herder argued that for primitive people, language is an immediate expression of spirit, indeed of an entire way of life.[62] Citing Herder, Peabody echoed this same argument in the first essay, "Creation." "Poetry is the expression of abstract and spiritual truth by sensible objects, by the forms, colors, sounds, changes, combination of external nature. The foundation of the possibility of such an expression is the fact, that the human mind in its original principles, and the natural creation, in its simplicity, are but different images of the same Creator, who has linked them for the reciprocal development of their mutual treasures. The primitive languages, therefore, were naturally poetic, that is, synthetic in their genius, like the minds that used them."[63]

Language, then, is not arbitrary, but deeply meaningful. Traced to its origins, it is synonymous with nature itself; "one is seal and one is print," as Emerson would say a few years later. Even more, all language derives from a common source and thus reveals the fundamental unity of humanity. These issues would become enduring concerns for Peabody, who returned to them again and again, in her essays on language, in her teaching techniques, and in her advocacy of the work of linguist Charles Kraitsir.

By the late 1820s, some of Peabody's psychological and emotional makeup was also coming into focus. She had come from a family where women, not men, held intellectual and even financial power, a family whose "myth of origins" linked mothers and daughters in an unbroken line back to the seventeenth century "Ann Sisters." Men were failures, seducers, or tyrants. Elizabeth's mother's vigorous embrace of liberal religion led to a rejection of the Calvinist God, who figured in Elizabeth's childhood memory as an old man in eighteenth-century costume wielding a corrective rod. In its place Elizabeth put a head and face of love, an image confirmed by Channing's feminized God as a loving parent.

Closely identified with her mother, with liberal religion, and with a woman-centered world, Peabody quickly took on the same burdens that her mother shouldered in caring for the large family, opening her first school when she was only sixteen. The Palmer side was particularly quick to criticize Nathaniel Peabody's failures. Regarding Elizabeth's departure from Lancaster for Boston in 1822, Aunt Sophia Pickman noted acerbically, "Dr. Peabody has added so much to his embarrassments by his removal [from Salem to Lancaster] that nothing but the success of Elizabeth's school in Boston can keep them from the most serious trouble." A year later, Elizabeth's grandmother commented on the young woman's responsibilities in a letter to her daughter Mary.

Noting Elizabeth's eyestrain, Mrs. Palmer wrote, "I hope she will be *prudent* enough to forbare [sic] reading—or studying—her success will greatly depend on her being [?] steady and attentive to her duties—she has an [ambition?] for so young a creature—but so much depends on her, for her father's family, I feel very anxious for her."[64]

It is not surprising, given this family history, that Peabody should keep eligible men at a distance, much preferring either the company of women or the association of men who were not realistic romantic partners. Peabody saved her most passionate outbursts for her sisters, as is abundantly evident in the letters they exchanged from the 1820s through the 1880s, and she became a relentless supporter and advice-giver for her sisters and their often-resistant husbands. The nature of these sometimes quasi-spousal and always emotionally intense relationships is clear in a comic episode that Mary Peabody told their mutual friend Maria Chase. Walking back to Brookline from Cambridge, in June 1825, the sisters found themselves exhausted and out of sorts. Mary "actually dragged Elizabeth home—her feet were swollen and rather pinched, and I plainly saw that we should be a little forever getting home if I did not do something energetic—so I proposed being horse—she took one corner of her handkerchief and I the other and threw it over my shoulder and thus dragged her home—stopping occasionally like all wearied donkies to take a *breathing spell*—We met lots of people—I suspect they never saw a poney [sic] with spectacles on before—we struck up a bargain to be husband and wife on the road—but E. insisted upon being husband—not considering that she was violating all the rules of chivalry by allowing me to be her Gustavus—or rather Gustav*a*."[65]

Unable or unwilling to imagine herself in a romantic and sexual relationship with a man that might have led to the forming of her own family, and early plunged into adult responsibilities, Peabody found herself in her early twenties giving advice and dispensing criticism to her sisters and her students. Nonetheless, it was hard for her to receive advice and criticism. Easily wounded by adverse comment, Peabody often sank into discouragement and depression, especially in these early years. Writing to Dorothea Dix in July 1827, when Dix was visiting the Channings at Newport and tutoring their children, Elizabeth revealed the depth of her pain at such criticism. The source and nature of that criticism are unclear; however, the impact is abundantly clear. "Every way in which it [criticism] *ought not to be done*—has left its burning trace upon my soul—which writhes even to remember it." Even her friends thought perhaps the criticism was well deserved and that Peabody was just trying to face it down. "I do not know why it was—but my mind instantly ran over the past with the thought of 'how little has my manner represented what was passing within,' and all seemed to concentrate into one agonizing sensation which before I was aware exhibited itself in that language which is understood by all human hearts altho' there are no articulate sounds—" that is, she burst into tears.[66]

In a series of letters to Sarah Sullivan, mother of one of her students, Peabody had more to say about the troubling issue of emotion. What is the relation between the intellect and feeling? She had written to Sullivan that she preferred the love of the "meanest" to the intellect of the "highest," and Sullivan had taken that statement to mean that Peabody had no powers of discrimination. Not so, Elizabeth responded; but she was convinced that intellect unbalanced by feeling is dangerous. "I would remark that there is a besetting sin to the cultivated of our imperfect age of the world—which breaks & scatters & palsies this noble energy of heart which is encouraged on every page of Scripture as the perfection of human nature;—& that is—the spirit of criticism—not of discrimination—but of criticism."[67]

This flurry of letters in 1827 on issues of criticism, emotion, misunderstanding, and intellect coincided with a time of serious crises for Peabody. The details of one such crisis, the "New Bedford Affair," are hazy, but it appears that Peabody went to New Bedford in the spring or early summer of 1830 to intervene on behalf of some of her students whose inheritance she felt was threatened by a conspiracy of relatives. She felt obliged to do so "because I could make a revelation to their legal guardian of the past action and character of those for whose pecuniary interest the conspiracy was devised."[68] This involvement got Peabody into a lot of trouble very fast, with the families of her pupils, with several of her good friends including Sarah Sullivan, and with such community notables as Eliza Rotch Farrar. Here indeed was criticism and conflict.

The issue was not only Elizabeth's perhaps intemperate intervention where she was not wanted, and her wounded response to "fault-finding." It was also that Peabody's interference violated cultural norms about women and the family. In a culture where women were increasingly seen as separate from the world of money and trusts and were placed in the realm of home and family, such "meddling" on her part seemed to challenge both the privacy of the family and the limits of appropriate female behavior. Most seriously, Peabody put her own reputation, and thus her career, on the line for the first, but not the last, time. She was, after all, dependent on the goodwill of parents. To be seen as an intrusive busybody would certainly drive away fee-paying parents of potential students.

Whereas others saw her as meddlesome, Peabody saw herself as the innocent and injured party, suffering for the sake of truth and her students. Her problem, she confided to Elizabeth Davis Bliss in July 1830, was that she "suffered intensely from contact with society all my life— for I chose to keep myself *unsheathed*—through fear of being selfdeceived." She liked to believe that she operated out of a disinterested ideal of "the lady and the Christian," in order "to guide those I love & those it is my duty to guide—into the right path" despite her selfdoubts.[69]

Besides the "New Bedford Affair," Peabody was also drawn into another scandal, one that attracted national attention. In 1880 she recalled to nephew Julian Hawthorne that she "had been greatly tired by intense sympathy with a great tragedy in a circle of my friends." This tragedy— about which she gave no details other than that it involved criminal behavior and subsequent punishment in her "circle of superior people," as she put it to Channing—was apparently the White Murder in Salem. Prominent merchant Joseph White was murdered on April 6, 1830, while he lay asleep in the White-Pingree House. His assailant was Richard Crowninshield, ne'er-do-well member of that notable Salem family. The Peabodys knew both families and had taught daughters from both. Rather than face certain execution, Crowninshield hanged himself in his jail cell. John Francis Knapp and Joseph Jenkins Knapp, who had paid Crowninshield $1,000 for the deed, were found guilty after a sensational trial with Daniel Webster as prosecutor, and they were executed in late 1830. The case, which was intensely covered by the regional press, spawned a flurry of popular broadside ballads and street gossip. For the distinguished families drawn into this melee and for the entire town of Salem, the case was an embarrassment and a disgrace.[70]

Warning Peabody not to become too emotionally involved in this case, Channing cautioned her "to watch over the health of your own soul. This is peculiarly your own care; nor are you to forget it in ministering to others. In truth, you cannot minister effectively without a calm, wise mind, conscientiously faithful to the will of God as expressed in all your relations."[71]

Then, on top of this scandal, one of Peabody's students got involved with a circle of "gifted young men" in Boston who pursued high living and sexual exploits. She described them as "disciples of Bulwer," who were "making 'Henry Pelham' their model." Edward Bulwer-Lytton's 1828 novel *Pelham, or, The Adventures of a Gentleman* was a must-read for the fast set in Boston in those years. Even though it criticized English high society and the dissolute lives of young aristocrats, it prompted much interest in exactly that "silver-spoon" life that Bulwer-Lytton deplored. The novel even effected a change in gentlemen's evening dress; where men had earlier worn evening coats of different colors, *Pelham* made black the only acceptable color. Elizabeth was probably glad to be on the giving rather than the receiving end of criticism about society propriety, as she intoned that "it was a frightful revelation to me to see crime committed, not by the access of terrible passion, but in mere frivolity and absence of all serious purpose."[72]

Without hesitation, Elizabeth wrote about this situation to her mentor. Channing's response of March 11, 1831, expressed his concern for her. "I fear that your mind is acting too exclusively and intensely on a few subjects. I trust, too, that your deep impressions of the guilt of a part of our community are to be ascribed, in a measure, to your position, your recent solitude, and your recent disappointments in what you thought tried virtue." Remember, he went on, that while "there is a terrible strength of moral evil in the world," there is also "an infinite fountain of moral energy and disinterested love. . . . I care not how faithfully and terribly human passions and crimes are portrayed to me; I want no deception,—I can bear the worst. But I desire to hear no language of despondency, not a moment's doubt of the triumph of virtue—" a suggestion that Peabody perhaps did feel despondent and doubtful of virtue.[73]

Still, Peabody did manage to feel that the power of goodness would triumph over evil, despite the shocking revelations of the depth of human iniquity. "I have suffered deeply this winter," she wrote in March 1831 to Sarah Sullivan, her friend who had been alienated by

Elizabeth's meddling at New Bedford but who was now reconciled to her. "*Theoretically* I had admitted the idea of evil which was all but infinite—& knew that Christianity outmeasured even this. But it has so happened that until now I never *saw the struggle*—for in the cases where there was this unmeasured evil (& I *have* seen such—I *have* seen people in whom the whole moral being was touched with evil—in whom the moral life was absolutely extinguished for this world)—there has been no attempt at repentance—*But* I have seen *virtue*—unsullied—unfailing—triumphant—which would have convinced me of immortality & Christianity & a God—had I never known it before."[74]

Even with this consolation, everything seemed to be coming apart. She had encountered deception and maliciousness on a level unaccounted for in liberal theology. Influential parents had called into question her discretion and propriety. She felt even Channing pulling away from her, impatient with her impetuousness, her deference, her generalizing cast of mind. Agreeing to leave his daughter Mary in her school for another term, Channing spoke of the qualities he wished Elizabeth could correct in her own character: "You are more given to general speculation than to the details that are so necessary to a teacher, and . . . you sometimes talk above your pupils, and bewilder instead of enlighten them . . . you have a noble mind in its moral and intellectual power; I want to see it unfolded in a manner worthy of itself and its Author." Channing made the same complaint in 1831: "You are led astray by slight connections and analogies, and are apt to see in past or present facts what other eyes cannot discover. I have thought, too, that your interpretations of life are not always to be trusted, and that you are in danger of substituting your own structures for reality. I would not trouble you with these remarks, did I not think that you have still a gifted eye, which looks far into the hidden wisdom of God."[75]

In many ways, however, Mary's and Elizabeth's lives went on as before, despite these trials. The rest of the Peabody family had moved to Boston in 1828, and Sophia was increasingly drawn into the literary and artistic world that her older sisters inhabited. They kept reading German and French books and ones by American authors as well. To Maria Chase, Mary wrote of their enthusiasm for Cooper: "I conclude by this time you have read and adored that transcendent book 'the Mohicans.' I think it is sublime. I am sure Cooper must be imbued with the very spirit of the woods," a judgment Elizabeth echoed, a bit confusedly, a few days later: "I think Hawk Eye, together with Natty—is the finest creation of American literature."[76]

The sisters even found time for romance, not their own but that of their former student Lydia Sears. Without other family, Lydia lived at the Peabody family home in Salem through much of the 1820s, until she met Samuel Foster Haven, Amherst graduate (1826) and student at Harvard Law School. Lydia married Sam in the Peabodys' rented house in Boston, probably Tremont Street, a little after 4 P.M., on May 10, 1830. Elizabeth described the ceremony, conducted by Channing, in a letter to Sarah Sullivan: "I brought down a tumbler of flowers and put it on the table after Mr. Channing came & took my seat. The bride & bridegroom came in, with their attendants, and without sitting down,— Mr. Hilliard gave Mr. Channing the certificate,—& he commenced with a prayer. I wish you could have heard the tones of his voice. Lydia told me, yesterday, that as soon as they touched her ear—every flutter was composed. . . When it was over I looked at her, and saw that the deep flush which had been in her cheeks all day had subsided & she stood perfectly calm."[77] That "deep flush" was likely a sign, though Elizabeth would not have known it then, of the tuberculosis that would carry Lydia off six years later. Still, despite joys like these and the continuing excitement of teaching and learning, the turn into the fourth decade of the nineteenth century had been emotionally and physically trying for Elizabeth. In late 1830 William Russell left Boston for Philadelphia, convinced by Bronson Alcott that they both could do better with alternative education there. Possibly Russell left his wife behind as well; at least Elizabeth thought that was the case.[78] Exhausted by controversy, drained by the changes taking place in her own mental and emotional life, and no longer able to draw on Russell's charm in recruiting new students, Elizabeth desperately needed a rest and a change of location. Mary and Elizabeth closed their Boston school in December 1831.

3

"You Think I Have No Judgment"
჻

IN THE EARLY DECADES of the nineteenth century, educational institutions and philosophy underwent important changes. Despite statutes in New England mandating public support for children's education, girls were regularly excluded from local schools, as were women who wished to teach there. Likewise, before the 1780s, girls were excluded from town-supported grammar schools, which trained college-bound boys in Greek and Latin. Parents who wished some education, usually limited to reading, writing, and simple arithmetic, for their girls sent them to a dame school, a local female academy, or to private tutors like the Peabody sisters. By the 1810s, however, girls were entering town schools, at least in Massachusetts, and by 1820 women had appeared in the classroom as teachers. These new teachers were young, unmarried, and paid significantly less than their male counterparts.[1]

Whether taught by men or women, publicly supported schools in the early nineteenth century were poorly equipped and poorly housed. Drafty windows, uncomfortable benches, and insufficient heat combined with an emphasis on physical discipline and rote memorization to make such schools appealing only to nostalgic adults or penurious taxpayers. Introducing exercise, nature study, and student-teacher conversation in the Cheshire, Connecticut, public school in 1825 brought the wrath of the taxpayers down on reformer Amos Bronson Alcott, who turned to private education as a more appealing venue for his reform ideas. When reform did finally take hold in public education in 1840s, spearheaded by Horace Mann, it was a combination of uniformity in curriculum and teacher training with a philosophy of self-culture and self-development that made such reforms acceptable to the Massachusetts public.[2] Private education likewise underwent changes in philosophy and practice around the turn of the nineteenth century. Boys' academies offered tracks that were either college preparatory or, in recognition of the growing commercialization of the new nation, training for crafts and trades. The most remarkable changes, ones in which Eliza Palmer took part, were the admission of girls into academies that had earlier been limited only to boys and the creation of new female academies.

Private in-house schools, like academies, were much more open to educational innovation than were tax-supported schools; wealthier parents who sent their children to private schools may have had more education and more tolerance for pedagogical experiment, or they themselves may have been interested in new ideas about education that were topics of intense discussion in the early nineteenth century. Like her mother, who was part of the previous generation's reformist demand for a more challenging curriculum for girls and young women, Elizabeth Peabody also participated in radical educational reform located in the private sphere. The decade of the 1830s began with Peabody's adult conversation classes for women on classical and historical topics; saw her active and critical role in Bronson Alcott's experimental Temple School; saw her involved, briefly, in an educational periodical called *The Family School*; and ended with the founding of her West Street bookstore and lending library, site of several of Margaret Fuller's more famous experiments in continuing education.

Peabody's exposure to educational theory began, as did so much in her life, with her mother. Mrs. Peabody offered the same curriculum to boys as to girls, and for both she insisted on the importance of historical study. But Elizabeth's mother was a teacher-housewife, not primarily an educational theorist, although her published work and unpublished letters testify to the sharpness of her insight and the range of her thought. For theory Elizabeth went elsewhere, to Pestalozzi, De-Gerando, Wordsworth, and ultimately Froebel, but first she turned to Richard Lovell Edgeworth and his daughter Maria Edgeworth.

Among the many volumes Elizabeth devoured in the library of Benjamin and Sarah Vaughan in Hallowell, Maine, was the Edgeworths'

Essays on Practical Education, first published in 1798. "E has been reading Miss Edgeworth on practical education & is exceedingly pleased with the book," Mary Peabody reported to their cousin Mary Tyler in January 1824. Unlike his friend Thomas Day, author of *Sandford and Merton*, who was a confirmed Rousseauist, Richard Edgeworth believed that society was humanity's natural element and that the best education fitted children for life rather than shielded them from it. A member of the "Lunar Group" that included Erasmus Darwin, Josiah Wedgewood, Matthew Boulton, and James Watt, Edgeworth proposed that education be considered a branch of experimental science and that the thinking about education should focus on questions like these: What could a child of a certain age be expected to understand? What could such a child reasonably remember? As she helped her father and stepmother prepare the manuscript for *Practical Education*, Maria Edgeworth learned lessons of careful observation and precise notation that would serve her well in her own career as an essayist and novelist.[3]

In *Practical Education*, the Edgeworths proposed that children be given simple shapes as toys, and clay and wax for modeling. They stressed the importance of visual education, drawing and perspective, as a means of training in skills useful for employment in a new commercial and mechanical society. Peabody would repeat the Edgeworths' fondness for sensory education and the use of simple shapes fifty years later in her advocacy of Friedrich Froebel's educational techniques.

The difficulty with the Edgeworths, Peabody came to understand, as she left Maine and resumed her place under Channing's influence, was that their educational thought was intended to fit children only for their place in the emerging social and commercial order. Left unexplored was the issue of the child's moral and spiritual nature. Ironically, this absence of any reference to religious education was precisely the criticism leveled at *Practical Education* by conservative evangelical critics in England, writing in the last years of the eighteenth century. Neither a conservative nor an evangelical, Peabody insisted that religious education is central to any system of pedagogy, and she faulted the Edgeworths for leaving it out. Writing to her friend Sarah Sullivan, Peabody observed, "Miss Edgeworth herself, in her life of her father, *says* that she thinks religion a necessary part of the character—but that she designedly *left it out* [in her fictions for children]—intending that it should be supplied by the parents.—But do you not think her works evince that she herself is wanting in a deep—allpervading—lively sense of a Moral Governor & father of the Spirit?" Echoing Wordsworth and forecasting Bronson Alcott's linkage of pedagogy and a Romantic idealization of the child, Peabody continued, "Now I hold—that the child,—between whose conscience & whose God—early instruction has at the very dawn of reason—opened a communication, carries not a little of Paradise in his own breast—therefore I think it is an object to find out a means of opening this communication."[4]

"Opening this communication" would prove to be Peabody's lifelong work, in one form or another. The question was not Elizabeth's ability to teach effectively and intelligently; her own rigorous education had guaranteed that. The real issue, she was coming to see, was the training of the whole person, shaping not just the intellect but also the moral and spiritual sensibility, together with a sense of collective identity, of belonging not simply to oneself or one's family but to the entire human race. Each of these tasks would prove challenging. Maintaining her own intellectual edge exposed Peabody to her culture's ambivalence about the "female pedant," the overeducated bluestocking who violated the norms of society in overreaching her limited female potential and thus becoming a kind of social freak. Seeking to shape her students' moral lives inevitably involved her in highly charged emotional issues and resulted in bruised feelings and angry parents. Because Elizabeth herself was not fully in control of her own feelings about her family, her own sexual identity, and about her spiritual values and experience, she often projected her own struggles onto others.

Peabody began her forays into educational theory cautiously, with the anonymous *First Lessons in Grammar on the Plan of Pestalozzi* published in 1830. Like Bronson Alcott, whose reading of the Swiss reformer encouraged him in attempting changes in the public school curriculum in Connecticut in the mid-1820s, Peabody was quite taken by Pestalozzi's practical application of Lockean psychology. "Pestalozzi does not attempt to introduce anything into his pupil, but to develop what he finds in him," wrote Joseph Neef, one of Pestalozzi's disciples. "His pupil always sets out from the known and plain, and proceeds with slow speediness to the yet unknown and complicated." For the Unitarian Peabody, this statement would have struck just the right note; education is the key to self-culture, encouraging and shaping the powers latent in each person. Typically, Mary's comment on her sister's accomplishment was less theoretical and more personal: "Here sits E. just finishing her grammar, which is to appear before the public immediately.—It is a cappadocious little book and I solicit your patronage," she wrote to Maria Chase. "Her brow has a true authorfied knit and in the course of her ruminations she has chewed up the feather of her pen all to nothing."[5]

Peabody's other early attempt at educational theory was, like the grammar based on Pestalozzi, also a popularizing of another's ideas. This was her translation, done in conjunction with Channing and published in early July 1830, of Joseph Marie DeGerando's *Self Education; or, the Means and Art of Moral Progress*. Just as Pestalozzi showed Peabody how theory might give substance to practice, so DeGerando reinforced her growing sense that education was not merely about mastery of information nor was it limited to the young. "The fundamental truth," DeGerando wrote in his preface, "which solves all the problems that agitate the youthful heart, and trouble growing reason, the truth which may direct and regulate everything in our earthly career, is this:—*the life of man is in reality but one continued education, the end of which is, to make himself perfect.*"[6]

Elizabeth was able to ponder and refine her ideas about education not simply in these grammars and translations but also in conversation with others. Channing's Federal Street Church, which Elizabeth and Mary began attending after their move to Boston in 1826, had adult education classes as well as those devoted to the young. Peabody devoted many pages of her *Reminiscences* to accounts of these classes. In the fall of 1827, she joined in a conversation group on the education of children that included Channing, his wife Ruth, Mary Peabody, Charles Follen, Jonathan Phillips, and several others. Held in Channing's study, these exchanges exposed Peabody to conflicting philosophies of education. Follen, an émigré professor from the University of Berne who had married the Peabodys' friend Eliza Lee Cabot, argued that education should lift children out of narrow individualism and acquaint them with "patriotic and humane sentiments." Phillips, who would later become a prominent Boston banker, took the opposite position, stemming in part from his own stifled childhood under the tyrannical rule of a Calvinist father.

In some ways, Peabody and Channing agreed much more with Phillips than with Follen. "The common management and domination of

children was the opposite of education," Peabody remembered the clergyman saying. "It ignored the child's consciousness, instead of drawing
it out and making it understand itself, to the end of giving it the clew
of self-direction." Peabody was prepared to go even further: "All great
acquisitions come from voluntary thought, and voluntary thought
alone," a position Channing thought too extreme and "sure to leave
undeveloped both the intellectual conscience and the sense of the moral
duty of study."[7]

As was so often his approach, Channing offered a middle way, but it
was one that Peabody could embrace as well. He proposed that education involved both self-culture and an exposure to that which is not
the self. Here the study of history would be crucial, he thought, offering as an example the study of "such works as Plutarch's 'Lives' and
other biographies, which he thought the best reading for the young,
because the immediate causes of historical events are to be found in
gifted, energetic persons, who show that men are responsible for the
catastrophes of history." Despite the sometimes heated differences, Peabody found these exchanges "interesting & instructive," she wrote to
Dorothea Dix.[8]

〰 IN FEBRUARY 1832, Elizabeth and Mary found rooms for living and teaching in a boardinghouse on Somerset Court, managed by
Rebecca Clarke, mother of Sarah Clarke and James Freeman Clarke,
who would both become lifelong friends of the Peabodys. Not quite
ready to resume teaching, Elizabeth set to work on the first in what
would be a series of historical study guides. Mrs. Clarke's proved to be
an excellent place for such work, since one of the other boarders turned
out to be the Lancaster schoolmaster-turned-historian Jared Sparks,
who brought his considerable library into the house with him. "We
have access to Mr. Sparks' library," Mary wrote their former student
Lydia Sears Haven in May, "which is immense & choice too. On one
side of his room stand a dozen shelves of large books containing 20,000
of Washington's letters in manuscript! of which there are only 5000 that
are duplicates."[9]

Sparks's presence at Somerset Court must have reinforced Elizabeth's
growing conviction of the importance of learning and teaching about
history, as she and Mary watched the "queer man" select materials and
work on his monumental edition of Washington's letters. Later that

year Elizabeth published her own work, *First Steps to the Study of History: Being Part First of a Key to History*. Like her other early publications that act as prefaces to the ideas or words of others, this volume contains lists of questions keyed to several works of American history, including Washington Irving's *Life of Columbus* and Robertson's *History of America*, but here the introduction is longer and much more original.[10]

Nothing is more central to intellectual freedom than a knowledge of the past, Peabody writes, yet "in this country, no study is more neglected in schools, and even in colleges" than history. The fundamental skill that underlies historical understanding, she thought, was comparative thinking: "To see . . . in what different circumstances human nature is placed, and the different forms which the same elements assume, before the mind has made any arbitrary associations as to what is beauty and truth, is the surest means of destroying the principle of dogmatism."

This comparative and chronological approach would be valuable not just for males, who would exert power and influence in politics and business, but also to females. Self-understanding requires women to understand the past, since the past "has the most direct influence in forming them for the duties peculiar to their relations in life." In a bold move, Peabody suggests the formation of historical schools, targeted particularly on women, "which would not take up more than an hour in the day; but which would help to give a regularity to the reading of history at home, and also afford an opportunity of receiving instruction and assistance from mature and highly cultivated minds [.] There are ladies who are capable of keeping such schools and of communicating therewith such cultivation of mind . . . but where schools of history are out of the question, this Key may be still more important;—serving in a humble degree the place of an instructor to a family of sisters, or a party of friends, or a solitary student, that feels the importance and the interest of the subject." Within a year Peabody would be relying on exactly such "historical conversations" for badly needed income. She even hoped that *First Steps* would bring in some cash. As she wrote to Sophia, "Hilliard & Gray offer to print my book & give me ten percent on the retail price—which I believe is very good pay."[11]

While Elizabeth saw her book into print, Sophia visited the Havens in Dedham, and Mary spent part of the summer tutoring the Channing children at Portsmouth, Rhode Island, where the Channings had gone to escape the danger of cholera. "We hear of nine cases of cholera in Boston, all deaths," Mary wrote Elizabeth. The Channings were very worried about William Ellery's health in view of the epidemic. "He only goes from the easy chair to the bed, & does not sit up much, and scarcely speaks, and cannot bear even to hear anything interesting read—or any conversation except the merest trifles—he coughs a great deal . . . & has a constant fever."[12]

Elizabeth had been feeling a certain coolness in her relationship with Channing. Doubtless he disliked her worshipful attitude toward him and recoiled from her intense and sometimes obsessive advocacy of her students and their causes. For her part, Peabody was critical of the Channings' skills at parenting their children William and Mary, and she had tactlessly but truthfully said as much. Mary Peabody dissected the clash this way: "I think one explanation of the difficulties you had in regard to Mary [Channing] is that neither Mr or Mrs Channing like to hear about the children's faults, though they probably would not acknowledge the fact to themselves. I think it is the only fault in their government which I admire and respect more and more every day. . . . Mrs. Channing cannot let even William be accused of wrong—all his faults are in her eyes but the effervescence of his spirits." Channing seemed largely uninterested in these disagreements over the education of his children, possibly because of his illness that summer, but Ruth Channing, as Mary suggested, was more difficult and intrusive, "so lovely & interesting in many points of view, & so curiously wanting in others that I am in a sort of mase [sic]. . . ."[13]

Despite these tensions, Peabody set to work on *Key to History: Part Two: The Hebrews*. She brought to bear much of her earlier reading in theology and church history, including the liberal insight that the Bible was an historical document as well as a record of God's revelation. The events narrated in Scripture were recounted by reputable witnesses and so qualified as truth made available to the senses, if not of present-day readers, then of earlier eyewitnesses whose accounts we can believe. This was the Lockean reasoning followed by Andrews Norton in his insistence on the historicity of miracles. For Peabody, who would find herself a few years later on the opposite side in the argument over the necessity of belief in miracles as a test of one's faith, this historicizing of the Bible made it possible for her to consider it as secular rather than sacred history.

That treating the history of the people of Israel as history rather than as revelation would be controversial was apparently much on Peabody's mind as she wrote the introduction, as it was a concern for Jacob Abbot, who wrote a "recommendation" as preface. "I ought however to add that 'The Key' while it recognises the divine authority of the Scriptures, does not exhibit at all the religious bearings and relations of the sacred narrative. It leads the pupil simply to such an analysis of the institutions and history of the Hebrews, as would be proper in the case of any other nation. There will be undoubtedly a difference of opinion in the community in regard to the propriety of this course."

Although this was perhaps not quite the ringing endorsement she had hoped for, Peabody echoed Abbot's words in her own introduction. "The present work being historical, and for young persons, its only object is to bring the student acquainted with the facts of the history of the Hebrews, in the first place; and the views taken of them by modern historians, afterwards. It is not the intention to impress any particular view of religion, but to present those facts to the mind, on which a judgement is made up." One needs to understand what the Israelites believed in the context of their times, she insisted. "That all [Moses's] views of cosmogony, morality, and even of providence, should bear the test of modern science and Christian philosophy, is not necessary, even to establish Judaism a divine revelation."[14]

Indeed, one steps into a past time not simply through a mastery of events but also through an awareness of its inner life, which often comes through its art. Hebrew history can truly be grasped only when one reads the creation accounts, Miriam's, Moses's, and Deborah's songs, David's laments and psalms, and many others. In support of this claim, Peabody appended a long section from Herder's *The Spirit of Hebrew Poetry*. This strategy, of linking her own introductions with long selections from or questions about scholarly sources, marked the entire work, which contains long lists of complex questions based on Josephus's *Antiquities of the Jews* and the Old Testament histories of German scholars Johannes Jahn and Johannes Müller.

Given the continuing religious antagonisms between liberal and conservative Christians, Peabody probably awaited the publication of this book with some anxiety. "Mr Emerson & Abbot are going to write recommendations to it," she wrote Sophia, although Emerson's preface never appeared and Abbot's was lukewarm at best. Still, she wrote after publication, the editor of the *Boston Daily Advertiser* actually seemed interested in her work. "Mr [Nathan] Hale is going to write a little notice of the Key to History (editorial) & is going to say a little about my school—." But even that turned out badly; in a postscript Elizabeth added, "Mr. Hale's notice is very slight."[15]

➣ IN JUNE 1832, as she worked on this and the final volume, *Key to History, Part Three: the Greeks,* Peabody reopened the school that she and Mary had suspended in December 1831. Living and teaching in the same place certainly had its advantages, despite the sharp eye and quick tongue of the gossipy Mrs. Clarke. Still, the other boarders provided intellectual stimulation, as did new students who began to fill up the little school. The problem was that neither her publications nor her teaching were bringing in nearly enough income. So in the last months of 1832, pioneering the technique later to be made famous by Margaret Fuller, Elizabeth held a conversation, "a reading party," she called it, or an adult education seminar as we might call it, on the Greek history and art she was then studying in preparation for her last *Key.* Describing this "party" the following spring in a letter to Sarah Hale, wife of Nathan Hale the editor, Peabody wrote that "we have been lamenting that we could not have heard Mr. E. Everett's lectures of olden time," referring to Sarah Hale's brother Edward Everett and his famous lecture "Antiquities" delivered in December 1822. Perhaps, Elizabeth went on, Sarah could intercede with her brother and encourage him to loan the manuscript to the class. How this suggestion turned out is not known; the letter to Sarah Hale refers back to Peabody's primary school and ends on a sober economic note: "I have—dear Mrs. Hale—concluded to *give up* in regard to my price—& take children under ten years of age for fifteen dollars (but they must know how to read)—& those over ten years of age for twenty—." In any event, Elizabeth wrote to her sister Sophia, sometime early in 1833, "tell Pa—that I think my historical school will enable me to pay him what I borrowed last fall—& for the washing this winter—at least."[16]

Surprisingly, Peabody's finances were somewhat improved by the "spontaneous forming" of a class on historical and literary topics in spring 1833. The group consisted of twenty women, six married and fourteen unmarried, she reported to Maria Chase. "We employed six days in reading various beautiful things about Socrates—including some manuscript translations I have of Plato—& now we are reading Herder on the Spirit of Hebrew Poetry—which is an exquisite book.—"[17]

No matter how difficult it might have been to make ends meet, Peabody's mind was as much on the Greeks as on personal finances. From her letters to her family and friends, it seems clear that this volume gripped her imagination much more than the other two volumes. Peabody received special permission from the trustees of the Boston Athenaeum to borrow books on her own, rather than through the courtesy of one of the members, all males. Extended this privilege throughout 1833, she borrowed Potter's translation of Aeschylus and Niebuhr's history of Rome each twice, Mitchell's translation of Aristophanes, Mitford's history of Greece, and Flaxman's copies of classical sculpture. She was particularly excited about the possibility of including illustrations of Greek art along with selections of Greek poetry and prose. To Sarah Hale she sent a detailed list of the illustrations she had in mind: Flaxman's work, outlines of ancient statues including the Elgin marbles, and copies of illustrations from books on Greek architecture.[18]

Copying and preparing these illustrations for press would be the particular task of her artistic sister Sophia, Elizabeth hoped, proceeding to bombard Sophia with assignments and suggestions. "The first part of it [her book] is to consist of questions on Senecas Theogony & Mythology—together with the Heroic legends—& I wish to have every thing illustrated by a drawing either of a statue or a gem—or a cameo— I shall make tracings at the Athenaeum of every thing that is there which will suit my purpose (on thin paper)—I enclose your Michael Angelo's Moses—and would like to know if you think you could copy from such models." By no means tire or sicken yourself, was the elder sister's constant refrain in a series of letters, yet Elizabeth seemed to pressure Sophia continually to copy more, not only for the *Key* but also for book covers and cards to sell at fairs, and to continue her work copying paintings. Elizabeth was indefatigable, busying herself both with finding copies to be copied as well as with the details of art supplies, paper, and printing: "The whole cost will be 4770 dollars—for paper—stones—letterpress & printing . . . there will be baggage waggoning for 100 stones—each weighing I fancy nearly an hundred pounds—." Sophia, whose headaches were intensely painful during the early 1830s, must have felt overwhelmed by Elizabeth's enthusiasm and likely was relieved that the volume on the Greeks appeared in 1833 without illustrations.[19]

↬ PREOCCUPIED AS SHE WAS with writing the *Keys* and teaching children and adults, Elizabeth Peabody could hardly have been unaware of the difficulties and disappointments afflicting the male members of her family. Never very adept at providing a livelihood for his wife and children, Dr. Peabody had moved the family to 128 Colonnade Row in Boston in 1828 in hopes of expanding his medical and dental practices. Even though he went into Salem every other week to practice dentistry, the move must have made his Salem patients wonder whether he had abandoned them, and in 1830 he felt obliged to take out an advertisement in the Salem *Gazette:* "Dr. Peabody continues to visit Salem the first and third Wednesday and Thursday of every month— for the purpose of operating upon Teeth. His office is at Mr. S. L. Page's, corner of Essex and Summer Streets." The announcement went on, "As a report is abroad that Dr. Peabody has raised his fees for operating upon teeth, he takes this opportunity to state that it is not true; his fees are the same as they always have been—He further states, that he operates according to the latest and most improved methods— and being permanently settled, will be responsible for his operations."[20] Even this apparently was not enough to satisfy his suspicious patients, and Dr. Peabody took his family back to Salem in 1832, leaving Mary and Elizabeth to carry on with their school on Somerset Court.

The problem, of course, was not simply location; it was Dr. Peabody's keen sense of his own precarious place in a family of highly educated and increasingly prominent women. He was, after all, the "son of an unlettered New England farmer," as his son Nathaniel noted, whose dreams of professional success were fading in the 1830s, replaced by more ordinary anxieties about money. Her husband's charges that Mrs. Peabody was secretly borrowing money from the girls prompted a remarkably frank letter to them: "It is necessary for me to tell you, that the peculiarities of his mind are best known to me; & that you cannot conceive how sensitive it is when he imagines his prerogatives infringed upon. It struck him, that because you felt interested that I should have what was comfortable & respectable, that I must have complained that he did not provide for me."

Much of Dr. Peabody's feeling of inferiority came from his background, his wife understood. "The sterling excellencies of yr Father's character are sometimes shaded by feelings, which originate from his early associations & from the great difference in our educations. He was always accustomed to see the female part of his family labour hard, dress coarsely & think themselves happy to be allowed a decent garment for holidays," and so she was reluctant to ask for anything new. "You will say, & very justly, these feelings are owing to forming too romantic notions of married life. But did you know how many such notions I have eradicated, you would give me some credit for the work I have done."[21]

The deficiencies of Nathaniel's early education gave him a surface demeanor of diffidence that masked deeper hostility, Mrs. Peabody thought, much the way their eldest son Nathaniel was turning out. He always used the same written prayer at family devotions, even though he had many others that were excellent. These are sensitive matters for their father, Mrs. Peabody observed to her daughters, whose intellectual accomplishments were likely to heighten his sense of failure. "You must ever recollect, in transactions with your Father, that he feels so conscious of the deficiencies of his early education as to be easily impressed with the notion, that he is thought inferior. This is almost always the case, perhaps, with those who have been taken out, as it were, from a family so uneducated as his were. *They* had little information, were constitutionally jealous, and had strong prejudices against expressing much feeling. I mention these facts, that you may shape your course accordingly."

Dr. Peabody's suspicion that his wife and daughters were conniving about family finances was not wholly misplaced. "Whatever your present feelings may dictate in relation to relieving your Father from present calls [of creditors], I think . . . that his best good will be secured by your obtaining a permanent fund . . . so as by & by to have interest upon it. These remarks are confidential, therefore burn this hasty notice of my anxiety. I humbly trust his children will so succeed as to discharge, in time, all his debts . . . and he is growing old and will need assistance more when he cannot exert his own industry."[22]

Like father, like sons. Nat picked through his studies with Eames, the Salem Latin School master (a violent man who flogged his students for mistakes in recitation), but he much preferred to hang about the wharves with his friend James Cleveland, talking of battles and shipwrecks, or at least until he and James got into a fight at North Field; then James was "all talk and no sense and no thinker." George, who studied for a time at Round Hill School in Northampton, was enrolled in Mary and Elizabeth's school in the late 1820s, but not doing too well there. In a letter to him enclosed in one to his sisters, Mrs. Peabody "exhorted him to pay strict attention to all your directions and advice; given him, as far as in my power, an idea of the sacrifices and exertions you are making for him and his Brothers."[23]

By the early 1830s, the Peabody boys were becoming serious concerns to their parents and sisters. George had taken a low-paying clerking job in Boston. Wellington, the youngest, had entered Harvard College in fall 1831 but left (or "took up his connections," as the official transcript puts it) in February 1832, no official reason being given for this hasty departure. Doubtless eager to flee family disapproval and to make some money, Wellington shipped aboard a New Bedford whaler early in 1832, much to his mother's dismay. "He is suffering all that the hardest and most disgusting labour can inflict in addition to an abrupt change from the luxury of study, easy and good Society, to watchings, storms, stern commands, vulgar oaths and gross actions." Two years later, in June 1834, Wellington returned, but he jumped ship in New York and forfeited his share of the ship's profits. In what was becoming a family pattern, Wellington wrote his father to borrow $60 to pay off his debts, prompting an exchange of letters and promises of industry and frugality. But meanwhile their cousin George Putnam wrote to Elizabeth to say that Wellington had taken Putnam's sisters to the theater on borrowed money. "Was there ever any thing like this mania for spending other people's money?" Elizabeth exploded in a letter to Mary.[24]

George Peabody was a quiet, sweet, bookish young man, whereas Wellington was a kind of romantic hero. It was not hard to like these brothers despite their stumbling approach to adulthood. Nat was another story. He seemed to possess a kind of seething inner rage compounded of bitterness against his sisters, against intellectual culture, and against the modern commercial world. Perhaps, as the eldest son, he was particularly stung by his father's sense of professional failure and inferiority in the world of educated women. Following the dubious family tradition, Nat got into the habit of borrowing money from his father. In 1833 Dr. Peabody bought for Nat the stock of Henry White's apothecary shop at the corner of Court and Tremont Streets in Boston, prompting Elizabeth to worry: "I am sorry to hear that Nat depends on Pa for ready money—I fear it will do him no good. I wish to my soul he was a clerk instead of on his own account—I fear he will fail—& then what can he do? To fail as an apothecary will not do him any good in reputation—it is so safe a business."[25]

Apparently Elizabeth's fears were well-founded. This business failed by the end of the year, whereupon Nat worked in an apothecary shop nearby. In 1834 his father helped him to fit out a shop in South Salem that sold both drugs and groceries. This enterprise too was a failure; Nat took in about a dollar a day, not enough to keep it going without help. Early in 1835 Nat wrote his sisters Mary and Sophia, trying to put the best face on what was in fact a failing business and a considerable indebtedness to his father. "You see: by the great exertions of father, money to the amount of $400 was procured in Boston, and so divided among my creditors that I received a full discharge of all debts. . . . My store is a very pretty one indeed—I sell groceries as well as medicine. My business has been such as to pay the expenses of the store and it would pay my board if I chose to take it. . . . Father's interest here is as great as, or greater than mine, because he became responsible for everything."[26]

Not quite everything, however: three months later, in May 1835, Nathaniel married Elizabeth Hibbard, whom he had been courting for at least a year. Had he seen it, Nat's mother's comment on the engagement would have enraged him, for its comparison of his situation with his father's and for the slap against the elder Nathaniel. "I shall be truly glad when the young people can settle down. I have much more hope that N. will make a good husband than I once had, that is, a kind, disinterested one. He is truly attached to E [Elizabeth Hibbard] and labours to improve her mind."[27]

A year after his wedding, Nat added to his responsibilities with the birth of his first child, Ellen. "She is quite pretty, & is a hearty, fat little specimen of incipient humanity," he wrote to his brother George, adding acerbically, "[w]hen it is considered that she is the only offspring of one out of five or six grown up members of a family, it is a desirable thing, perhaps, that she has come into the world, to perpetuate to future times the name of the Peabodys, together with the haps & mistakes of that notorious family." As for his shop in Salem, "my own affairs are in statu quo. I have applied to four different monied people, for loan of a sum to set me on a good footing," but so far without success. Mrs. Peabody too had her doubts, which she shared with the long-suffering George. "Of N's ultimate success we can form no certain opinion. I believe he does all he can & that he is honest and industrious, and if he has not all the requisites for a trader, we can only regret that it is so; he is not to blame for it."[28]

In the fall Nat moved his family to Boston, where they boarded with the Hibbards and he opened a drugstore, but this plan quickly fell apart. "Nat has got a rival in S. Boston, which diminishes his gains—& Mr. Hibbard thinks of moving away—which will oblige him to go to a more expensive boarding place," Elizabeth wrote to George in October. Even worse, Nat resumed his habit of borrowing money from his father, this time $400 to pay Salem debts. "When do you think there will be an end to this?" A month later Nat lost that business and was on the street, searching for work. "Our poor Nathaniel is paying dearly for his hasty marriage," Mrs. Peabody confided in George. "He is now utterly without money and without business. He means to try to get a clerkship in some Apothecary's establishment. If that fails—he must try Teaching. . . ."[29]

In early 1833 the company of boarders at Mrs. Clarke's was enlarged by the addition of lawyer and recent widower Horace Mann. A representative to the Massachusetts General Court in the early 1830s, Mann had tirelessly advocated state support for hospitals for the mentally ill. Despite the strain of sponsoring such unpopular legislation, Mann managed to win significant victories. He also courted and married the young Charlotte Messer of Dedham. In September 1830 they married, despite her already declining health from incipient tuberculosis. Less than two years later, on August 1, 1832, she died, plunging Mann into an abyss of grief. In an effort to help him reconstruct his life, Mann's friends, especially his Litchfield Law School classmate Edward Loring, encouraged him to move from Dedham to Boston and to enter a legal partnership with Edward's cousin Charles. Mann took rooms at Mrs. Clarke's, conveniently located near the Massachusetts State House.

There Mann encountered Jared Sparks, Washington scholar and future president of Harvard College; George Hillard, in later years a prominent Boston lawyer; Mrs. Clarke's daughter Sarah; and Elizabeth and Mary Peabody. In this circle, which Mary described as a "hodge-podge," Elizabeth's prodigious intellect led her to have something to say about every topic of conversation, while Mann, masking his grief, appeared to be "intolerably witty," having "an anecdote, a story or a saying for every emergency." Some of the boarders were sure that Elizabeth was romantically attracted to Mann. Mrs. Clarke recalled that Elizabeth once volunteered to take a meal tray up to Mann's room, where he nursed his grief. "'No,' said I 'it isn't proper Miss Peabody. I don't want you to.' 'Oh but I must' said she, 'I've got something to say to Mr. Mann.' Then they all began to talk about Mr. Mann's marrying again. Elizabeth declared indignantly that he'd never be married again. 'In your presence,' said Mr. Fairbanks, laying his hand on his heart, 'In *your* presence Miss Elizabeth I think he will.' Great fool! He really seemed to think he'd said just the right thing."[30]

Mary Peabody, as it turned out, proved Fairbanks right and her sister wrong by marrying Horace Mann in 1843. She was attracted from the start not so much by the brooding Byronic intensity that was so compelling to Elizabeth, but by his tenderness toward children. Sometime in the spring or summer of 1833, Mary went to Father Edward Taylor's church to observe a children's temperance meeting, for which she wrote a brief anonymous review for the *Christian Register*. But, as she wrote to her sister Sophia, "I could not for the newspaper write a con amore account of Mr. Mann's electrifying part in it: it is impossible to convey by description the beautiful way in which he told that story of the doves, or talked to the children about their playing & behaving well for each others' & their own sakes . . . the children looked at him as if they thought he was a creature of light, just as he looked to be standing above that mass of little bodies . . . I was in a sort of little ecstasy."[31]

Despite Mann's ability to get out of his grief through such public appearances as these, his sorrow grew as the first anniversary of Charlotte's death approached. He seemed to find the company of the Peabody sisters some consolation, or perhaps only an audience, for his struggle. To Sophia, Elizabeth described one such scene: "In the evening after pacing the room an hour or more—while I sat alone—and silent—he said in a voice that seemed a sigh—''Tis vain to speak—'tis vain to sigh—But in the heart—and in the brain—awake the thoughts that pass not by.'" On another occasion, Mary and Elizabeth held his hands in sympathy. Mary went out of the parlor "& then [he] drew me nearer & throwing his arm round me—let the tears flow—which seem ever to wait this touch of sympathy." Perhaps aware that such demonstrations of affection might be misunderstood, Elizabeth warned Sophia, "pray do not let any body read what I say of Mr Mann—for sorrow is too sacred to be made a subject of speculation."[32]

Despite these sympathetic young women, Mann was unable to master his feelings or deal with his fellow boarders. In late July or early August, he abruptly left Somerset Court and set up housekeeping in his offices at 4 Court Street. "Mr. Mann is going away from here—going to take a room and live alone, and dine at the Tremont—he thinks it will be better for him, at least for the present," Mary wrote Sophia. "I don't know but what he is right, for he seems to grow more depressed and unhappy all the time. It is a family & it is not a family," she continued, referring to Mrs. Clarke's boardinghouse, "and Sarah [Clarke] & I agreed the other night that *ergo* it was the abomination of desolation—a 'social solitude' as Byron says."[33]

Still, Mary and Elizabeth felt that somehow they, or perhaps the other boarders, had offended Mann, and wrote to apologize. His departure had only to do with his grief, he responded: "When I first went to the house where we are, I had hoped, that the intellectual and refined society of its inmates would do something towards filling up the void in my life. But . . . I only found so much of that which I mourned, as to be a perpetual remembrance of it. . . . At this time, too, the anniversary of that fatal day, when all the foundations of earthly happiness sunk beneath me, was approaching and drawing me into its vortex. I will not attempt to describe to you the power of imagination where memory supplied it with such materials. . . . [I]n the hope of being able to break the spell that bound me, I resolved upon the proposed change."[34]

To "break the spell that bound" him was precisely what Elizabeth intended. From late summer 1833 through at least early spring 1835, she was engaged in a grand project to convince Mann that the universe was presided over by a loving God who, despite appearances to the contrary like the death of Charlotte, desired only good for His creatures, and whose existence and behavior could be best understood intuitively and emotionally. If you could but *feel* God's love, Peabody said a hundred different ways, you would be cured of your soul-sadness. As she would so often in life, Elizabeth appointed herself the evangel of this good news, a task that involved, naturally enough, the sharing of emotions as well as the sharing of ideas.

Much to Peabody's chagrin, Mann was unmoved by the gospel of liberalism, of Channingite Unitarianism's becoming Transcendentalism. This drama of the handsome, grieving widower and passionately serious young schoolteacher intellectual, with all its attendant sexual tensions and played out in the larger context of competing religious worldviews, was likewise performed for the unwilling audience of Mary Peabody. For Mary, who had probably already fallen in love with Mann, could only read about Elizabeth's long walks, talks, and embraces from afar, from Cuba to be exact, where she had gone with her sister Sophia in December 1833.

⤳ THROUGHOUT THE NINETEENTH CENTURY and well into the twentieth, cures for illness were sought not just in medicine or diet or better attitudes but also in travel to what seemed more salubrious locations. After the Civil War, invalids sought health in the Adirondacks or, later still, in the desert climates of the Southwest. In the antebellum decades, many Americans, particularly women, also sought out sanitariums where, in many cases, hydrotherapy was practiced for such conditions as prolapsed uteri. Bronson Alcott's wife Abigail once abruptly left him and the rest of their children for such a health resort in New Hampshire, taking only Beth, their second youngest child, with her as company.

Travel abroad for one's health was more exotic, possibly more dangerous. Cuba, in the early decades of the nineteenth century, was to New England taste both exotic and dangerous. Still, it attracted a number of pilgrims seeking better health. In 1859 Richard Henry Dana's *To Cuba and Back* noted the number of such people, especially young women, on Cuba-bound ships: "That pale thin girl who is going to Cuba for her health, her brother travelling with her, sits on the settee, propped by a pillow and tries to smile and to think she feels stronger in this air. She says she shall stay in Cuba until she gets well." Others of the Peabodys' aquaintance had already made the voyage, including Abiel Abbot and Oliver Prescott, or were thinking about it, like their friend Sarah Perkins.[35]

When Sophia first broached the subject of traveling to Cuba for her health, her friend Dorcas Cleveland, who had helped her family settle in Lancaster and whose husband was now a customs officer in Havana, responded forcefully that Cuba, or at least Havana, was no place for such a refined flower of New England:

> Your olfactories are continually offended even to sickness, with the hot steaming effusion from jerk beef half spoiled salt fish, & dried fish spawn fried or rather burned lard garlic, old tobacco mingled with the filth of streets never dry, & the slimy mud of which, is daily increased by the slop & trash of houses, & the whole kept constantly impregnated by the natural solution of urisalts from horses, mules & dogs innumerable & also by the black & white male population which contribute, by copious streams from the side of every door & at every post & corner, to keep up the rank odours of the city.[36]

In place of the redolent Havana, Dorcas Cleveland suggested that Sophia board with the Morrells, a family living inland at a plantation called La Recompensa. After some negotiation Mary Peabody agreed to accompany her sister there and act as tutor to the Morrell children, while Sophia would teach drawing. With a mixture of excitement, anticipation, and anxiety that we might only imagine, the sisters left Boston for Havana on December 10, 1833, on board the *Newcastle*, accompanied by a young Boston businessman named James Burroughs and a Madame Gerault, wife of the overseer at the plantation of Nathaniel Fellowes, a neighbor of the Morrells.

Mary and Sophia were linked to their family and friends back in New England through a series of long journal-letters called the "Cuba Journal," which Sophia kept on the Cuba end and to which Elizabeth, and occasionally other family members, contributed on the Massachusetts end. Sophia's "Cuba Journal," which details the people and environment that the young women encountered, is a clear indication of the keenness of Sophia's aesthetic sense. Mary's letters home reflect her abundant moral sensitivity regarding slavery, which would much later find form in her novel *Juanita*, published in 1887.

☙ FOR OUR PURPOSES, however, the real drama continued to take place back in Salem and Boston, and for those events Elizabeth's "Cuba Journal" provides essential insight into her daily life, educational work, publications, causes, and evolving thoughts and feelings. Much of these, in the weeks and months around her sisters' departure for Cuba, had to do with Horace Mann.

Elizabeth Peabody grew up in a family where male leadership was constantly in doubt, where men were untrustworthy and unreliable, and where women held the intellectual, emotional, and financial authority. While she was inventing a series of fantasy-males, like Sylvanus Robinson, Channing, and Mann, to replace her real-life unacceptable males, she was also struggling with the Unitarian heritage of her mother and her Salem culture. That heritage stressed universal order, law, control, even a form of determinism that she absorbed from reading Thomas Brown. But her conviction that the universe was an orderly and explicable place seemed to fit less and less her own life circumstance, which appeared anything but orderly. What Peabody needed was a system that seemed to integrate her own tumultuous and disorderly emotional life with a belief in an overarching order and sense of purpose, a larger order that would embrace even her life's evident disorder. She found such a framework, or the beginnings of it, in Channing's Unitarian pietism, his efforts to describe and validate religious feelings. But she wanted even more. Repelled by strong feelings of any kind, Channing was always a devotee of the faculty psychology and its central principle of balance and order. Emotion is necessary but must always be controlled. Although Peabody would never overtly disagree with that belief, she was searching for a way in which moral truth could be *felt* as true, not simply understood to be so. Here, of course, the Common Sense philosophers had gone before, in their emphasis on conscience as the inner principle of moral truth. But she did not reach for that language. Instead, in her exchanges with Horace Mann, she groped for a way to say that the emotional life was not merely private fantasy needing always the discipline of judgment and will but that it was an important guide to universal truth; that which is felt in the heart and the blood resonated in history and in nature.

This heady brew of erotically charged language and religious liberalism marked Peabody's encounter with Horace Mann. Elizabeth was probably not "in love" with Mann. Rather, as her letters to her increasingly distraught sister Mary, who was in love with him, make clear, she was in love with an image she had constructed, a perfectly gentle, perfectly understanding, perfectly intuitive "elder brother," whose grief it was her project to heal through the ministry of good feelings. Central to those "good feelings" was the feeling of the love of God, Peabody insisted. Mann had no sense of this, she reported to Mary: "He asked me how love of God could be born amidst such sufferings." Could he not feel, she replied, through his sufferings, that the other world and its inhabitants were very near? "He said he did not know whether it would help him to believe there was this *nearness* combined with the wall of separation. There was for a moment a pause. Do you think, said he, I could sleep tonight if I thought my wife was in the room. . . . This thought of nearness overwhelms me. . . . I said I fear you have been excited to no purpose, my dear friend. *No*, said he, and he stood still leaning upon me as I also arose, and fixing his eyes with an inward look of calm still endurance upon my features."[37]

As Mann's visits to the Clarke boardinghouse continued in the winter and early spring of 1834, it became clear to Peabody that his stoicism and inability to believe in a God of love stemmed from his rigidly Calvinist upbringing. He simply did not have piety, he told her,

> nor anything of which it could be compared or from which it would grow, for not only was the theology of his childhood all horror and gloom, but his life had been a chain of suffering and disappointment, and every body he loved was in misery, suffering from calamities they were irresponsible for. He had never seen happiness but in one [his dead wife Charlotte]—there every thing was indeed concentrated—but to be consumed! He made much more words in this speech than I have made, and said it with so much desperation, that I involuntarily moved up to him and took his hand with my left hand and put my right over his shoulder, and said, "not consumed, but *translated.*" He laid his head upon my shoulder and pressed my hand, and said, "I trust so."

Later, in this same vein, he said to her, "I have the energy of a desperado, which makes me try to bear up like a man, while I *must live* I look forward to life *with clenched teeth* and say, *Come*, come and do your worst—the worst is done—let come what may." During all this, Elizabeth wrote, "he pressed my hand again and again."[38]

Conversations like this must have disturbed Peabody very much, for they collided with her own belief in the essential goodness of the universe. In an undated letter that directly addresses Mann's stoicism, Peabody returns again and again to this theme of God's love and boldly insists that she herself is the avatar of that love. "To myself—there is one short sentence '*God is happy*' which has quieted me and consoled me when all lesser truths, and nearer means have failed. But these words would be cold—aye ferocious—to the soul that did not feel without a shadow of doubt that He loved it. . . . Can love spring from the bosom of suffering? You asked me this last Sunday night. *Yes* [underlined twice]—and you have experienced it. For *me*—dear friend—you have expressed a very affectionate friendship—Before you did it in words, you did it by the most confidential manner."

Elizabeth was sure that his sorrow was a way station on the way to acceptance. Even if her words of consolation brought even greater grief and tears and caused him to embrace her, these were not signs of despair. "It was because you believed that sympathy and tenderness dictated my painful words. . . . You saw & could not doubt the simplicity & sincerity of my friendliness. . . . So love acts in its faintest form." And not just human love, either. "*The Love of God!*—to this you are now called—I cannot but think. No other blessing—no lesser good—can be to you a *good* now—till your soul is *consciously* anchored on this Rock—the Rock of Ages."[39]

There was nothing in Elizabeth Peabody's experience that prepared her for this sudden turn into psychotherapy. She must have felt on shaky ground indeed, given her own recent turmoils and trials at the beginning of the 1830s, now to feel called upon to counsel a deeply grieving and emotionally repressed man. It was wise of her, then, to turn for help to her mentor Channing. In March 1834 Elizabeth organized an evening's conversation among Mann, Channing, and several others. Mann was reluctant to go, he later confessed. It seemed that he was mired in confusion over human suffering: "minds with any sensibility were distressed, detoned and destroyed by the suffering they experienced for themselves and others." To say that God "understands" human suffering through the sufferings of Christ made no sense to him, he observed. "Mr. Mann told [Channing] that till he was sixteen years of age he had never heard the divinity of Christ questioned—he never knew it was questioned—but neither had he ever heard a trait of his character which could be considered moral set forth, that he was merely a name, conversive with that of a deity whose nature was vindictive and terrific."[40]

By now it was pretty clear how far Mann's post-Calvinist stoicism was from the views of Peabody and her friends, but she persisted, inviting him to a conversation about James Walker's recent sermon "The Evidences of the Spiritual World." Walker, pastor of the Unitarian Charlestown Church and editor of the *Christian Examiner* from 1831 to 1839, had argued that "spiritual impressions & perceptions" were evidence of the existence of a spiritual world and thus were the foundation of all religion. Channing argued that not every spiritual impression was religious, but only those that were corroborated by moral law. Mann, not surprisingly, insisted that "moral impression & feelings . . . could not be experienced without involving a conviction of *laws*—& that these laws were the spiritual world."[41]

And so it went. As these conversations, dutifully reported to Mary, unfolded, it became clear that Mann had replaced the Calvinism of his childhood, which taught that acquiescence in the divine will is humanity's duty, with a determinist view of the universe. But in such a universe there was no room for undeserved suffering, and the death of Charlotte had called Mann's Enlightenment view into question. The more he rejected a belief in a loving God as a cynical deception, the more he elevated Charlotte and blamed himself for not living up to her standards of purity. Out of this crisis, Mann gave up his former love of stylish dress and amusement and became prim, censorious, and moralistic, seeing in propriety the only fit way to honor Charlotte's memory.[42] It would take, not Elizabeth's labored arguments, but Mary's gentler and more instinctive touch, to bring Mann out of his sustained suffering into a new life.

In 1835, months after the intensity of their "affair" had cooled, Peabody wrote Mann a kind of epilogue to the encounter. For two years, she wrote, she had "entered into your feelings and thoughts, and meditated day and night upon them . . . *with reverence* for their character and the most unbounded *faith in their object*." In all that time she had hoped to convince Mann that a universe of love could encompass and heal the individual griefs that we experience. The principle of growth and change argues for the possibility of moving beyond these seemingly ineradicable sorrows. "The Creator forever creates, and the universe ever expands, so that the emanating stream which constitutes our particular being, finds the field which it traverses forever expanding," Peabody insisted, against Mann's fixed belief that "a person of decided character must be the same, and cannot change, and cannot turn their thoughts."

But her argument had failed, she realized. "There are doubtless great advantages in studying the spiritual philosophy in this world, looking through the *glass darkly*," she wrote with surprising bitterness, "or you would not be bound to the stake of life for that purpose." She offered this final shot: "You bid me once think of my feeling toward God, in order to understand your devotion and self-annihilation in the thought of your wife. I will ask you to think of that sentiment of confidence she inspired in you to understand the nature and character of my faith in God. And then you will comprehend how *intimately* I feel *desirous* that a *beloved brother like yourself* should not *hold back* in doubt and scepticism. . . . Despair is the only fatal error."[43]

⁊ WHEREAS ELIZABETH must have felt flattered and excited by Mann's attentions and by the "cause" of ameliorating his grief, Mary must have felt increasingly troubled by the intimacy between the two. How was she to take, for example, a letter from Elizabeth in May 1834 that seemed to indicate both Mann's interest in Mary and Mann's willingness to lean on Elizabeth? Mann was deeply interested in news about Mary and begged Elizabeth not to omit anything as she read Mary's letters aloud, Elizabeth related. She also reported a conversation in which she said "well now I do not feel half done—I have not said what I wanted to say. He took hold of both my hands—and drew me for one moment absolutely into his arms—& said—well and can you not say it now? not now I believe said I—It wants *time*—well—you can *write it*." In parting, Mann "held me very affectionately to him—with the most confiding brotherly manner until he went—It was a perfect comfort to me to think he could feel free to do this—without fear of misapprehension."[44]

It was of course precisely the issue of misapprehension that drove the sisters apart. What would others think of this intimacy, Mary wondered? And what in fact was going on between Horace and Elizabeth? In tackling this issue, Mary Peabody found a weapon that would wound her older sister immediately, painfully, and recurrently, the issue of propriety. Elizabeth had already been accused of impropriety earlier in the decade, and now to have it raised again made her bewildered and angry.

> Last night I had a very disagreeable dream—I dreamed you came home—& that every thing you said was very provoking—and that you treated me precisely as if you had made a resolution you would never thwart me—and as a means of doing this—you intended to keep at a distance from all collision—& that you did not intend to know what was passing in my mind—I felt as if the ground of all this was a deep scepticism as to the fact that human beings of different temperaments could be one in the unity of the spirit.—I thought you carefully avoided saying anything that you thought would wound me—& that you had taken for granted that there were things which you must *bear*—which still you thought were unnecessary for me to do—but which you had come to the conclusion I would never submit to the test of right & wrong—but would go on doing to the end of my life—out of wilfullness—& wrongheadedness—Well I dreamed that this made me very angry—and all your kindness I rebuffed—everything you said I contradicted & was as cross & wicked as I could be. . . . This morning I awoke feeling very unhappy & wicked—& I tried to trace the association & concluded that it was the last page of my letter . . . yet it seems to me true that you do entirely misapprehend my character—when you think I have not as quick & nice a sense of propriety as yourself.

The Rices, with whom Elizabeth was now staying, "understand exactly the terms of our [Elizabeth's and Horace's] intimacy," she concluded, implying that it was a mystery why Mary could not.[45]

Mary's accusation that Elizabeth lacked a sense of propriety blew up again just a few weeks later, this time in Mary's face. James Burroughs, whom Mary and Sophia had met aboard ship on the voyage down to Cuba, was apparently quite attracted to Sophia. The two struck up a correspondence and exchanged gifts, with Burroughs even proposing marriage. Taking all this as lighthearted romancing, Burroughs read some of Sophia's letters aloud to the inmates of his Havana boardinghouse, while Mrs. Cleveland, hearing of this intrigue, told everyone she knew in Salem and Boston. Elizabeth was mortified at such gossip about her absent sister and was furious that Mary had been lax in her guardianship. Elizabeth must have been relieved that the propriety is-sue was in someone else's court, and not soon enough. In this letter to Mary, she sensed the charge being returned to her:

> But that is a *dark* affair on *JB's account.* He *knew better* than to expose S to be talked about for he knows the country & I do not believe he is a person who *ought* to talk sentiment to any lady.—If he *did* do it I cannot doubt he was *refused*—But you ought to have insisted on seeing & knowing the whole—I [double underlined] should have done so—or have quarrelled outright—& even at the expense of being called a highhanded tyrant—for the relations of sister & the situation of guardian has a *divine right* of certain pre-rogatives—I do not wonder you [are] still in agony—I should have told her that if she intended to have secrets—she had better go straight home—for you could not take the responsibility unless you shared the confidence. . . . I did not read (without being pro-voked) your remark that I should "lose my reputation in a week in such a country"—but you are so full of such random things to me—I have learnt to try to believe that they mean nothing—of all the subjects that ever came into your mind to judge upon—there never was any one in which you showed such utter want of com-prehension as of my character.—If I should judge of your under-standing by what you have said of me from first to last—I should set you down for being utterly stupid. You have sometimes been provoked that I suppose you were influenced by other people in your judgment but this has been one of the resorts of my imagina-tion to account for the fact of your always mistaking me. . . . Be-cause I have sometimes made mistakes you think I have no judg-ment—no good sense—nay no virtue I should think [written in left margin: that is, if I thought of any body as you do of me—I should despise & pity them—heartily & unreservedly—I should feel there was one of the noblest of God's works—in all but ru-ins] and as my sensibility always anticipates the conclusions of my mind—you think I have no guide but passion—*not observing* that I seldom act—till the latter has confirmed the decisions & impressions of the former. However I live in hope that this separa-

tion may produce *an acquaintance* which our intimate association
has prevented.[46]

For his part, Horace Mann backed away from any "misapprehension" about his relationship with Elizabeth Peabody, perhaps because
he sensed that it was causing Mary unhappiness, perhaps because it
might be endangering his career to be associated with such an eccentric
young woman. In September 1834 Elizabeth wrote her sister that she
and Mann "talked very delightfully about a great many things—and the
differences between love and friendship—And delicate as the subject
was the conversation was perfectly unembarrassed and [several words
unclear] I feel a great deal more certain than ever I have done that no
misunderstanding can ever come between us—however affectionate we
may be [as a?] brother or sister."[47] With Mary, however, the issues of
propriety and discretion would surface again and again to agitate their
relationship.

4

"The Only Practical Transcendentalist There Is"

ॐ

WHILE ALL THIS TUMULT of bruised feelings and uncertain relationships surged back and forth, Elizabeth Peabody still needed, and needed desperately, some paying work. The Boston class on historical and literary topics, formed in early 1833, had brought some relief, as had her own ongoing class at Mrs. Clarke's. But it was not much. To Mary she confessed this in February 1834: "I am so poor. I have paid last quarter's board, and for my wood and lights for all winter. Historical school will give fifty dollars the next quarter. I do not know how much the reading party will give, but I hope fifty, and I have saved some money from last quarter which will, altogether, pay in April for this quarter. My present prospect is to go home in May pennyless and prospectless, except for what I may hope from the Christian Examiner," referring to the articles on the Hebrew Scriptures she expected to publish in that journal. Still, Emory and Anna Lowell had joined her reading party, and by late February she could report a total of twenty in that class.[1]

By June, Elizabeth had yet another idea: a school for little boys, a departure from her usual contingent of girls and women in private schools and reading groups. She hoped to recruit pupils from among her circle of Boston acquaintances—the Rices, Borlands, Blisses—and "teach them Latin and the first things . . . enough to make a school of

112

ten at our old price." Elizabeth was careful not to let this plan interfere with the possibility that she herself would replace Mary as Sophia's chaperone in Cuba, allowing Mary to return to Boston and to Horace Mann.[2]

But a month later this plan, and much of Elizabeth's life, was upset by the return of Bronson Alcott to Boston, full of new energy and a new plan to open a private school.[3] Alcott and William Russell had left Boston for Philadelphia in December 1830, drawn by that city's reform-minded reputation and by the support offered him by such wealthy reformers as Roberts Vaux and Reuben Haines. Although Alcott's schools in nearby Germantown and in Philadelphia had failed to attract enough students, his years in Pennsylvania saw decisive changes in his philosophical and religious views and in his pedagogical practice. Indifferent to institutional reform, voluntary societies, and political organizations—the means that thousands of Americans were choosing in the early nineteenth and mid-nineteenth century to effect social change—Alcott focused his energies on what he believed was a more fundamental question: what were the laws of the human mind? If the mind were properly understood, then its effective training would lead inevitably to social improvement. This philosophical approach to education led Alcott to the work of phrenologists like Caspar Spurzheim and George Combe, to several rereadings of Locke, and to Victor Cousin's *Introduction to the History of Philosophy*.

Alcott's fascination with the workings of the individual mind and his conviction that a proper understanding of one such mind would lead to truths about human nature itself intersected with the birth of his and Abigail May Alcott's first child, Anna Bronson, in March 1831. A mix of empirical observation and deductive speculation about the growth of the child's moral sense, "Observations of a Child During Her First Year" reflected Alcott's growing sense that given freedom of choice and behavior, the child would choose the virtuous path. The birth of a second child, Louisa May, in November 1832, led to another child-study manuscript. In these pages and in his voluminous reading and writing, Alcott pursued the question of the laws of the mind. He had become convinced, in line with his idealist thinking, that the soul was primary and divine, and the body merely its shell.

All this reading and thinking coalesced for Alcott in 1832 when he read Coleridge's *Aids to Reflection*, in the edition prepared by University of Vermont president James Marsh. Coleridge argued there and in his *Biographia Literaria* that in addition to the power of Understanding, based on sensation and the normal powers of reasoning, humans possessed the power of Reason, the creative and divine ability to combine sensations and insights into truly new truths. Coleridge's Reason was spiritual insight, intuitive power, innate truth, called into being by the sights and sounds of daily life. The task of the parent, like that of the teacher, was to surround the child with appropriate stimuli, to call out of the child those truths and powers that were already present.

Alcott had already been thinking along these lines as early as the late 1820s, during his teaching stint in Connecticut. In 1830 this celebration of the child's intuition (along with an acknowledgment of the need for instruction and guidance from teachers of the highest character) had shown up in his *Observations on the Principles and Methods of Infant Instruction*. There Alcott wrote that of the intellectual faculties—imagination, association, attention, taste, memory, judgment, reflection, reason—imagination "should receive special attention since . . . infant happiness depends much upon its activity and guidance." In fact, Alcott went even further, strikingly anticipating Coleridge's great insights: "Infant education when adapted to the human being, is founded on the great principle, that every infant is already in possession of the faculties and apparatus required for his instruction." Still, reading Coleridge began "a new era in my mental and psychological life," Alcott wrote in his journal. Like Coleridge, Alcott saw in the imagination, whether child's or adult's, the power to discern and express spiritual truth.[4]

Bronson Alcott's and Elizabeth Peabody's reunion in midsummer 1834 brought together two brilliant and unconventional teachers whose remarkable agreement about much masked, briefly, their equally vigorous divergences. Both believed that truth came not only from intellectual learning but also from nurturing the nonrational, intuitive powers as well, though Alcott had the Coleridgean vocabulary for expressing this insight, while Peabody was still testing the limits of faculty psychology. Both were educational empiricists, grounding their teaching in experience, trying to give pupils as much firsthand engagement with the objects of study as they could.

Peabody was certainly impressed with how much Alcott had read and synthesized in the intervening four years, with his visionary sense of education as the primary reform. To Mary she wrote of her first encounter with Alcott on July 14: "Alcott is a man destined, it appears to me, to make an era in society, and *I believe he will*."[5] Abigail Alcott told Elizabeth more about Bronson's Pennsylvania schools: "The children keep journals & a perfect passion for composition is developed in them before they are nine years old—He teaches them a great deal by allegories—& they write allegories & fables." Five days later Alcott came over with some of these journals, together with letters from his students, "all under ten years of age!" Peabody's rapid progress from enthusiasm to commitment deserves to be told in her own words:

> He stayed and talked like an embodiment of intellectual light, and yet calm, solemn, and simple as ever. I told him I wanted him to make an effort for a school here, and he said he wished to, but he thought he could not do it without a modification of his plan. He must have a school at different hours from other schools and for a shorter session—two hours and a half, say. I told him there would be a difficulty in this. . . . I told Mr. Alcott that I would inquire about the children in town, and see whether there was not a chance for him. When he went away I took up the journals &c and was *amazed* beyond measure at the composition.

In that afternoon alone, Elizabeth was able to recruit four children for a not-yet-established school. Later in the day, she found Abigail Alcott at the home of her brother Samuel May and told her about the growing possibility that her husband would have a school in Boston.

> She thought it would never succeed without more book learning, and that Mr. Alcott could never put [?] his mind to that; he needed an assistant, and yet it was out of the question to find an assistant that was competent, and that he could afford to pay. I told her I would be his assistant, that is, I would teach two hours and a half a day for a year at his school, for such compensation as he could afford to pay. When she found I was really in earnest, she was in a *rapture* and Mr. A too when he came in I told him I could only engage until your [Mary's] return—on these terms.—They both said the terms were altogether too small—but it is not a partnership—& he could give me no more possibly—with thirty scholars as his expenses would be great.[6]

It seemed practically providential. Alcott found in Peabody a brilliantly educated and experienced teacher with vast contacts in Boston Unitarian society, while Peabody saw in the Alcott school an opportunity to stay in Boston for yet another year. The Lees, the Rices, the Tuckermans, the Blisses—all promised their children to the school. "Every body seems all alive at the idea of Mr. Alcott's coming back . . . the plan goes on pretty well—marvellously well I think. Every body that hears of it—hails its success." To top it off, Elizabeth "wrote a very pretty letter to Dr. Channing telling him about it."[7]

By early September, through Peabody's and Channing's efforts, there were thirty pupils promised for the new school that, Alcott and she had decided, should be located in some rented rooms in the Masonic Temple on Tremont Street near the Parker House hotel. The schoolroom had a distinctly churchly appearance, illuminated at one end by the upper half of the Temple's gothic window. In front of the window on a table was a bust of the "Image of Silence 'with his finger up, as though he said, Beware.'" Across the room was a table Elizabeth loaned for the cause, at which Alcott was to sit. "Very pretty desks all round the room—with pretty chairs . . . for the scholars" and plaster casts strategically placed: "Plato on a pedestal in one corner—Socrates on a pedestal in the other. Christ in bas-relief larger than life over Mr. Alcott's head." Plants, Elizabeth's green sofa, a long table at which she sat and worked, coat closets, library shelves, two landscape paintings, and a portrait of Channing completed the furnishings.[8]

On the first day of school, September 22, eighteen students came— "Willy Rice, S. G. Williams, J. Sewall, H. Higginson, three Gustavus Tuckermans, George Kuhn, Robert Rogers, August Shurtleff, Helen Shurtleff, Luisa Peabody, Susan Wainwright, Lucy Channing, Mary Rogers, Sarah Barret, Emma Savage, Pamela Colman—a lovely set of children," Elizabeth noted, although "the three Tuckermans will be the hardest to manage." At ten o'clock Alcott had the children draw their chairs around him in a semicircle—"the chairs so far apart that they could not easily touch each other—" and asked them why they had come to school. "To learn," said one, and Alcott pursued this response in a conversation designed to draw out the various subject they might study there. What else? "To behave well," came another response, and this led to conversation on right behavior and right feeling. What about punishment? "After a consideration of its nature and issues, they all agreed that it was necessary, and that they preferred Mr. Alcott should correct them rather than leave them in their faults, and that it was his duty to do so." Actually, not all agreed, as Elizabeth's more spontaneous "Cuba Journal" report indicates: "They all said too that they preferred to be punished when they did wrong. The little Tuckermans demurred, however in this a little."[9]

The school schedule gradually took shape, Alcott beginning each day with conversation with the children, followed by lessons with Elizabeth in Latin, arithmetic, and geography. School was usually over by early afternoon, but by December 1834 Elizabeth kept some of the brighter students on Tuesday and Friday afternoon to hear her read the Homeric hymns, the *Iliad*, and the *Faerie Queene*. In December she also began to keep a journal of the school, which she would occasionally read aloud to the students. Alcott put it this way: "Miss P—is now present every day and keeps a Journal of the *operations* and *Spirit* of the *Instruction*. . . . I deem the opportunity of being observed and interpreted by her, during my *professional* life, as propitious in every respect."[10]

Given such a remarkable chance to shape a school exactly as he wished, Alcott swiftly blended a pedagogy of conversation and collective learning with Coleridge's theory of the imagination in a way that remarkably echoed Peabody's own first efforts at teaching language. Words are signs of thoughts, he taught, not simply markers for external objects and events. Language is imagery, and images awaken our sense of the congruence between inner thought and outer thing. The real work of the school lay in the children's self-exploration, the study and expansion of their own native powers of imagination. "Can you understand this definition?" he asked the children. "Imagination is the power that represents, re-presents? Yes. Imagination represents spirit, soul, mind, the outward world, and God, said Mr. Alcott. Imagination is the power by which you picture out thoughts that never were realized in the world, as in 'Pilgrims Progress,' said a child under six." So the school days went, painfully slowly some children thought, through words, definitions, narratives like Maria Edgeworth's *Frank*, Krummacher's fables, Spenser, Bunyan, and the Bible. The children were required to think about ideas, to articulate their views, to write their thoughts in journals. "I never knew I had a mind before," said one.[11]

Still, it was not easy, as Peabody's journal makes clear. The children were not used to Alcott's strict discipline, which centered on complete silence and motionlessness, on strict attention, and on full participation. The pages of *Record of a School* are filled with references to Alcott's interrupting the lesson to quiet some whispering students, to comment on noisy actions, to focus their wandering attention. Although he believed in the freedom of the spirit, he insisted on the complete discipline of the body; "autocratic" is the word Peabody chose to describe his discipline. The school enrolled, after all, a sizeable number of boys ten years old or younger, "who were creatures of instinct more than any thing else, with undeveloped consciences and minds; but well-disposed, good-natured, and overflowing with animal spirits, and all but intoxicated with play."[12] Control of such a classroom under any system of discipline might be considered a challenge. Alcott had no sense of the possibilities of using children's energy and curiosity as part of the educational process; later Peabody would discover that that was the great insight of early childhood specialist Friedrich Froebel. *Record of a School* is a record of Alcott's struggle to maintain order so that the entirely mental work of expressing imagination might go forward.

The children were not the only challenge to Alcott's visionary pedagogy. Some parents considered Alcott too dogmatic; others wondered about this constant focus on the self; still others were concerned that no natural sciences were taught; and yet others asked, "Will children ever be willing to study from books, who have been educated by Mr. Alcott?" To these concerns Peabody addressed an Explanatory Preface in the second edition of *Record:* the focus of the school is inward nature, not outward; and yes, students are quite capable of learning from books, including the several texts that Alcott did in fact use.[13]

All this excitement among reformers and their privileged backers about the sensational new school, however, obscured a simultaneous failure and injustice. Charles Follen had joined the American Antislavery Society in early 1834, despite warnings that the Harvard Corporation would not tolerate one of their faculty advocating such radical views. Follen's poorly paid apppointment as German professor was not renewed, and his friends rapidly fell away. Meanwhile, Eliza Lee Cabot Follen, the Peabody's friend, had tried to open a girls' school of her own in Boston, which Elizabeth feared might be a "death blow" to her and her sisters' efforts to have their own school.[14] But this plan failed, as did Charles's plan to found the "Boston Seminary," a private academy to prepare young men for Harvard. The Follens left Boston for Watertown and then Milton, creating an opening filled in part by Alcott's and Peabody's school.[15]

Much as Temple School reflected Bronson Alcott's educational philosophy, it equally mirrored Peabody's views. In her schools in Maine and Massachusetts, Peabody had sought to combine rigorous training in academic subjects with efforts to draw out and shape her students' moral natures. Indeed, much of the intellectual rigor at Temple came from Peabody herself as she trained the older students in Latin and geography. There is a sense of Peabody's commitment to academic subjects in a letter to her friend Elizabeth Bliss, who was pondering withdrawing her son William from the school and enrolling him in a college preparatory academy:

> It was a horror and consternation to my mind to think of William Bliss being put into any Latin school for a considerable time. . . . If he leaves Mr. Alcott's school in the fall—he will not have gone thro' much of his course. He will not have been taught Geography; Arithmetic; the Art of Writing; facility in Composition;—English Grammar; all of which things it is very desirable to learn before entering a Latin School. Neither will he [illegible] have come into the first class of Latin. . . . He can also learn Plane & Solid Geometry with me before he leaves us, and if I were you I would not think of his removal yet. I am more & more convinced that Mr. Alcott's school is not understood, even by those who are most interested in it; and long for the first of August to come, when my Record of a School will be published.

But it was not just the subject matter that made Temple School unique; it was Alcott's pedagogy. As a test, Peabody reported to Elizabeth Bliss, she once asked Alcott to say to the children that he was giving up his conversations on "mind—and soul—& spirit and conscience—& such things;—and teach them exclusively about rocks—and trees—and mountains—&c &c and machines & engines." The children were dismayed by this: "*Oh it is too bad—too bad—too bad . . .* and shan't you read in Pilgrims Progress—& Spenser—& Krummacher?" With some prodding, all the children assented in the school's present curriculum, "full of thoughts & feelings about conscience, God, the mind, the soul—with all my punishments & all my disagreeable fault finding & the necessity of self-control & self-knowledge."[16]

Mary Peabody also caught some of her sister's enthusiasm. Upon returning to Massachusetts from her stay in Cuba, she wrote Horace Mann about the new ideas that were much talked about in Boston and Salem, and the new language of Reason and intuition. "I am not quite clear about the transcendentalists yet and if you know I wish you would give me some intimation of it. Elizabeth says she is the only practical transcendentalist there is, but even that does not clear up my mental vision entirely." Even so, she was quite taken with Temple School, and promptly joined in the instruction. "I am extremely interested in Mr. Alcott's school," she wrote Rawlins Pickman that summer.

> What Mr Rodman calls the steam-engine system with children is entirely laid aside in this school—it is his object to cultivate the heart, and to bring out from the child's own mind the principles which are to govern his character. The outward manifestations of learning are not great, therefore, but the self-control that the children exercise is of the first importance, and a foundation for all future good. I am reading Columbus to them, and am able to give life to it by talking of the W. Indies from my own experience, which delights them very much. I only teach in the afternoon, but often go in the morning for my own edification, and hear Mr. A talk to the children.[17]

ALL THIS ACTIVITY—teaching, correspondence, writing, publishing—around Temple School might suggest that the school was the center of Elizabeth Peabody's life in the mid-1830s. That would be far from the case. By 1836 she was increasingly critical of some aspects of Alcott's teaching method and offended by the treatment she received from the Alcotts while she boarded with them. Even more, Peabody was developing a rich intellectual and associational life quite apart from the Alcotts and Temple School.

As Peabody recruited for Alcott's school and began her dual tasks as teacher and recorder, she was also shepherding her essays on the "Spirit of Hebrew Scriptures," written back in 1826, through the publication process. Only three of the six essays were published, and Peabody blamed Andrews Norton for the partial publication. In her *Remi-*

niscences of Channing, Peabody recalled that the editor, who was then James Walker, said that "I must needs be incompetent to the subject from want of learning." In a letter to Orestes Brownson around 1840, however, she said it was "Mr. Norton" who "cut off untimely my little series."[18]

These essays were, as we have seen, an effort to integrate the historical scholarship of people like Andrews Norton with the more language-centered and aesthetic approach of theorists like Herder. Perhaps Norton did not agree with Peabody's efforts to synthesize two very different approaches, or perhaps he agreed with Horace Mann that the essays were far too dense and difficult. Consider the reader, Mann begged, and make the argument clearer: "The truth is that the depth and purity of your views on moral subjects ought not to be lost by any dimness [?] in the medium through which alone they can be made visible to others." If the Almighty was concerned enough to lay down rules to the Hebrews about cooking utensils and the right ways to slaughter animals, "may you not descend to means almost unsuited to the dignity of your subject to avert the attention of those who have so much need of instruction and moral impulse?"[19]

Peabody shared her interest in language with her one-time Greek tutor Waldo Emerson. Elizabeth had translated the first part of *Le Vraie Messie*, first published in Paris in 1829 and later published by Peabody herself as *The True Messiah; or The Old and New Testaments, Examined According to the Principles of the Language of Nature*. Reading Peabody's translation, Emerson found yet more confirmation for his growing belief that language is symbolic of nature, including one's own body, and nature is symbolic of the spirit. "I find good things in this mss of Oegger & I am taken with the design of his work," he wrote in his journal in July 1835.[20] As Emerson would in *Nature* and other works, so Peabody would find several avenues to express her ideas about language, especially in the 1840s through her association with Charles Kraitsir.

These exchanges of ideas and manuscripts certainly caused Emerson to notice the energetic young schoolteacher, busy as he was with his engagement to Lydia Jackson and with lecturing, reading, and journal-keeping. Emerson certainly took Elizabeth seriously, writing her a dense letter in August 1835 regarding the development of character. The moral life has primacy over the intellectual, he agreed (apparently he had said something that made her think otherwise): "There's a kind of falsehood in the enunciation of a chemical or astronomical law by an unprincipled savant." Still, we should hold out for the fullest human development in all spheres, moral, intellectual, spiritual, and physical: "The blacksmith has a strong arm, the dancer a strong foot . . . such lobsided one eyed half men we are now, & such a yawning difference between our esse & our posse." Even Jesus was not a perfectly proportioned human being, "but a very exclusive & partial development of the moral element" and not enough of the intellectual.[21]

Now, with Temple School in full swing, Peabody found herself even more drawn to Emerson. She attended his series of lectures on biography, which ran from January 20 to March 5, 1835, delivered in the same Masonic Temple that housed Alcott's school. "Waldo Emerson's lectures have *inspired* me, and encouraged my heart, and made me think better of myself than I have ever done before," she wrote to Horace Mann. By early summer she felt confident enough to ask Emerson to read her manuscript journal account of Temple School, which she had been preparing for publication since April. His response was both generous and specific:

> I have read your manuscript with greatest pleasure. It will bear to be tried by the test of all speculation, [that is, by] practical value. It has to [sic] much that I wish it may be printed speedily. I am delighted with the whole piece & I hope you will not curtail it for I wish to read it a third time in print. If an objection may be made, I suppose it will be the danger of the joke which one gentle dulness is sure to find in sudden transitions from the real to the phenomenal, as in the first page of the third sheet, "rudely interrupts his spiritual exercises," &c &c & which perhaps might be forefended by a premonition that truth is always jocose to such as do not apprehend it. Anyhow, we wish to be advertised from time to time even by Plato, that he speaks that which is not that which appears.[22]

Record of a School was "printed speedily" by James Munroe in Boston and advertised for sale on July 20. Emerson was again unstinting in his praise, this time in his private journal. "I read with great delight the 'Record of a School.' It aims all the time to show the symbolical character of all things to the children, & it is alleged, & I doubt not, truly, that the children take the thought with delight. It is remarkable that all poets, orators, & philosophers have been those who could most sharply see & most happily present emblems, parables, figures. Good writing & brilliant conversation are perpetual allegories." To Peabody he wrote, "I have left myself but little room to thank you for the pleasure & hope the Rec. of a School has given me. It is the only book of facts I ever read that was as engaging as one of Miss Edgeworth's fictions. The best success attend the sch. & reward its teachers."[23]

Elizabeth found herself quite involved not just with Waldo but with the extended Emerson circle. Like other friends, reformers, and hangers-on who were beginning to take Emerson as their informal leader, Peabody was deeply interested in his engagement with Lydia Jackson of Plymouth. Not simply nosiness or possessiveness, although having those traits to be sure, Peabody's interest in Jackson had to do as well with the sense that this second marriage would have an enormous impact not simply on Emerson but on the entire circle. Peabody met Jackson first in February 1835 at the home of her friend Elizabeth Bliss. "Bye and bye she descended. She looks *very refined*, but neither beautiful nor elegant, and very frail, and as if her mind wore out her body. She was *unaffected* but *peculiar*. When she came down I was reading a letter which Thomas Carlyle wrote to Waldo Emerson—who saw him when he was in Europe. It was very interesting, indeed, and full of genius and love. She sat down by me, and we had a beautiful talk about a variety of most intellectual and spiritual things. And I should think she had the rare characteristics of genius—inexhaustible originality." Sarah Clarke, who was also at that first meeting, recorded a sharp exchange between Peabody and Jackson. Speaking of the Unitarian heritage, Lydia said, "I respect Unitarianism, for without it we should never have had Transcendentalism. That was a foothold." "It was terra firma," Peabody responded. "And nothing else," Jackson rejoined, "cold and hard, with scarceful a firmament above it."[24]

Perhaps it was this independence of mind, or perhaps some other anxiety, but for a few days in the last week of February 1835 Elizabeth Peabody and Elizabeth Bliss seemed to entertain serious doubts about Jackson's suitability. But after another visit with Jackson, Peabody wrote this to her friend: "I wish you would dismiss all fears—I am so much inclined to admire your friend [Jackson] & have so many sympathies with her—there is really no fear of not doing justice to her—You may have surmised from my letter to her—that I felt some of the anxiety you expressed—& I confess I did—I wanted to know much whether she thought & felt in such a way as that the natural & beautiful contrast of her character & Waldo's was to be productive of a more perfect union— or of disunion—And her answer—which you saw—entirely settled my mind at peace on that point."[25]

This inspection is a little odd—Elizabeth Peabody and her friends setting themselves up as a screening committee for Emerson's future wife. Lydia Jackson seemed to take it all calmly, responding directly and lucidly to Peabody's concerns that she might be too different from Waldo to be a suitable spouse. While not a Swedenborgian, she wrote, there is much in Emmanuel Swedenborg's teachings that she found attractive, particularly his sense that each person exists not simply for his or her own sake, but as part of a larger whole. We find our place in the human community by cultivating what is most essentially ourselves and then by seeking others to compensate for our deficiencies and fulfill the "harmonious whole." Families are such communities, she thought, as are intimate relations to others. "Each human soul has its own relation to the universe—to its race at large—to its country—its neighbourhood—its family circle;—and yet more, has it, I believe, a very peculiar relation—such as it has to no other being—to some chosen friend—perhaps of the same sex but generally of the other. In the latter case it is probably the most perfect. The union between friend & friend—the fraternal tie—but more specially the conjugal union—is strengthened and perfected and made productive of mutual goal by the very dissimilarity of the natures thus joined by the order of Providence."

Jackson's claim that we are most ourselves in community, in relationship, certainly conformed to Elizabeth's beliefs about history and society. The way that she linked the balancing of individual strengths and weaknesses with the institution of marriage, thus effectively answering Elizabeth's doubts about her suitability for Waldo, may have made logical and even psychological sense. But in Peabody's experience these dissimilarities of nature inevitably found expression in unequal marriages, like Lydia Sears's or her mother's, in which female intellect and ambition faltered in the face of unceasing domestic duties. While her main concern was that Emerson marry well, she may have been thinking hard about how rare it would be to find a mate with whom one could achieve that "more perfect union."[26]

↘ FROM MARCH to about September or October 1835 was a period of intense and fruitful activity for Elizabeth. She published *Record of a School*, deepened her friendship with Emerson, and met other noteworthy people like James Freeman Clarke. She seemed always to be on the move, attending lectures and conversations, having tea with Lydia Jackson, teaching at Temple. In September she wrote to Boston bookseller Nahum Capen, who was about to leave for Europe, asking him to carry letters to de Gerando, Maria Edgeworth, and William Wordsworth, the letter to the poet being one of ten that she wrote to him from 1825 to 1845. This particular letter had to do with the powerful impact that reading "Peter Bell" had on one of her pre–Temple School classes of girls. To Capen she appended a list of titles she wanted him to find for her in Europe: dictionaries of the Basque language, François Huber's studies of bees and ants, and books in Latin. In Capen's spare time, she wanted him to arrange for the European publication of *Record of a School*! While all this activity is amusing (to us, probably not to Capen), it does suggest the enormous range of Peabody's intellectual interests.[27]

By the last months of 1835, however, things began to come apart for Elizabeth, her friends, her family, her causes and career. For one thing, she was beginning to have some doubts about Bronson Alcott. His emphasis on introspection and journalizing worried her, for it seemed to encourage a kind of moral competitiveness among the children. To have these journals read aloud only worsened the matter. More deeply, Peabody disagreed with the way Alcott described evil in specific forms and situations, "clothed in *forms* by the imagination." Reflecting the ancient view that evil is the absence of good, not an independent substance, Peabody wrote that evil "acquires the existence it has from want of faith and soul-cultivation, and that this is sufficient reason why all cultivation should be directed to give positiveness, coloring, shape, etc., to all kinds of good,—God alone being eternal truth."[28]

As if in sharp punctuation to this view, the warehouse storing the unsold copies of *Record of a School* burned, probably just as Peabody was writing this letter to Alcott. Mary Peabody gave the details to Rawlins Pickman: "I presume you have heard of Elizabeth's loss by the late fire—the burning of the books has swallowed up not only the profits of the whole edition but left her in debt—about four hundred were burnt, the rest of the thousand being already disposed of—she intends to have another edition out immediately. It seems as if she were fated to make no money by books."[29]

Mary was right about her sister's intention. In January 1836 Elizabeth oversaw the publication of a second edition of *Record*, this one with an essay of her own called "Method of Spiritual Culture," which was also released as a separate pamphlet. This essay was something of a balancing act for Peabody. She was still very much associated with Alcott and largely agreed with his pedagogy and principles. But there were areas of disagreement. "The point from which I diverge from Mr. Alcott, in theory, is this: I think that a private conscience in the young will naturally be the highest. Mr. Alcott thinks a common conscience is to be cultivated in a school and that this will be higher in all, than any one conscience would be, if it were private." Drawing on her own experiences in Maine and Brookline, Peabody described a system in which she established a "separate understanding with each particular scholar . . . while in general assembly no reference should be made to any moral wrong-doing of any one . . . this method also tends to preserve all the delicate individualities of character, and to give appropriate and differing atmosphere and scope to those flowers of delicacy and of sensibility." This system did, after all, work best with a handful of students with whom one could establish personal relationships. Temple School was different, she acknowledged: "Here was a school of thirty children, mostly boys under ten years of age." Still, she worried that "the instinctive delicacy with which children veil their deepst thoughts of love and tenderness for relatives, and their reasonable self-gradulations, should not be violated . . . in order to gain knowledge, or for any imagined benefit to others. . . . And Mr. Alcott, I believe, agrees with me in this, notwithstanding that he practically goes sometimes upon the very verge of the rights of reserve. . . ."[30]

Alcott took this mixed review with surprising equanimity.

I am not sure of the effect of this attempt of Miss Peabody's to explain the *Theory and Practice of Spiritual Culture* as regarded by myself. Yet, I have felt willing to let the experiment be made, in the belief that some good would ensue. . . . This *Introductory Essay* is to be inserted in the *Second Edition of the Record*—now in press—and 1000 copies have been struck off, and stitched in pamphlet form, for distribution among friends, and others. It contains some lucid statements of the methods and principles of the school, and is, I think, an improvement upon the first edition of the Record. . . . These efforts of Miss P are praiseworthy endeavours to present truths of value before the public.[31]

That was January. In April the relations between Peabody and the Alcotts shattered, with nasty accusations flying back and forth. In a remarkable journal that Elizabeth kept during the second week in April, she detailed this collapse. At first things went well in the house on Front Street, where the Alcotts and Peabody boarded together, as they had since Temple School began—on Somerset Court, Bedford Street, and Beach Street, the first behind Park Street Church, the last two in residential neighborhoods in south Boston. She had her own room, where she could have her much-desired solitude. But she could not easily avoid the Alcotts and their reform enthusiasms. In late winter and spring, it was Sylvester Graham, whose lectures on physiology and the spirit found eager listeners in the Alcotts.[32]

At dinner, Peabody referred to Graham's assertion that with the proper diet and spiritual elevation, people could live to be two hundred years old, and suggested that she found it "no desirable thing to live so long but rather a misfortune." Alcott replied that this was in effect a *"suicidal statement."* After a few more heated exchanges and in an effort to change the subject, Peabody observed that Graham's class in Salem consisted principally of physicians, but this was an unfortunate reference since it then brought up Alcott's distrust of physicians. Although he denied it, Peabody insisted that Alcott had said physicians "fed like vampyres on the community for the sake of money—& I also read in his articles—expressions of a like kind." As the daughter of a physician, Elizabeth doubtless felt this slur keenly. More bitter exchanges followed, with Alcott's finally accusing Peabody of not being able to observe properly. Retiring to her room and "feeling very uncomfortably," she reflected on the exchange and found herself blameless. "I am quite sure that he has planted himself on dangerous ground—for his own humility & selfestimation without a doubt of having the key that unlocks all wisdom—in his own metaphysical system—he subjects every thing to the test of his talismanic words—and as they answer to them in his predisposed ear—they take their places."[33]

Worse was to come. Abigail Alcott began opening Elizabeth's mail and concluded that Elizabeth had influenced Mary Peabody and Horace Mann to think poorly of the Alcotts. Bronson joined this chorus of denunciation, tipping off Elizabeth that Abigail had shown him the purloined letters. Sarah Clarke, who was quickly brought into the controversy, agreed with Elizabeth that she had to leave the boardinghouse and to sever all her ties with the Alcotts. The worst part of all this was that Sophia took the Alcotts' part against her own sister, believing that somehow Elizabeth had misjudged and slandered them. Indeed, Sophia, who said that she could not "sufficiently thank my Heavenly Father for the gift of Mr. Alcott as a friend," would come to live with the Alcotts in July.[34]

Now the nasty bickering and disagreements over pedagogy began to spill over into larger conflicts, as Alcott's experimental school and method came under increasing attack. Temple had always been controversial, as Peabody's "Method of Spiritual Culture" preface indicated. Parents had wondered about the lack of textbooks, the focus on the imagination and the inner life, the lack of science study, and the fitness of Temple students to study in other, more conventional schools.

But nothing aroused parental concern quite so much as rumors of talk about conception and childbirth. Peabody had tried to head off this problem in "Method of Spiritual Culture" in dispelling the notion that Alcott taught the "Oriental doctrine of pre-existence and emanation." "Mr. Alcott indeed believes that birth is a spiritual act and fact prior to embodiment. And does not every one believe this, who does not think the soul of an individual the temperament of a body, the effect of matter? For my own part, I believe that this is the only way of conceiving the unity of a spirit; and that it is the pre-existence meant in Wordsworth's ode on Immortality, and that which Plato himself meant to teach; and that it certainly is the doctrine of Christianity taught by Jesus Christ."[35]

To these doubts and suspicions, Alcott was largely oblivious. Despite the sharp arguments with Elizabeth Peabody, the spring and summer of 1836 represented an extraordinary moment of self-confidence and success for the reformer. Good reviews of *Record of a School*, enthusiastic supporters like Rhode Island's Hiram Fuller and Elizabeth's sister Sophia, and the company of fellow intellectuals like Emerson, William Henry Furness, George Ripley, Orestes Brownson, and Frederic Henry Hedge in the informal discussion group, the Transcendental Club—all served to confirm Alcott's position as one of the leading thinkers and activists in the Transcendentalist movement.[36]

Equally intent on being part of the avant-garde circle, Elizabeth was also keeping up with the new ideas and their avatars. She was reading Furness's *Remarks on the Four Gospels*, Orestes Brownson's *New Views of Christianity, Society, and the Church*, and George Ripley's *Discourses on the Philosophy of Religion Addressed to Doubters Who Wish to Believe*, all published in 1836. But although it was an "annus mirabilis" (as Perry Miller has said) for many in the circle of reformers and intellectuals, Peabody was preoccupied with her growing misgivings about Alcott and Temple, with her always fragile relationship with her sister Mary, and with the deaths of people close to her.[37]

In the summer Alcott had decided to issue a set of *Conversations with Children on the Gospels*, drawn from such interactions as Elizabeth had recorded. Some readers, now as then, would find amusing, even ludicrous, Alcott's fierce insistence that the children interpret every event in the gospels as pointing to a spiritual truth. Others, perhaps more theologically conservative, were offended by the children's simplistic religious interpretations. But the real issue was talk about sex and birth. Elizabeth Peabody saw this instantly and recognized its implications. In a "Recorder's Preface" to the first volume, she observed that what the children said was not necessarily the view of Alcott; "still less are they to be regarded as any intimation of the recorder's; who, though occasionally an interlocutor, was, in general, a passive instrument, and especially when she felt that she differed from Mr. Alcott, on the subject at hand, as was sometimes the case."[38]

It had all become too much—the personal hostility with the Alcotts, the disagreements over private versus common conscience, probably her own dissatisfaction at not having her own school, Alcott's inability to pay her, and now this looming scandal with *Conversations*. Elizabeth resigned from the school. Alcott laconically noted her departure in a journal entry for Monday, August 1: "Miss Peabody left me today for Salem. She will not resume her connections with the school after the holidays."[39]

Six days later Peabody wrote Alcott a now-famous letter, attacking his plan to publish the children's comments on sex and birth, and defending her departure from the school: "Whatever may be said of the wisdom of pursuing your plan as you have hitherto done in the schoolroom . . . I feel more and more that these questionable parts ought not to go into the printed book, at least that they must be entirely disconnected with *me*."

> In the first place, in all these conversations where I have spoken, I should like to have that part of the conversation omitted, so that it may be felt that I was entirely passive. And I would go a little farther: there is a remark of Josiah Quincy's about the formation of the body out of *"naughtiness of other people"* which is very remarkable. Please to correct that in my record. But if you wish to retain it, you can add a note in the margin saying: "the Recorder omitted Josiah's answer in this place, which was &c &c"—putting Josiah's answer in your note. There are many places where this might be done, and thus the whole responsibility rest upon you. I should like, too, to have the remarks I made on the Circumcision omitted. I do not wish to appear as an interlocutor in that conversation either. Besides this, I must desire you to put a preface of your own before mine, and express in it, in so many words, that on you rests all the responsibility of introducing the subjects, and that your Recorder did not entirely sympathize or agree with you with respect to the course taken. . . .
>
> Why did prophets and apostles veil this subject in fables and emblems if there was not a reason for avoiding physiological inquiries &c? This is worth thinking of. However you as a man can say anything; but I am a woman, and having feelings that I dare not distrust, however little I can *understand them* or give an account of them.[40]

It is a remarkable letter, springing from fear and alarm, filled with stumbling efforts to reframe the conversations to make her appear passive, pervaded by a sense of the coming catastrophe of publication. To Alcott partisans, it proves Peabody's weakness and fickleness, her desire to get inside at the first hint of trouble. Still, it was not as if Peabody and Alcott were exactly on good terms that summer. They had quarreled fiercely in April, and Peabody had tried to indicate her independence from Alcott in the "Method of Spiritual Culture" preface to the second edition of *Record*. Even more, she revealed a keen awareness of the limits that Boston Unitarian society, indeed, all urban middle-class society, placed on the discourse of sex. The society in which she and Alcott moved set strict limits to what was discussable in public, in mixed company, and in the presence of children. As a single woman, dependent on the goodwill and good opinions of others for her very livelihood, Peabody was deeply aware of these rules of propriety. She was in fact often accused of violating them through her gusty enthusiasms and bluestockinged love of learning. But in this case, however awkward it must have been to insist that Alcott rewrite her own dialogues, Peabody understood where the boundaries were. In choosing not to violate them, she saved her career and her always fragile reputation, and she came in from the storm.

It broke shortly after the first volume of *Conversations* was published in December. Alcott had borrowed the spirit, if not the letter, of one of Peabody's suggestions and had placed all the "questionable" passages in an appendix at the end, thus presenting an unavoidable target for his opponents. These began to appear in the early months of 1837, led by *Boston Daily Advertiser* editor Nathan Hale. He indicted Alcott's experiment for unnatural stimulation of curiosity, lack of exercise, and moral laxity. "The essence of the system appears to be, to select the most solemn of all subjects—the fundamental truths of religion as recorded in the gospels of our Saviour,—and after reading a chapter, instead of offering any illustration of what is there recorded, to invite the pupils to express, without discrimination or reserve, all their crude and undigested thoughts upon it—and especially on those points which are most difficult to be understood and not excepting those upon which inquisitiveness is useless, and often improper and mischievous." Joseph Buckingham thought that *Conversations* was "a more indecent and obscene book (we say nothing of its absurdity) than any other one we ever saw exposed to sale on a bookseller's counter." Andrews Norton, the voice of conservative Unitarianism, thought it was "one third absurd, one third blasphemous, and one third obscene." Added to this chorus of domestic critics was the voice of English writer Harriet Martineau. Although she had never visited Temple School, Martineau boldly linked the absence of organized play with Alcott's penchant for seeing the physical as only emblematic of the spiritual: "His system can be beneficial to none, and must be ruinous to many. If he should retain any pupils long enough to make a full trial of his methods upon them, those who survive the neglect of bodily exercise and over-excitement of the brain, will be found the first to throw off moral restraint."[41]

Alcott's friends, including Emerson, Francis, James Freeman Clarke, Ripley, and Alcott's cousin William Alcott, all rose to his defense. So did Elizabeth Peabody. If she had been solely concerned about her reputation or status as a single woman, she might well have decided not to call attention to her close association with Bronson Alcott and Temple School. Nonetheless, she defended her old colleague in the pages of the *Christian Register and Observer.* Alcott's conversations are rambling and disjointed, true enough, she writes; he should not have talked with children about birth, nor should he have connected their real names to their conversations, also true. But these dialogues, like all of Alcott's teachings, illustrate his central passion, that "tyrannical custom, and an arbitrary imposition of the adult mind upon the young mind, is not substituted . . . for the *true method* of nature, in which the imagination leads the understanding." Had Alcott's critics, especially Nathan Hale, read all the conversations, she concluded, they would have seen beyond the occasional immature expression of unformed ideas to the profound expression of deep spiritual truth.[42]

↪ TEMPLE SCHOOL was not the only thing occupying Elizabeth's attention in 1836. Personal matters, including the deaths of her former student Lydia Sears Haven and Waldo Emerson's brother Charles, and the always emotionally charged relationships with her sisters, equally filled her mind and her correspondence. Samuel Foster Haven, whose sister Catherine was once engaged to Horace Mann, must have been dubious about his wife's intense relationship with the Peabodys. In a postscript to a letter from Mary Peabody to Lydia, Elizabeth addressed this issue directly: "Now that I have *proved* I *think* to your gude man by my long cessation of intercourse—that it is no part of my plan of loving—to endeavour to *govern* my scholars—especially when they are married. The truth is—my darling—I love you too truly—too *purely*—to express any particular jealousy of Sam's opinion of me."[43]

Two years later Sam Haven had apparently learned to tolerate the Peabodys, carrying letters and the "Cuba Journal" to Lydia, but had shifted his hostility to Horace Mann, who had, he felt, strung his sister

Catherine along too long. Haven thought that Mann was "revengeful, spiteful, malicious, *demoniacal*, irritable in respect to personal slights, taking pleasure in giving pain. . . . I defended him but very composedly," Elizabeth wrote to a very interested Mary, "and asserted his freedom from whatever could spring from selfishness." Elizabeth's spirited defense put Haven in a better mood; "he went away with a smile of benevolent indulgence at my enthusiastic estimation, which he allowed was the most natural thing in the world!"[44]

But the real problem was Sam's wife Lydia and their new son Foster. In August 1834 when Elizabeth went to Dedham to visit the Havens, she was shocked at Foster's appearance. "Little Foster is a peaked little thing—but very lovely and sweet in his character. I could not think what made him look so—miserably—*not peevish*—for there seems not a particle of that—but attenuated." Gradually, Elizabeth pieced together the story, taking careful notes.

At the death of her mother some thirty years earlier, Lydia's expressions of grief were met with the severe response that God had willed this death and that God would punish her if she did not acquiesce. "Little did the thoughtless and heartless person who thus dealt with the distressed little heart think, how disastrously she was emasculating the word GOD of good by associating it with such an image of ruthless power divorced from tenderness, as she unheedingly did." When Lydia married and had her own child, she determined not to refer to God or death until she felt the child was old enough to understand such truths. But by not nurturing the child's imaginative and creative powers, she was creating a taciturn and unresponsive creature, much as she herself still was. "His face continued to be an infant's countenance, and he was strangely without that childish joyousness called animal spirits, and grew more and more peevish as he grew older; for he was sequestered to the society of his silent mother, who would not even be read to in his presence, lest, as she said, some chance word which he could not understand should excite some fear."

Elizabeth must have been dismayed by the lack of nurture that Lydia gave her son. This neglect was not exactly the child-rearing they envisioned coming from one of the Peabodys' star pupils. "[I]t appears that Lydia *starves him*—she will only let him eat so many times a day," and if he does not the food is put away. All this—the neglect of his intellect, the starving of his imagination, the stunting of his physical growth—appeared to come from some unnamed child nurture book. Sam's mother was in despair over the treatment of her grandchild, but Lydia had nothing but contempt for her, Elizabeth reported to Mary. During this August visit, Elizabeth mostly kept silent, or so she said, only making up a story about a boy, a brook, and a drop of water, based on a picture in the "Story Without an End." Foster was transformed at this telling, begging Elizabeth to tell it again and again, "Story!" and "Story again!" By this simple expedient, Foster came to obey her voice *as if it were a physical law.*[45]

Sometime early in 1835, Lydia was diagnosed with tuberculosis, and Elizabeth traveled to Lowell to be with her, arranging for Mary to take her place at Temple School. Lydia's "physician says she never can be well, that the disease is radical and spreading rapidly," Mary wrote to Rawlins Pickman. "She may linger all summer—in the mean time she needs ministration to her mind, and only finds comfort and tranquility by Elizabeth's assistance."[46] Doubtless much of her tranquility came from what Peabody was able to accomplish with her difficult child.

As Elizabeth sat at Lydia's bedside, Foster, now four-and-a-half, was carried into the room by his nurse. The child instantly recognized his "Aunt Lizzie." "Immediately the large eyes filled with intelligent light, and with a cry of joy he sprang toward me, climbed up into my lap, clasped his arms round my neck, nestled upon my bosom, and looking up with a joyful expression of confidence said, 'Story—little boy—drop of water!'" From this reunion, Peabody began to nurture Foster's imaginative, moral, and intellectual life. "You see, my dear friend," she observed to Lydia, "that the child has mind enough, heart, enough, and a moral nature. He can understand and feel sympathy; feels the symbolism of nature; and can obey a self-denying motive. No fatal harm has been done after all by your delay, but he needs now to know he has a Heavenly Father. . . ." To Lydia's demurral that she had no genius to educate the child, Peabody responded firmly, "No, no, . . . it does not require genius to talk with children, but only simplicity of heart trusted in." Gradually Peabody educated the child in the existence of a loving God, in the way nature symbolizes invisible and spiritual truth, and in the love revealed in the way that God takes away the sick and dying. Sometime toward the end of the summer, Peabody gave this report to her sister Sophia, softening considerably her earlier estimate of the damage Lydia had done to her child:

Never was anything so interesting as Foster—I am thinking of writing a little memoir of this summer—for it has been very rich in psychological facts—I have some memoranda—Lydia has done a vast deal for him by her ceaseless care—there is no evil thought in him—& her rigid temperance with him has made him free from all gross & selfish tendencies—& to have the greatest selfcontrol I ever saw for his age. His affection for me is perfectly spiritual & most ardent—He will declare that he not only loves my love & thoughts & mind—but my body—everything that belongs to me—And his conversation about God & heaven—the new ideas that come to him in the train of those I give him are all proofs of Spiritualism the most delightful & satisfactory.[47]

Peabody based her "memoranda" on "notes that his mother made, who was watching every word said, with the most intense interest. She always had pencil and paper at her side, because the danger of hemorrhage caused her to avoid speaking." It was indeed remarkable, that as Foster's imaginative and intellectual powers waxed, Lydia's health, though not her powers of observation, declined. Elizabeth gave a graphic description of her student's illness in the summer of 1835: "Lydia is very sick and although she does not suffer much pain will die. Her lungs are all tuberculous & the tubercules are soft in many places—Ulcers have discharged—She has had three hemorrhages & is in daily danger of another.—She does not speak but talks with her finger, signs, & the lead pencil—Death is rather terrific for her—She is so timid—& it is the greatest comfort to have me talk to her all the time upon the spiritual life & life beyond the grave."

Lydia Haven clung to life for nearly another year, her tuberculosis "so lingering that every trace of her former beauty was lost in the ghastly emaciation." Peabody had returned to Boston, but in the spring of 1836 she went back to Lowell as Lydia sank toward death. Foster had accepted his mother's impending death, she reported later, but could not bring himself to look at her in her emaciated condition. He would come into the room, head down, sit with his back to her, take her arms over his chest and cover them with kisses. "He refused, as it were, to recognize her, under that ghastly mask; which, however did not shut off from his *remembrance*, her former loveliness; for, as soon as she was really dead, and he began to think of her *in heaven*, she became his standard of beauty."[48] It fell to Elizabeth to break the final news to Sam Haven: "The Dr. commissioned me to quench her husband's last hope yesterday, and it was more painful to do than if I had been able to show him that where the finite joy ended, the *infinite* certainly commenced for him," she wrote to Horace Mann. But Sam's lack of faith in an afterlife made such hope impossible.[49]

Elizabeth persuaded Sam to let Foster come to live with the Peabodys in Salem. Mother Peabody immediately put herself in charge of the little boy: "For dear Lydia's sake I will do all I can for those she loved best." Foster stayed there for more than a year, attending Mary Peabody's school, watching with delight Sophia at her easel. But his mind was never far from his mother's death. His conversation, if Elizabeth's forty-year memory can be trusted, turned often to death, to the many ways people die, and to ways that their souls are released from the body. Sophia reported one such incident to her brother George: "He very often says he wants to see his mother—& one day he called to her as loud as he could to come down out of the sky." Perhaps Elizabeth's insistence on the reality of the afterlife had its own ill effect on the sensitive child. In any event, Foster's father abruptly ended this phase of the boy's education, enrolling him in boarding school and then Harvard College. After medical training in Europe, Foster Haven became a doctor in Worcester and then enlisted as a surgeon in the Union Army. He was killed at the battle of Fredericksburg in December 1862. Two years later Elizabeth loaned some of her notes on Foster's childhood to his father, who mislaid them. In the 1870s she reorganized and rewrote her account of Foster Haven as "A Psychological Observation," a lecture she delivered to students at kindergarten training schools and published in 1888.[50]

Lydia's was not the only death in the spring of 1836 to shake the Peabody family and the larger circle of reformers and thinkers. On May 9, Emerson's brother Charles died suddenly in New York City. Bonded together by their common literary interests, Waldo and Charles had grown close as brothers and friends. Charles had a darker and more pessimistic streak than Waldo had; or perhaps Waldo, who also had his bouts with despair, was able to transform his darkness into sparkling prose by the sheer force of his will. Charles brooded on death and could often imagine himself dead, despite the intense connection to life signalized by his engagement to Elizabeth Hoar. In the first years of the

1830s, Charles's health, weakened by the family's heritage of tuberculosis, deteriorated. Visiting his brother William in New York in May 1836, Charles collapsed after a walk and died.

Like Waldo Emerson's engagement to Lydia Jackson, the death of Charles was both a public and a private event. The news swiftly made the rounds in letters and conversations. "Have you not sorrowed for the death of Charles Emerson? I had not heard of any indisposition, and when the news came to me with the sad mingling of his Aunt Mary's bitter regrets, I felt as if a light had been transferred to Heaven whose radiance we could ill spare in these times of moral darkness," Eliza Guild wrote to Mary Peabody on May 15. Sophia Peabody wrote on at length to her brother George, determined to draw out of those "mournful circumstances" moral lessons about the preeminence of soul over body. "His most pure & lofty & seraphic spirit was plumed for its flight. He was ready even at the threshold of our allotted life—for the eternal change. . . . How thankful I am that I heard that thrilling burst of eloquence last winter from his lips. I felt then that he already belonged to the radiant band of the translated." And Sarah Clarke wrote Mary that when she met Waldo after Charles's death, "I looked away. I could not help it, for it seemed like intruding on his sacred sorrow to demand so much as a look of recognition—but I could not help seeing that the seraphic smile was quenched."[51]

For her part, Elizabeth Peabody was provided some glimpse of what the loss meant for Waldo Emerson when he let her read his letter to his wife, written from New York after Charles's funeral: "And so, Lidian, I can never bring you back my nobler friend who was my ornament my wisdom & my pride. . . . Thanks, thanks for your kindest sympathy & appreciation of him. And you must be content henceforth with only a piece of your husband; for the best of his strength lay in the soul with which he must no more on earth take counsel. How much I saw through his eyes. I feel as if my own were very dim."[52]

Elizabeth wrote to Mary that this was "a wonderful letter for the idea it gave of friendship." The depth of Waldo's despair over Charles's death, Elizabeth thought, might also be glimpsed in the account of Waldo's behavior at Charles's funeral, given in a letter Robert Waterston wrote to Peabody. "He said he stood at the grave with Waldo—& that when he turned away from it—compressed nature found its way *in a laugh*—and an ejaculation 'dear boy'—'when one has never had but little society—and *all that society* is taken away—what is there worth living for?' said he."[53]

    THE EMERSONS were increasingly the hub around which the small circle of reformers and thinkers turned, so that their private tragedies had public consequences. But Waldo's grief over the loss of his brother must have touched not merely a sympathetic chord in Elizabeth Peabody. It likely prompted her to think again about her own relations with her sisters, particularly with Mary, and to reflect on the peculiar bond of heritage and experience that siblings share.

    Mary said it best when she wrote of her relationship with Elizabeth, "my existence has never been a separate one from hers since I can remember."[54] They shared so much in common: their commitment to education and educational reform, their common circle of friends, even their mutual attraction to Horace Mann. But temperamentally they were strikingly different. Mary was quiet, funny, sharply observant of the human and natural worlds. She knew that single women like the Peabodys would attract notice and comment, especially as they moved into the world beyond their circle of reformers and intellectuals, and that discretion was after all a usefully self-protective trait. Elizabeth, serious, ponderously learned, was, for all her anxiety about propriety and discretion, increasingly involved in situations, like that at Temple School, that attracted public attention. She was becoming a public intellectual, publishing articles and reviews, attending lectures, associating with the religious and intellectual avant-garde. Such activities caused men like Bronson Alcott and Waldo Emerson to catch public criticism for their unpopular views. Peabody, an intellectual woman, was also putting herself in the way of public commentary and the kind of criticism that might cost her the parental support and pupils that were the basis of her livelihood. Therefore, the issue of discretion and propriety, which Mary raised constantly with her older sister, was a difficult and ambiguous one for Elizabeth.

    These swirling issues—love and competition with Mary, anxiety over propriety, concern over her own public image—surfaced again and again in the sisters' correspondence, and nowhere more bluntly than in a letter Elizabeth wrote shortly after Charles Emerson's funeral, a remarkable piece that summarizes and interprets the entire history of the sisters' relationship.

You say "When the question is of discretion, I must say that I should not choose you for my confessor." Now this is the beauty of your letter & why I like it—that you tell the simple unvarnished truth.—I hope you never will desert this point again—but that you will always acknowledge to yourself & to me whenever this subject is up—that *you do not confide in me because you do not think I have discretion*—Now as I think *I have discretion* & as I think *discretion is an entirely essential thing*—Your coming to this decision—& acting upon it—as it has ever been perfectly plain that you have—with the most entire confidence that your impressions in regard to my *indiscretion* are correct—& without making me either explain the cases away—or acknowledge their character—*is & ever has been the wound that I have felt perpetually irritated between us.*

Still, she has never been easy to live with, Elizabeth acknowledged, especially since their return from Maine in 1825. The New Bedford affair made her irritable, as did the "terrible winter of 1830," probably the White-Crowninshield affair. She felt that "life lost its character of Moral *Beauty.*" Only Horace Mann "mended my heart with his essential approbation—& unshadowed sympathy." Even there, she went on, Mary seems to have misunderstood her intention: "I *did* hope no bitterness would ever mingle with this new stream of friendship—where we both could drink without visitations from the demon peopled Past—I did feel that he drew us together in becoming a common object of affection to us—& in respecting us both *equally* as it were." Here, of course, Elizabeth was only deluding herself, since the romantic interest that Mary, and then Horace, developed toward the other could not admit a third.

Perhaps also, Elizabeth wrote, in her relations with Mary, with the family, and with the Alcotts, she did not "adjust the virtue of *forbearance* correctly with that of *frankness*—Feeling that forbearance was always a concession to human weakness. . . . Here is my sin—& I shall try to *sin no more* in that way."

Finally, Mary had advised Elizabeth not to keep a journal so as not to be so self-absorbed. Elizabeth replied, "I have found that the study of myself the last two years—has produced none but good effects—that I am calmer—clearer—wiser—stronger—I am sorry to find that you do not see the advantage of it—& that your advice finds no echo of suitableness in my mind." It is not self-sacrifice she needed more of; since the beginning of her teaching career in Lancaster, she had been sacrificing her whole life. "And here I suppose I may as well end this discussion.—That there is a better world you believe as well as I.—I believe it is nearer than you do—even *at hand* & *within*.—You think it is above the region of Circumstance, & thus thinking you can never find it till beyond the grave.—Whatever may be the circumstances—we certainly cannot *enter it together*—till we be agreed concerning this possibility—."[55]

It is a striking letter, much like Peabody's August letter to Bronson Alcott, a dense brew of self-justification, muddled thinking about relationships, and clear analysis about her own personality. Mary, naturally, saw things differently, particularly with regard to Horace Mann. Some time later, after her marriage to Mann, she wrote angrily to Elizabeth: "My own opinion is that he thinks you have lorded it over me in a certain way & that has always made him indignant—as long ago as when we were at Mrs. Clarke's he used to express indignation about it to Sarah [Clarke] for she told me of it then. . . . I think you not only do but *never have* seen my husband exactly as he is. . . . There are chords in me that you have severed that vibrate only with agony—It might cease to be so from this day if you could only *practically* realize that you are sometimes in the wrong in your intercourse with people."[56] These things are not, after all, so easily resolved.

〜 By AUGUST 1836, Elizabeth was back in Salem, in a house on Charter Street, with her parents and sisters. Having withdrawn, just in time, in the face of the coming explosion of opposition to Temple School, she was by no means withdrawn from the intellectual world or from her larger circle of friends. Lidian Emerson wrote of her concern that Elizabeth find some new project and added that "Mr E too feels the kindest interest in your success and happiness—and hopes you will soon be able to arrange some plan that will be altogether—-eligible—He has none to suggest—(management of the concern of this present life not being his forte you know)—but he asks me if you would not like to visit us before you decide upon any new arrangement—and in the quiet of our Lethean town—clear your ideas of what you wish to do, or shall be able to undertake. . . ."[57]

One of Peabody's plans was to write and publish a "manual of Educa-

tion," intended mainly for women readers. Hoping to entice John Sullivan Dwight to contribute an article on music, she described the other
essays she hoped to include: one on education and the family, another
on religion, yet another by Francis Graeter on drawing. From Emerson
she extracted the promise of an essay on biography. She even imagined
a second volume, devoted to the "Moral Poetry of England" and its
impact on education.[58]

Nothing ever came of this project, but a second plan, a periodical
called *The Family School*, showed brief signs of life. Still, Horace Mann
was skeptical of its success in the current climate. He warned her not to
include anything about anatomy or disrobing, as she had done in *Key to
History*, in her stories for Foster Haven, and in passages in *Record*, because he believed that most people simply do not have enough purity of
mind to discuss such matters. Mary thought that this was good advice:
"I hope she will learn not to be in a hurry about compassing even good
ends. You are perfectly correct in telling her that that is her great
mistake. I have often told her that very thing, but coming from such a
wise man as you, it will make more impression. I always have a parox-
ysm of terror when I see her getting interested in imperfect mortals,
and there are so few of any other description, and her sympathies are so
widespread, and so earnest, that I am subjected to not a few. If she
would only be as prudential and doubting as I am, her heart would be
saved from many a wringing."[59]

Judging from the two numbers of *The Family School* that were published, Mary had little to worry about. Following conventional wisdom
about the family as divinely inspired and culturally central, Elizabeth
wrote the following in the "Prospectus" for the first issue: "Originat-
ing in the deepest instincts of humanity, it [the family] is accepted by
the Affections, the Imagination, and the Reason, as the play-ground of
their first efforts, the nursery of their energies, and the school of their
Heaven." Even with the addition of Romantic language about Reason
and Understanding, *The Family School* steered away from the controversies of progressive education, and into the safer waters of little articles
and stories about duty, piety, and obedience.[60]

The only really remarkable thing about the paper was its subscription
policy. In the first issue, Peabody announced that a second would appear only if there were enough subscribers for the first, a policy she
would follow, with equally disastrous results, in her single-issue journal

of 1849, *Aesthetic Papers.* At least two subscriptions came from Concord. "My wife is so dyspeptic that she cannot well write you a letter as she would," Waldo Emerson wrote in September, "but not so ill but that she rejoices in the fair promise of The Family School, & begs to be set down as a subscriber. Our Sunday School also subscribes for one copy. I hasten to send you my little Tract of Nature before its week is over." Even Bronson Alcott was generous in his hopes for "Elizabeth's paper," as he called it, hoping that "she will carry her purpose into execution. Such a periodical is extensively wanted." But *The Family School* never went beyond two numbers, for, as Elizabeth observed in a note she appended to Emerson's letter, "I could not get enough subscribers to pay for it, though the subscribers I did get were very flattering to me—."[61]

Now, with the failure of *The Family School*, Elizabeth returned to what she knew best, teaching. She had to start all over again building up a clientele, this time in Salem. It was a struggle, to be sure. In October Mrs. Peabody wrote to George that "our dear E is to be at home now—she has one Pupil at 25 dollars—to read History &c." Other than that, as Peabody wrote stoically to Elizabeth Bliss, "this is a grand place for study—and reflection. I do nothing in the world by way of helping in the world save teach a Sunday School—& *act the nurse* occasionally to my invalid sister—who is very miserably this winter *(bodily)*—The rest of the time I read German & write letters—& occasionally write in a Common book. It seems another world than Boston. You cannot imagine how different it is.—"[62]

Mary Palmer Tyler
(1775–1866), from a
daguerreotype.
*Royal Tyler Collection, Gift of Helen Tyler
Brown, Vermont Historical Society.*

Profiles of the Peabody family, November 8, 1835. Top row, left to right:
Mrs. Elizabeth Peabody, 57, Dr. Nathaniel Peabody, 61, Elizabeth, 31,
Nathaniel, Jr., 24. Bottom row: George, 22, Sophia, 26, Mary, 29,
Wellington, 20. *Courtesy Peabody Essex Museum, Salem, Massachusetts.*

Concord center, Concord, Massachusetts, ca. 1865. *Courtesy Concord Free Public Library.*

The Wayside, showing Nathaniel Hawthorne and his wife. *Courtesy Concord Free Public Library.*

Elizabeth Palmer Peabody in middle age.
Courtesy Concord Free Public Library.

Orchard House and School of Philosophy (Alfred W. Hosmer).
Courtesy Concord Free Public Library.

The Faculty of the Concord School have decided on the arrangements for the summer of 1884 as follows : (1). Six or seven days devoted to a discussion of *Emerson's Genius and Character;* beginning July 23, 1884, and including the subjects and writers named below. (2.) Three days devoted to a discussion on *Immortality,* with essays by Dr. PEABODY, Dr. HOLLAND, Prof. DAVIDSON, Dr. HARRIS, and Mr. JOHN FISKE, the latter taking for his subject *The Origin and Destiny of Man.*

(I). THE GENIUS AND CHARACTER OF EMERSON. To be considered July 23–30, 1884, under the following heads :

1. *Emerson's View of Nature,* by W. T. HARRIS, LL. D., of Concord.
2. *Emerson's Religion,* by Rev. C. A. BARTOL, D. D., of Boston.
3. *Emerson's Ethics,* by Mr. EDWIN D. MEAD, of Boston.
4. *Emerson's Manners and Relation to Society,* by Mrs. JULIA WARD HOWE, of Boston.
5. *Emerson as seen from India,* by PROTAP CHUNDER MOZOOMDAR, of Calcutta.
6. *Emerson as an American,* Mr. JULIAN HAW- THORNE, of New York.
7. *Emerson in the Pulpit,* by Miss E. P. PEA- BODY, of Boston.
8. *A French View of Emerson,* by M. RENÉ DE POYEN BELLEISLE, of Paris.
9. *Emerson in Boston,* by Mrs. E. D. CHENEY, of Boston.

10. *Emerson as an Essayist,* by Mr. JOHN ALBEE, of Newcastle, N. H.
11. *Emerson and Thoreau.*
12. *Emerson's View of Nationality,* by Rev. G. W. COOKE, of Dedham.
13. *Emerson Among the Poets,* by Mr. F. B. SANBORN, of Concord.
14. *Emerson's Relation to Goethe and Carlyle,* by W. T. HARRIS, LL. D., of Concord.
15. *The Genius of Emerson,* by Mr. W. E. CHAN- NING, of Concord.

(II). The question of *Immortality* will be opened July 31, 1884, by Rev. A. P. PEABODY, D. D., of Cambridge, who will be followed by Mr. JOHN FISKE, of Cambridge ; Rev. R. A. HOLLAND, D. D., of New Orleans ; Dr. HARRIS, of Concord, and others ; the discussion closing on the 2d of August.

In the absence of Mr. SNIDER, Prof. HARRIS will take his place.

PROGRAMME OF LECTURES.

JULY, 1884.

23d, 9 A. M. Opening Exercises.
A Sonnet by Miss Emma Lazarus.
Readings from the Diary of Mr. Alcott.
7.30 P. M. Mr. Hawthorne.
24th, 9 A. M. Dr. Bartol.
7.30 P. M. Prof. Harris.
25th, 9 A. M. Mr. Albee.
7.30 P. M. Mr. Mead.
26th, 9 A. M. Mrs. Howe.
28th, 9 A. M. { Mrs. Cheney. Miss Peabody.
7.30 P. M. Mr. Sanborn.

JULY, 1884.

29th, 9 A. M. { Prof. Harris. Mr. Mozoomdar.
7.30 P. M. M. de Poyen Belleisle.
30th, 9 A. M. { Mr. Channing. Mr. Whitman.
7.30 P. M. Mr. Cooke.
31st, 9 A. M. Dr. Peabody.
7.30 P. M. Mr. Fiske.

AUGUST, 1884.

1st, 9 A. M. Dr. Holland.
7.30 P. M. Prof. Davidson.
2d, 9 A. M. Prof. Harris.

Portion of the Concord Summer School of Philosophy program, July 22, 1884.
Courtesy Concord Free Public Library.

Elizabeth Palmer Peabody in old age. *Courtesy Concord Free Public Library.*

Elizabeth Palmer Peabody and William Torrey Harris.
Courtesy Concord Free Public Library.

5

"One's Inward Instinct Is
One's Best Guide"

᠅

THE ONLY LIKENESS we have of Elizabeth Peabody in her early adulthood comes from a set of silhouettes cut of her and her family in November 1835. Hers shows a woman of sharp chin and short hair, holding a small book in her left hand, the other hand on her hip in an appraising, self-assured manner. A year earlier, Mrs. Peabody sought to lay to rest Mary's concerns about Elizabeth's appearance: "Your sisterly heart would be satisfied, my dear Mary, with her personal appearance. She puts up her hair most becomingly in Grecian mode, and though still less willing to decorate her own person than to give her hard earned money to others, she has everything necessary to that personal neatness of appearance, which is the limits of your ambitions."[1]

But the personal unhappiness with Mary and Horace Mann, and the professional crisis with Temple School, had taken a toll on Elizabeth and her appearance. Easily distracted, always more interested in ideas than in appearance, Peabody impressed observers in the last years of the 1830s not just with her intellect but with her untidiness as well. Nathaniel Hawthorne, who had his own reasons to be nasty toward her, referred to Elizabeth, at age thirty-five, as "a good old soul" who "would give away her only petticoat, I do believe, to anybody that she thought needed it more than herself." In a passage included in his journals for 1848 but written some time earlier, Emerson observed that

Peabody was "superior, & really amiable, but took no pains to make herself personally agreeable, & was not neat,—& offended." It seems likely that Elizabeth was gaining weight, too, judging from this letter from Sophia in 1838: "You are horridly lazy about locomotion—I know that the reason why you tire so immediately upon any exertion of mind is because your physics are so inert. I should respect you infinitely more if you would make an effort to walk constantly. . . . I do not believe you would have any uneasiness upon the surface of your skin if you would exercise & never drink coffee."[2]

If we are uncertain about Peabody's physical appearance, we are on safer ground with estimates of her intellectual powers. In the same undated journal entry that contains his remarks on her lack of neatness, Emerson writes of the workings of Peabody's mind, reflecting at the same time his own masculinist blindness:

> A wonderful literary head, with extraordinary rapidity of associa-
> tion, and a methodising faculty which enabled her to weave sur-
> prising theories very fast & very finely, from slight materials. Of
> another sex, she would have been a first-rate academician; and, as it
> was, she had the ease & scope & authority of a learned professor or
> high literary celebrity in her talk. I told her I thought she ought to
> live a thousand years, her schemes of study & the necessities of
> reading which her inquiries implied, required so much.

In spite of such praise, Elizabeth must have been depressed at her prospects. She was back in Salem, canvassing for a new group of students, disconnected from her family home, and alienated from the gendered work that culture required and so many women assumed. "Never was ever a *woman* creature made so little calculated to live out of woman's only true abiding place *(home)* as *I*," she wrote sadly to Horace Mann.

> I have always known it, though I have striven to see it as little
> as possible while it could not be helped. . . . My early home was
> clouded with sorrows and cares:—but still it was a region of *liberty*,
> and I could always follow my own ideas and act my own feelings,
> and say my own *say*. Here I became acquainted with God in the
> silence of my own heart, and in a sanctuary where an *angel* minis-

tered. . . . In renewing old impressions [now that she is back in Salem] I wonder that I have ever strayed from that religious peace which grew up in my heart, while my *mind* wandered unchecked through every path of speculation and intellectual doubt.

Too early in her life she had assumed the burdens of teaching and caring for her siblings, and these responsibilities distorted her own development. "Just as it destroys the strength of the body to be put to work before it is grown, it destroys all harmonious action of mind to be put to the mental labour of one's life before one is ready. Everything has been imperfect because everything has been premature." She continued to feel the results of this premature adulthood in the years of her work in Maine, Brookline, and Boston, this sense that she had never been allowed to grow up, that she had been asked to learn and teach and do before she was really emotionally mature. "I have had *fifteen years* of this intense worry, this feeling that I could not possibly perform *actually* what I was *potentially* capable of in slightly different circumstances, and through it all I have preserved the essential element of hope and joy, and if I have been at times in a state of considerably exquisite *irritability* and sometimes *felt* pretty near the insane hospital, yet I believe I have never lost my *benevolence.* . . ."[3] What she needed was an intellectual holiday, a rest from warring ideas and a break from the public attention that her status as an unmarried female intellectual occasioned.

So, in the fall of 1836, Elizabeth Peabody seemed gradually to shift her focus away from teaching the young toward larger intellectual concerns. In the 1860s she would return to teaching the very young, and in the 1870s and 1880s she would teach their teachers, as she wove together her classroom experiences, her thoughts about language, and her new devotion to the kindergarten pedagogy of Friedrich Froebel. For now, however, private-school teaching seemed a dead end.

From her perch in Salem, Peabody observed the intellectual scene, writing some reviews, mostly anonymous, and keeping up her voluminous correspondence. Emerson once wrote his wife, who was visiting in Plymouth, "I found here a letter, when did I not? from Elizabeth Peabody[.] The kind gods never let us choose our benefactors or benefactresses, or never me mine." While visiting the Emersons in November 1836, Elizabeth wrote a long letter to Mary detailing the argument between George Ripley and Andrews Norton on the importance of

miracles for Christian belief. In an article in the *Christian Examiner* of
that same month, reviewing James Martineau's *Rationale of Religious
Inquiry*, Ripley asserted that a belief in the historicity of miracles had
never been a test of Christian faithfulness and should not be seen as a
confirmation of Jesus' divinity. In an angry rebuttal, Andrews Norton
restated his position that a belief in miracles is absolutely essential to
Christian faith. Peabody reported in her letter on a confrontation between the editor of the *Examiner*, James Walker, and Norton, who
charged him with publishing material at odds with the views of "sensible men." Although he did not agree with Ripley's view, Walker replied,
it did conform with the views of a large number of readers and of a
"portion of the association of Ministers." "No, said Mr Norton—only
of *women & very young women!!*" The sisters must have enjoyed Norton's
discomfort, being among those who distinctly agreed with Ripley.[4]

The Ripley review and controversy was a *locus classicus* of the Transcendentalist movement, as were books by William Henry Furness,
Convers Francis, and Orestes Brownson. Of Brownson's *New Views
of Christianity, Society, and the Church*, Peabody wrote to Horace Mann
that she wished he would read it and "lay it to heart and thought that
the Church and Christianity are *two*, and that all your arguments and
feelings of a warlike character belong to the Church, and none to
Christianity. Would that I could make you *take in that fact*. Mr. Brownson's views are not *new*, however; in our religious world they are as old
as Dr. Channing at least."[5]

But no person prompted so much reflection and correspondence in
the last months of 1836 as did Emerson. By now, Emerson had become
a respected, even idolized, intellectual figure in the Peabody household.
Mary, whom Horace Mann described as being "Emerson-struck," reported to Rawlins Pickman that "Mr. Emerson is the most beautiful
converser that can be imagined. You know there is a great difference
between talk & conversation. . . . A sentence of Mr. Emerson's is a
volume from which other people may converse a great while—he talks
very much as he lectures—his conversation full of beautiful allusions,
aptly applied & a sincerity & truth of mind & expression always that
you make you feel that this is the real thing." Sophia called him "the
most complete man that ever lived."[6]

The Peabodys' admiration was not universally shared, of course.
Their friend Sally Gardiner sharply responded to a similar letter from

Mary that she was surprised "at the unqualified approbation you say you have bestowed upon Mr. Emerson. He is the sage and the enchanter of a few, but all our ministers are opposed to him, and the grave, sensible people who never hear him, think it necessary to their own character for staidness, &c, to pass him by on the other side. . . ." After the publication of *Nature* in 1836 and the delivery of the "Divinity School Address" in 1838, the social and religious establishment would have much more to oppose in Emerson's teachings.[7]

It is a little surprising, given Emerson's standing among the Peabody sisters, that Elizabeth should be so lukewarm in her attitude toward *Nature.* "Mr. Emerson's book on Nature has come out," she wrote her brother George in October—the book had been published in July— "and a very provoking book it is. It beats all nature in unintelligibleness—not that every separate sentence is not plain enough—But these sentences are taken out of different lectures of his—& arranged under the heads of the Commodity—the Beauty—the Discipline—the Idealism—& the Spirit of Nature—without being connected together with a sufficient degree of illustration. . . . I do not think you will enjoy it much—& you have your wit's work I am sure at present in Sartor Resartus," referring to Thomas Carlyle's book which Emerson had just had published in Boston by James Munroe.[8]

With all Horace Mann's skepticism about Transcendentalism, Peabody was sure that he would not like *Nature,* and she tried to preempt some of his criticisms. "Have you seen Mr. Emerson's book on Nature? I know you will find fault with its reserved style and the want of illustration and development of the ideas. And you will *smile,* for even *I do,* at the ultra idealism of its last chapter but one. But in spite of all its faults, I hope you will be attracted to read it more than once." To Emerson himself, Peabody must have expressed the same criticism that the book seemed disjointed, for he wrote this in response: "You express overkind opinions of my little book, but think it wants connexion. I thought it resembled the multiplication table. I hope however to offer you something better by & by when the lectures are finished."[9]

These private comments were sharper and more critical than her published ones, judging from her unsigned review of *Nature* and "The American Scholar" published in February 1838 in *The United States Magazine and Democratic Review.* Calling *Nature* a "Prose Poem," Peabody reminded her readers that Emerson did not intend to write a

treatise on physics, as some readers assumed, but rather a metaphysics
of nature, composed "in the midst of the dust of business and the din of
machinery." Expressed like a good poem in figurative language, Emerson's *Nature* seeks to recover and reexpress the truths of nature in an
age of commodity.

More than Emerson probably intended, Peabody restated the essay
so as to emphasize its theism and its didacticism. She defended his
philosophical idealism but noted correctly that Emerson did not go so
far as to make nature the product of the human imagination. Nature is
the necessary clothing for the life of the Spirit, Emerson claims, and
Peabody agreed. But Emerson would not agree with Peabody's efforts
to restate his insights in liberal Christian language. To his assertion that
"the problem of restoring to the world original and eternal beauty is
solved by the redemption of the soul," Peabody responded that "we
should like to hear Mr. Emerson's philosophy of Redemption. It is very
plain that it consists of broad and comprehensive views of human culture; worthy to employ the whole mind of one who seeks reproduction
of Christ within himself. . . ." This reference to Christ reminds us that
Peabody was working hard to bridge the distance between Emerson
and her mentor Channing. Emerson had begun his career as a Unitarian clergyman reflecting his denomination's view of the distinctive ministry of Christ, but in the early 1830s, as David Robinson has noted,
Emerson began to question that status, seeing this reverence for Christ
as an obstacle to full self-culture and self-reliance. Comfortable as she
now was with the Romantic intuitional philosophy, Peabody still
wanted to hold on to the figure of Christ, at least as symbolic of the
perfected self.[10]

In December, Elizabeth traveled to Concord to visit the Emersons,
who were also hosting the English writer Harriet Martineau. She had
been touring about the northeastern United States, gathering impressions that she would publish as *Society in America* the following year. For
all her nascent eccentricities, Elizabeth Peabody was no match for the
redoubtable Miss Martineau, with her ear trumpet and decided opinions. Elizabeth, Mary reported, found Martineau a woman of "prodigious understanding and talent" but decided that she had had quite
enough of the writer by the end of the visit. It was interesting, however,
to find out how Martineau wrote all those books on political economy.
Elizabeth learned that she would immerse herself in all the sources and

then sit and write as fast as possible, without corrections, "pick up her manuscript, send it to the publisher, take out new books & new paper & immediately commence upon another."[11]

Of course, Elizabeth had her own limitations as a guest. Although she is not named in this December journal passage, it seems as if Emerson was speaking of Peabody (rather than Martineau) when he reported that "I have been making war against the superlative degree in the rhetoric of my fair visiter [sic]. She has no positive degree in her description of characters & scenes. You would think she had dwelt in a museum where all things were extremes & extraordinary. . . . But besides the superlative of her mind she has a superlative of grammar which is suicidal & defeats its ends." Her writing suffered from the same defects, "unelaborated thought," a "hurry of images & ideas," all arising from "undisturbed exuberance." He even recommended that Elizabeth follow his custom and keep a "manuscript book—& write down every train of thought which arose on any interesting subject with the imagery in which it first came into my mind." Afterwards she could write thematic headings on each page, "& when I wanted to make up an article—*there* were all my thoughts *ready*." For such reflective journal writing and indexing, Emerson recommended what Peabody was perhaps finding a bit too much of, "quiet study—and all calm influences."[12]

❧ EMERSON COULD not have known, in mid-1836, just how disturbing to "quiet study" and "calm influences" Jones Very would be for Elizabeth Peabody, for Emerson himself, and for many others in Concord and Salem. Very shot like a meteor across the path of the Transcendentalists, illuminating the territory between orthodox Christianity and liberal religion, and then burning himself out in three years of creativity and notoriety.

The son of a sea captain who died when Jones was ten and of a woman famous for her outspoken atheism, Very graduated from Harvard College in 1836. Later that year he began divinity studies and accepted the post of tutor of Greek at the college. In 1837 Very began to meet the people who would decisively affect his life and introduce him to a larger public. In the evening of December 27, Very addressed the Salem Lyceum on the topic of "Epic Poetry." More than forty years later, Elizabeth Peabody recalled that "he was alone on the platform and when his lecture was finished stood for a moment—uncertain, shy, and embarrassed.—Being on the front seat with my father, I said 'Let us ask him to go home with us'—and stepped up to him—to do so—He grasped my outstretched hand like a drowning man . . . and accepted the invitation." On the walk to the Peabodys' Charter Street house, Elizabeth "found that he was an enthusiastic listener to Mr. Emerson" and heard about Very's interpretation of Shakespeare. "Mr. Very, that evening, did not seem at all excited or mystical."[13]

Peabody immediately wrote to Emerson about her discovery and encouraged him to invite Very to lecture at the Concord lyceum. Emerson's invitation brought Very out to Concord in April for a lecture and the first of many visits with the Emersons. He was delighted with this new acquaintance and wrote Elizabeth "to thank again your sagacity that detects such wise men as Mr. Very, from whose conversation and lecture I have had a true and high satisfaction. I heartily congratulate myself on being, as it were, anew in such company."[14]

Meanwhile, Very came to the Peabody house whenever he was in Salem, and gradually Elizabeth learned more of his story. In response to his mother's lack of faith, Very had adopted a rigorous and yet eccentric orthodoxy. He preferred to preach to his Greek students than instruct them in the ancient language, and he would take a favored few for walks in Mt. Auburn cemetery for conversations on "the deepest spiritual subjects and in the most devout tone." During his years as a Greek tutor (1836–1838), Very became convinced that union with God would come only after a surrender of the individual will.

Toward the end of 1838, Very's sense of divine mission intensified. He was sure he had achieved perfect self-emptying and that his words were not his own but were God's. He understood himself as one authorized to speak prophetically to his generation, believing that he had attained oneness with that other example of perfect *kenosis*, Jesus. It was in this spirit that Very suddenly cried out to his students, "Flee to the mountains, for the end of all things is at hand." Later that day he told some other students that they were merely men but that he spoke with the voice of God. Shocked by these outbursts, Harvard president Josiah Quincy relieved Very of his classes.

Two days later, Sunday morning, September 16, Very called on Elizabeth Peabody, who was home alone. "He looked much flushed and his eyes very brilliant and unwinking—it struck me at once that there was something unnatural—and dangerous in his air," she recalled. Very announced, "I come to baptise you with the Holy Ghost and with fire." "I trembled to the centre—But it was my instinct—not to antagonize but to be perfectly quiet—I felt he was beside himself and I was alone in the lower story of the house." After an uneasy silence, Very asked if she felt any change. "I replied gently, 'I feel no change'—'But you will'—said he hurriedly—'I am the Second Coming—Give me a Bible'—There was one in the room to which I pointed. He went to the table where it was and turned to Christ's prophecy of the Second Coming—and read it ending with the words, 'This day is this fulfilled in your hearing'—I was silent but respectful even tenderly so."

After Very had left, Peabody learned that he had already visited John Brazer, minister of the Unitarian North Church, the Baptist minister Lucius Bolles, and Charles Upham, minister of the Unitarian First Church, to bless and baptize them. Bolles had physically thrown Very out of his house; and Upham, "who at that time was a good deal excited against the transcendentalists, calling Mr. Emerson an Atheist—and declaring that it was wrong to listen to him—had told Mr. Very that he should see that he be sent to the Insane Asylum." Despite his mother's strenuous resistance to this idea, Very agreed to enter McLean's Asylum in nearby Somerville the next day, and spent a month there.[15]

Eager to inform Emerson about the implications of the case, Peabody wrote him while Very was still at McLean's. Diagnosing Very's condition as the result of overwork and possibly "water on the brain," Peabody connected the tutor's outbursts with the equally mistaken spiritual individualism of Quakers. *"These impulses* from above I think are never sound minded—the insanity of Quakers—(which is very frequent under my observation) always grows out of it—or rather begins in it.—I wonder whether some thing might not be written by a believer in the doctrine of Spirituality—which would show the difference between trusting the Soul & giving up one's mind to these *individual illuminations."*

This whole question of intuition and inspiration was vexing, because people like Brazer and others "impute to his transcendental ideas—this misfortune—considering that his notions grow straight out of the idea that the evidence of Revelation is a more inward one than *miracles,"* the same issue that divided Andrews Norton and George Ripley. Very himself was not much help. "He used Christ's words all the time & in the whimsical manner an insane person might. But the thought which has pressed itself on my mind *most* is—how some people have taken it all—as nothing but *transcendentalism*—which shows how very entirely they do *not* apprehend the *ground* of a *real belief* in *Inspiration.*—What a frightful shallowness of thought in the community—that sees no difference between the evidence of the most manifest insanity & the Ideas of Reason!"[16] But Emerson appeared unconcerned about fallout from the Very situation. To Margaret Fuller he stressed Very's gift of expression. The essay on Shakespeare "is a noble production: not consecutive, filled with one thought; but that so deep and true and illustrated so happily and even grandly; that I account it an addition to our really scanty stock of adequate criticism on Shakespear [sic]. Such a mind cannot be lost."[17]

Released in mid-October, Very spent much time with the Emersons, occasionally testing the limits of their hospitality. When not in Concord, Very closeted himself in his mother's house in Salem, producing over a hundred poems, emerging on occasion to visit the Peabodys. In Elizabeth's view, Very was still "as crazy as ever." Even though he claimed to be free of the delusion of being a prophet, he still spoke like one, she wrote to Emerson. His enemies in town, particularly John Brazer (whom Elizabeth called "the doubly distilled old woman"), still wanted him institutionalized or sent to sea. The whole Peabody family was drawn into this imbroglio, with both Mother and Father Peabody stirred up about the threat to the harmless Very.[18]

Beyond the danger to Very was the continuing danger to Emerson, or so Elizabeth thought. Brazer went around linking Very's insanity with Emerson's teachings, while Very "thinks you *and he* are persecuted—& he goes expecting full sympathy," Peabody wrote to Emerson. She had some advice in light of Very's upcoming visit to Concord: "I would not—if I were you—stretch your charity so far as to invite him to stay in the house—or if he comes late & you have to—in charity—limit your invitation—else you may not easily get rid of him."[19]

When the danger of Very's abduction had passed and the threat to Emerson's reputation had quieted for the moment, Peabody reflected on Very's message. He was, after all, treated with respect and seriousness by her mentor Channing in an interview in early December. James Freeman Clarke had written a graceful introduction to a selection of Very's poems published in the *Western Messenger,* connecting Very to the radical wing of Protestantism that claimed divine guidance by the inner light and intuitive knowledge of God's will, much like the Quakers whom Peabody distrusted. Therefore, she was perhaps more open to Very's message when he came to call on December 2. "He was very charming and when he explained & explained in answer to my questions and self-analyses—it seemed to me as if I thought & believed exactly so—though I did not acknowledge it quite—that is—I contended for a less violent & more compromised expression of the same ideas." Of course Very was not so charming everywhere. She reported to Emerson that when Very visited Salem's social and intellectual luminary Susan Burley, he was much more violent in his language and gloomy in his manner, possibly because Burley had less patience with Very's "excessively conceited" and lofty view of his own insights than had the Peabodys.[20]

Very passed as quickly out of Peabody's life as he had entered it. She suggested that Emerson edit Very's poems for publication, an idea he had already come to. Although Very was reluctant to accept any editing, Emerson managed to assemble a manuscript that appeared as *Essays and Poems* in September 1839. In the following year, Peabody moved to Boston, where she opened her West Street bookshop and where Very visited at least once. She sent him a copy of the *Dial* in 1842. For her and others in the Transcendentalist circle, as for Very himself, 1837 to 1840 were indeed Very's "effective years," in the apt phrase of his biographer.[21]

Jones Very made such an impact on Elizabeth Peabody in part because she was ready for intellectual stimulation, feeling bored and useless in Salem's intellectual backwater. Very drew her back into the kind of intellectual controversy that she had surrendered in leaving Temple School and threw her into close connection with her hero Emerson.

Even more, Peabody must have found Very strikingly reminiscent of her mentor Channing. True enough, Channing never thought of himself as a prophet or a new messiah. But both men were slight and frail in appearance, both seemed possessed of a truth that almost overpowered them, both had a sweet disposition, and both aroused vigorous and sometimes vicious opposition. Peabody's descriptions of Very do not have the eroticism of her letters about Channing. But Very must have seemed that same kind of physically weak, spiritually strong man that she had found so irresistible in Channing. Like Channing, Very forced Peabody to rethink her ideas about spirituality and religion, in this case her views of Transcendentalism and her place in the "movement." Her Unitarian upbringing and experiences with Channing had taught her that religious language was figurative speech for psychological and moral life. Words like grace, spirit, redemption, salvation, sin, and the like functioned as tropes to refer to conditions of the self in its growth toward ethical maturity. Personal growth was understood as the corollary of social growth, and history was seen as the record of God's plan for humanity, unfolding in an orderly and linear fashion.

What made Jones Very so unsettling for Elizabeth Peabody was the possibility that religion was not synonymous with gradual growth toward divine perfection. Liberal Christianity even offered the possibility of mystical experience as part of the shaping of a spiritually harmonious self.[22] But Very revealed another kind of mysticism, one in which one is beside oneself, possessed, protean, or else emptied of self and filled with a new identity. Even if one claimed, as Channing and Peabody did, that emotional states are indicative of spiritual states, what happened when one's emotional life seemed out of control? For Peabody, whose emotional life was often erratic, charged, and intense, and whose behavior seemed sometimes to challenge convention, this was a charged and lively question. Very's case exposed society's views of the unconventional self; it is not surprising that Peabody echoed the general view that he was insane, and deflected onto him the criticisms that might, and sometimes did, land on her.

For Peabody the most fascinating and dangerous part of Very's message was his insistence on self-emptying and will-lessness. For Channing and Peabody, self-emptying had to do with overcoming selfishness or self-preoccupation in favor of what was perceived as a higher social good. One found a new will as one practiced moral rectitude. Very also believed in *kenosis* but came at it from a completely different vantage point. For him it entailed a prophetic message that had no particular application to society or to others. Peabody kept wanting to channel intuitive insight back into the world of social institutions, but Very simply wanted to inspire perfectly self-emptied, spirit-filled selves who were led, as he was, to speak their message regardless of social convention or propriety.

Jones Very was, to borrow Taylor Stoehr's happy phrase, a "nay-sayer," whereas Elizabeth Peabody was most definitely a "yea-sayer."[23] For her there was no radical break between the Unitarianism of her

teens and twenties and the Transcendentalism of her thirties and for-
ties. Transcendentalism was an extension of the beliefs that Channing
nurtured—that all creation is fundamentally spiritual, that all things are
symbolic of universal truth, and that such truth exists in all people and is
progressively unfolding throughout human history. Unlike some others
in the Transcendentalist movement, notably Emerson and Alcott, Peabody was convinced of the importance of history as the central record
of that spiritual perfectionism, and she preferred to read the text of the
past rather than the text of nature for such illuminations. Still, immersed in its central texts, employing its characteristic language, involved in its central institutions like Temple School, the West Street
Bookshop, and the *Dial*, she certainly thought of herself as a participant
in the movement informally led by Emerson.

Charges that Transcendentalism was synonymous with atheism contradicted Elizabeth's sense that it was, rather, purified Christianity. Such
charges also warned her of the implications that her being in this movement might have for a young, unmarried woman. The collapse of Temple School and her inability to get subscribers for *The Family School*
reminded Peabody that teaching functioned within a market economy.
Like Bronson Alcott, she was selling her ideas and skills in the marketplace and depended on the goodwill and active support of parents for
her livelihood. The exchange nature of teaching was often obscured in
the highly personalized and emotionally charged "gift-like" relationship of teacher-student, and by the privileged status of the Unitarian
parents whose children she taught. Charges of immorality and atheism
against Transcendentalism seemed wide of the mark. But they endan-
gered her livelihood, frightening parents away from a teacher who associated with such disreputable people and ideas.

This situation was not a new problem for Elizabeth Peabody, but
the Transcendentalist movement sharply focused the issue for her in
the late 1830s. To the extent that Peabody understood her livelihood
to depend on the goodwill of a large, educated, religiously liberal audience for her classes and publications, she was intent on interpreting
Transcendentalism as an extension of liberal ideas and on downplaying
its radical and socially disruptive aspects. It was, in this interpretation,
the opponents of Transcendentalism, like Andrews Norton and John
Brazer, who were indecorous and improper in their violent language
and menacing behavior, not its adherents.

On the other hand, Peabody was herself often charged with impropriety and lack of decorum. She was unmarried, had no home of her own, and stood just outside the domestic conventions so widely accepted in her time, no matter how much she might have craved such conventions. Very, Emerson, and the whole Transcendentalist movement appealed powerfully because she already found herself on the margins of society in her social arrangements, in her practice as a teacher, and in the intensity of her emotional life. "I feel as I never felt before that to be true to one's self is the first thing," she wrote to Sophia in July 1838. "—that to sacrifice the perfect culture of my mind to social duties is not the thing—that what we call disinterestedness of action is often disobedience to one's *daimon*—that one's inward instinct is one's best guide."[24]

⅋ NOT EVERYONE appreciated Peabody's efforts to find her place in the "Newness," as Transcendentalism was sometimes called. Margaret Fuller, for one, was often critical and occasionally cruel. Elizabeth had first encountered Margaret in 1828. Twelve years old and a student at Dr. Park's school, Fuller impressed the young schoolteacher with her ability to talk "pure mathematics with her father" although she also "had not religion." Margaret seemed even then amused by the earnest young teacher. After Fuller's death, Peabody recalled that first meeting: "Margaret said almost nothing, but I thought she was laughing at me, for which there seemed good cause. I was impressed strongly with her perfect good nature. It seemed her eyes overflowed with fun, & this fun was a pure sense of the comic,—inevitable to an intellect as sharp as a diamond; the conviction was irresistable that she had no malice in her heart." This was perhaps overgenerous on Peabody's part.[25]

Elizabeth kept up with Margaret into the 1830s; when the Peabodys moved into Mrs. Clarke's boardinghouse in Boston, Mrs. Clarke's son James Freeman and Margaret Fuller had been studying German together for a year. By 1835 Peabody thought her own career and Fuller's sufficiently similar to hope that Park Benjamin, editor of the *New England Magazine*, might help both of them "in making our thoughts known." The following year she encouraged Emerson to invite Fuller to visit Concord, even though she admitted that she had at first felt a "strong but unjustifiable prejudice" against Fuller. That visit, the first of many, lasted three weeks in July and August 1836, and at its end, despite some uncomfortable moments, Emerson wrote to Peabody that "I believe we all here shared your respect for Miss Fuller's gifts & character. She has the quickest apprehension & immediately learned all we knew & had us at her mercy when she pleased to make us laugh. She has noble traits & powers & cannot fail of a permanent success."[26]

Despite this mediation from Fuller's "faithful booster," as Charles Capper has called Elizabeth, Margaret could not resist making fun of the overserious and sometimes garrulous Peabody. To the worldly Fuller, whose vision was much more Hellenic than Hebraic, the Peabodys' filiopiety toward New England was quaint and amusing. In 1837, Elizabeth was helping her brother Nathaniel find yet another job, this time teaching school. Fuller passed along an advertisement for a position teaching Latin and Greek at a school in Virginia. Perhaps Nathaniel would be interested, she wrote, adding that "a residence in that pleasant part of Virginia would I should think have its charms—unless your brother is as great a fanatic about N. England as his sisters."[27]

The Peabodys did not follow up on Fuller's suggestion. In fact, two months later, in July 1837, Elizabeth traveled to Bangor, Maine, in search of a position for her brother. There she stayed with Frederic Henry Hedge, the brilliant scholar whose occasional visits to the Boston area gave the name "Hedge's Club" to the group of Transcendentalists who were gathering for conversation and mutual inspiration. Fuller, who shared a passion for German language and literature with "Germanicus" Hedge, as he was sometimes called, was amused that Peabody was staying there. "I cannot but laugh when I think of your former way of talking about 'Dr Channing's women' to hear of Miss P. as domesticated with you." Hedge, though, did not join in the joke and defended Elizabeth in his response. "I cannot sympathise in her enthusiasm or her personalities, but these things are so balanced by other qualities that they trouble me much less than I had supposed they would."[28]

Hedge's generous response notwithstanding, Fuller would rarely find reason to be very charitable toward Elizabeth Peabody. "I admit that I have never done you justice," she wrote to Elizabeth in 1844. "There is so much in you that is hostile to my wishes, as to character, and especially as to the character of woman." Besides that, Fuller deeply disliked what she thought was Peabody's inclination to idolize, to hero-worship.

Such a habit invariably causes the hero to withdraw emotionally. Even more, hero worship affected intellectual judgment and expression. "A little, only a little less of this in you would give your powers the degree of fresh air they need. Could you be as generous and sympathetic, yet never infatuated; then the blur, the haste, the tangle would disappear, and neither I nor any one could refuse to understand you."

It is suggestive, as Charles Capper notes, that Fuller should so dislike a woman whose career in teaching, writing, and literary entrepreneurship resembled her own, and ironic that Peabody, so often maligned by Fuller, was in many ways her most faithful champion. William Ellery Channing, who caught this irony immediately, is reported to have said to her once, "Miss Fuller, when I consider that you are all that Miss P[eabody] wished to be, and that you despise her, and that she loves and honors you, I think her place in Heaven must be very high."[29]

Fuller and Peabody were both, after all, "literary" women, unmarried for all or most of their careers. Although there was a growing number of women working in literary occupations in the antebellum years, few chose, or were able, to support themselves in this fashion. Both women were acutely aware of the interplay among ideas, expression, and audience. Both were constantly seeking new outlets for their insights, including the literary and historical conversation that Fuller popularized but that Peabody pioneered.

For all their similarities, striking differences remained. Fuller was the more original thinker. In her views of gendered relations and particularly in her understanding of androgyny, in her critiques of American writing, and in her own often-brilliant journalism, Fuller shaped new paradigms still relevant today. On her side, Peabody was a much more pragmatic and synthetic thinker. She combined ideas, tried things out, and sought to build intellectual alliances, as in her effort to lessen the gap between Emerson and his Unitarian critics. Just as significant is the fact that Fuller was a post-Christian intellectual, who lived in what she increasingly took to be an alienated and fragmented world. As she once said, "I have no belief in beautiful lives; we were born to be mutilated; Life is basically unjust." For her, Transcendentalism theorized self-trust in the midst of a radically disordered world. In contrast, Peabody's Transcendentalism led to cosmic, although not naive, optimism, a desire to weld self-trust and self-reliance together with a liberal Christian belief in an ordered universe and a loving God. She was a good example of William James's "once-born" personality, tempered but not defeated by adversity and disappointment.[30]

〜〜 TEACHING always called out Elizabeth Peabody's gifts of synthesis, good explanation, and nurture of character. But much as Margaret Fuller disliked Peabody's hero worship and probably resented her presence in the Transcendentalist movement, so Horace Mann quarreled with some aspects of her pedagogy. Although she had no class of students at that time in Salem, nor would she have until the late 1860s, Peabody did have one student right in her family home, Foster Haven. Foster had attached himself to Aunt Lizzy when she visited his dying mother, and now in the year that he lived with the Peabodys, Elizabeth quickly took over his education.

In her 1886 "Psychological Observation," based on notes she had lost, Peabody observes that she taught Foster reading and spelling, and through her sister Mary's school, the rudiments of natural science. But her real interest was moral and spiritual education, and central to that, she recalled, was instruction in prayer. By that she meant not memorization, but rather an understanding of the self as a spiritual being in contact with a spiritualized universe. Given her own theological bent, it is not surprising that Elizabeth taught young Foster that "good" exists and that evil is the absence of good, a concept she held in common with Emerson and many other thinkers.

This concept was exactly the point, however, that Horace Mann, caught up in his own endless struggles with his Calvinist inheritance, disputed. Commenting on the scene in Elizabeth's "Foster-Biography," probably the memoranda she had lost by 1886, in which Foster was tempted to take some fruit from his dying mother's bed stand, an act that Peabody interpreted as the absence of good, Mann wrote, "now this is not true, either religiously or philosophically; and if the child has any causality, he will soon drive you from the point. Has his desire to eat his mother's fruit the absence merely of good, or was it as positive an entity as was ever subjected to his consciousness? The desire to eat good things at a proper time and in proper quantity is right and not wrong. Had you not better keep the things away from the mind until it can understand the right, than to give the wrong, which must be so soon taken away, until a child's confidence that anything is right is destroyed."

Elizabeth was clearly hurt by this criticism. "I told him [Foster] . . . that *naughty* was not from a source of power, but was the absence or the mind's unconsciousness of God, and *so it is.* Surely you think so. You do not believe in any evil spirit—you will allow that a wrong state of mind always arises from taking a partial view—a view which leaves out *the good.*" Mann's criticism was not just pedagogical, but theological as well. "I wish you would not dismiss my views of evil so lightly," Peabody wrote. "I should think it a crime to take advantage of a feeble mind as you suggest. But I do not think evil an entity. How curious it is that you should deny that good is an entity, as you always seem to do, and stickle for evil as an entity." Margaret Fuller, so hostile to Elizabeth for her hero worship, might have been pleased at how Peabody was cutting her former demigod down to size.[31]

↜ As CONTROVERSIES about Temple School and Jones Very swirled around her and as Horace Mann and Margaret Fuller disputed her ideas and manner, problems and tragedies much closer to home filled many of Elizabeth Peabody's days in the late 1830s. No males— neither William Ellery Channing nor Jones Very with their gaunt bodies and otherworldly spirituality, not Horace Mann with his long, self-indulgent crisis of faith, not Bronson Alcott with his dreamy utopianism—so illustrated masculine struggles for vocation and self-respect as did Elizabeth's brothers and father. Dr. Peabody had settled into his dental and medical practice by now. The intellectual and emotional energies of his family had long been given over wholly to his wife and daughters, but at least his work was prospering, partly because by 1836, he was no longer supporting his son Nat and his family. But in this family he was simply a nonentity, a loved and tolerated figure who made no difference at all in the intellectual and emotional climate.

The brothers, on the other hand, blew up great storms of controversy and concern. Landing in New York in June 1834 after a two-year stint on a whaler, but forfeiting his pay by jumping ship, the youngest brother Wellington was full of improbable schemes for making money. Perhaps his cousin George Putnam could find him a clerkship in a bookstore; and then there were even more outrageous possibilities. "Association with inferiors has made him overrate his talents infinitely," Elizabeth wrote Mary, then in Cuba. "He said he should write a book of observations upon the countries he had visited. I beg him to do nothing so absurd. He said he had written to the Duke of Wellington to ask him to take him into his employ! I told him not to tell of such an extravagant [word unclear]—& believe I made him ashamed of both—the latter thing especially. He says he is willing to work entirely—to do anything." Their brother George was even less kind about Wellington. "He *thinks all* Welly's talk is *palaver.* He does not believe a *word* of his resolutions &c—He does not think he has any principle whatever."[32]

Elizabeth and George were right in their assessment. In July Elizabeth visited Salem and saw Wellington, "who has got a dandyish cut & look again." A packet of letters from their Aunt Catherine Putnam confirmed their worst fears about the young man, detailing "Wellington's extravagances & lies in New York—& showed how many lies he had told since he came home—about matters there. . . . Yet Wellington holds up his head and thinks he has nothing to be ashamed of. I do not know what will become of him . . . the only business that offers him any thing like *subsistence* is going to sea." Part of the problem, Elizabeth admitted years later, stemmed from Dr. Peabody's indifferent parenting. "My father was most indulgent, not a particle of the disciplinarian in him, and Wellington, who was his youngest son, a darling pet, though he was occasionally thoughtless, and we all at the moment were frightened lest he should be led into dangerous and expensive habits, in consequence of his popularity with some rich fellows, of whom he was tempted to borrow money."

Wellington managed to hang on in Salem for the next few years, aimlessly pursuing jobs and studies, including a course in physics. In 1837 he decided to go down to New Orleans to study tropical diseases, especially yellow fever. He arrived just as the city was being devastated by a cholera epidemic that had brought yellow fever in its wake. Nearly all the doctors had fled, leaving Wellington, who had signed on at a marine hospital with no significant medical training, "to be nurse, servant, and physician to 120 patients, of whom only 20 died, and he had no nurses but black men (slaves)," Elizabeth wrote in 1886. Wellington himself contracted yellow fever as he ministered to the dying, and died, at age twenty-one, on September 29.[33]

George Peabody spent his last days in Salem, in the Peabody family house on Charter Street. Like his brothers, George could never find his path, his calling, and spent years working at unchallenging jobs and traveling to South Carolina and to Turkey. He was in New Orleans around the time of Wellington's death; his family begged him in a collective letter to return home lest he expose himself to diseases there or risk the recurrence of his paralysis. George was, in fact, in the first stages of spinal meningitis, which he had contracted somewhere on his voyages.

The last two years of George's life passed in increasing pain and immobility, interspersed with a few periods of remission. When he came home in early 1838, Elizabeth said, "he knew he must die." His brother Nat and his sisters wrote to him when they were away, and they ministered to him when they were at home. By spring 1838 he was taking doses of morphine and quinine for the pain and could just barely pull himself upright in bed by means of a rope.[34]

George's sufferings affected the whole family. Elizabeth wrote Horace Mann that "for seven years at least—no calamity has ever oppressed me like this condition of George's—worse than death to him for it has not like death a glorious reverse—in which the heart can repose—Next to vice—to be a helpless cripple is the most terrific thing." Sophia was distraught at George's condition. The invalided youngest sister, whose headaches originated with the overdoses of medicines given to her by her father and other doctors, was in the habit of seeing everything through the "'couleur de rose' medium," as she put it. Her brother's increasing pain and the hopelessness of his condition strained both her optimism and her nerves.

> One day I heard him groan in my chamber, and I can truly say that such a pang of anguish never rived my heart. This is a new trial to me, and perfectly unimagined with all my imagination. I never have thought, you know, that it was any trial to bear my own pain. I could always manage it, and arrange it in the grand economy of events; but I must yet learn to be patient and serene at the sight and consciousness of his. . . . The slow and ever increasing suffering is the most appalling prospect that can be to such a hypersympathetic person as I am.

Her own suffering she could bear; that of her brother created "momentary anguish which the terrific sensitiveness of my nerves renders it [sic] impossible to control. I mean for George."

In his last days, at the end of November 1839, George was conscious but completely paralyzed. Five days before he died, wrote Elizabeth, "he said he had nothing more to say or to hear and did not fear to lose his tranquility of mind in the death struggle—which lasted 45 hours! I was with him all the time, but my mother had to leave him some hours before he died, for she could not bear it, and he was long past recognition. I never saw death before. How wonderful it is—that final look of distress, that convulsion, and then that *sudden peace and sweetness.* That night we could only be thankful that he was gone and could hardly leave the witness of his rest, left in his corpse."[35]

The family circle was shrinking. It had contracted twice in 1837, once with the death of Wellington, and again when Nathaniel, reduced to being a shop hand in a drugstore on State Street, decided to try his hand at teaching, his sisters' chosen profession. Elizabeth was willing to help him find a post, and in June she traveled to Bangor, Maine, close to her old haunts on the Kennebec River. She found it "curious & painful & pleasurable too to come to a place so strongly associated with some of the most intense feelings of one's life."

But her business was Nat, not nostalgia. She was not too sanguine about what she found there. Perhaps Margaret Fuller was right: "If a very good place & a large salary could be obtained, it would be worth while for him to go to the South." Still, Nat was willing to give it a try. Elizabeth described his school as consisting of "nine young ladies. . . . He is very fortunate in their loveliness and good manners as well as in their intelligence & wellgrounded education." The teaching post came with a house and a landlady who was once a student of Mrs. Peabody.

As was so often the case, Nat's perceptions were utterly at odds with those of his sisters. By the end of the summer, he had had his fill with these lovely and well-mannered young ladies:

> I use no violent language. I have expressed myself decidedly several times, but it does nothing toward affecting my object. . . . I cannot obtain proper attention. The great girls behave twice as bad as the young. As a last resort I have made the girls read each the same passage, it may be more or less, over until all have read. . . . My remonstrances and remarks, let them be ever so sage and decided, produce effect for about the space of one minute. As to listening to reading, it is impracticable: it is a waste of time and exhausts me. . . . You see that very little respect is gained by good

nature. Scholars take advantage of it. There ought to be strictness in a school. Pupils ought not to sit with one another to study, but if they want help come to the teacher. They will abuse the confidence placed in them, and when you expect they are studying together, they will be eating currants or cherries or drawing figures. . . .

and so on and on, a bitter and resentful explosion about his frustrations in a career that seemed so effortless to his sisters.[36]

Again Elizabeth came to the rescue of her luckless brother. She arranged for him to have a school in West Newton, a town about ten miles west of Boston. Not just that: she got back her furniture that she had loaned Alcott for Temple School; brought Nat's wife and child out to Newton; located a house, in which she would also have rooms; figured out what should go in each room; and even determined which rooms needed carpeting, painting, and wallpapering. What Elizabeth Hibbard Peabody thought about this domestic tyranny is not recorded.

Perhaps this school would be better than Bangor's; at least Elizabeth Peabody hoped so. She must have been doing some "master-teaching," to give Nathaniel some tutoring in the kind of moral education that she and her sisters so loved. "I shall part with N—very pleasantly—there were some developments the last day I was in school—which convinced him of the value of my moral lessons—& my going away after I had set him a going—seems to open his eyes to the fact that I did not come merely to gratify my own wilfulness but to set him up in life." Nathaniel was bitter at what he interpreted as his sister's patronizing intervention in his affairs. Back in April he had written Elizabeth sarcastically, probably after receiving yet another letter of good advice: "I read your remarks attentively, but I think we had better not say any more on these matters by letter. There are some things on which my mind has never been fully made up, and if it can be convinced by any future conversation with you, I shall be glad. In the meantime I can have no better example of entire disinterestedness and self-sacrifice for imitation than your own life, for I have not forgotten your story told me of your early trials in school keeping in Boston."[37]

᧥ No event in Elizabeth Peabody's life so fused private and public spheres as her encounter with Nathaniel Hawthorne. In the midst of her life as writer and sometime teacher, in the midst of her profound connections with Jones Very and Waldo Emerson, and in the midst of these family tragedies and imbroglios, came the famous evening with Hawthorne and his sisters, the consequences of which echoed throughout Peabody's long life, even into its last decade.

In 1811 the Peabody family lived on Union Street in Salem, in a house that backed up to the Hathorne (as it was then spelled and pronounced) family house on adjacent Herbert Street. In that year Mrs. Peabody was preoccupied with two-year-old Sophia's difficulty in teething and was trying, without much success, to teach Elizabeth to read. Elizabeth much preferred to listen to stories, including those about the widow Hathorne, "who had shut herself up after her husbands death & made it the habit of her life never to sit down at a table but always eat her meals above in the chamber she never left." But listening to stories was not the same as learning to read, and Mrs. Peabody in desperation sent a note to Mrs. Hathorne, asking if her eldest daughter, also named Elizabeth, might come to the Peabody house for an hour or two a day to be taught, and also to be "a companion to stimulate a dull little girl of her own by example." Elizabeth Hathorne did come to instruct and be instructed, but her example was lost on Elizabeth Peabody, whose "youthful admiration for the astonishing learning of Elizabeth reacted to discourage me who had no power of utterancy at all—at that time."[38]

Mary Peabody remembered playing with the Hathorne children, and Elizabeth was prompted by a glimpse of Julian Hawthorne at age three dancing across the backyard to recall a similar image of his father, "a boy of the same size, with the same head of clustering locks, and the same broad shoulders, do just the same thing, in the old yard at Herbert Street." But the connection was lost when the Peabodys moved away to the corner of Cambridge and Essex Streets, although they heard that Mrs. Hathorne had returned to her seclusion and that Elizabeth Hathorne had begun doing the same, "spending all her days lying on the bed and reading, and never getting up except in the night."[39]

In the early and mid-1830s, Elizabeth had been reading stories in Samuel Goodrich's *New England Magazine*, which, as she said, "arrested her attention." Notable among these was "The Gentle Boy." When she returned to Salem in 1836, after her resignation from Temple School, she was told that the author was, in fact, the son of the reclusive widow

Hathorne. This she refused to believe, thinking that the author was probably the brilliant Elizabeth Hathorne. Always on the lookout for new talent and fresh ideas, and more than a little bored in her hometown, Peabody made her way to the Hathorne house and inquired for Elizabeth. Elizabeth, she was told, "never saw visitors," but there was another sister, one she had not met or remembered, Louisa, "who was more like ordinary people." It was from Louisa that Elizabeth learned that Nathaniel, not their older sister Elizabeth, was the author of "The Gentle Boy" and other tales.

"'But if your brother can write like that,' said I, 'he has no right to be idle.' 'He never is idle,' she replied laughingly; 'but I will go and see Lizzie and tell her what you have said.' She soon returned laughing and said, 'Lizzie says if you will come some time in the evening she will see you.' But she did not appoint any particular evening, and a year passed." This odd story, with Elizabeth stumbling into a bizarre household where Louisa acted as intermediary for her silent and hidden relatives, is repeated both in her reminiscences for Julian Hawthorne and in her letter to Francis Lee.[40]

Still there was no connection with the real author, until in late 1837 Elizabeth Peabody received a copy of the recently published *Twice-Told Tales* inscribed "to Miss Elizabeth Peabody, with the respects of the Author." Elizabeth seized this opportunity to write to Elizabeth Hathorne, explaining that she wanted help from her brother in getting an article into the *United States Magazine and Democratic Review* and requesting that they all please come to the Peabody house that very evening, November 11.

Surprisingly, they did, just as Elizabeth was looking at a new version of the *Iliad* edited by Harvard's Cornelius Felton. Its Flaxman illustrations broke the ice, "and they all drew up their chairs to the table, and we were all at ease at once, as we looked over the whole five volumes, and talked of Homer and Hesiod, Aeschylus and Dante, with all of whom they were perfectly at home." As they studied the drawings and talked, Elizabeth observed Nathaniel Hawthorne (as he was now styling himself) and his sisters: "Louisa was quite like other people. Elizabeth with her black hair in beautiful natural curls, her bright rather shy eyes, and a rather excited frequent low laugh, looked full of wit and keenness. . . ." But it was for Nathaniel that she reserved her fullest description: he "first looked almost fierce with his determination to conquer his sensitive shyness, that he always felt was weakness . . . but as soon as he forgot himself in conversation, all this passed away, and the beauty of the outline of all his features, the pure complexion, the wonderful eyes, like mountain lakes seeming to reflect the heavens, made a wonderful impression on both Mary and me."

A few days later Hawthorne returned and this time had a chance to meet Sophia, who had refused to come downstairs during the first meeting.

> She came down in her simple white wrapper, and glided in at the back door and sat down on the sofa. As I said "My sister Sophia— Mr Hawthorne," he rose and looked at her—he did not realise how intently, and afterwards, as we went on talking, she would interpose frequently a remark in her low sweet voice. Every time she did so, he looked at her with the same intentness of interest. I was struck with it, and painfully. I thought, what if he should fall in love with her; and I had heard her so often say, nothing would ever tempt her to marry, and inflict upon a husband the care of such a sufferer.

"Painfully," because Hawthorne did not yet know the extent of Sophia's illness, but "painfully" too because of the attraction Elizabeth herself was feeling toward the shy, handsome author.

For his part, Hawthorne seemed a little dazed by the bright light of society that the Peabodys shone into the dim Hawthorne household. Nathaniel himself felt that his family's seclusion was unhealthy, producing "a morbid consciousness that paralyzes my powers," he is supposed to have said to Elizabeth. He was absolutely "cataleptic" at a dinner party at Caleb Foote's, she reported, until Elizabeth and Mary "each took a hand in ours, which he grasped like a drowning man a straw, and we drew him toward to the table, where we all sat down."[41]

Hawthorne's seclusion in Salem should not be exaggerated, his biographer Edwin Haviland Miller warns: Hawthorne was often given to bouts of overexaggeration and self-dramatization. Although he did spend considerable time in his attic room, he also spent much time with his lifelong friend Horatio Bridge, often rambling around the Salem countryside or taking trips to others regions of New England; he enjoyed playing whist with his sister Louisa, cousin Susan Ingersoll, Horace Conolly, and David Roberts; and he shared the company of Salem's middle-class Democrats, often rowdy and intoxicated, "all of whom," Miller suggests, "he no doubt met in Salem's disreputable taverns. . . . In such company he lost the shyness and tied tongue that consigned him to the role of silent observer in genteel gatherings."[42]

"Such company" was remarkably different from the companionship of genteel intellectual women into which Hawthorne was now thrown. He now frequently walked back and forth between Herbert Street and Charter Street, often in the company of his sisters and of Elizabeth and Mary Peabody. Elizabeth, with her customary assertiveness and knowledge of the literary world, took upon herself the management of Hawthorne's career. Horace Mann, she knew, was seeking authors for a series of books meant for the Massachusetts district school libraries, and Peabody wrote him in March 1838 recommending *Twice-Told Tales*. "There is a young man in this town—not so very young either—(he is between thirty & forty years old)—of whom you have heard—the author of the 'Twice told Tales.' He is I think a man of first rate genius—To my mind he surpasses *Irving* even—in the picturesque beauty of his style—& certainly in the purity—elevation—and justness of his conscience." Even though Hawthorne in fact had had a dismal time writing for the children's market, Elizabeth felt obliged to say that he wished to create "a new literature for the young—as he has a deep dislike to the character of the shoals of books poured out from the press." Mann, however, was not impressed. "I have read several of the 'Twice Told Tales.' They are written beautifully—'fine' is the true word. But we want something nearer home to duty and business. . . . Such a story as the 'Wedding Knell,' wherefore is it and to what does it tend? Miss [Catherine] Sedgwick has her eye fixed on the true point. Such stories as hers would make a fire to consume the Alexandrian Library of our book shops. But we want something graver and sterner even than those—a development of *duties* in all the relation of life."[43]

Even such an unmistakeable rebuke failed to slow Elizabeth in her efforts to promote Hawthorne's career. She reviewed *Twice-Told Tales* in the pages of the *New-Yorker*, noting the difficulty of writing fiction in a culture dominated by business and politics. Still, such artists do exist, although "we have heard that the author of these tales has lived the life of a recluse." Such withdrawal may be necessary, she thinks, for the development of his "Wordsworthian philosophy," which proposes that "ideal beauty may be seen clearest and felt most profoundly in the common incidents of actual life." Peabody also urged his sisters to encourage his writing.

> If, in the first ten years after leaving college, a man has followed his own fancies, without being driven by the iron whip of duty, and yet has not lost his moral or intellectual dignity, but rather consolidated them, there is good reason for believing that he is one of Nature's ordained priests, who is consecrated to her higher biddings. I see that you both think me rather enthusiastic; but I believe I say the truth when I say that I do not often overrate, and I feel sure that this brother of yours has been gifted and kept so choice in her secret places by Nature thus far, that he may do a great thing for his country.[44]

Hawthorne's visits to Charter Street allowed him to spend more time with Sophia, to whom he was undeniably attracted from the first, and she to him. But there was something attractive as well in Elizabeth, in her enthusiasm and rush of speech so different from his own melancholy and silence. When Elizabeth was in West Newton in spring 1838 helping Nat get settled there, she and Hawthorne engaged in a correspondence exchange, which has not survived. What we do know is that Hawthorne keenly awaited visits and letters from Elizabeth. When he came to dinner in May and found that Elizabeth was not there, he thought it "'too bad,' 'insufferable,' 'not fair' and wondered what could be the reason. . . . He looked very handsome and full of smiles." In June he came to visit Sophia, and she wrote Elizabeth that she had never seen him look "so brilliant and rayonnant. He said he had a letter nearly written to you, but should not finish till you wrote. He seemed quite impatient to hear from you, said he had not since you were here" last.

Hawthorne's gratitude for Elizabeth's standard-bearing, muted by an uneasy sense of obligation and entanglement, was not, could not be, the same as romantic attraction. He quickly discovered that it was Sophia's grey eyes rather than Elizabeth's blue stockings that captured his attention, as Norman Holmes Pearson observes. But, as students of Hawthorne know, there was yet another woman in Hawthorne's life in 1838, besides the Peabody sisters: Mary Crowninshield Silsbee.

Mary Silsbee was the daughter of Nathaniel Silsbee, former United

States Senator from Massachusetts, and of Mary Crowninshield, member of one of Salem's most distinguished families. A beautiful young woman to judge from her portrait, Mary was at home in the sophisticated ways of Salem's, Boston's, and Washington's cultured high societies. Into her elegant home on Washington Square East came witty and brilliant talkers to entertain the young hostess; into that company somehow Nathaniel Hawthorne, the shy, often tongue-tied, mysterious young Salem author, also stumbled.

The central evidence we have of the confusing, funny, and tragic involvement of Mary Silsbee and Hawthorne comes from Julian Hawthorne's biography of his parents. Long dismissed as a product of Julian's romantic imagination, the story was given new plausibility with the discovery of the manuscript journal of interviews and notes on which he based his biography. Included was the account given by his Aunt Elizabeth Peabody of the Hawthorne-Silsbee affair. This discovery does not quite transform the account into fact, however; Elizabeth was seventy-eight when she told Julian this story, and she was, after all, not an uninvolved bystander.[45]

The story, as Elizabeth told Julian, is this: attracted by Hawthorne's reputation as the author of *Twice-Told Tales*, Silsbee probably invited him to her house in early 1837. Actually, Elizabeth thought that it was the other main player in this affair, John Louis O'Sullivan, who invited Hawthorne to visit Silsbee at her request, but that possibility could not be since the two men did not meet until April 1837, after the initial encounter. Fascinated with the shy author and wanting to draw him out, Silsbee told him very personal details of her private life and invited him to share some of his. Hawthorne, shy to the point of "catalepsy," as Elizabeth said on another occasion, refused to be drawn out.

Seeking another way to find out more about this odd genius, Silsbee apparently made up a story about Hawthorne's new friend, John O'Sullivan, whom Silsbee had known in Washington. Claiming that he had attempted "to practice the basest treachery upon her," she appealed to Hawthorne to rescue her honor. Although he knew only slightly the man who would later have much to do with his career, Hawthorne challenged O'Sullivan to a duel. At this dark moment, Hawthorne reached out to his good friend Horatio Bridge, in a letter of February 8, 1838: "It is my purpose to set out for Washington, in the course of a fortnight or thereabouts—but only to make a short visit.

Would it be utterly impossible, or extremely unadvisable, for you to come to Boston or this place, within that interval?" Hawthorne was sometimes given to the overdramatic, but the end of the letter seems just right for a man facing death through his own foolishness: "I repeat that you cannot exercise the slightest favorable influence on my affairs—they being beyond your control, and hardly within my own."[46]

Fortunately for them both, O'Sullivan responded with a letter rather than a weapon. Refusing to accept the challenge, he explained the situation as he understood it and, in Julian's words, "claimed the renewal of Hawthorne's friendship." According to Elizabeth, the story had one final, and tragic, turn. Hawthorne's classmate Jonathan Cilley, now a Representative from Maine, was challenged to a duel by William Graves of Kentucky, over a complicated bit of sectional politics and offended honor. Cilley tried to shrug off the challenge, but Graves insisted; in Elizabeth's and Julian's account, Cilley rallied to the duel after being taunted that his friend Hawthorne had not hesitated to enter into a duel; why should he? On February 24 the two met in a Maryland field outside the District, and after two unsuccessful exchanges of rifle fire, Cilley was struck and killed.

Elizabeth Peabody's narration of this story is filled with the kind of high-minded language we expect from her, drawn equally from her strong Unitarian sense that morality was the highest religion and from her concealed sense that she herself had not always behaved decorously or conventionally. Her language is replete with harsh moral judgment: Mary Silsbee was afflicted with a "sort of moral insanity . . . she was a coarse-minded woman. She liked to create difficulties and intrigues." Part of Elizabeth's strategy here may have been to distinguish the rivals; Mary Silsbee the scheming socialite, and Sophia Peabody the invalided saint.

Still, Elizabeth's rhetorical excesses aside, and her charges seem essentially just: Hawthorne did challenge O'Sullivan to a duel, prompted by Mary Silsbee's casual (and casually vicious) plotting. Someone might have died. At least one other source, Ann Gillam Storrow, also commented on Silsbee's character. In a letter to Jared Sparks, who would, ironically, marry Silsbee in 1839, Storrow wrote: "Her thirst for display and admiration is so utterly insatiable that it leads her I verily believe to sacrifice for the sake of it much that is lovely and beautiful in a woman's character—properties which you my susceptible friend, love and admire as much as anybody when you have the clear possession of your faculties," that is, when you are not head over heels in love with the stunning Miss Silsbee.[47]

Even though she may not have known all the details of this intrigue in the spring of 1838, Elizabeth did sense that Mary Silsbee was up to something, if only to judge from Hawthorne's gathering gloom. "I came to suspect that M.C.S. was coquetting—I interpreted their hieroglyphics—by means of that—in some measure," she wrote Hawthorne's sister Elizabeth in September. To give Hawthorne something else to think about, she encouraged him to study German. But his heart was not in it; as he wrote to his friend Henry Wadsworth Longfellow at the end of March, "I am somewhat doubtful of the stability of my resolution to pursue the study." Sophia thought the same, writing Elizabeth in April that Hawthorne did not want to come to study German now that Elizabeth was away in West Newton. By the end of July, she said it even more strongly: Hawthorne "could not take the trouble" to study the language, even though his sister Elizabeth "went on famously."[48]

We can imagine Hawthorne, in late winter and early spring 1838, in torment over the sudden abundance of eligible women in his life. After O'Sullivan had cleared up the matter of his imagined insult to Mary Silsbee, Hawthorne went back to the Silsbee mansion and managed to end his relation with her. Julian says, quoting his aunt Elizabeth, that his father "crushed her," but that outcome seems unlikely, since Mary "managed to renew relations with him, and told him (with no encouragement on his part) that she would marry him when he had an income of $3000." Silsbee's effort to frame their relationship as a financial one must have broken her spell over the author. Hawthorne responded, we are told, that "he never expected to have so much," and we can imagine the dawning amusement with which he said those words, or something like them.[49]

Having disposed of Mary Silsbee, Hawthorne was likely in a clearer frame of mind to deal with his feelings about the eldest Peabody sister. Elizabeth would be an intellectual peer, or perhaps rival, but not a romantic partner. That much is clear in his correspondence with O'Sullivan, vigorous and confidential now that the duel business was put behind them. On April 19, 1838, Hawthorne wrote the editor, asking whether he were willing to look over an essay Peabody had written, "On the Claims of the Beautiful Arts." "She is somewhat too much of a theorist, but really possesses knowledge, feeling, eloquence and imagination." She had not done justice to Emerson's *Nature*, but this essay was stronger. Then, in May, as if to seal the end of any possible attraction to Elizabeth, Hawthorne wrote O'Sullivan in amusement and some exasperation about Elizabeth, a tone that would mark many of his letters to and about his future sister-in-law. Apparently Elizabeth had sent a second essay to O'Sullivan, which she was now demanding back. She was irked, he reported, that Hawthorne had intervened on her behalf with the editor, although this was exactly the effort she had wanted him to make, and she was now refusing to accept any pay for the essay on the "Beautiful Arts," "the article having been in a manner forced upon you. But I told her that I should do no such thing, nor that you would consent to such an arrangement. Nevertheless, it will make you easier to know that she is not in immediate want of the money. She is a good old soul, and would give away her only petticoat, I do believe, to anybody that she thought needed it more than herself."[50] A most distancing comment that, since Hawthorne and Peabody were the same age.

On her side, Elizabeth found Hawthorne Byronic, mysterious, romantic, and inevitably, a cause. She may even, as Norman Holmes Pearson thinks, have seen Hawthorne as hers by "right of discovery."[51] But it seems unlikely that Elizabeth could have moved from fascination and hero worship to romantic love and attachment. As with Channing and Mann, so with Hawthorne: Peabody transformed an erotic, emotional connection into an intellectual one, perhaps arising from a deep sense rooted in her family experience that men disappoint, or perhaps springing from a realization that lasting emotional attachments bring unwelcome limitations to career, particularly in that era. She found herself, perhaps not wholly willingly, making Hawthorne into an idol. Certainly she would have found herself unable to respond to any of Hawthorne's own psychic and emotional needs, perhaps because her own deeper needs were so rarely satisfied that she did not fully know how to respond on that level.

In any event, Elizabeth was deeply attracted to Hawthorne, perhaps even briefly in love with him. She was not, as Caroline Dall later claimed, ever secretly engaged to him. In 1894 Dall wrote to Thomas Niles that "Sophia never knew of her sister's engagement to N.H., but Hawthorne lived in terror lest E.P.P. should tell her. Many an hour of bitter weeping has she passed in my house because of his insulting

letters about it—after he was married." There is no evidence to substantiate this claim. Much later in her life, Elizabeth acknowledged that
rumors about her and Hawthorne circulated in Salem in early 1838, but
she recalled being convinced "from the first week of our acquaintance
with Hawthorne, that *he* was so much in love with Sophia—at first
sight—that he would probably never marry any *other* woman."

This statement has the unmistakeable ring of rationalization about it.
Undoubtedly, Elizabeth hoped in late 1837 and early 1838 that she
would be his choice. A little later in this same letter, she breaks out of
her Panglossian spell and speaks the truth: "Had Hawthorne wanted to
marry me he would probably not have found much difficulty in getting
my consent;—but it is very clear to me now, that I was not the person to
make *him* happy or to be made happy *by* him, and Sophia *was*."[52]

With the passage of years, Peabody found a way to interpret her
relationships with Mann and Hawthorne, husbands to her sisters, as
intimate friendships. To some readers Elizabeth's relationships with her
sisters' husbands demonstrate her worst traits of aggressiveness and
interference, combined with a fuzzy idealism that made it impossible to
see human relations clearly. But these views of her ignore both the
larger issues in her personality and the many situations in which she was
remarkably sharp and clear-thinking. In her assessment of her connection with her brothers-in-law, Peabody was close to the target in thinking of them as both intimates and friends. For contemporary readers
(though not for Peabody) "intimates" hints at the erotic charge that
pulsed through her early contacts with these men, and yet the word also
suggests the containment of those feelings within the sturdy walls of
friendship. She would have required an extraordinary man for a romantic partner: someone who could break through her wall of talk and
intellectualism, through the emotional reserve that lay behind the emotional excess; someone who somehow could guarantee her intellectual
life and career in an age that demanded their surrender at marriage.
Elizabeth understood the difficulty of finding such a partner: "It is
because I believe marriage is a sacrament, and nothing *less*, that I am
dying as an old Maid," she wrote in 1886. "I have had too much respect
for marriage to make a conventional one in my own case."[53]

Despite Hawthorne's growing preference for Sophia, Elizabeth Peabody continued to work on behalf of Hawthorne's career, with more

enthusiasm, it must be said, than he was working for hers. In October 1838 she wrote to Orestes Brownson, congratulating him on his appointment as overseer of the United States Marine Hospital in Chelsea, outside Boston. This patronage post had come his way when George Bancroft became Collector of the Port of Boston, a position given Bancroft, a Democrat, by the new Democratic President, Martin Van Buren. Peabody asked Brownson about the possibilities of a patronage post for Hawthorne, who needed a position "requiring very little time & work—& having abundant leisure & liberty" or else he might leave New England. Brownson wrote back saying that sinecures were always available but that he had supposed Hawthorne would not stoop to take one.

In early November, Peabody renewed her campaign, this time having an interview with Bancroft himself. It was an awkward conversation; she found it difficult to explain that Hawthorne really was fitted for "an ordinary part in life," even though she also thought of him as a rare genius "capable of extraordinary things." She appealed to her old friend Elizabeth Bliss, who had just married Bancroft, to intercede on Hawthorne's behalf. All this behind-the-scenes maneuvering worked. In January 1839, Hawthorne was offered the post of measurer of salt and coal at the Boston Custom House, and he accepted it in a letter to Bancroft dated 11 January.[54]

⟡ IT WAS NOT JUST Nathaniel's, but also Sophia's career that revealed Elizabeth Peabody's shaping influence. Sophia's first instruction in drawing came in 1824, not as a student but as the teacher of a little class of children in a school taught by a Miss Davis, which Sophia undertook in order to learn to draw. She offered ten lessons, but the "exertion was too much for her, and she was thrown into a sickness, from which she never rose into the possibility of so much excitation again; and by a slight accident was disabled in the hand and could not draw."

Six years later, Sophia finally had her own teacher in the German émigré artist Francis Graeter. Graeter would later be employed at Temple School, but in 1830 he taught drawing in Elizabeth's and Mary's school on Colonnade Row in Boston. Sophia would come downstairs into the classroom on drawing days. "Mr. Graeter occasionally went and looked over her shoulder. At last she looked up and said, 'Have

you no word of criticism for me?' He replied, 'I can only envy you.'"
Graeter was succeeded by Thomas Doughty, who kept a painting
school in Boston with the unorthodox method of having students come
and watch him paint, "but he never explained or answered a question."

It occurred to Elizabeth that Doughty might be induced to paint in
Sophia's presence, who was too weak to attend these pseudolessons.
Doughty was willing and painted in Sophia's room; after he left, she
would copy his canvases. Eventually "her copy of his landscape was
even better than his, so that when they were displayed side by side,
everybody guessed her copy was the original Doughty." Sophia also
took lessons from Chester Harding, who painted Sophia's portrait in
1830, and Elizabeth's, now apparently lost, in the late 1820s. Harding's
portrait of Elizabeth occasioned some family tension in 1828. Mrs.
Peabody loved it for the maternal sentiments it aroused toward her
firstborn, "the pride and joy of my heart; for amid all the faults of her
childhood & her youth has been blended so much moral courage, so
much intellectual wealth, such pure & elevated views, that I felt sure the
good would triumph." However, Elizabeth's grandmother disapproved
of the portrait and went about "screaming, Elizabeth! why Elizabeth!"
Little Wellington tried to intervene and make peace in the disrupted
household, pleading with his mother not to cry: "'Mother, don't,
Mother. I will tell you something. Don't you know Mr. Harding's children go to school to Lizzy, she did not spend any money about it.' The
dear Child, thinking my tears flowed, at the idea of Elizabeth's spending
her money to get the picture."[55]

As Sophia's gift of copying became more pronounced, Elizabeth began actively to encourage her sister and promote her work. Sophia was
involved in recopying copies of classical sculpture for Elizabeth's *Key to
History* volume on the Greeks, as well as working on several other
projects Elizabeth had concocted: book covers, illlustrations on cards
for sale at fairs, and copies of artworks. Some of her sister's work Elizabeth liked, others she did not: "Your head of St. George is sublime—the
face is just what it should be—the idea of Una is also perfect . . . the
only defect is the proportion &c of the horse—you should not attempt
such parts without models."[56] By the mid 1830s, Sophia was copying
large-scale oils by Salvator Rosa and Washington Allston, and even
attempting her own original work, most notably *Flight into Egypt*, now
hanging in the House of the Seven Gables. She entered copies in local

fairs and artshows, completed a portrait medallion of Emerson's brother Charles, and executed a sweet, albeit clumsy, illustration for Hawthorne's story "The Gentle Boy."

Sophia's budding career as a copyist took shape in the midst of a good deal of interest, in the circles of educated people in Boston, Cambridge, and Concord, in art and artists. Living at the time of the Greek Revival, these middle-class folk shared with the social elites an appreciation of classical and neoclassical art. They admired Greek and Roman statuary, which most New Englanders knew in plaster-cast reproductions at the Boston Athenaeum. They pored over Flaxman's illustrations of Homer and Dante, and loved the work of Raphael and Michelangelo, which again all but a handful knew only in copies. They admired the sculpture of Hiram Powers and even liked the wild romanticism of Salvator Rosa. After Hawthorne and Sophia Peabody married and moved into the Old Manse, Sophia demonstrated current aesthetic taste by replacing "the grim prints of Puritan ministers" and redecorating the rooms according to neoclassical taste.

The contemporary artist who attracted most attention from the Transcendentalists was Washington Allston. Elizabeth had first encountered Allston in 1822, during an early visit to Cambridge and Boston. Like William Ellery Channing, his brother-in-law, Allston did not impress the eighteen-year-old Elizabeth with any conventional good looks, "but his features plain as they are, are harmonized so exquisitely, and there is a softness in his sallow complexion and a refined enthusiasm sitting on his forehead and beaming from his mild eye and a gentle dignity in his manners that wins the heart while it throws one at a distance." A few years later, Sophia echoed the same theme, that Allston's manner and appearance were transparent of his artistic genius and intense spirituality: "That fortunate chicken, Elizabeth, went to Dr. Channing's as usual a few evenings ago and whom should she meet there but Washington Allston. You know he is quite unparalleled in the fascination and polish of his conversation as well as in perfection of manners, and music of voice."[57]

Nathalia Wright notes that Allston was the first American painter to go beyond the portraiture and historical scenes of the Revolutionary era and to project the drama of his inner life onto the canvas. In his poems, gothic romances, theoretical essays, and paintings, Allston applied a single standard of judgment, says Wright; "the great works are representations of the artist's own inner experiences rather than of natural forms." A hundred years later, the Russian artist Wassily Kandinsky offered a similar perspective on his then-revolutionary art. "A picture is not necessarily 'well painted' if it possesses the 'values' of which the French so constantly speak. It is only well painted if its spiritual value is completed and satisfying . . . [the artist must] create a spiritual atmosphere which is either pure or infected. . . . *That is beautiful which is produced by internal necessity, which springs from the soul.*"[58]

This perspective is nearly identical with Emerson's view of the artist. Emerson believed that art springs from an original intuition in the artist. The artist's ability to create comes from that inner gift, rather than primarily from skill or training. Emerson was relatively indifferent to the completed artwork, preferring to focus on the creative process that preceded it. In 1838 Emerson wrote in his journal, "why should we covetously build a Saint Peter's, if we had the seeing Eye which beheld all the radiance of beauty and majesty in the matted grass and the overarching boughs? Why should a man spend years upon the carving of an Apollo, who looked Apollos into the landscape with every glance he threw?"[59]

This perception is very close to the grounds on which Peabody understood and praised Allston. In her 1836 essay, "Allston the Painter," she stresses the religious intensity and purity of his character as qualities central to his artistic gift. He possesses a "holy life, flowing from a deep sensibility to religion . . . and from a severe and uncompromising self-restraint as to every questionable indulgence." Despite poverty and ill-health, Allston's works "come forth more soft, delicate, gentle, and tender than in his youth." Peabody had little to say about Allston's works themselves, except to ask the public's patience while the artist completed his huge painting of "Belshazzar's Feast."[60]

Peabody's approach to Allston's art echoes the artist's own view that the mind and the soul of the artists are paramount, the actual work only secondary. Allston had already known of Sophia Peabody's work, offering her pieces of his own to copy, and now the eldest sister's praise brought him more squarely within the Peabodys' circle. Elizabeth and Bronson Alcott visited Allston, who was living in Cambridgeport, in May 1836, a rather surprising pair of guests given their angry exhanges and charges just a month previous. But no hint of that blowup is given either in Alcott's version or in Elizabeth's account of the visit.

Alcott noted that Allston thanked Elizabeth for her essay on his life and work, which he had just read. Writing to Sophia, Elizabeth naturally elaborated on the encounter. She was nervous about seeing him now that the article had come out, "lest he should be in some way wounded—or pained about it—he is so shrinking—he took my hand—& giving it a very kind grasp—he said in the most expressive voice—I am very much obliged to you." Elizabeth was flustered by his response, leaving behind her hat, and overwhelmed by his praise, lying awake that entire night out of "pure ecstasy." She did remember to tell Sophia that Allston also inquired after her and was pleased that she was selling her pictures.[61]

In 1839 Peabody took advantage of her connection to Allston by writing a series of articles for the Salem *Gazette* and Boston *Evening Transcript* on an exhibition of the artist's work. This show, running from April to July 1839, was the first retrospective of a living American artist ever held in the United States, attracting thousands of viewers and scores of reviews and assessments. Held at Chester Harding's Gallery on School Street in Boston, the retrospective was an enactment, as Elizabeth Garrity Ellis says, of Unitarian aesthetic theory and moral philosophy. The paintings revealed and enhanced Unitarian beliefs in the power of individual artistic genius tempered by a sense of social responsibility revealed in the mostly Biblical subjects. This combination of expression and restraint took on new meaning in a time marked by economic depression and rapid social change. In this setting, among these genteel patrons, Allston's art was inflected with new cultural meanings.[62]

Peabody's reviews of the show, collected in June into a pamphlet called *Remarks on Allston's Paintings*, reveal her indebtedness to this Unitarian view of art and culture. In seeing all these paintings, she writes, "you feel anew how great a thing one human mind is. You see how it may be a mirror of the whole race, of nature, and of something above nature. The appreciation of the supernatural, the sensibility to all that is sublime and all that is beautiful in external nature, the sympathy with all passions . . . all is manifested before your eyes, at once." Allston is able to paint the solidity of his subjects, "the depth of the flesh," but always transcends the material in quest of a deeper, higher truth.

It is in the depictions of women, and particularly of Dante's Beatrice, that Peabody sees Allston's spiritualizing aesthetic most clearly at work.

This was a familiar painting for her, having seen it in 1826 when Allston exhibited at the Boston Athenaeum. "I used to go and sit before it day after day, and it unlocked streams of thought and feeling, which, as unuttered presentiment, had burdened me before." Disturbed by the painting's revelations, Peabody nonetheless returned to it often, "impelled by an irresistible attraction." This work revealed "celestial wisdom embodied in nature's masterpiece," she writes. The inner vision of the artist, expressing the "intuitive intelligence" of his subject, is no mere subjective effusion but reveals "celestial wisdom," the existence of a moral universe. Exactly in these years, when Peabody was being challenged by the example of Jones Very and by her own strong feelings toward Nathaniel Hawthorne, Allston's art spoke of the possibility of a reconciliation of emotion and restraint, subjective vision and social responsibility. But such a reconciliation, of the kind offered in most of Allston's works, existed only in a safely spiritualized and harmonious aesthetic world, not in the ambiguous relations of real-life men and women.[63]

Washington Allston benefited greatly from this exhibition. He earned almost $2,000, and his reputation rebounded after the nearly universal critical praise. Elizabeth Peabody's contribution to the burnishing of his reputation, her essay in the *American Monthly Magazine* and her *Remarks on Allston's Paintings*, earned her Allston's respect and admiration, but little else. With teaching apparently closed to her as an occupation and with writing an insubstantial and unpredictable source of income, Peabody found herself, at the end of the 1830s, surrounded by colleagues, new ideas and publications, and new projects of her own, but desperately short of funds. She had been living at home in Salem, supported in part by Dr. Peabody's fees as dentist and doctor and by Mary's income as schoolteacher. Financial obligation must have only heightened Elizabeth Peabody's desire to find an independent career path.

Trained by her mother in the importance of history, Peabody had long understood the need for collecting and preserving important documents. She admired the work of Jared Sparks, editor of Washington's letters, when she and Mary shared Mrs. Clarke's rooming house with him in the early 1830s. Elizabeth's interest was not merely antiquarian, though; she sensed the need to preserve the manuscripts of contemporary writers and thinkers, particularly those associated with Emerson. She wrote to him in 1838 asking whether he would "leave me *in your will*—all your sermons—to keep for two years giving me leave to make extracts according to my judgement & *print them.*" In this same letter, she reminds Emerson that Jones Very's manuscript essay on Shakespeare belongs to her "and is to come to me when you are done with it." This message is repeated in a line written in the left margin of the second manuscript sheet, reinforcing the point: "It is to say that that manuscript of Very's *belongs to me.*"[64]

This desire to preserve the written record of the movements and ideas of her times fused with Peabody's need to move on, to find another outlet for her energies and talents. The result would be the most successful economic venture of her life, the bookshop and lending library on West Street in Boston.

6

"A Transcendental Exchange"

⌘

EXACTLY HOW Elizabeth Peabody got the idea of opening a bookstore is something of a mystery, although bookstores and lending libraries were sprouting up everywhere in the Northeast in the early decades of the nineteenth century. In Boston, literary culture was relatively far advanced, and in the countryside, literacy and its elements—books, newspapers, periodicals, libraries, itinerant peddlers—were transforming rural life.[1] Wherever the idea came from, Elizabeth was willing to embrace it if only to get out of the backwater of Salem, "another world from Boston," as she put it to her friend Elizabeth Bliss. Her sisters were engaged to be married to men for whom Elizabeth had intense and complicated feelings; perhaps some distance would help clarify those relationships. Her brothers George and Wellington were dead, and Nat was stuck in unhappy, low-paying jobs, bitter at his sisters' abilities to move easily in intellectual circles while he failed at everything he tried. His hostility is hot to the touch in this comment to Elizabeth in 1850:

> I have very little sympathy with those who admire and worship
> brilliant men, and the enthusiasm which many persons feel for art,
> and the almost man-worship they practice rather disgusts me than
> otherwise; and this not because I cannot understand and appreci-
> ate as well as they whatever is beautiful or godlike in art or nature,
> but because they apply the term divine (and other attributes dread-

fully misapplied) to individuals who are remarkable only for saying brilliant things, uttering striking thoughts or broaching profound views, but who are detestable in respect to personal character— and it seems to me that the aesthetic portion of our community indirectly support vice, by the countenance they give to individuals who ought to rank with stable boys in spite of all their genius.[2]

Nat did not name these "brilliant men" and "divine individuals." Did he mean Emerson or Alcott, Very or Fuller? In any event, his rancor towards Elizabeth's circle was growing all through the late 1830s and the 1840s until it burst out in that remarkable letter. Perhaps some distance from Nat and his family might be wise. Of course, distance is a relative term: the Peabody parents lived at West Street throughout the 1840s, as did Sophia and Mary until their weddings. Nat, probably hating every minute of it, worked at the bookshop on and off throughout the decade, selling homeopathic medicines to his sister's earnest and intellectual customers.

By this time, Peabody had come to realize that for her, "family" would mean her family of origin, not a new family formed through marriage. Bonds composed equally of injury, competition, misunderstanding, and affection tied her to her sisters, while links of duty bound her to her parents. Still, as a single woman from a genteel but unprosperous family, she was responsible for her own survival and success. Peabody had extended her concentric circles of work outward from her first schools in Lancaster, Boston, and Maine, to her private schools in Brookline and back in Boston, to the controversial Temple School. All these efforts required the patronage of wealthy parents willing to hire a bright young woman with advanced ideas about education, morality, and the intellectual potential of females. That patronage came to an abrupt halt with the collapse of Temple. Shaken by this revelation of the fragile base on which her own career was built, and shaken likewise by the thin commitment of Boston Unitarians to progressive education, Peabody returned to Salem and found herself drawn into an alternative community of reformers with radical ideas.

Throughout the 1840s, Peabody continued to identify herself as an educator, but her field of operation shifted from classroom and children to other institutions of society and toward adult learners. Her bookshop, her publishing business and single-issue magazine *Aesthetic Pa-*

pers, her involvement with Hungarian linguist Charles Kraitsir and with Polish educator Josef Bem, all suggest a steady widening of her circle of involvement in education. Pressing beyond the small circle of familiar faces to a larger, anonymous public, Peabody addressed her educational and reformist concerns to that audience by means of the commercial, market-oriented aspects of society—buying, selling, merchandising, dealing with strangers in anonymous relationships made possible through specific and limited interests.

↪ THEN AS NOW, West Street is a one-block lane between Tremont Street and Washington Street in Boston. Tremont bordered Boston Common, across which one could glimpse Bulfinch's State House at the top of Park Street. At the corner of Park and Beacon, in the shadow of the State House, was George Ticknor's house, and up Beacon, the new site of the Boston Athenaeum after 1849. Behind the State House were the mansions and row houses of Beacon Hill. All this represented the alliance of money and learning, whose representatives had smiled indulgently on young Elizabeth in the early 1820s as she made her way among high society along these streets.

Washington Street was Boston's "publishers' row" in the nineteenth century, whose entrepreneurs were often "new men" who had come to the city from the countryside, determined to make a fortune in the market's maelstrom. Clustered along the street and up and down Cornhill, just north of School Street, were the offices and bookstores of Boston's book trade, each with its particular specialty. Gould and Lincoln concentrated on works for a growing evangelical population; Crosby and Nichols served Unitarians, while Crocker and Brewster published and sold for the Trinitarians. Lee and Shepard published children's stories and works from social reformers. The American Tract Society, the New England Sunday School Union, James Munroe, Phillips, Sampson and Company—all and dozens more lined these streets. Perhaps most famous by midcentury was William D. Ticknor and Company, half of what later became Ticknor and Fields, which dominated the belles lettres field from its perch at the Old Corner Bookstore. Like Ticknor, most of these publishers also had bookshops on their premises, where patrons could look over their wares.[3]

Poised between the worlds of Beacon Hill and Washington Street, Peabody shrewdly perceived an opening for herself. Transcendentalism had generated a sizable body of printed literature and was itself stimulated by ideas gleaned from English and European publications. But where would one find these foreign books and journals? Some were brought back by American travelers and passed around from hand to hand. Bronson Alcott had brought back a copy of the Vienna *Jahrbuch* from his 1842 trip to England, which he had left at Munroe's. Emerson wrote Peabody to ask whether her father could pick up the *Jahrbuch* and bring it with him on his next trip to Concord, and also could she meanwhile pick up journals waiting for Emerson at Munroe's? Sometimes American readers simply subscribed to foreign publications themselves, rather than relying on the kindness of others; Emerson subscribed to all the major British quarterlies and regularly received shipments of foreign-language books. Not all readers were so fortunate, and alternatives were scarce. The Boston Athenaeum was closed to the ideas and the publications of "The Newness"; and the Boston Public Library would not open its doors until the early 1850s.[4]

Into this gap Elizabeth Peabody moved. In July 1840, in a two-story house at number 13 West Street, Peabody set up shop, with a bookstore and lending library in the first-floor parlor and rooms upstairs for her family, who moved to Boston with her. It was, as Sarah Peter recalled, an "atom of a shop," into which Elizabeth packed domestic and foreign books that she either sold or loaned for a small fee, her father's homeopathic medicines, and art supplies. Peabody described her venture this way: "About 1840 I came to Boston and opened the business of importing and publishing foreign books, a thing not then attempted by any one. I had also a foreign library of new French and German books." This library of over 1,100 items "stood on shelves in brown-paper covers," Edward Everett Hale remembered. "Here any one could subscribe a small annual fee," he went on, "and carry home the last German or French review. 'The "Revue des Deux Mondes" is a liberal education,' said one of the bright girls who first saw it there."[5]

In the early 1840s, the bookshop and library became an intellectual nucleus, attracting the leading reformers and writers in the Boston area. James Freeman Clarke was delighted to find publications other than the usual English quarterlies; Thomas Wentworth Higginson found the French eclectic philosophers, the text and music to Schubert's "Geschichte der Seele," "and many of the German balladists who were beginning to enthrall me." West Street became a kind of "Transcendental Exchange," wrote George Bradford. "Many persons of high culture, or of distinction in the sphere of religious philosophy, philanthropy, or literature, were often here, and likely to meet others, like themselves, interested in the questions then agitating the community, or to talk on the calmer topics of literature and philosophy." The shop even became a kind of mail drop, where Emerson and Fuller would leave letters and parcels for one another. Presiding over this intellectual buzz and hum was Peabody herself, "the learned and active-minded proprietor," in Bradford's words. Higginson remembered her as "desultory, dreamy, but insatiable in her love for knowledge and for helping others to it," while Clarke thought of her in those days as "always engaged in supplying some want that had first to be created."[6]

Peabody had high hopes for the bookstore, hopes which in the first years were being fulfilled. In September 1841 she wrote Samuel Gray Ward, a wealthy Boston banker and intimate friend of Margaret Fuller, for advice on whether she should take a partner in order to increase the shop's stock of books and journals. She agreed with the sentiments of the man who proposed this move: "He said it was so desirable to have this foreign bookstore—where people could obtain some information—& so desirable to have the matter so much in my own hands as for me to be able to have only that in my shop which I *chose*—& could in a measure recommend.—This was the original plan of my store—that I should keep one in which were to be found *no worthless* books—shadows of shadows—and nothing of any kind of a secondary quality." There is no record of Ward's response, nor evidence that Peabody took a partner, but the letter does suggest that she felt confident enough in the shop's success to imagine stocking and selling only items she approved of, rather than those she thought would sell.[7]

↬ THE WEST STREET bookshop quickly became part of that Transcendentalist social network about which Anne Rose has written so well. At West Street, people, ideas, and texts moved and merged. But the shop was devoted not simply to buying and renting books; it served another purpose, as home to several important conversations. Margaret Fuller held her first Conversations there. George and Sophia Ripley conversed there with others interested in forming a utopian community along Transcendentalist lines. Although occasioning more argument than conversation, several numbers of the financially hard-pressed Transcendentalist quarterly the *Dial* were published there.[8]

Although records are scarce, it appears that Peabody leased the West Street house in late 1839, for it was there, on November 6, that Fuller held her first Conversation. Earlier that fall, Fuller had written to Sophia Ripley on the possibility of gathering a group of women for a form of adult education:

> The advantages of a weekly meeting, for conversation, might be great enough to repay the trouble of attendance, if they consisted only in supplying a point of union to well-educated and thinking women, in a city which, with great pretensions to mental refinement, boasts, at present, nothing of the kind. . . . I do not wish, at present, to pledge myself to any course of subjects. Generally, I may say, they will be such as literature and the arts present in endless profusion. Should a class be brought together, I should wish, first, to ascertain our common ground, and, in the course of a few meetings, should see whether it be practicable to follow out the design in my mind, which, as yet, would look too grand on paper.

There were, it turned out, twenty-five women willing to commit to thirteen weeks of Conversation, meeting once a week from noon to two. Elizabeth Peabody's journal of these Conversations, now mostly lost, forms the basis for Emerson's account of them in *Memoirs of Margaret Fuller Ossoli*. In the first Conversation, Peabody reported, Fuller observed that men have the advantage of being able to put their education into action, whereas women's education seems only for display. To remedy this, Fuller proposed a series of Conversations on Greek mythology, in which ideas and instincts could be discussed without reference to the political and religious controversies of the present day. Peabody ended her report by observing that "Miss Fuller's thoughts were much illustrated, and all was said with the most captivating address and grace, and with beautiful modesty. The position in which she placed herself with respect to the rest, was entirely ladylike, and companionable. She told what she intended, the earnest purpose with which she came, and, with great tact, indicated the indiscretions that might spoil the meeting." This was, we recall, the same Margaret Fuller who mocked Elizabeth and her brother Nat and who ridiculed Elizabeth's devotion to Channing. Perhaps Peabody either had forgotten those digs or had suppressed them in light of the free publicity that Fuller's Conversations were bringing to the bookshop. It must have given Elizabeth pause, since she too had conducted conversations with adults and was equally knowledgeable about classical history and mythology. But she was not usually a fierce fighter or a keeper of grudges, and she preferred to think generously about most people, even her competitors.

In any event, the series went well, both from Fuller's perspective and from that of her auditors. One woman wrote that "I know not where to look for so much character, culture, and so much love of truth and beauty, in any other circle of women and girls." Not everyone liked the Conversations, to be sure, or participated very conscientiously: Elizabeth Hoar went mostly to see her friends and complained that one session she attended was "too much like a performance," on Fuller's part no doubt; Caroline Sturgis "quietly disposed herself to sleep on the arm of the sofa" at the same meeting.[9]

Others were vigorous participants, including Elizabeth Peabody. Besides keeping a journal of the proceedings, Peabody often entered the discussion. In the fifth Conversation, an explication of the myth of Psyche and Cupid, Fuller argued that this narrative and the Biblical account of the tree of the knowledge of good and evil made the same point, "that analysis instead of faith makes the origin of evil." True to her Unitarian beliefs that education itself was the key to the kingdom, Peabody proposed that "faith itself might lead to knowledge—and that it was only a premature analysis that originated evil—that the time would come when the God himself would reveal himself." Still, she admitted, "I did not make my meaning clear," while Fuller drove home her point, that the soul "was at first the victim of temptation by means of its own credulous simplicity & at length it was purified by the sufferings that its own errors involved."

Margaret Fuller's paradoxical view, a restatement of the ancient doctrine of the fortunate fall, sat well neither with Peabody's liberal anthropology nor with the more conservative views of other members. Was there no evil? she was asked, "for if evil was but the condition of a necessary & desirable development—it was a good—She replied that evil was *temporary*—but it was *real* while it lasted," an echo both of St.

Augustine's view and of Emerson's more recent restatement in 1838 before Harvard Divinity School's graduating class that "good is positive. Evil is merely privative, not absolute."

Several sessions were given over to definitions of beauty. Participants had been asked to write out their definitions, and at the seventh session, Elizabeth read hers:

> Beauty is the *Spirit of Proportion*. We could never see it at all if we had it not within us an element of our being—but having it a fair proportion waked it in our consciousness. Symmetry is however the lowest form of beauty—When the proportion is covered over & adorned as it were with grace, we are sensible of a more exquisite pleasure—we draw nearer the living spirit. Thus the more latent the beauty is, & the farther it is from its material envelope— the more does the perception of it delight us & the more at home do we feel in it.—Sublimity is not so much as a perception of beauty. . . . It is only an approach to the perception. It is naturally connected with material magnitude when our senses cannot command the materials of the proportion—And when we speak of the moral sublime we are in the same position—one term of the proportion lies out of sight. It is through a kind of faith that we are susceptible of the sublime. But we always feel that what is *sublime* to us, is *beautiful* to a higher being & we look forward to the sublime's being swallowed up in the beautiful— as we speak of faith being swallowed up in fruition—In saying Beauty is the Spirit of Proportion I avoid a petrified idea of beauty—Beauty lives—It forever makes proportion—To every new glance of the eye & the mind there is a new, fresh, immortal Beauty.[10]

Here Peabody reflects the newer Romantic philosophy. Beauty is not imitation of conventional forms. Instead, it arises from an inner quality of proportion that is only partially visible but available to the self's intuitions. There is no record of Fuller's response to this view. Perhaps she found this an adequate, even inspired, restatement of Emerson's view of the matter. "Beauty in nature is not ultimate," Emerson wrote in *Nature*. "It is the herald of inward and eternal beauty, and is not alone a solid and satisfactory good. It must stand as a part, and not as yet the last or highest expression of the final cause of Nature."

In the last sessions of this first series, Fuller read aloud the remaining definitions of beauty. "She remarked that she was delighted with the elevation of thought in all. All spoke of men & women as equally souls. None seemed to regard men as animals & women as plants." The group was amused by this definition, but Fuller pressed her point, that women are all too often, even in intellectually advanced societies, regarded as ornamental. "These false views haunted society with regard to women," Peabody recorded, doubtless with approval, "or else mother & father would not wish to [replace?]or annihilate faculties—as a means of making their daughters happier—a thing we constantly saw—We constantly heard that it was not well to cultivate this or that faculty—because in the boy's case it would not contribute especially & certainly to his worldly success—& in the girl's case because it might make her discontented as a woman."

A second series of Conversations followed in the spring of 1840, this one on the fine arts. Here, although records are scanty, Fuller seemed to be at the top of her form. Beautifully dressed, she would begin each session with some extended remarks of her own and then invite others to comment. "A very competent witness," probably Peabody, observed that "it was not easy for every one to venture her remark, after an eloquent discourse, and in the presence of twenty superior women, who were all inspired. But whatever was said, Margaret knew how to seize the good meaning of it with hospitality, and to make the speaker feel glad, and not sorry, that she had spoken." Emerson added that Fuller seemed to reach her pinnacle of creativity in conversation, where she was "quick, conscious of power, in perfect tune with her company." She would "pause and turn the stream with grace and adroitness, and with so much spirit, that her face beamed, and the young people came away delighted, among other things, with 'her beautiful looks.'"[11]

Fuller's views on art and the artist must have been familiar ones for Peabody, fresh from her own essays and reviews on the work of Washington Allston.

> Miss Fuller labored to show that the artist was distinguished by discovering in beautiful things or scenes the *law* of Beauty, Power—& then making use of the sights he had seen to express this law directly to the mind of a spectator—She thought the human interest a man's work inspired waked the spectator into inter-

est, roused his confidence in himself & induced him to ask of the picture its significance. Art was therefore the finishing touch of Nature—Without Art Nature in the highest sense would not be complete. By art the Divine manifests continually more & more of its inexhaustible self.[12]

Both women agreed that art reveals transcendent truth, which lies hidden in character, action, or scene. But Fuller went beyond the notion that art can so reveal these truths because of the moral character of the artist, who acts, in this view, as a kind of passive medium. That was Peabody's argument in her essays on Allston. Fuller proposed that the artist actually completes or fulfills nature, revealing truths that nature on its own was powerless to reveal. Here, it seems, the stress is not so much on character as on genius.

Inspired by the success of these two series, Fuller agreed to offer another, beginning in November 1840, on fine arts. Once again, the front parlor of Elizabeth Peabody's West Street bookshop served as the classroom for this "noble meeting," as Fuller called it. The number of participants, in fact, taxed the limitations of that small house, but it seemed not to matter. The participants had caught something of Fuller's enthusiasm, "glowing" and "kindling" with excitement, so much that Fuller went home with "a long attack of nervous headache." Many of these Conversations, to judge by Peabody's notes, were extended monologues, some successful, others, like the one on painting, not so successful. Peabody's own experience in art criticism is reflected in her judgment of Fuller's insights: "She seemed to think painting worked more by illusion than sculpture. It involved more prose, from its representing more objects. She said nothing adequate about *color*."[13]

In early 1841 Fuller was approached with the possibility of offering an evening class on Greek mythology open to both men and women. A group immediately gathered, which included many of her female conversationalists, together with a male contingent including Emerson, Alcott, James Freeman Clarke, Hedge, Ripley, Very, Charles Stearns Wheeler, and Theodore Parker. They met from March 1 through May 6, nearly weekly, nine times at the Ripleys' house on Bedford Place and once at Peabody's bookshop.[14]

Fuller may, in hindsight, have regretted this decision. She considered the class a failure, in part because of the mixed audience. She appeared to prefer female company: "Certain it is that Margaret never appears, when I see her, either so brilliant and deep in thought, or so desirous to please, or so modest, or so heart-touching, as in this very party," Peabody observed. In mixed sessions the men dominated, unfamiliar, as Emerson said, with the organic flow of conversation or, more likely, with the possibility that women might have ideas. "I remember that she seemed encumbered, or interrupted, by the headiness or incapacity of the men, whom she had not had the advantage of training, and who fancied, no doubt, that, on such a question [as mythology] they, too, must assert and dogmatize." Emerson's comment is remarkably obtuse, since he virtually shanghaied the second session, dominating the discussion with his obsession about present-day heroes and myths.[15]

Nonetheless, that session and the others provided an opportunity for another scribe besides Peabody to record her impressions and recount the Conversation. This new voice belonged to nineteen-year-old Caroline Healey. Having been given a superior education by her banker father Mark Healey, Caroline developed a sometimes unnerving self-confidence and acidity of response. These were, of course, also Fuller's traits, and led inevitably to the clash of rivals. Caroline had found her way to the West Street bookshop, where Peabody invited her to attend this new session on Greek mythology, knowing that Fuller needed every possible attendee and fee. Fuller was irritated by her presence and berated Peabody several times for inviting Caroline, but the young woman stood her ground because "I had paid a certain number of hard dollars for my place in [the class], & valued it too much as a means of culture, to give it up."

Healey at first sat "a little out of sight," at the first sessions, but Peabody and Eliza Rotch Farrar apparently drew her into the circle, where her presence doubtless irked Fuller session after session. Caroline had mastered shorthand, and after each session she wrote out a transcript of the Conversation. In 1895 she published these transcriptions as *Margaret and Her Friends, or Ten Conversations with Margaret Fuller. . . .* This volume, together with manuscript journals from 1859 and 1895, provides vivid insights not only into the give-and-take of the Conversations but also into Elizabeth Peabody's place and participation.

Caroline Healey prided herself on being reserved, insightful, even "clairvoyant." Elizabeth Peabody, she recalled, was just the opposite. A

boundless, tireless talker, Peabody would go on for hours in monologue. "I have watched the rapids above Lake Erie, and the opening of
the Gulf of the St. Lawrence, with precisely the same feeling," Caroline
wrote. Elizabeth would run her life for her, Caroline was convinced, all
out of a serene sense of "loving sympathy"; but the young woman was
determined to "hold the helm, with all my strength, to escape the
Maelstromn [sic] of her affectionate mistakes."[16]

Some of the funniest and most telling of Healey's remarks about
Peabody and the Conversations have to do with Caroline's nearsightedness and its consequences. Once Elizabeth chided her for not wearing
her glasses; had she worn them, she would not have missed Emerson's
look of contempt in response to something Healey had said. Caroline
turned the older woman's criticism aside by saying that she already so
keenly felt people's responses that she didn't need glasses to see them;
besides, she suffered from a disease of the optic nerve that glasses would
only worsen!

At the March 19 session, Caroline's nearsightedness got her into
deeper trouble. Engaged in a conversation with Peabody about Edward
Hale, Healey said some indiscreet things about Hale, whose brother-
in-law William Wetmore Story happened to be sitting next to her,
unnoticed by the myopic Caroline. Later, Peabody roundly criticized
her: "'How can you *dare* to speak before persons whom you do not
know?' she exclaimed, as if she were not constantly doing it herself!".
Elizabeth Peabody followed this up with a note to Caroline, suggesting
that she not speak so freely in the Conversations unless requested to
do so.

Fuller's Conversations revealed their feminist implications not simply because they provided opportunities for women to speak freely
about religious and philosophical topics; they also threw men and
women together in new and uncharted social arrangements, setting
aside the usual limits of marriage and family and exploring relationships
based on common interests and passions. This was Elizabeth Peabody's
milieu, without a doubt, a place of intellectual freedom and personal
liberation. We have a wonderful glimpse of her, by way of Caroline
Healey's pen, sitting with Caroline in the center, Elizabeth on her left,
and William Story on her right, with Elizabeth leaning across Caroline
and resting her arms on Caroline's knees. "For some time I said nothing
and pretended to be engaged in other thoughts, but she spoke loud,

and finally said she was so much in love with Hale, that she was afraid to think of it, when our three pairs of eyes met, and we burst into laughter."[17]

Lydia Maria Child was also vastly amused by reports of Peabody's comments on love, which Child saw as characteristic of her vague, hopelessly idealistic outlook. Sifting through hundreds of letters prior to burning them, Child came across an account of Fuller's Conversations by Louisa Loring and wrote this to Loring in March 1849: "I kept smiling, smiling; but when I came to your attendance upon Margaret Fuller's conversations, and the prolonged discussion upon love & marriage, between Elizabeth Peabody and Miss Haliburton, I shouted with laughter, here all alone by myself. Miss Peabody thought the perfection of love was to love the object so well, that it was perfectly immaterial whether you ever saw him or not. What a comfortable, cozy idea! I advise all such high spiritualists to fall in love with the *idea* of Plato. I say the *idea* of Plato, two thousand years off; because the man himself I apprehend was made of other metal. At all events, history records that he left a legacy to his son. Miss Peabody's shadowy sentiment amused me, and your 'real' indignation amused me much more."[18]

Meanwhile, the Conversations went on, less well recorded than the earlier ones. Caroline Healey never came to another, and Peabody's notes appear scattered or lost. Sessions on "Ethics," the influence of women, and "Education," carried Fuller and her students to April 28, 1844, the last day of class. "How noble has been my experience of such relations now for six years," she wrote to Emerson, "and with so many and so various minds. Life is worth living is it not?"[19]

 THAT ELIZABETH PEABODY seems to have left no record of her opinion of Fuller and the Conversations is disappointing, but not puzzling. The early 1840s was a time of intellectual achievement for Peabody, a time when demanding activities were layered one on top of the other, interacting and interpenetrating. Alive with new commitments and ideas and pulled in many directions, Peabody nonetheless managed to write several of her most powerful and polished essays. Published in the *Dial*, these analyses of Brook Farm reflect her interest in the social implications of Transcendentalism and illustrate the rich interaction of causes, ideas, and expression in this period of Peabody's life.

Peabody had long been interested in social arrangements and in the cultural values articulated by different societies. These concerns, which stemmed in large part from her mother's instruction in history, continued in her own *Keys to History* series. Sometimes expressed as an anxiety about propriety, other times as a concern for the legitimate claims of society on the individual, Peabody tempered the more radical individualist and immediatist claims of Jones Very, Bronson Alcott, or Margaret Fuller with counterclaims of social responsibility and gradualism, reflective of her characteristically practical blend of thought and action. Interested in maintaining the privacy, even the sanctity, of individual life (as in her concern about the Temple School students' journals being read aloud, or, earlier, in her hostility to revivalist methods), Peabody was nonetheless concerned about the reformation of society and not simply about the apotheosis of individuals.

In the early 1840s, Peabody's concerns merged with those of many other reformers disturbed by industrialization, the growing gulf between rich and poor, and the shift away from handcraft to industrial labor. William Ellery Channing, Theodore Parker, and Orestes Brownson all spoke vigorously on the "labor question," agreeing that the arrangement of society dictated by capitalist economics was fundamentally immoral. But how to reform it? Brownson saw the problem as one of power; the rich held the economic power in society, and no improvement was possible until workers seized the tools of investment and production. As Brownson put it in a striking presentiment of Marx, "the truth is, the evil we have pointed out is not merely individual in its character. . . . [It] is inherent in all our social arrangements, and cannot be cured without a radical change of those arrangements. . . . The only way to get rid of those evils is to change the system, not its managers." Channing and Parker, more given to Protestant individualism, could not see any solution beyond the personal: working people could raise themselves beyond poverty through dint of enormous personal sacrifice and self-discipline.[20]

There was a third way, communitarianism. The 1840s saw hundreds of intentional communities organized in the United States, ranging from those based on specific religious teachings like the Shakers to the Transcendentalist communities of Fruitlands and Brook Farm, which sought to combine a sense of individual freedom and responsibility with alternative social and economic institutions. Sure that the artificial division between intellectual and physical labor lay at the root of American class inequities, these reformers encouraged participants to seek the rewards of both manual and mental effort. Such communities could act as models for the rest of society, demonstrating the possibilities of personal growth and communal prosperity.

During the spring and early summer of 1840 and into the following fall and winter, George and Sophia Ripley talked of their hopes for such a Transcendentalist community. Elizabeth Peabody was an eager listener to their plans for reforming American society. In the fall she wrote Emerson of these plans, and his response was much in tune with his preference for the private solution. "I must honor what you tell me of Mr Ripley's purposes & I look at him with great curiosity, & hope. One would not wish to be always canting on this matter, & yet it seems that if the man were democratized & made kind & faithful in his heart, the whole sequel would flow out easily, & instruct us in what should be the new world; nor should we need to be always laying the axe at the root of this or that vicious institution."[21]

Emerson's reluctance and final refusal to join the Brook Farm community is well known. In Robert Richardson's words, "the decision about whether to join Brook Farm forced Emerson to make a hard choice. Between the community of others, which he believed in and which he was always trying to gather or foster around him, and the self-determination and independence of his present way of life, he took the latter." In his journal Emerson linked his decision with the distinction between individualism and collectivism, among whose advocates he listed Peabody: "The young people, like Brownson, [William Henry] Channing, [William Batchelder] Greene, E. P. P. & possibly Bancroft think that the vice of the age is to exaggerate individualism, & they adopt the word *l'humanitie* from [Pierre] Le Roux, and go for '*the race.*' Hence the Phalanx, Owenism, Simonism, the Communities."[22]

For Elizabeth Peabody, managing the bookshop and caring for her aging parents after her sisters' departures with their new husbands, made joining the community impossible. But she welcomed the idea of community, as long as it preserved the sacredness of the self. Perhaps her openness stemmed from her single state, which rendered her less defensive of the private institution of marriage, or from her relative poverty, which made her less defensive of private property. For whatever set of reasons, Peabody was in on the planning of Brook Farm from the first. On September 20 she wrote John Sullivan Dwight of two meetings of the Transcendental Club, one at Theodore Parker's and one at West Street, which were dominated by discussions of social reform. "Mr Ripley said his say—very admirably too—& making no small impression of the reality of the evils he deplores—the key of which is—that the ministers & church are upheld in order to uphold a society vicious in its foundations—but which the multitude desire should continue in its present conditions."[23]

Throughout the fall and winter months, the Transcendentalist circle discussed the community idea. "Yesterday George and Sophia Ripley, Margaret Fuller and Alcott discussed here the Social Plans," Emerson recorded in his journal on October 17, adding, "I do not wish to remove from my present prison to a prison a little larger. . . . Shall I raise the siege of this hencoop, and march baffled away to a pretended siege of Babylon?" Later that month, Fuller wrote William Henry Channing, "in the town I saw the Ripleys. Mr. R more and more wrapt in his project. He is too sanguine, and does not take time to let things ripen in his mind; yet his aim is worthy. . . ."[24]

In April 1841 the Ripleys and the first of the Brook Farmers moved out to a farm of some 200 acres in West Roxbury, southwest of Boston. They were soon joined by Nathaniel Hawthorne, whose arrival at the "polar Paradise" in the midst of a spring blizzard is thinly fictionalized in *The Blithedale Romance*. Elizabeth knew all about these early days and the heroic work done by a handful in setting the place up. Her letters to Dwight suggest the scale of the task. "In a fortnight Hawthorne and Mr. Warren Burton joined them and Hawthorne has taken hold with the greatest spirit—& proves a fine workman—but Frank Farley is the crown etc—He knows how to do every species of work—from cooking & other kinds of domestic labor & through all the processes of farming & dealing with livestock. . . ." But it was all still in the formative phase, Elizabeth observed, and Ripley had determined to hold a meeting on May 11 to get the community on a more solid financial basis. Ripley hoped to attract investors from whom at least $10,000 could be raised. In describing all this to Dwight, Peabody identified the community as a "school," not a surprising term from her, and not even very surprising given the exemplary intent of the community. In fact, in her essay "Plan of the West Roxbury Community," she refers to Brook Farm as an "embryo University." Peabody also uses "school" in the more institutional sense, and notes that investors would be able to send pupils to the community's school, which would be conducted by such luminaries as George Bradford, Sophia Ripley, and occasionally Elizabeth Peabody herself.[25]

Still, for all the flurry of activity on the farm and in Peabody's parlor, Ripley had not been very forthcoming about its plan or his expectation; at least that is what Elizabeth Peabody thought.

> With respect to the Community—I do not see how it is to step out of its swaddling clothes—unless Mr. Ripley makes known in some regular way or allows some friend to do so the plan in detail & in connection with the Ideal.—He enjoys the *"work"* so much that he does not clearly see that his plan is not in the ways of being demonstrated any farther than it is being made evident—that gentlemen if they will work as many hours as boors will succeed even better in cultivating a farm.—But I trust something will be done soon of a magnetic character—to find the steel which is scattered in the great heap of lead which make up our Society. I am more & more interested in it—as I see the evils arising out of this present corrupt—or petrified—organization.[26]

It was exactly to this "magnetic" task that Peabody set herself in the early fall, to write descriptive and interpretive essays on Brook Farm and on the communitarian effort to reform modern society. The first, "A Glimpse of Christ's Idea of Society," appeared in the October 1841 issue of the *Dial*, Emerson's and Fuller's new Transcendentalist journal. When we inquire as to Christ's understanding of society, Peabody observes, we typically think of churches as models of what he intended. But churches do not do justice to this issue; Jesus referred the question not to institutional life but to the life of the soul. That is, society as Jesus intended is that medium in which individuals achieved their full personhood. "The Problem of the present age is human society, not as a rubric of abstract science, but as a practical matter and universal interest; an actual reconciliation of outward organization with the life of the individual souls who associate; and by virtue of whose immortality each of them transcends all arrangements."[27]

Christian societies have addressed this question of "Christ and culture," as H. Richard Niebuhr would later term it, either by ignoring social arrangements altogether and cultivating the individual soul; or by heavy-handed organization, the method, Peabody thought, of the Roman Catholic Church. Both are in error because of their false separation of the material and spiritual dimensions of life. The time is coming, she writes, when every aspect of social life must be judged by the principles of "Love to God and Love to Man": "The church of Christ, the Kingdom of heaven, has not come upon earth, according to our daily prayer, unless not only every church, but every trade, every form of social intercourse, every institution political or other, can abide this test."

Paradoxically, this immense social transformation (the thought of which outrages and terrifies social conservatives) begins with individuals who live as Jesus lived, from an inward principle of love, individuals who seek out others who share their dream of social change based on living according to Jesus' model of life. "There are men and women . . . who have dared to say to one another; why not have our daily life organized on Christ's own idea? Why not begin to move the mountain of custom and convention? Perhaps Jesus' method of thought and life is the Saviour,—is Christianity! For each man to think and live on this method is perhaps the second coming of Christ." There have been, to be sure, Christian communities—Moravians, Shakers, Rappites, others—and secular efforts, like European socialism. But so often the light of the individual self has been extinguished by the needs of the group.

The ancient problem of Christ and culture resolves itself into the more modern problem of self and community. For Peabody, the priority is clear: "The final cause of human society is the unfolding of the individual man into every form of perfection. . . ." Therefore, the key to *true* community, Christ's idea of society, must be education, the development of each person's gifts and calling. "When we consider that each generation of men is thrown, helpless and ignorant even of the light within itself, into the arms of a full grown generation which has a power to do it harm, all but unlimited, we acknowledge that no object it can propose to itself is to be compared with that of educating its children truly." Education must not be seen as inhabiting yet another social institution, but as "the generating Idea of society itself. . . . In the true society, then, Education is the ground Idea. The Highest work of man is to call forth man in his fellow and child. This was the work of the Christ in Jesus, and in his Apostles."

"A Glimpse" is one of Elizabeth Peabody's finest essays, clearly written in prose that serves to convey rather than obscure her meaning. Grounded in liberal Christianity, the essay portrays Jesus not as supernatural god but as inspired visionary and hero. Jesus's uncompromising devotion to an ethic he found within himself and simultaneously within each other person, forms the basis for social transformation, namely, the vision of a society that encourages and develops each person's unique selfhood. Therefore, Peabody preserved her sense of individual power and agency against those who, like Orestes Brownson, would see social problems as requiring only collective solutions; and she preserved her sense of the need for social structures that nurture and protect these fragile selves, against radical individualists who, like Emerson, feared social constraint. "To form such a society as this is a great problem, whose perfect solution will take all the ages of time; but let the Spirit of God move freely over the great deep of social existence, and a creative light will come at His word, and after that long Evening in which we are living, the Morning of the first day shall dawn on a Christian society."

"Plan of the West Roxbury Community," appearing in the *Dial*'s January 1842 issue, is in many ways a much safer and more conventional essay. She accepts without question the community's decision "to come out in some degree from the world," in contrast to the call for global transformation and conversion in the first essay. Here, nature is community's true home, set against the violence and crush of the city. Much of this essay is devoted to a detailed account of the operation of the community—its farm and school, its principles that all should combine mental and manual labor and thus develop both mind and body—from the perspective of the "interested spectator." She warns against factionalism, and against the inevitable clash of temperaments. Most of all, she warns the community not to allow as members anyone who is not willing to work, since doing so would surely introduce class differences. "'My Father worketh hitherto, and I work,' is always the word of the divine humanity."[28]

A third Peabody essay inspired by the West Roxbury community took up the theme of "Fourierism" and appeared in the *Dial* in April 1844. As befit the outlook of its founders, Brook Farm depended on the voluntary labor of its members, and emphasized, as Peabody happily reported, spiritual and intellectual culture just as much as agriculture. But another school of thought was working a powerful influence on

American communitarians in the early 1840s, the work of French reformer and theorist Charles Fourier. Fourier, arguing that the root of
social injustice lay in the incorrect organization of society, proposed in
the place of the current haphazard schemes a precise plan for communities, or phalanxes, each numbering 1,620 persons.[29]

In late December 1843 reformers from all over New England met in
Boston to discuss the implications of Fourier's work for the reform of
American society, and in January 1844 Brook Farm's amended constitution reflected his influence. Seeing the need for a more detailed organization of labor, the members divided themselves into various working
groups and granted membership to those who brought labor, as well
as capital, into the community. This ready acceptance of Fourier's ideas
suggests something of the bold thinking current among the Brook
farmers, since Fourier, or at least the Fourier Americans knew through
the work of Albert Brisbane, was a highly controversial figure.

Elizabeth Peabody reflects in her essay the reservations many felt
about Fourier. "The works of Fourier do not seem to have reached us,"
she begins, accurately enough if she means that Americans know about
Fourier only through his chief American exponent Brisbane, but clearly
her words are an evasion of the larger truth, which is that American
reformers had been discussing little else besides Fourier. "For ourselves we confess to some remembrance of vague horror, connected
with this name," by which she probably means Fourier's criticism of
monogamous marriage and nuclear families. Her anxieties were somewhat abated, she notes, when she heard William Henry Channing defend Fourier's system as a means of understanding the Divine Mind.
Ever the lover of complex systems, Peabody spends several pages out-
lining what she understood to be Fourier's scheme of the twelve human
passions and the social means necessary to refine them.[30]

Peabody's central criticism of Fourier could be forecast from her
previous essays on community. There is no place, at least in the system
as she understands it, for the institutionalization of spirit, no permanent presence of religious life. "Let the Fourierists see to it, that there
be freedom in their Phalanx for churches, unsupported by its material organization, and lending it no support on its material side. Inde-
pendently existing within them, but not of them . . . and pressing on to
the stature of the perfect man, they will finally spread themselves in
spirit over the whole body."

Intimately involved as she was with the *Dial*, Margaret Fuller undoubtedly read Peabody's essay. There is no record of her comment, but she surely would have felt that Peabody missed the point of Fourier. Like Emerson, Peabody saw the nonmaterial self as one of the constituent elements of all human life, a given. But Fuller, like Fourier, saw the self as socially constructed. The need was to reconstruct society so as to free selves rather than inhibit them. Family, marriage, and monogamy were among the most serious inhibitors, Fourier thought, and Fuller agreed. "The true source of human power will remain thwarted," Christina Zwarg has written of Fourier's theory, "and the successful transformation of society into a system of mutual trust, labor, and sharing will remain impossible until women and men are equally free to choose their sexual partners and openly express their desire."[31] Permanently anxious about passion, Peabody would not have seen or not have recognized such implications in Fourier's work, indeed arguing in "Fourierism" that his system purifies the institution of marriage.

While Brook Farm challenged her to work out her views of self and society, other issues and opportunities competed for Peabody's attention in the first years of the 1840s. She filled pages of correspondence to John Sullivan Dwight about Dwight's ambivalence with ordination, his dubious gifts for ministry, his conflicts with his Unitarian congregation in Northampton, Massachusetts, and his eventual resignation. Dwight was also the recipient of Peabody's excited remarks on the controversies surrounding Theodore Parker and his exclusion from several Unitarian pulpits because of his theological radicalism.[32]

Although it is hard to know where she found the time, Peabody also conducted a series of "Historical Conferences" throughout the 1840s and 1850s. Long committed to the study of history and to women's education, she believed that history "should take the place that law, medicine, or theology takes in the liberal education of men." In six-month terms of fifty sessions each, she took up history before the eighth century, the history of ancient Israel, and Greek and Roman history. "Our text-books were Herodotus, Thucydides, Zenophon, Livy, and Plutarch," Karl Otfried Müller on Greek literature, and her own key to Greek history. "There were some Harvard students, brothers and friends of my scholars, who came to me *sub rosa* [much as male students at Atkinson Academy had come to her mother] while this conference was going on, and asked my advice as to their historical reading, who followed out this course and read the tragedies, and I advised them to read the Greek historians and Livy in the originals." In 1844 she led her class through a discussion of the eighteenth century, with much focus on the French Revolution.[33]

Given her intense activity and visibility in the early 1840s, it comes as no surprise that Elizabeth Peabody should be invited to some of the sessions of the Transcendental Club. Founded in September 1836 by Emerson, George Ripley, Frederick Henry Hedge, and George Putnam, the Club brought together the leading figures in New England religious, social, and educational reform. Variously called "The Symposium" or "Hedge's Club," after the Bangor, Maine, minister whose visits to the Boston area usually prompted a meeting, the club's discussions reflected the various controversies that its members and their ideas occasioned.[34]

Elizabeth Peabody attended three sessions of the Club. The first was on September 6, 1837, at James Freeman Clarke's house. She attended two in September 1840, as controversies swirled around George Ripley and Theodore Parker. One session, possibly on September 2, was held at Parker's house in Roxbury, and the next on Sepember 20, at Peabody's West Street address. "At both places it was the same subject," she wrote John Sullivan Dwight; "& Mr. Ripley said his say—very admirably too." Parker "is really inspired. . . . He has got on fire with the velocity of his spirits speed." Peabody thoroughly admired his insistence on remaining within the Unitarian fold regardless of the opposition of conservatives, and equally admired his ability to look upon institutions as merest shells of their transcendent meaning.[35]

☙ In the early 1840s, as in the mid-1830s, events and people in Elizabeth Peabody's life overlapped and interwove, making a dense fabric of literary and intellectual heft. If West Street was the busy workshop to which the many strands were brought—Fuller's Conversations, Transcendental Club meetings, conversations about Brook Farm, books, and ideas—then the Transcendentalist quarterly the *Dial* became the loom on which the strands, briefly but memorably, were woven.

In the late 1830s, the members of the Transcendental Club had sought vainly for a publishing outlet for their ideas, realizing that no existing journal had the capacity or the willingness to act as their vehicle. Nothing would do except that "The Newness" have its own journal with Emerson as its editor. But Emerson steadily refused to take the post, citing his own difficulties in editing and publishing the works of Thomas Carlyle. Instead, in late October 1839, Margaret Fuller agreed to be the journal's first editor, and she began laying plans for its first issue as she conducted her first Conversation in Elizabeth Peabody's bookshop. Through the spring she gathered material for that first issue, scheduled for publication in July 1840.

In April, aware that Peabody's bookshop was the journal's boon companion, Emerson wrote Fuller to suggest an "Intelligencer" column for the *Dial*, with Peabody involved in gathering information for it. Nothing came of this, nor of Emerson's further suggestion that the bookshop itself be mentioned in such a column. Perhaps Emerson wanted to do Peabody a good turn or possibly to make her look useful in the eyes of the critical Fuller. But such positive feelings did not stand in the way of Emerson's decision in October 1840 when, acting as a kind of selection committee for Fuller, he rejected Peabody's offer of an essay on patriarchal religion. This was the fourth in her series on Hebrew religion, which she had published back in 1834 in the *Christian Examiner.* As she explained to Orestes Brownson, whom she also tried to interest in this essay for publication in his *Boston Quarterly Review*, she intended to publish six essays on this topic; but Andrews Norton "cut off untimely my little series" as coming from one who had insufficient knowledge of the subject.[36]

Emerson too was uninterested, though from a different perspective. No one seems to care much for history these days, he wrote, a shockingly casual dismissal of Peabody's primary passion. "Instead of reverently exploring the annals of Egypt Asia & Greece as the cardinal points of the horzon by wh. we must take our departure, go where we will, it is too plain tht the modern scholar begins with the fact of his own nature & is only willing to hear any result you can bring him from these old dead men by way of illustration or ornament of his own biography." To the modern reader, these ancient biblical figures "have a certain air of unseasonableness, like octagenarians at a young party, & one would willingly spare such valued friends the shadow of a disrespect." Emerson reported his decision to Fuller: the essay "had great merits, but the topics Abraham, Isaac Jacob & Esau, I told her, were a little too venerable for our slight modern purpose. Yet the first ten pages could make a very good paper (there were 40 or 50 pp) if you want one." Margaret did not.[37]

A year later Peabody had better luck with Fuller and Emerson. Her essay on Christ's idea of society appeared in the second volume of the *Dial*, in October 1841, and her sketch of Brook Farm the following January. These two, and a third essay on "Fourierism" which appeared in 1844, were all she could manage to get into the journal. Although usually her well-wisher, Emerson was impatient with her digressive and verbose style: "You would think that she dwelt in a museum where all things were extremes & extraordinary," he wrote Fuller. Still, Peabody's involvement with the *Dial* went far beyond writing for it. From January 1842 to July 1843, she published the quarterly from her West Street bookshop address, adding that title to several works she had begun publishing in the decade of the 1840s.[38]

As with the idea of opening a bookstore, it is not altogether clear where Peabody got the notion of going into publishing. Her records seem not to have survived, and what does remain is spotty and contradictory: the Boston *Daily Advertiser* for March 26, 1842, contains an advertisement announcing her publishing office at 109 Washington Street, but Boston City Directories from 1840 to 1850 do not list Peabody as having any other business address besides West Street. To complicate matters, a "Catalogue of the American and Foreign Circulating Library, kept by E. P. Peabody," contains the 109 Washington Street address, although whether as a publishing location or a library location is not clear.[39]

In any event, Peabody's first publishing venture was not the *Dial*, but children's books by Nathaniel Hawthorne. In December 1840 Hawthorne's *Grandfather's Chair* appeared under the imprint "Boston: E. P. Peabody," followed by *Famous Old People* in January 1841 and *Liberty Tree* in March. Until the middle of the nineteenth century, publishers acted as agents for authors, arranging for printing and binding and advertising their wares to prospective readers. By March 1841 Hawthorne had grown restive with the slow pace of sales. Perhaps seeing the need to position Hawthorne's works more decisively in the marketplace, Peabody negotiated with James Munroe to print another edition of Hawthorne's children's books together with another edition of *Twice-Told Tales*. In this she acted without Hawthorne's permission, it appears, prompting this rather acerbic response in the third person: "Mr. Hawthorne particularly desires that the bargain with Mr. Munroe, in respect to the remaining copies of Grandfather's Chair, &c may be concluded on such terms as Miss Peabody thinks best, without further reference to himself. Being wholly ignorant of the value of the books, he could do no other than consent to any arrangement that she might propose."[40]

Seven months later Hawthorne took a more active role in the fate of his books. He engaged Tappan and Dennet to publish succeeding editions, probably irked by Peabody's refusal to take her share of royalties on *Grandfather's Chair.* From Tappan and Dennet, Hawthorne moved on to Ticknor and Fields, who would become his preferred publisher for the rest of his career. Still, Hawthorne was not Peabody's only author. In 1842 she edited and published a version of St. Augustine's *Confessions,* a copy of which Thomas Wentworth Higginson bought at her bookshop in January 1844. At the beginning of the new decade, she was publishing her own textbooks, including *The Polish-American System of Chronology* in 1850.[41]

Despite this mixed record at publishing, Peabody was entrusted with the task of publishing the *Dial* from 1841 to 1843. In October 1841 the magazine's first publisher—Weeks, Jordan—went bankrupt, and Margaret Fuller suggested Peabody as their successor. Early in the following year, Peabody and James Freeman Clarke were asked to inspect the books of Weeks, Jordan. They found that there were only three hundred paying subscribers, not the five hundred to six hundred as had been assumed. This number would ensure an annual income of $750, but since costs of paper and printing would come to $700, little would be left to pay the editor or publisher. "I am sorry to hear no better tidings of the Dial in the past," Emerson wrote Peabody upon receiving this bad news, but added cheerfully, "'let Bygones be Bygones & fair play for the time to come.'"[42]

As Peabody settled into the work of arranging for the printing, binding, and marketing of the magazine, together with handling its finances, Emerson thought that he and Fuller had made a reasonably good choice of new publisher. "As to pecuniary matters, Miss Peabody I have found more exact and judicious than I expected, but she is variable in her attention, because she has so many private affairs." But it might not be so wise to trust her with publishing Fuller's own work: "A connection with her offers no advantages for the spread of your work whatever it may be." For her part, Fuller, as usual, had little good to say about Peabody. Elizabeth's publication and advertisement of Fuller's translation of the correspondence of Bettina von Arnim and Karoline Günderode, the latter a young woman who committed suicide in 1806 over a failed love affair, drew scathing commentary. "Let me before I forget to guard you," Fuller wrote Emerson in April, "if need be, against trusting E.P.P. to write the slightest notice or advertisement. I never saw anything like her for impossibility of being clear & accurate in a brief space. She wrote one notice about 'the importance of public patronage to secure the *identity* [rather than "indemnity"] of Editors' which I fortunately arrested on the way and I see she had advertised Günderode as 'Correse of Bettine Brentano with a *Nun*' [Karoline was a member of a lay religious order] as if people could not make mistakes enough of themselves without putting the grossest in their way."[43]

In the spring of 1843, Emerson took Peabody's warnings about the fragile condition of the magazine more seriously. Subscriptions were now down to 220, with many readers' preferring to buy single copies rather than to purchase subscriptions. "I think to end the Dial with this number for Miss P assures me that the subscription is less than at the beginning of the year and is less than the expense: a plain leading from above or from below to an end," he wrote resignedly to Fuller. Some of the responsibility for this state of affairs Emerson laid at Peabody's door. She was not up to the kind of aggressive marketing and distribution necessary for survival, he thought, and her inability to get the April 1843 issue to the booksellers at the beginning of the month seemed to prove his point. In response to her "careless" policy, Emerson turned over the publication duties to his own publisher, James Munroe. Still, the journal continued to lose subscribers, and a year later, in April 1844, the journal published its last issue.[44]

Despite this dizzying pace of writing, publishing, conversing, and bookselling, Elizabeth Peabody still managed to find time for private and family life. She continued to be close to the Emerson family. Lidian had written her several letters in the late 1830s, combining accounts of her Swedenborgianism and her concerns about Jones Very with anecdotes of baby Waldo, born in 1836. "Having no other baby to compare him with we [cannot] of course say what he is comparatively—but we think that he is *positively* all that we can wish," she wrote in early 1837. "(Pardon my writing," she begged in a letter from around that same

time; "baby is in my arms & his 'footies' touch my elbow occasionally)—we were very much interested in what you say of Mr. Very & his
opinions. Mr. E will I think be glad to know him personally."[45]

Having shared in their happiness, Peabody also shared in the Emersons' sorrow at Waldo's untimely death in January 1842. She had invited Emerson to be among a group of citizens meeting Charles Dick-
ens when he arrived in Boston in late January. But Emerson wrote this
response: "Thanks for your kind invitation, my friend, but the most
severe of all afflictions has befallen me, in the death of my boy. He has
been ill since Monday of what is called Scarlet Fever, & died last night
& with him has departed all that is glad & festal & almost all that is
social even, for me, from this world. My second child is also sick, but I
cannot in a lifetime incure another such loss. Farewell."[46]

Gains and losses must have also been very much on Peabody's mind
as she watched her sisters marry men for whom she had once had strong
feelings. Sophia married Nathaniel Hawthorne on July 9, 1842, in a
ceremony conducted by James Freeman Clarke in the West Street parlor, with the Peabodys, Sarah Clarke, and Cornelia Park in attendance.
Nathaniel and Elizabeth were still in the throes of argument over book
publishing and royalties. Six years later the indomitable sister-in-law
was still very much a presence in Hawthorne's life, in his dreams as in
his family life. In 1848 when Sophia was away visiting her sister Mary in
West Newton, Hawthorne had a terrifying dream:

> The other night [he wrote his wife], I dreamt that I was in New-
> ton, in a room with thee, and with several other people; and thou
> tookst the occasion to announce, that thou hadst now ceased to be
> my wife, and hadst taken another husband. Thou madest this intel-
> ligence known with such perfect composure and *sang froid*—not
> particularly addressing me, but the company generally—that it be-
> numbed my thoughts and feelings, so that I had nothing to say.
> Thou wast perfectly decided, and I had only to submit without a
> word. But, hereupon, thy sister Elizabeth, who was likewise pre-
> sent, informed the company that, in this state of affairs, having
> ceased to be thy husband, I of course became hers; and turning to
> me, very cooly inquired whether she or I should write to inform
> my mother of the new arrangement! How the children were to be
> divided, I know not. I only know that my heart suddenly broke

loose, and I began to expostulate with thee in an infinite agony, in the midst of which I awoke. . . . Thou shouldst not behave so, when thou comest to me in dreams.[47]

Confirming Hawthorne's deep sense that Elizabeth had some prior claim on him, this nightmare of being married to both sisters would become a living reality again and again ten years later when Elizabeth intervened vigorously and often in the Hawthornes' political opinions and child-rearing practices.

In July 1849 Hawthorne's mother became ill and declined rapidly. In his journals Hawthorne contrasted his mother's final days with the incessantly cheerful play of his children Una and Julian. Later Julian wrote that his grandmother's death, in August, "passed me by unknowing, or rather without leaving a trace upon my memory." But the tension of the household must have made some impression on the boy, for between Elizabeth Manning Hawthorne's death and his own falling ill, he acted out that tension.

I was standing in a chair at the nursery window, looking out at the street-lamp on the corner, and my aunt Lizzie Peabody, who had just come on from Boston, was standing behind me, lest I should fall off. Now, I was normally the most sweet-tempered little urchin imaginable; yet suddenly without the faintest warning or provocation, I turned round and dealt my loving aunt a fierce kick in the stomach. It deprived her of breath for a space; but her saintly nature is illustrated by the fact that the very first use she made of her recovered faculties was to gasp out "Sophie, the child must be ill!"[48]

In 1843, Clarke performed a second wedding for the Peabodys, this time for Mary and Horace Mann. A rainstorm prevented other guests from attending, so only Elizabeth and her parents witnessed the rite. "I enclose you some geranium leaves which garnished the wedding thinking you might like to press them," Elizabeth wrote Rawlins Pickman. "Mary was dressed in the beautiful grasscloth—& handkerchief that Mrs. John Forbes gave her. With the gold band around her head that Mr. Mann gave her & no other ornament—though she had many given to her that were beautiful—The illuminated countenance of Mr. Mann, so full of joy & tenderness was the ornament you would have most enjoyed: as I did.—We waited the ceremony for you till your messenger arrived & were all most disappointed that you could not come."

When the ceremony was over the couple went down to the dock and boarded the *Britannia* for their honeymoon voyage to England, Germany, the Netherlands, Belgium, France, and Ireland. "I went with them down to the steamer & saw their stateroom as they intended you should also do—We parted with smiles—not tears—& when I saw the great monster creep away with her there was no discord in my heart," Elizabeth added in a postscript. The "great monster" is of course the steamship. But as Horace Mann took Mary away from the family and from Elizabeth, it is altogether possible that she harbored some mix of resentment and envy toward the man whose agony had so entranced and aroused her ten years earlier.[49]

These changes in Peabody's family life were matched throughout the 1840s by shifts in her professional contacts and in her own thought. Bronson Alcott was off in England, after the failures at Temple School and his experimental community at Fruitlands. A lawyer had told Peabody that remaining copies of Alcott's *Conversations with Children on the Gospels* were going to be sold at five cents a pound to trunkmakers to line trunks with, so far had Alcott's public reputation fallen.[50] Emerson had thrown himself into lecturing, writing, and editing the *Dial*, hoping to assuage his grief over the loss of Waldo. Margaret Fuller had left Boston to travel in the Midwest and to write for Horace Greeley's *Herald Tribune* in New York City.

Meanwhile, Peabody continued to run the bookshop, attracting adherents of mesmerism, vegetarianism, phrenology, hydropathy, as well as the curious and the combative. Among the latter was William Batchelder Greene, who had come to Boston in 1841 after serving in the U.S. Army's campaign against the Seminoles in Florida. Attracted at first to Orestes Brownson, then to the reformers in West Roxbury, Greene found his way to West Street in hopes of finding a translation of Kant. The circle of intellectuals to whom Elizabeth introduced the young man found him strikingly opinionated, as in his lofty acceptance of Emerson and his equally lofty dismissal of Theodore Parker. Others besides the Transcendentalists did not much like Greene either. Emerson's Aunt Mary Moody Emerson found "the Green" at West Street and "tea[']ed and eve[']ed" with him. "When I first saw him on the

Couch at West St. I thought him an unconscious hearer of his praise as invisible spirits might. The time at Concord I lost sights of his wings—and now I believe that Waldo had done him full justice & that Miss Fuller was correct in thinking his vanity obvious. Unfortunate connection his with my friend E.P.P."[51]

In Peabody's view, Greene did not really understand current thought, "lumping together the errors of pure mind—with the bad passions of *modern french novels* and the moral indifferentism of Goethism." What was worse, Greene treated Peabody with rudeness and indifference, reminding her constantly of her "various intellectual, religious,—& even *moral* deficiencies," because he supposed she had "no feelings to be wounded, and no *respectibility!*" On his side, Greene thought that Peabody was "a strange character—entirely too hard for me. Every general remark that I make she applies to herself, and she wants me to ease her mind upon difficult points of which I cannot even conceive. If I had known that this would have been the consequence, I should have been very careful of letting her become so well acquainted with me. I never saw a woman like her before." This statement suggests some kind of intimacy between them, but a brief and comic one at that. Greene would reenter Peabody's life in the 1860s, writing her a series of strange letters on human cultural evolution.[52]

Much more intense and consequential was her relationship with Charles Kraitsir, who was a Hungarian-born linguist and philosopher of language. Involved in the Polish Revolution of 1830, Kraitsir had led a group of refugees first to England and then to the United States in 1833. He established a language academy in Maryland in 1837, and in 1840 he was appointed Professor of Modern Languages and History at the University of Virginia, a position he held simultaneously with an appointment at Charlotte's Hall academy in Maryland. But Kraitsir's antislavery sentiments put him at odds with his southern hosts, and he left Charlottesville in 1844 for the more congenial atmosphere of Boston. In 1845 Kraitsir gave a series of lectures on the philosophy of language. Elizabeth Peabody, who was already serving as an assistant at Kraitsir's language academy that had opened that same year, attended those lectures and took careful notes. She developed those notes into a fifty-page pamphlet, which she published in 1846 as *The Significance of the Alphabet.*

The reigning view of language was that taken by Unitarian theorists like Andrews Norton, who followed Locke in believing that language was arbitrary, a culturally derived system that had no universal or transcendent meaning and no organic relation to the ideas being conveyed. In sharp contrast, Transcendentalists were coming to believe that language was symbolic both of the natural order and of the spiritual world. Following the lead of the Swedenborgian Sampson Reed, Emerson in *Nature* argued for a three-fold parallel: language was symbolic of nature, and nature symbolic of spirit. Elizabeth Peabody was equally vigorous in her pursuit of the language key. In 1834 the first of her essays on Hebrew scripture appeared, in which she argued for the peculiar fit between the poetic language of ancient peoples and the natural world they inhabited: "The human mind in its original principles, and the natural creation, in its simplicity, are but different images of the same Creator. . . . The primitive languages, therefore, were naturally poetic, that is, synthetic in their genius." In that same year, Peabody reviewed J. G. Herder's *Spirit of Hebrew Poetry*, making much the same point. Philip Gura, the closest student of Transcendentalism and language theory, writes that "for Peabody, the chief lesson of Herder's volume was the suggestion that, if one went back far enough in his study of language, he could not only locate the original roots of a tongue but ascertain how these roots *themselves* were derived from 'external and internal nature.'"[53]

Into this rich stew of theory and speculation was stirred another element, the work of the Rhode Island industrialist Rowland Gibson Hazard. A self-taught philosopher, Hazard wrote *Language: Its Connexion with the Present Condition and Future Prospects of Man* "in fragments on steamboats, at hotels, and during such hours as could be spared," and published it anonymously in 1836. Elizabeth Peabody read it aloud to William Ellery Channing during one of her secretarial sessions with him. He immediately "recognized a rare metaphysical genius in its author," she recalled. Hazard's contribution to the discussion was the claim that speech originated in "primitive perceptions" that people had before they uttered a sound; language existed first in the mind, as immediate intuition of an object or situation. But this primal stage of language development passed quickly and was replaced by a "language of narration" or a "language of abstraction" in which words acted simply as counters rather than as deep symbols of natural and mental reality.[54]

Charles Kraitsir put all the pieces together—the natural poetry of primitive speech, the linguistic intuitionism—and showed Emerson, Peabody, and others who opposed the Lockean approach exactly how, in his view, languages were connected. He distinguished between language, the culturally and socially derived system of semantics and vocabulary, and speech, the actual physical production of sound. When we (or our primitive ancestors) encountered nature, the result was a vocalization, or an "explosion of reason," as Kraitsir put it. These primal sounds, or germs, are universal. By collecting and systemizing these germs, Kraitsir thought, we could offer the scientific basis for a belief in the unity of language, and therefore, the unity of humanity.[55]

Notions of unity and development were addictive to Elizabeth Peabody. During her career, she described a common human nature working with varied cultural and historical materials throughout history; she argued for the intellectual and cultural development of civilization through the ages; in each person as in each culture, she took note of moral and spiritual development. Channing was Peabody's first mentor in this paradoxical lesson of continuity and change, and Emerson echoed that paradox in much more subjective and personal language in his lectures and essays. Now Kraitsir seemed to put a belief in fundamental unity amid the array of diversities on a firm scientific foundation.

↬ THERE WAS SOMETHING in Kraitsir's work that appealed to Peabody in the mid-1840s that was not simply a restatement of her old lessons from Channing. Something was happening to her in these years, a change and deepening of her perspective. As she aged, Peabody was becoming more confident of her views, less anxious about propriety, and more willing to complicate the Unitarian synthesis that had marked her earlier years. While she still used specifically Christian language in her thought and writing, she was open to the post-Christian influence of Emerson and Fuller; and while she was resistant to notions of direct revelation, she found Jones Very's prophetic speech compelling and disturbing.

Nothing else demonstrates the way Peabody was personalizing these intellectual issues better than "A Vision," a meditation she published in *The Pioneer* in 1843. This three-issue journal was edited by James Russell Lowell and Robert Carter. Lowell's first number was apparently well regarded, but when Lowell stepped aside after eye surgery and turned the reins over to Carter, the magazine foundered. In particular, as Sculley Bradley has pointed out, Lowell and his sister Mary Lowell Putnam, were dubious about Carter's acceptance of Peabody's "A Vision" for inclusion in the March issue. Writing to her brother, Mary Putnam was sharp in her criticism: "I hear that the first article in the next number is to be a *Vision* by E. P. Peabody. Now, with all my regard for Miss Peabody, I cannot think that her abilities qualify her to write a leading article for *any* periodical. Her name alone would be an injury to any work to which she should be a contributer—& her vision should be something very *transcendent* indeed to enable it to make head against this prejudice."[56]

Despite her hostility, the essay was published. Mary Putnam was proven true in one respect at least: the essay is "very *transcendent* indeed."

A record of what appears to be a personal mystical experience, "A Vision" is part of Peabody's long and complex history with the issue of personal revelation. She had rejected the emotionalism of the Maine revivals but had equally found academic Unitarianism too arid for her soul. Wordsworth and Channing had reminded her of her "childhood faith," in which she felt the loving presence of God imparted in images of a "kind Face." Convinced that one can feel within oneself the same divinity that is implicit in the universe, Peabody was still unprepared for the individual illuminations of Quakers or of mystic prophets like Jones Very, whose messages had no social corollary or application but were simple and powerful utterances of possessed individuals. Even the founding of Brook Farm raised the question of social needs versus individual genius. "A Vision" comes out of the ferment of the 1840s, reflecting the continuing struggle between the competing claims of self and other. This piece is distinctive, Diane Brown Jones notes, because it is one of the few times when Peabody "casts off her typical stance as literary priest to assume the voice of literary prophet."[57]

"A few evenings since, while sitting in deep reflection over a pamphlet that contains a new definition of life, and seeming to catch a gleam of light upon that mysterious *death-in-life* which so extensively characterizes modern genius, suddenly I found myself taken off my feet, and realized before my eyes at once all Time," Peabody begins, a Poe-like moment in which the self's powers of reflection and analysis are suddenly suspended and the self is whirled into another layer of consciousness.[58]

As Peabody finds herself taken back to ancient cultures, she is struck by the pervasiveness of music. "Vainly should I attempt to describe the ancient music. Its effect was not—like the modern—to plunge the soul into dreams and prophecies and vain longings. It acted on my senses, and whirled me into an intoxication of delight." This music brought her deeper understanding of ancient rituals, fables and legends, and art forms: "In this music life, Forms unfolded to me their meanings,—I mean more especially those forms which owe their existence to the plastic genius of men. I saw Architecture was solid harmony, and Painting liquid harmony; every statue a single chord, every picture a melody." Presaging her essay on "The Dorian Measure," which would appear in *Aesthetic Papers* at the end of the decade, this treatment of music is striking for an intellectual who had seemed, to this point, quite tone-deaf.

Her vision allowed her to see the building of ancient Asian civilizations, with all their grandeur and cruelty. Each new culture seemed to repeat the same pattern: "While everywhere were traces of an energy and reach of intelligence so marvellous, from all the monuments of it the life was ever departed or departing. Each succeeding generation was degenerate . . . the more gigantic the first generations, the more puny appeared their descendants; till, at last, the contrast became ghastly of lofty customs with the miserable abortions of humanity that wore them as splendid chains."

As her vision moved to western civilizations, she perceived the same contradiction. Living people seemed to move as ghosts among the great works they had created. To the claim that art represented the spiritualized essence of individual people, Peabody protests that "Expression—Beauty, is not life; it is only the aspect of life." For all the material glories of Greek civilization, it is hard to ignore the dismaying social record of continual revolution and repression. Even "the land of Thought is dead" because it separated itself so firmly from matter, from daily social life. The music that had accompanied her vision had died.

Now, in her grief, she begins to hear a different melody: "This simple and venerable strain came up from the chaotic abyss, and, as it touched my soul, the world of art and policy dissolved,—temple and tower, statue and picture, became shadowy and dreamlike, going up like an exhalation." Creation seemed to move backward, from human culture, through the state of nature, and finally "to ancient night." But this Transcendental sublime was not terrifying to the visionary; rather, it "seemed to invigorate my fading life with a new faith in Being."

As she praised this fecund Chaos, this ground of being, Peabody found that it transformed into "a Personal Presence, tender as Love, beautiful as Thought, terrible as Power, and a voice that was based, by the roar, as of artillery, and yet was sweeter in its articulation than the accents of childhood, said to me, 'I am the way, the truth, and the life; whosoever cometh unto me, I will in no wise cast out.'"

In recognizing Christ as the foundation of all human culture, Peabody had come to a further understanding of the limitations of "the world of Thought, which had declared itself to me as Heaven, though it was indeed Hell; for while it was Death, it thought itself Life, and thus forever receded from Life." Echoing her essay on Christ's idea of society, Peabody sees in his message a call to build human community on the basis of respect for the divinity in each self. Christ represents not so much a savior from individual sin and a guarantor of eternal bliss as a figure of reconciliation, a trope of synthesis in the eternal war between self and other.

Peabody's new appreciation of the vocabulary and figures of Christian orthodoxy extended beyond this appropriation of the religion's central figure. She turned again to the question of sin, an issue that had troubled her deeply as a child and young person. Because of their belief in total depravity, Calvinists among her family and acquaintances were able to come to terms with human failure much more effectively than liberals, who saw every wrong deed as a failure of individual will. Now, years later, Peabody opened this issue again.

"I have been trying to think out *into words* that change in my opinions and creed which makes me feel that I have *changed*—without having lost that aspect of truth either, or that truth which Unitarians as a body have gained over the Orthodox as a body," she wrote to Mary Moody Emerson sometime in 1845 or 1846. "My change consists in having got some notion of life on the one hand and of sin on the other. I have discriminated life at once from the creative essence, and from dead existence. Perhaps I may say with the Germans—It is a becoming—and yet I cannot *exactly*, for there is an objective as well as a subjective condition of life, and neither of the conditions are *the life*."

The value of the orthodox approach to sin is that it has to do with the very stuff of life, whereas the liberal sees sin as circumstantial. "The orthodox man looks upon the wrong thing done as a comparatively trifling matter when compared with that fault of his organic self whence this wrong thing came, and which makes all his action, when he looks to it narrowly, have some wrong tinge or bias in it." Although she finds the words "total depravity" confusing, she is convinced that orthodox Christianity is right in saying that sin is organic rather than episodic. But her way of understanding sin is not Pauline, it is Romantic and developmental: *"Arrest a man at any moment* and observe him arrested—cut him off—and he will revolve forever in a vicious circle—or cease to revolve—and die like a plant or animal of longer or shorter date. This is the idea I meant to express in that 'Vision' which you have. . . ."[59]

Peabody's words are ambiguous. In one reading, Sin is the breakdown of development, a violation of that principle of growth that is revealed most fully in the life of Jesus. In another, Sin could be understood as the sign of our collective existence, our organic and interconnected nature. In any event, she is led to make a bold claim: "Perhaps sin is [God's] minister, introducing us into deep secrets of the Divine nature. . . . And it is a wonderful Minister indeed! I speak however of the abstract *Sinfulness*—not of *concrete sins*—when I make the bold proposition that as far as I can understand myself—*Sinfulness* has been the greatest Angel to me."[60]

Once Elizabeth Peabody had brooded over issues of propriety, concerned about offending the views of parents whose children were her livelihood. Now she can claim, echoing Luther's "peccata fortiter," the redemptive power of sin. "It seems to me certain," she wrote to Mary Emerson in 1845, "that characters which have the most life and joy are those which are not scrupulous. And that the excessive fear of doing wrong which we Unitarian children were all brought up with, strikes a blow at something within us—which is *vital.*"

You lived before that day, and do not exhibit any of this death-in-life which I complain of, but coquette with life like a girl of fifteen, who knows herself sovereign and can afford to play with *All.* You remind me of Mr. Emerson's saying in his first essays,—something of this kind—that if a person acts consistently "according to their

constitution["] *they are justified.* This is subjective transcendentalism I think you must acknowledge, but it is very exciting to see it
done. I confess it makes my blood dance and is altogether more
entertaining than the conscientous nicety of some people. Is it the
Satan in me that is conciliated and tickled? or is it the freedom
wherewith Christ doth make us free? I am *really in doubt.*[61]

Recognizing the organic oneness of humanity led Peabody back to
the issue of language as the key to that oneness. "Since I knew Dr.
Kraitsir I have seen a little into the reason why we puzzle ourselves so
much and perpetually lose the truths which the great God gives us
whereby to live," she wrote to Mary Moody Emerson.

We have lost the key to language, that great instrument by means
of which the finite mind is to compensate itself, for its being fixed
to a point in space and compelled to the limitations of the succession we call time. We use words that are no longer symbols but
counters—Our logomacy does not coincide with the eternal logos,
and yet we are so constituted that words affect us according to
their nature in some degree, and talking about one thing while we
are thinking about another, and inextricable confusions arise. I
have literally begun at my a b c and I mean to understand the
languages of those men who have made some advance, and enter
into their labors.[62]

In its supposed scientific modernity, Kraitsir's language theory served to
bolster for Elizabeth Peabody an ancient teaching about the unity of
humanity: "In Adam's fall we sinned all."

There would be no one better to remind Peabody of those ancient
truths than Waldo Emerson's Aunt Mary. Mary Moody Emerson was a
deep and highly original thinker, whose letters reveal a profound engagement with the major intellectual issues of her very long life. In a
manner reminiscent of Jonathan Edwards, Mary Emerson believed in a
grand and mysterious God of whom one had knowledge through mystic and intuitive experiences. Combined with that lofty view of God was
an equally lofty view of human dignity and potential. At one time, Mary
Moody Emerson thought that Elizabeth might make a suitable wife for
Waldo, after Ellen Tucker Emerson's death. It would not have been a

wholly implausible match—two vigorous intellects engaged with the issues of their age. But temperamentally the talkative, brilliant, but unfocused Peabody and the intensely disciplined Emerson would have been incompatible.[63]

Still, there was much in Elizabeth Peabody (whom she called "Miss Pea") that Mary Emerson found interesting and admirable, and clearly much in her that Peabody found stimulating and original. Both were unmarried, viewed by their contemporaries as "eccentric," and both "homeless," without fixed abodes for long periods of their lives. Their intellectual lives, like their letters, were spiral-like, spinning off into tangents of related thought and then returning to the central point. Both were, above all, intellectual women who hungered for a diet of new ideas and new insights.

Mary Emerson knew of Elizabeth Peabody as early as 1832 when the younger woman "sent me a long long letter some time since—mostly of the history of breaking up care of her family &c," as she wrote to her nephew Charles. Peabody both intrigued and irritated her, even in these early years. "She is a gifted mind—pupil & inmate of Dr. C[han-ning]. Becoming an Autheress. Her letter was also fraught with the natural complainings of genius and disappointed aspirations—w'h in this exile state attend talents & virtue as the most beautiful body has it's shadow," Mary observed to Ann Sargent Gage the following year.[64]

Despite these "complainings," Mary Emerson clearly wanted to know more about Peabody and so agreed to begin a correspondence with her. It was, at best, a fitful exchange, as she observed tartly to her nephew Waldo: "Tell Miss Pea. she really coaxed me out of my silence and now neglects to notice my letter." By the end of the year, the exchange seems to have broken down. To Elizabeth Hoar she reported that Peabody "proposed a 'brisk correspondence,' & we have written two or three times—'tis best—& then let it rest—for in the lapse of months we lose sight of each other."[65]

But Peabody had not dropped out of Mary Emerson's life. In fact, the decade of the 1840s saw renewed and intense interaction between them, as well as the breakdown of their relationship for which Mary felt considerable regret. That came in the last years of the 1840s; earlier on Elizabeth and Mary were in close contact. When they were not, Mary Emerson was distressed: "What can be the *cause* of her silence perplexes me more than the silence pains," she wrote to Elizabeth Hoar and

Samuel Ripley in 1843. Elizabeth helped her with health issues and also hosted her in Waltham, where she and Horace Mann escorted Mary to a performance of *Hamlet* with the touring English actor William Charles Macready. "If you see EPP please say how very devoted to me was her & hers in attentions. Was glad to have H. Mann there all the time," Mary wrote to Lidian Emerson and Ruth Haskins Emerson in October 1844.[66]

Mary Emerson was likewise involved in Peabody's intellectual life. "Her change of views has interested me," she noted. What was particularly interesting was a series of twenty "letters" Elizabeth published in the *Christian Register* from September 1845 to February 1846, called "Letters to a Pole on Religion in America." Attempting a survey of Christian denominations in the United States, Peabody's analysis had its predicable aspects and its startling and original points. Ever her mother's daughter, she both celebrates and disparages her New England ancestors. "The Pilgrims came to New England for the express purpose of finding a sphere large enough to practise the Bible in; and as they held to no authorised interpretation of it, this was equivalent to a sphere for the development of an immortal spirit, whose exercises should not respect material good alone, but spiritual good in its highest sense. But they were men of short sight, and by no means understood the scope of their principle." Likewise predictable is her dismissal of the Roman Catholic Church as "the very decay of nature . . . the tomb of Christ."[67]

More interesting, however, is Peabody's structural analysis of ecclesiastical types. For her, religions in America form a triangle, whose apexes are the Baptists, Quakers, and Catholics. "The Baptists assert independency of Church and State. . . . The Catholics identify Church and State. The Quakers annihilate the State." Of these possibilities Peabody distinctly prefers the Baptist, which most readily reveals the spirit of Christ in the modern democratic state. Doubtless Mary Moody Emerson, who was closely following this series, found Peabody's dismissal of Calvinist theocracy irritating. Still, she kept reading. "How her letters increase in interest," she allowed to Elizabeth Hoar.[68]

In September 1845 Peabody and Christopher Cranch accompanied Mary to New York City. Mary wanted to visit her nephew William and to pay her respects at the tomb of her much loved nephew Charles. The older woman was grateful for the younger's "benevolent smiles—her visits on board the boat to look after me." But there was apparently some falling out in September—"I seem deceptive not to tell the whole truth & regret that I went to N.Y. as it has lessened your esteem & confidence"—made much worse by Mary's reading an opened letter written by Mary Mann and addressed to Elizabeth. No one in *her* family would read opened mail addressed to another, Peabody wrote her in October, and she could not imagine such a thing happening elsewhere. "*I* never had heard of the *rule* which you declared to me was universal in good society, viz, that letters left open on a table were to be read." In any event, Elizabeth went on, people invariably differ in their assessments of one another. "If I should tell *Mr. Alcott* that you read a letter in the above circumstances, *he* would consider it the evidence of a pure and exalted mind, which had entered into the region of the *Universal.* But if I were to tell *Mr. Mann* the same thing, *he* would tell me to take care of my purse—for a person who would do *that*—would break any commandment of the decalogue."[69]

Mary Emerson was briefly penitential for her social sin. Writing to Elizabeth in December, she recalled their happy times on the trip to New York, memories "like beautifull visions that are past & clouds are hovering at moments round them—and Mr. Manns supposed anathema 'to take care of her purse.' Yet why take time (so doubly inhanced) to name these things when my health predicts a termination to all ills owing to sin or weakness. . . . If I live till the beauties of summer I do depend on your promised visit," appealing both to her delicate health and their continued friendship to bridge any difficulties.[70]

That visit in 1846 and another the following year would, however, prove fatal to the friendship. Elizabeth agreed to visit Mary at Elm Vale, her farm in Waterford, Maine, in August. At first the visit went well. Peabody had brought "a large machine full of letters from the great & good & read them here & to Gages, whom she captivated & to Hannah," Mary Emerson wrote to Elizabeth Hoar, referring to Waterford friends and to her niece Hannah Haskins. "Miss P. busy in writing. I am glad of it as she must rely on herself for society," since she so much preferred solitude, she noted in another letter to Hoar.[71]

But soon enough that fragile equanimity broke down. Confused about whether Mary Emerson wanted Elizabeth to accompany Hannah Haskins on a walk or to keep her company, Elizabeth finally went out. "For sixteen years I have been trying to get to this place of mountains and lakes, and perhaps in my whole life may never see another mountain." It was, however, the wrong choice from her hostess's perspective, Peabody wrote to Frances Gage. "[S]he said to me today . . . in rather a forced way—'you are not to go upon the mountain *however long you may stay.*' If she had been thirty years younger I should certainly have asked her if she would tell me in what the principle that prompted this petty piece of tyranny differed from the principle of slaveholding."[72]

Then there was the affair of the spectacles. Someone—possibly Mrs. Houghton, wife of the local doctor, or possibly Peabody herself—had misplaced Mary's glasses, throwing her into "such wild excitement. One would have thought there had never been another pair of spectacles in the Universe." Elizabeth commanded the distraught Mary, "you *must* bear it till tomorrow night when another pair shall come from Portland." Mary Moody Emerson did not readily take orders from another, and snapped back that "she did not want my *advice*, but I think it recalled her a little to the inconsistency of such emotion about a circumstance, in one who talks so much of the composing influence of *solitude*." The next day Elizabeth paid for a new pair of glasses, which were to arrive in two days' time.[73]

Whether out of possessiveness for her niece Hannah, with whom Elizabeth was friendly, or from a critical sense of the deficiencies of Peabody's religious views, or some combination of factors, Mary Moody Emerson now found Peabody "frivolous, irreligious, and without love for her." To one like Mary Emerson who lived so much in solitude, Peabody's "swarm of intimates" seemed coarse and alien. "I always believed her without that earnest & delicacy dignity (w'h one of her Praisers possesses) & never trusted her with a secret or even to trade as Waldo said something of her extreme carelessness[.] As to her 'beneficence' the go between for subscriptions are many busy old maids. . . . That her smile & meddlesom kindness is certain & that she was born with good feelings w'h still live—but her trials & business have weakened the basis of virtue." Mary later grieved that her intemperate words caused a breach between her and the Gages, but she never changed her mind about Elizabeth Peabody, whom she called "a rediculous pet" whose "propensity to meddle & divide" had ruined the friendship with the Gages.[74]

For her part, Peabody still found much to admire in Mary Moody

Emerson. Even after the affair of the spectacles, she found the older woman

> an extraordinary creature [she wrote to Ann Gage]. I think I never received a greater impression of her genius:—the ploughshare of experience never seems to have broken the wild beauty of her character, which like a wild country of great natural sublimity of feature, retains its untamed rocks and woods and cataracts. . . . She is so original, and then I like mountains and valleys—cataracts and wild woods—in character as well as nature. I love her though she does stick hard things into all tender places, and I have a faculty to guard myself. I am surprised to think how little pain I felt. Nothing she said to me hurt my feelings—it merely stimulated my imagination.[75]

Still, Mary Emerson's version of Calvinism must have given Peabody pause in her own exploration of that once-hostile territory. Mary's strength of character seems to have sprung in part from the grandeur of her beliefs, but the rigor and discipline of those beliefs seem also to have led to a rigid and domineering personality, at least so Peabody thought. Mary Emerson was devoted to the *"creative power of God"* but seems to have missed "the redeeming power of Christ. How this last would shock her who has such a passionate love of *His Name*, and so fine and just an idea of the necessity of his redemption." What Mary lacked was a transformation of self: "It grieves my heart however to realize how entirely impossible it is for her—with all her genius and all the noble views and deep truths before her mind—to be serenely and beautifully *happy*. She has certainly missed that truth of Christianity which gives the power of selfgovernment and takes away the lust of power over others. . . ." Added to that was Mary Emerson's insistence on sabbath observances, what Peabody called "Jewish notions about Sunday, the minister, and spoken or stated prayers" that "bothered my feelings and ideas . . . it seemed conventional and to make a certain impression."[76]

Hungry as she was for a more experiential and intense spiritual life, Peabody found in Mary Moody Emerson's Calvinism not quite the answer she was looking for. Mary distrusted Elizabeth's "calvinist conversion," calling it "a Specie of extravagance." And Elizabeth found that Mary refused to understand how her questions had led her to reencounter the old orthodoxy: "I think she had a falser idea than when I arrived there."

Despite this disaster in 1846, Elizabeth Peabody made one more visit to Waterford in the following summer. Waldo Emerson was surprised to hear of this event. He had heard of last year's imbroglio from his aunt, who had written for information on Peabody's religion. "To day Mr Emerson called—exclaiming 'indeed!' when I said you had gone to Waterford—'I did not know she thought of going. I hope the change of air will do her good,'" Mrs. Peabody wrote to her daughter in late June 1847. This must have been a strained visit as well, prompting Mrs. Peabody to write, "I am sorry about Miss Emerson. The poor old lady has not many joys and her love for you was a real one, and I cannot but hope the breach made in it may be repaired. I trust you meet her more than half way, in consideration of years and loneliness. There may be truth in the idea that she is not quite sane." A few weeks later, she returned to this idea in another letter to Elizabeth, still in Maine: "Miss E, remember, is in her second childhood & probably this sensitiveness about being exclusively loved grows strong in Death."[77]

When Mary Moody Emerson grew "strong in Death" in 1863, Elizabeth Peabody wrote an obituary remarkable for its clarity, insight, and generosity.

> She had a great heart, although she was not tender, like most women; for it was her theory that what was noble and prevailing in human nature was to be brought out by provocation rather than by nursing. The womanly qualities of wife and mother were never developed in her. But she had great love. . . . She seemed hard— was hard—upon those who disappointed her . . ., and was not very tolerant of the concentrated mediocrity of people in general. . . . She commanded the homage of her illustrious nephews, to whose early nurture and education, she gave not merely the mental but the physical energies of the meridian of her life. . . . One of them has said of her, that in their youth, "her residence in the family was an element as great as Greece or Rome." Any woman of whom such a thing could be said by such a person, might feel it was worth while to have lived amid all the disturbing influence of this

"workday world," however much she might personally enjoy contemplation.[78]

Undoubtedly Elizabeth Peabody would want such a thing to be said of her.

⤳ CHARLES KRAITSIR had been the link between Elizabeth Peabody's interest in language and history and her brief "calvinistic conversion" in the mid-1840s, and Kraitsir was never far from her mind in the last years of the decade. He boarded with the Peabodys at West Street in 1847 and was always short of funds. In 1848 Kraitsir returned to Europe but by 1849 was back again in Boston. Peabody continued to find his ideas fascinating, writing out sometime in the late 1840s a draft of what would later be a chapter on Kraitsir's philology for *Aesthetic Papers*.

As was the case with Jones Very and briefly with William Greene, Kraitsir became something of a "cause" for Elizabeth. After his return from Europe, he was troubled by personal problems. He had been separated from his wife, who now lived in Philadelphia, but he wanted custody of their child. Elizabeth went down to Philadelphia to determine whether the mother was fit and found her to be a "non compos Caliban." Demanding that Mrs. Kraitsir return to Boston with their child and submit to care in a mental asylum, Kraitsir and Peabody were quickly embroiled in a nasty controversy with the wife's defenders, in the pages of the popular press in both cities.[79]

As part of her efforts to defend his reputation, Peabody drafted a letter to Charles Nagy, a Hungarian acquaintance of Kraitsir. Asking for a letter of reference for the philologist to be addressed to Rufus Choate, whom Kraitsir had retained for his defense, Peabody wrote that "you should not say you have been directly asked for this letter— but you can explain the writing of it by saying that you have learnt that Dr. Kraitsir's reputation has been most cruelly assailed in some Boston papers, which began by calling him a 'rabid monarchist,' a vagabond 'maitre de langue,' and & then proceeded to assail the purity of his private character. . . ." For her part, wrote Elizabeth, "my motive is to make him feel better—and more willing to remain amongst us."[80]

Peabody had left a copy of this letter with her mother at West Street, with instructions to get prominent people to co-sign. James Freeman

Clarke's response after reading it was so instructive that Mrs. Peabody wrote her daughter a long letter recounting Clarke's views. If Clarke had signed it, he told Mrs. Peabody, Kraitsir might well ask him what business he had meddling in his affairs. Even more, "Elizabeth runs the risque of really injuring the Dr by medelling [sic] in his affairs unasked, and calling down upon herself more censure than she has yet endured." "People will say—even the best and the wisest—" Mrs. Peabody went on, reporting Clarke's concerns, "'You see how it is, nothing will stop her—She has now plunged into a deeper gulph than ever.'" Finally, in her own voice, Mrs. Peabody added this guilt-inducing plea: "If you love us, if you feel that any deference is due to parental authority—any return due, for years of untiring love and devoted affections, be advised in this. . . . Farther efforts [on Kraitsir's behalf] will render our motives doubtful—both to him and to the world. Self respect demands of you now redoubled caution in all your intercourse with him."[81]

There is no evidence that Peabody ever sent her letter to Hungary. Kraitsir left Boston in 1851 and moved to New York City, where he spent his last years. Kraitsir was not the first nor the last man whose faltering career or unrecognized genius Peabody would attempt to up-lift. She seemed to have a genius of her own for such cases. Perhaps Peabody women inherited a capacity for rescuing their dimmer spouses, siblings, or colleagues.

The risk that Elizabeth took and that her mother warned her about was the old one of propriety, the limits to a single woman's actions and advocacies. James Freeman Clarke's phrasing of what people might say about her championing of Kraitsir—"She has now plunged into a deeper gulph than ever"—suggests that the Boston public already had some fixed notions about Elizabeth Peabody.

෨෨ As THE DECADE WORE DOWN, Elizabeth Peabody focused her enthusiasm on the work of another little-known figure. This was Josef Bem, a Polish general who had devised a system of teaching history by the use of chronological charts. Peabody first heard of this method through a Polish émigré named Joseph Podbielski, who had brought charts to the United States in 1845 and had boarded with the Peabodys at West Street. Because Podbielski could lecture only in French, Peabody recalled in 1882, "he brought the charts to me, and told the history of the origin of the method in Poland, and of the introduction of it between 1832 and 1840 into the higher schools of France by General Bem, and, as he told me, it was also introduced by Polish exiles into Oxford and Cambridge, England."[82]

At first Peabody was put off by the idea of teaching history through chronology, preferring to use narratives about each era's "leading actors, and their aims." Learning dates seemed such a waste of time. But her own experience in teaching had suggested that learning each nation's history required learning about its predecessors. There was simply no time to master all the necessary information. "But were I to keep school again I should use the Polish charts. . . . For I have found that it is possible for grammar-school children, certainly for the high-school class, to master the outlines of human history without any agonizing effort of memory."

Each chart represented twenty centuries through a grid of five squares across and four down. Each square is divided into ten decades, and each decade into years. By counting grids and squares, students can identify specific years. Overlaid on this grid system is a system of color and shape, "a different color being used for each nation; and the class of event is indicated by the part of the square in which it is represented. Thus the succession of striking events in a nation's history can be represented to the eye, and the synchronistic events of other national histories will be seen in relation without effort of recollection, for they mutually help to fix each other."

Peabody's crusade to have public schools adopt these charts occupied much of her time in the following decade. At the end of the 1840s, however, she was still mastering the system and was practicing on her nephew Julian. Years later Julian recalled that his aunt, "a very learned woman, and a great student of history, and teacher of it," attempted to teach him history "by the aid of huge, colored charts, done by my uncle Nat Peabody and hung on the walls of our sitting room." Using these, Aunt Lizzie "labored during some years to teach me all the leading dates of human history—the charts being designed according to a novel and ingenious plan to fix those facts in childish memory. But as a pupil I was always most inapt and grievous, in dates and in matters mathematical especially; so that I gave her inexhaustible patience many a sad hour."[83]

Despite Julian's academic deficiencies, Elizabeth was captivated by this system; and, adding her own charts on the common era centuries to

Podbielski's ancient history charts, she published *Blank Centuries accompanying the Manual of the Polish-American System of Chronology* under her own imprint in 1850. Revising Podbielski's charts required further research. In 1849 she wrote to Charles Folsom, then the librarian at the Boston Athenaeum, asking for permission to consult works on Chinese history. She reminded Folsom that she had been granted the right to withdraw books when she was preparing *Key to History, Part III, The Greeks,* and wondered whether she might have that privilege again. To sweeten her request, she even offered to donate a collection of Polish and French books, which had recently been sent to her by a Princess Czartorska, "who heard that I was going to publish a history of Poland." The Athenaeum accepted her donation, and she was allowed to visit and read in the library but apparently not permitted to withdraw books.[84]

ॐ PERHAPS BECAUSE Transcendentalism seemed so antithetical to institutional embodiment, or more likely because its principles were so unpopular or little understood, the print outlets for "The Newness" had shrunk to two by 1849. The demise of the *Dial* in 1844 and of the Fourierist journal *The Harbinger* in 1849 left only William Henry Channing's *The Spirit of the Age* and Theodore Parker's *The Massachusetts Quarterly Review.* Parker's journal very much reflected its editor's eclectic tastes, with articles ranging from political theory to natural history. Channing's, which began in July 1849, sought to continue the communitarian spirit of *The Harbinger.* It lasted only until April 1850.

In choosing this moment to begin a new liberal journal, her single-issue periodical *Aesthetic Papers* (1849), Elizabeth Peabody was perhaps unwise and incautious, but caution was often not one of her strong suits. Reform-minded people were being drawn in several directions by the end of the decade, including the growing women's movement, opposition to the Mexican War, the ominous sectional quarrel, the growing antislavery movement, to say nothing of continuing discussion and debate about communitarianism and other forms of social reform. Peabody herself had become deeply involved with several people and several movements simultaneously at the end of the 1840s—Kraitsir and the philosophy of language, Bem and the teaching of history, and her own brief but intense "calvinistic conversion."[85]

Peabody may have had all these competing claims in mind when she announced in the prospectus to her new journal, *Aesthetic Papers,* that "no person is asked to subscribe for more than one number in advance; but whoever is so far pleased with the current number as to desire another is requested to send an order to that effect to the Editor, who is also Publisher, No. 13, West-street, Boston. When a sufficient number of orders are given to pay for publication, including compensation to the authors, a new number will be printed."[86]

It would be difficult to do much advance planning for a journal with such an editorial policy. In late 1848 Peabody began telling people about the new journal and soliciting essays for inclusion. She had some trouble getting contributions, beginning with her own family. She pressed her brother-in-law Nathaniel Hawthorne for a contribution. Julian recalled that his father originally promised "Ethan Brand" but judged that story "too lurid for Miss Peabody's aestheticism," and so substituted "Main-street," a strange and disturbing social portrait of Salem.[87] From Emerson, Peabody extracted an essay on "War," delivered first as a lecture in Boston in 1838. In response to her inquiry, Henry David Thoreau wrote in April 1849, "I will send you the article in question [a lecture he had delivered in 1847] before the end of the week," and he added in a postscript, "I offer the paper to your *first* volume only."[88] This paper would turn out to be "Resistance to Civil Government," which later became known as "Civil Disobedience," one of Thoreau's most enduring works. Peabody herself contributed three essays, including the volume's introduction, and seven other contributors rounded out the volume. There was also a handful of poems by Peabody, Ellen Hooper, Thomas Wentworth Higginson, Louisa Higginson, and Ann Sargent Gage. Until virtually the last minute, Peabody was unsure about what to call the new journal; in a letter from February 1849 to Ann Sargent Gage, Peabody reported that "I have in the press a volume to be called *The Aesthetic Counsellor* or Magazine or something of that sort with choicest writers, & I am going to put in it those very beautiful monodies of *yours*—& I want to know if I shall call them *Monodies on Dr. L. Gage* or put them in with no name."[89] Eventually these went in as "Meditations of a Widow."

In her introductory essay, "The Word 'Aesthetic,'" Peabody distinguishes between the idiosyncratic element in art, championed in French criticism, and the German approach that emphasizes the universal and "disinterested" qualities in art. In its stress on idea rather than on taste and appetite, German criticism deserves the term "aesthetic," she argues.[90]

The majority of the essays follow and develop this broad approach to art and ideas. In "Criticism" Samuel Gray Ward maintains that although art is a personal product, it is rooted in natural genius that is universal in its appeal. In an essay privately circulated since 1821, Sampson Reed suggests in "Genius" that all authentic human expression springs from an inward divine spirit, which acts to unify what otherwise appears to be random and chaotic events. Samuel Perkins takes this concern for unity and universal standards into the political arena in his essay "Abuse of Representative Government." In a rather ill-tempered contribution, Perkins decries the degeneration of the system of representation from one in which legislators led and educated their constituencies into one in which elected officials mirrored the whims of the electorate.

Another set of essays develops Peabody's belief that the aesthetic sensibility is the result of a process of moral development. John Sullivan Dwight's essay "Music" makes heavy use of the notion of historical periods, drawn from Comte, and argues that music is a universal, mystic, religious, and emotional language. In "War" Emerson claims that in earlier cultures war was acceptable and functional but that in higher civilizations it has been supplanted by the "peace principle." Peabody's essay "Language" develops Kraitsir's notion that the common physical origin of speech shows the fundamental unity of all people. Parke Godwin proposes in his "Organization" that progress in all areas of life is marked by an increase in organization. Finally, in J. J. G. Wilkinson's "Correspondence" Swedenborgian doctrine is applied to the entire cosmos. All life is linked in sets of analogies, connecting truths of science with truths in philosophy.

Whereas these essays are predictable in their argument, the remaining essays in *Aesthetic Papers* are distinguished by their originality, complexity, and vigor of expression. Two of them, Hawthorne's "Main-street" and Thoreau's "Resistance to Civil Government," undermine the very assumptions of the periodical. Hawthorne's sketch is ostensibly a history of the social and moral progress of his native town, but that theme is challenged by a critic who ridicules the pasteboard, cut out figures who move across the stage, pulled by the author-"showman." The whole demonstration collapses when the wire breaks, suggesting the fragility of the notion of progress and subverting the optimistic theme of the entire journal.

Perhaps the most famous essay is Thoreau's "Resistance to Civil Government." In striking contrast to Parke Godwin's essay celebrating organization, Thoreau disdains government and civil authority, preferring the moral majority of one. In light of the essay's omnipresence in American literary culture, it is ironic that critic Thomas W. Parsons should write to James Russell Lowell that "I think that Mr. Thoreau has got into better company than he deserves and doubt if there is much in him."[91]

Peabody's "The Dorian Measure, with a Modern Application," is her best contribution here, and her strongest essay since "Christ's Idea of Society." Anticipating some of the ideas that she would develop in the next decade in essays like "Egotheism the Atheism of Today" and "The Philosophy of History in the Education of Republican Men and Women," Peabody saw in an admirable society like that of the Dorians (Spartans) a powerful model for contemporary America. Following the reconstruction of that culture in the work of Karl Otfried Müller, Peabody saw in them a balance of self and society, under the guidance of a monotheistic religion, that of the worship of Apollo. Such a community avoided the pitfalls of self-worship, which she would explore in "Egotheism" and "Philosophy of History," and those of self-annihilation, which she explored in "Fourierism." Since part of the recovery of the spirit of the ancient Greeks lay in an appreciation of their training of the whole self, in "The Dorian Measure" she calls for instruction in gymnastics, dance, music, and art in public schools as part of the education of the whole person. As for cost, she writes, "it is plain that, if we can spend a hundred millions of dollars in a year for so questionable a purpose as the late war of Mexico, we have resources on which we might draw for public education." Even more, she calls for an American society that would be as governed by the spirit of Christ as Sparta was by that of Apollo. The possibilities were all there: "Never before the birth of our political constitution, which was not made by men, but grew up from the instincts of Christian men who had brooked no control of their relations with God, was there any nation on earth, within which the life eternal could unfold its proportions."[92]

A handful of serious essays and some lugubrious poems attracted enough readers to cover John Wilson's printing costs of $163.20 for 750 copies, but not enough expressed interest for a second issue.[93] Perhaps the times were too distracting for such intense writing, or perhaps the ideas and practices generated in New England needed to find a larger and more diverse audience. Finding and educating that audience would be Peabody's task in the next decade.

7

"Inconceivable Power, Wisdom, and Love"

❧

IN THE FIRST FOUR DECADES of Elizabeth Peabody's life, her vocational and intellectual passions intersected with the life of her family. Elizabeth and her sister Mary kept school together in the 1820s and 1830s; Sophia was one of Elizabeth's first students and contributed artwork to Elizabeth's historical *Keys.* Mother Peabody was the most obvious link between family and vocation, for it was from her model that Elizabeth drew the outlines of the life of an intellectual woman. In the early 1840s, any remaining barrier between the life of the family and the life of the mind broke down. At West Street, domestic life upstairs blended fluidly with the lending library; the bookshop and counter with its art supplies and homeopathic medicines; and the parlor, which became, for a few years, a Transcendentalist salon.

In the last half of the 1840s and throughout the following decade, Elizabeth Peabody's life changed perceptibly, and in no way more noticeable than in this connection between work and family. She would remain devoted to education, in the broadest sense. But the close ties that had linked classroom, Unitarian parents, and liberal religious and educational philosophy with family concerns had begun to loosen. Peabody's involvement in the Temple School controversy and her affiliation with Margaret Fuller, Brook Farm, and the West Street bookshop itself damaged her reputation among parents seeking private education for their children. As the members of the interwoven circle of liberal reformers and avant-garde thinkers scattered, Peabody's own career shifted toward more national, if also more diffuse, causes. She continued her vigorous crusade for Josef Bem's chronological charts. She embraced the causes of Hungarian émigrés and of dissenters from the slavocracy of the South. She tried to make a living from her pen, as she said, and wrote several long essays, though none as powerful as her pieces on Brook Farm for *The Dial.* Until she discovered the kindergarten in the 1860s, nothing replaced the intellectual intimacy of the Transcendentalists.

Peabody's own family was likewise changing. Her parents were aging and sickening, and both would die in the 1850s. Her sisters, who had both married in the 1840s, were now moving away from the Boston area, the Hawthornes first to western Massachusetts and then to England, and the Manns to Yellow Springs, Ohio. As always, Nat's vocational struggles were unrelenting. Peabody tried hard to retain a place in her attenuated family, caring for her parents, writing long, prying, and moralistic letters to her sisters about child-rearing. Family and career now seemed utterly at odds. Not until Mary and Elizabeth were thrown back together, after the death of Horace Mann, would Peabody rediscover the issue that was both intimately domestic and vocationally fulfilling: early childhood education. Until then, she wandered in a wilderness of causes and issues, leaving in her wake a growing reputation as a warm-hearted, intrusive, scattered eccentric, in equal parts careless of her personal appearance and devoted to the well-being of others.

ᔪ BOUND VOLUMES of the blank charts still exist in various library collections, but Peabody's original Bem charts must have been much larger than even folio size. She would put these down on the floor, she wrote later, and invite her listeners to do the same to study the relationships among dates and events. This must have been quite a scene: Peabody, now "just as fat and solid and good humored as she can be," according to Mary, on the floor with various distinguished educators including Barnas Sears, George B. Emerson, and Thomas Wentworth Higginson.[1]

As public, tax-supported schools spread throughout the Northeast and Midwest in the 1850s, Peabody discerned a new field in which she could work. These schools, and the state teachers' colleges that provided their faculties, aimed at systematized and bureaucratized education, with organized curricula, graded levels, and established standards. In this new regulated environment, textbooks were crucial, together with methods that could reach large numbers of students at the same time. Bem's charts provided both text and method. Although some of the charts she carried as examples were printed in color and included in books like *Blank Centuries* and *Chronological History of the United States*, most had to be drawn and colored by hand, that is, by Elizabeth's hand. "Just now I am *aching* from the fatigue of *making Charts* for the Schools who will take the book," she wrote to her friends the Wards in September 1850. "—Every school must have a mural chart—& there is but one way of making them (until they can be made by ten thousands) & that is by stencilling. . . . I can do one a day. But I must sell them cheap. . . . To day I worked *15 hours*—only sitting down to take my meals—& so I have done all week—so much fatigue stupifies one—but as soon as it is adopted in a few towns I shall be able to hire somebody to do this drudgery for me."[2]

In the early and middle 1850s, Peabody crisscrossed the northern and central United States, urging the adoption of the charts. She began with her own impressive network of contacts, including Horace Mann's sister Rebecca Pennell, now women's principal at the State Normal School in West Newton, and spread outward. Following the railroad lines, she traveled west in Massachusetts to Worcester, Northampton, up to Brattleboro in Vermont, back down to Pittsfield, Lenox, Lee, and Great Barrington, then across the Hudson River into New York to Albany, Syracuse, Rochester, and Buffalo, and then on to Detroit. She swung back east and south to Cleveland, Columbus, Cincinnati, Louisville, Marietta, Pittsburgh, Baltimore, and Washington. She ventured to Richmond, then back up the coast to Wilmington, Philadelphia, Newark, New York, and Providence. Everywhere in this exhausting itinerary, she spoke to schoolteachers, school boards, leaders of normal schools, college presidents, and journalists.

Few of Peabody's letters from this period of intense travel still survive, if in fact they were written at all. Other western travelers have provided vivid accounts of the hardship of public transportation and western roads, hotels and inns, and the sometimes dubious hospitality of private homes. Still, some records survive. The Reverend F. A.

Adams of Orange, New Jersey, wrote to Peabody that "in your chart facts are, as it were, nailed to their places, and its simple, definite and rigorous statements, afford the best possible opportunity of obtaining an ineffaceable impression of historic dates." A Brooklyn teacher observed that "I have never known a system which placed the events of the history of all nations before the mind with so much clearness, so little confusion, and so much permanency; it will hardly be possible to efface them." Eliphalet Nott, president of Union College in Schenectady, New York, and his faculty were likewise much interested in the charts.[3]

For Peabody herself, the charts were crucial not simply for the teaching of events and their sequence, to show students that Herodotus was a contemporary of Nehemiah, as she once said. Far beyond that, the charts revealed the providential and unfolding nature of history, the divine hand at work amidst the welter of events.

> There is a peculiar wisdom to be derived from the outlines of history [she wrote to an official of the State Normal School in Albany], considered in discrimination from the details, and compared. Details show the activity of the finite mind, and the action of second causes; outlines mark the decisions of the Divine mind interpreting events; and the workings of the Divine will controlling them; and it is the part of the teacher to suggest to the pupil the terms of this antithesis, which he is able to do by means of this chart. . . . The lesson to be learned is, how to employ one's energy, whether in antognizing or cooperating with Providence. The will of God will certainly always be brought about, in the long run, but the weal and woe of nations depend upon whether it is brought by French revolutions, or American revolutions; by the growth or destruction of the instruments.[4]

Bem's charts provided Peabody with yet another compelling argument for unity, plan, purpose in history, a belief all the more fiercely held in the face of her life's disunities and disappointments. History was the key to national survival, she pointed out to Rawlins Pickman: "Our people *need* to be instructed by *History*, and to learn that the free will of man has a scope that is rounded in by the Eternal Laws of God after all—& this instruction must be given in the public schools & effectively. Our young republicans must be made as familiar with the fields of Time . . .

as they have been made the last forty years with the surface of the earth of [sic] geographical maps."[5]

Peabody's essay "The Dorian Measure" and her introductions to her several texts based on Bem's charts cast light on the particular nature of Peabody's "providential" history. Like many other historians and theorists in the century preceding, Peabody believed history was a linear unfolding of a singular though complex divine intention. One read the past as a vast code, God's language of chronology. Elizabeth had learned this typological way of interpreting history from her mother, who "loved to compare [the people of Israel] with the Pilgrim bands, who left the despotisms of Europe to plant a nation of freemen, by which all the nations of the earth were to be finally blessed. Born and brought up in the midst of a family all of whom devoted all their means to their country, in its birth struggle, she looked upon national life as God's education of mankind, and it was the pattern on which she modelled the education of every citizen."[6]

But what exactly was being unfolded, being articulated in the divine tongue? For evangelical Christian providentialists and millennialists like Jonathan Edwards, William Miller, or Charles G. Finney, it was the kingdom of God on earth foretold in scripture, ushered in by Christ's return and the final apocalypse. Peabody read history a different way: for her its message was the gradual improvement of the political and religious climate in which the perfected individual self, of which Christ was the avatar, emerges in radiant wholeness. For her, American exceptionalism, Romantic perfectionism, and Christian language (interpreted in her own distinctive way) blend in a unique vision of past and future.

Meanwhile, Peabody's parents and sisters contributed their own share of encouragement and caring for Elizabeth. Mrs. Peabody followed her daughter's travels with concern. "This vast body of snow with which the earth is covered," she wrote in January 1852, "will make the travelling hazardous for a long time. You must keep us informed as well as you can, how you get along, we shall think much about you, alone in the midst of a multitude—no protection but your own resolution and dependent on the good feelings of our citizens for the many comforts needed in such rapid changes from place to place." She peppered Elizabeth with questions about her plans: "Do you mean to go to Cincinnati before you return in June. . . ? Shall you be able to command cash enough to liquidate your most pressing debts? . . . I do not know anything about this journey to Richmond. Do you know any body there, or are you going among entire strangers? By whom are you invited and with whom will you reside?"[7]

Worried as they were about their migratory daughter, the elder Peabodys also had reason to be concerned about the house on West Street, a concern they shared with Nat and Mary. In spring 1851 the family retained Caroline Hinckley, from Hallowell, Maine, to care for the house in return for room there. Her duties, Elizabeth noted in a letter to Caroline's brother Eugene, involved "tak[ing] care of my bookroom, sweeping & dusting it in the morning, & seeing to the selling—letting—& dispensing of medicines when my brother was not there between 1/2 past 5 P.M. & 9 A.M." Nat needed somebody who was particularly neat and methodical, to match his own very precise manner, and Elizabeth wanted someone whose manner would not remind Nat of the radical contents of some of the books and periodicals in the shop and lending library. "He and I are somewhat at issues about transcendentalism, and *transcendentalism* will have to bear the blame of any short comings you may show," she wrote Caroline, "& so I have *that* interest that you should not leave on him the impression of incapacity—I am myself rather jealous in that score—for I think that transcendentalism fosters certain weaknesses unless in very remarkable minds—It has made *Waldo Emerson practical* & efficient—but it seems to have confounded & deranged the minds of a great many of those who count themselves his disciples."

"Incapacity" was, however, exactly what the Peabodys discerned in Caroline Hinckley. She left the shop at odd hours, sat up all night or dozed with a fire lit, which terrified Mrs. Peabody and Mrs. Poole, who lived in the garret, and ate badly. All that behavior offended the genteel Peabodys and threatened to drive customers away. From somewhere on her Bem tours, Elizabeth wrote Caroline to "give you a little advice" about appearing more efficient and organized, while Mary Mann wrote Eugene Hinckley to complain about her odd hours and behavior. In her own defense, Caroline told her brother that the Peabodys praised her to her face, noting that Nat said "I had let more books from the Library than his mother *ever* had in the same time when she tended" but that they criticized her behind her back, filled as they were with "utter selfishness and avarice." By the end of summer 1851, the conflict had sunk to mean-spiritedness and name-calling. On August 30 Elizabeth complained to Eugene that Caroline would not speak to her in the shop, whereas Caroline scrawled on that letter, "what misrepresentation this wicked letter contains! It is more base than her undisguised abuse to me. It is adapted to deceive even the very elect."[8]

While this crisis at West Street involved the Peabody children, two other crises drew the parents into their daughter's life more directly. They were deeply involved in the business end of Elizabeth's promotion of Bem's charts, arranging for color lithography, stocking boxes of paints, and tracking shipments and distribution. In January 1852 Mrs. Peabody wrote Elizabeth that Henry Codman, the owner of the West Street house, had decided to convert the property into more profitable shops. Nat, who had been selling homeopathic medicines at the house, would have to find another venue. Elizabeth, in whose name the property had been rented, owed Codman some back rent, adding that much to her growing debts for the printing of *Blank Centuries*.[9]

Anguishing about what would make Codman look more favorably upon the family, Mrs. Peabody wrote Elizabeth that she really had to clean up all the boxes of unsold books that had accumulated in the house. The treasures listed in her letter are enough to stagger the lover of nineteenth-century literature and culture:

> I have thought that those innumerable packages of Dials & periodicals might be boxed up and stored away in the attic or somewhere, for of them you will not probably make any sales for years to come, if ever. You can advertize that you have Nos. of the Dial, if wanted—so also your Aesthetic Papers. . . . If I were you I would dispose of St. Augustine—the ideal man—and Hawthorne's little books, at even what it would cost to bind them. . . ., What shall be done with the Gentle boys, already eaten by mice and otherways damaged? I should say, give them to the trunk makers. They will make beautiful linings. They are only encumbering us now.

Eventually Codman relented and allowed the Peabodys to stay. Nat recalled that he was given the lease to the house in 1851, a memory at odds with Mrs. Peabody's letter from January 1852. In any event he continued on at the house, selling homeopathic medicines, well into the 1850s.[10]

The second crisis reported by the Peabody parents had to do with the unexpected publication of "Chronological Atlas of bl[ank] Centuries with information how to learn history in the shortest time according to Polish Menemonics [sic]," by one Poblielski. Although the spelling differs, this is apparently the same as Joseph Podbielski, the Polish émigré from whom Elizabeth learned the system of charts. Mrs. Peabody immediately saw the threat to Elizabeth's livelihood: "Is he playing the villain and snatching from you the chance of realizing the fruit of your arduous labours?" Podbielski even had the effrontery to inscribe the pamphlet "to Miss E. P. Peabody from her respectful friend T [probably a misreading for J] Poblielski."[11]

Mrs. Peabody need not have worried. Neither Elizabeth nor her rival stood to profit much from Bem's charts. Even so, after the publication of the *Polish-American System of Chronology* in 1850, she began to work on a textbook history of the United States for use with Bem's charts. She had put off publication of this work for a few years in the early 1850s but quickly regretted that decision. School districts in Richmond and Schenectady that had been anticipating her text were obliged to choose its rival, Samuel Goodrich's *History of the United States*. Peabody's friend Eliza Clapp called Goodrich's text "the driest reading I ever looked at," but she warned Elizabeth to be "strenuously accurate about your dates & such minor things, because it is upon such defects that the critics will be most likely to fall upon you."[12]

In May 1856 Elizabeth signed a contract with the New York publisher Sheldon Blakeman to publish *Chronological History of the United States Arranged with Plates on Bem's Principle*. American history is rooted in all that has gone before, she wrote in the introduction; God's will and the course of Progress are the engines that drive republicanism as it emerges from the Greek city-states and the Swiss and Dutch republics to its present glory in America. Bem's charts are the perfect means of demonstrating this progress: a "chronological outline of the chain of events may certainly be impressed on the mind, by means of that natural memorizer, *the sense of sight, addressed by these colored symbols.* . . ." Divided into ten rows of ten squares each, the charts were to be colored in to mark defeats, victories, foundings of states, falls of states, births and deaths of remarkable people, and individual deeds. For her narrative, Peabody closely follows Bancroft's *History of the United States*, Irving's *History of the Conquest of Florida*, Gayarre's *Lectures on the Romance of the History of Louisiana*, and Hakluyt's *Voyages*.[13]

For all her labors, Bem's charts never caught on. The system required charts and murals for teachers, blank workbooks filled with tiny, Mondrian-like grids for each pupil, and boxes of paints, all often beyond the means of hard-pressed school districts. Compared with the vivid illustrations and bindings in children's books published by McLoughlin and other presses in the 1850s, Peabody's texts and accompanying blank "centuries" must have appeared baffling and abstract to young readers and adult teachers alike.

Except for a fond memory of the historian Hannah Adams, whom she had once read and taught, Mrs. Peabody had nothing much to contribute to her daughter's thinking about chronology as a key to the divine plan. In fact, Mrs. Peabody's health declined rapidly in the early 1850s. Now in her mid-seventies, she was subject to frequent colds and debilitating lethargy. In early 1851 she had an attack of flu, and then another a year later, both of which left her weakened and with a persistent cough.[14]

Elizabeth was so alarmed at her mother's decline that she made the momentous decision to close the bookshop at West Street in April 1851 and move her parents out to West Newton to live with Mary and her sons, who were renting a house there while Horace Mann was serving in Congress. Sophia agreed with the decision, playing on Elizabeth's sense of guilt for being away so much with Bem's charts and leaving the shop to her mother's care:

> Your plan about West St. house seems very wise—I think if Mother is in the country—& free from the awful weight of that rent & the responsibility of the Book room—that she may revive for a long time—that city life has been a terrible drag upon her powers—& her anxious thoughts the worst possible thing for her health—I think too that your persecutions & sufferings took years out of her that winter. If you were pale & sad, she palpitated & was faint—I saw it when I was there—and she has missed you painfully this winter . . . oh do not leave her till she is in Mary's house.[15]

Her husband grumbled that all this furor about Mrs. Peabody's health was affecting Sophia's pregnancy, now in its seventh month. Hawthorne wrote to Elizabeth that "the intelligence contained in your letter, received yesterday, caused some symptoms that alarmed me, in Sophia's present condition. They have passed off, however, and I hope will not reappear. It appears to me that it would be most unsafe to agitate her with any further alarm, or vicissitude of feeling, as to your mother's health. . . . I trust, therefore, that your future advices will be as cheerful as the facts of the case may anywise admit, and that there may be no reference to dangers past and left behind."[16]

Mrs. Peabody, who understood the "facts of the case" much better than did Nathaniel Hawthorne, felt her life slipping away. In November she wrote out an "IMPORTANT MEMORANDUM" on a small piece of paper, enclosed in an envelope with a sprig of arbor vitae to preserve it.

> I am improving in health but still very weak and exercised with constant pain. Death may finish my earthly trials early and without giving me time for directions. Relative to my worthless body I have but one injunction to give respecting it. Be sure to let me be examined before I am buried. I wish to have it known of what disease I have suffered so long. I wish more than all to avoid the danger of being buried alive [underscored twice], a fate most horrible to think of. Excepting this desire of a post mortem examination I am perfectly indifferent about the disposal of my remains. In the bosom of my God I trust to find all that the heart can desire. In Him is my trust. Elizabeth Peabody.[17]

As their mother's life faded, Elizabeth and Mary were pressed into duty as her nurses. Mary was often preoccupied in caring for her own children, so much of the responsibility fell to Elizabeth. A bit of resentment toward the youngest, absent sister comes through in this line written to Sophia, now living with Nathaniel and their children in Lenox: "When Mr. Mann is at home, & the children are well—about once a week—Mary will come in & take my place & I shall get rest from care for a night." Mrs. Peabody died on January 11, 1853. It had been an eighteen-hour struggle, Elizabeth reported, but then "her life went out into the free spaces, and here she lies, for I am sitting by her bedside, this first night. Mary has gone home; father has gone to bed. We are all at peace—peace—peace."[18]

With her sisters married and now with the death of their mother, Elizabeth Peabody felt her female-centered family shrink perceptibly.

"Anna has told you of the close of my dear mother's life," she wrote Samuel Gray Ward, "& how I am left rather mournfully in freedom to do nothing but business—which I shall do without the burden on my heart that has weighed it down the last two years—when my mother had the pain without the peace of death."[19]

Mrs. Peabody's life had illustrated both the successes and the limitations of educated women in the early and mid-nineteenth century. She had caught the wave of female academies in the late 1700s and had ridden it into the private school phenomenon early in the 1800s. Her mastery of languages, belles-lettres, and history influenced her daughter's distinctly "humanistic" bent. But Mrs. Peabody deferred her intellectual interests and ambitions to those of her husband, who was, it turned out, much less ambitious. Her mental edge dulled under the burden of housekeeping and child-rearing, and her vigorous Enlightenment sensibility turned into a prosy evangelical moralism toward the end of her life.

Like her mother, Elizabeth Peabody sought inclusion—in circles of educators and reformers, in publications, in institutional life. The two Elizabeths worked vigorously to bring women into the public cultural life of their eras, to bring women's sensibilities to bear on intellectual issues. Margaret Fuller, who died in 1850, took a much more critical stance toward intellectual institutions, working skeptically and ironically along their margins. Always the educator and mediator, Peabody could never translate her personal eccentricity into an emblem of intellectual independence, as Fuller did. Still, she was shocked by Fuller's death but was glad, as she wrote Sam and Anna Ward, that "neither knew another died—till *all three*—met to part no more—above—& beyond!"[20]

Through the rest of 1850 (Fuller had drowned July 19 in a shipwreck off Fire Island, New York, while returning from Italy with her new husband and son) and 1851, Emerson, James Freeman Clarke, and William Henry Channing collected fragments from Fuller's journals and letters, and from her published work, together with the recollections of others. Emerson was the guiding light for this effort, since Fuller's use of language was so much like his own—pungent, original, intense, unexpected—and so unlike, it must be said, Elizabeth Peabody's, who seemed increasingly prone to the verbal or emotional cliché, as in that letter to the Wards.

Peabody's logorrhea amused and exasperated Emerson. So did her enthusiasm for the Fuller project. "E.P.P. ransacks her memory for anecdotes of Margaret's youth, her self devotion, her disappointments which she tells with fervency, but I find myself always putting the previous question," Emerson confided in his journal. "These things have no value, unless they lead somewhere. If a Burns, if a DeStael, if an artist is the result, our attention is preengaged; but quantities of rectitude, mountains of merit, chaos of ruins, are of no account without results—tis all mere nightmare; false instincts; wasted lives."[21] Despite this put-down, Peabody did after all contribute both anecdote and analysis to *Memoirs of Margaret Fuller Ossoli*, providing the unforgettable scenes of Fuller's Conversations at West Street.

༺༻ THINGS WERE definitely loosening, slackening, slowing down. Instead of the constant cross-reference of people and causes in the 1830s and 1840s, now in the early and middle 1850s, Peabody turned from one cause to the next, each worthy, none sustaining her interest for very long. She involved herself with the fate of European political exiles, fleeing the consequences of the failure of the revolutions of 1848. George Haven Putnam recalled seeing "successive groups of refugees" camped out in tents in Elizabeth's and Mary's backyard in Cambridge in the late 1860s. But her concern had begun much earlier, as hunted men and women wanted by imperial rulers scattered across Europe and out to the United States. One such group were the sisters of Hungarian revolutionary Louis Kossuth. Emilie Kossuth, wife of a Polish nobleman named Zulawski, fled both the wrath of the Austrians and that of her husband, whom she had divorced. Peabody worked hard to interest American liberals like Samuel Gridley Howe and Gerrit Smith in the purchase for Emilie and her children of a fruit farm in New Jersey, which would provide Antioch College with vegetables. Peabody likewise championed the memory of another sister, Susanne Kossuth Meszlenyi. She had been imprisoned twice for her liberal connections, despite her heroic efforts at opening hospitals for all soldiers injured in the revolution. She died of tuberculosis in 1854. In her pamphlet biography of Susanne, "Memorial of Madame Susanne Kossuth Meszlenyi," published in December 1856, Peabody calls her readers to greater involvement in the cause of political exiles. "[God] pours upon our shores the various victims of the Old-World despotisms, that they may plead with our hearts, which, by all their humanity, are interlinked, and must suffer, with other men. . . . For Americans to realize their relations and duty to the exiles for liberty is not only of vast importance to their own culture of intellect and heart, not only important to all the exiles, who will, if neglected, die by the slow torture of broken-heartedness, but it is important to the Liberal party of Europe, which is the vanguard in the march of humanity."[22]

So energized was Peabody with the situation of European liberal revolution that she cobbled together extracts from histories of central Europe into a volume called *Crimes of the House of Austria.* Because the first edition was "mutilated," she wrote to E. A. Duyckinck, she required a second edition. Current events like these revolutions require knowledge of history to understand them fully, she went on, and methods of teaching history like Bem's charts would help immensely. Peabody would continue to follow the cause of exiles closely and sympathetically, but references to the Kossuth sisters seem to vanish from the record by the end of the decade.[23]

Like Emilie Kossuth, Delia Bacon flashed across Elizabeth Peabody's sky in the 1850s and was gone by the decade's end. Bacon arrived in Boston in November 1850, recovering from a public scandal in New Haven, in which her fiancé Alexander McWhorter had been accused before an ecclesiastical court of violating his promise of marriage. McWhorter had been narrowly acquitted, but not before Catharine Beecher had picked up the story and written a highly dramatized account, *Truth Stranger Than Fiction*, which made Bacon's story into public property.[24]

Peabody became one of Bacon's most enthusiastic supporters, along with Eliza Rotch Farrar and Caroline Dall. They helped fill Boston's Cochituate Hall for Bacon's lecture series on history in the winter of 1850–51. Much like Elizabeth Peabody, Delia Bacon argued that history was an integrated and harmonious whole, each age contributing to the next in the grand unfolding of divine destiny. And like Peabody, Bacon believed that linguistics demonstrated the fundamental unity of all humanity. Despite Bacon's anxieties about speaking before highly educated and critical Bostonians, her lectures were a success, with many of her more liberal listeners finding in Bacon's poise and intellect a striking reminder of Margaret Fuller.

In the early 1850s, Bacon combined these public appearances (and another lecture series in New York City in 1852–53) with a growing interest in Shakespearean studies. To a group of Boston and Cambridge women who constituted an informal class for her historical ideas, Bacon apparently broached her belief that a group of Elizabethans led by Francis Bacon had really written the plays ascribed to "William Shakespeare." Although most of the women found this idea outrageous, Elizabeth Peabody found it perfectly plausible. "I entered into her investigation &c with a great deal of interest; & even pointed out to her some coincidences & made some suggestions that *helped* her," Peabody wrote later to Bacon's brother Leonard. "But although the whole affair was under a solemn promise on my part that I would never anticipate her, by even suggesting the discovery, but allow to her the whole glory of this remarkable piece of historical criticism. . . . Yet I saw that it worried her to see how completely I did get possession of her idea."[25]

Although her family and many of her friends, particularly Eliza Farrar, thought it a bad idea, Bacon went to England in 1853 to pursue her theory about the plays. In 1856 she managed to interest Hawthorne in her interpretation. Hawthorne promised to see what he could do in securing a publisher for Bacon's manuscript. In February 1857 Sophia wrote Elizabeth that "Miss Bacon's book is in course of publication & we have loose folds of it to read. She is very involved in her style—covert & rambling so that it is difficult to keep the thread. She drives six in hand; but it is to me profoundly interesting as all deep philosophical questions always are." Two months later Bacon's *The Philosophy of the Plays of Shakespeare Unfolded* appeared, to considerable bad press. Hawthorne too came in for some criticism for his perceived support for her ideas, but "Mr. Hawthorne does not at all agree with her theory," Sophia explained, "but he thinks her book very remarkable & a splendid criticism. I have been deeply impressed with her internal evidence, but I am by no means a convert yet."[26]

Exhausted and mentally disturbed, Bacon returned to Connecticut and died in September 1859. A month later Peabody wrote her brother to introduce herself, explain her connection to Delia, and make a request. "Now I think that if I could have all her papers—I might ferret out the whole matter with the hints she gave me, and in the course of time—& bring it out at last in an intelligible manner—giving her the whole credit.—Perhaps in a kind of *memorial* of her *as a scholar.*" But Leonard Bacon put her off; he had long been suspicious of his sister's enthusiasms, and would likely be equally suspicious of someone like Peabody who shared them. Just as likely, he was probably offended by her intrusion into the family's grief, saying that he could not share Delia's papers with anyone without permission of the entire family, a process that would take some time.[27]

The plight of the Kossuth sisters, the claims of Delia Bacon, the case of Mattie Griffith, a white antislavery Southerner whose situation interested Peabody in the mid-1850s—these causes symbolized Peabody's sympathy with European liberals, her deep interest in historical scholarship, her late-blooming loyalty to antislavery. To her second cousin George Putnam, such crusades scattered Elizabeth's energies and had the air of noble but hopeless lost causes. "Elizabeth's judgment was often at fault, but her integrity of purpose, her absolute unselfishness, her readiness for sacrifice of time and money . . . made her a distinctive personality," he wrote in his memoirs.[28] But from another perspective, Peabody was choosing to champion women who found themselves at the margins of acceptable behavior or beliefs, who were trying to carve out places in social or intellectual life on their own. Elizabeth could not help but recognize her own fate in their efforts.

Similarly, Peabody's involvement with spiritualism in the 1850s reveals something of her inner life. She had long been interested in "magnetism," a kind of holistic healing practiced by, among others, her friend Cornelia Park. Peabody recommended that Mary Moody Emerson be magnetized for her various ailments; one can imagine Mary Emerson snorting with amusement and rage at yet another one of "Miss Pea"'s hopelessly airy causes. But spiritualism, which involved much more than medical experiments, was embraced by far more people than the New England avant-garde.

Christianity has always taught that life does not end with the death of the body but that some immaterial essence of the self survives. For most Christians it has been enough to imagine that souls live on in a heavenly afterlife or else suffer torment in an eternal hell. But beginning in the 1840s and continuing into our own time, many have professed the ability to contact these spirits. In the nineteenth century, the most notorious case of such mediums was that of the Fox sisters of Hydesville, New York, whose claim to commune with the dead was amplified by the showmanship of P. T. Barnum. In the wake of the Foxes, who were later shown up to be adept not at interpreting the rappings of spirits but only at cracking their knuckles, came hundreds of mediums, magicians, and other dabblers in the occult.[29]

To people experiencing loss and change, spiritualism made a power-

ful appeal. This situation would be particularly true in the years immediately following the slaughter of the Civil War. Even before the war,
adepts like the Foxes appealed to large numbers of people anxious about
the possibilities of spiritual reality in a materialist age of railroads and
factories. From Channing and certainly through her own reading and
thought, Peabody understood humans to be spiritual beings, dwelling
in a cosmos that is a living symbol of its immaterial origin and meaning.
From Emerson and Very, and again through her own experience, she
recognized the power to apprehend that meaning directly and intuitively. Perhaps from her brief encounter with Calvinism in the mid-
1840s, Peabody pondered the continued existence of spirits in a life
after death, a literal afterlife rather than the metaphoric one taught by
many Unitarian clergy.

In the early 1850s, Peabody attended several séances in Boston, apparently met the Fox sisters, and encouraged her family to get involved.
Mrs. Peabody was doubtful, feeling that what Elizabeth needed was
more attention to her physical being, not to her spiritual essence. But
when Elizabeth suggested that her niece Una might make a perfect
medium, Mrs. Peabody was horrified and tried to warn Elizabeth off
this course. "Nothing astonished me more, relative to the spirits than
Una Hawthorne's being mentioned. Did Katy Fox ever hear about her
at all, especially about the peculiarities of her character and organization? I hope the suggestion of her becoming a medium will never be
mentioned to Sophia. She may not believe—and yet the idea will not
fail to give much anxiety, which she may as well be spared till time has
proved beyond all controversy the fact, that the Spirits of Departed
friends are always with us."[30]

Unfortunately for good family relations, Elizabeth did not take her
mother's advice, and proceeded to ask the Hawthornes if they would
consider letting Una be a vehicle for communicating with the dead.
"Mr. Hawthorne says he <u>never</u> [underlined five times] will consent to
Una's being made a medium of communication, & that he will defy all
Hell rather, so that he will have to disprove the testimony of the spirits,
if it comes to that. He says he cannot let you come here [Lenox] with
Rappers in train—for he thinks it would injure Una—physically and
spiritually to be subjected to such influence. Thus he bids me say—."
Although this is about as firm a "no" as one can imagine, Peabody could
not quite give up the idea. "Should it ever come of itself," she blandly

wrote her sister the following month, "the purity of the medium would be a fine chance to take an observation, and I should treat it to Una as if it were not at all *strange*—only rather curious. Then it will not agitate her." The emotional intensity of Hawthorne's portrayals of mesmerism and spiritualism in *The Blithedale Romance* originates in part from this episode, in which his sister-in-law, for her own reasons, sought to bring his little daughter into the carnivalesque atmosphere of mediums and rappers.[31]

Although her family would have nothing to do with spiritualism, Peabody found others who shared her interest. In March 1851 she received a letter from William Logan Fisher of Philadelphia, congratulating her on *Aesthetic Papers* and enclosing a pamphlet of his own, a tract on spiritualism. He thought he had recognized a kindred spirit in her: "This great principle is evidently working within you, and if my work should give any words to your feelings I shall be glad. If you are fond of Metaphysical investigation, I would ask your particular attention to the argument. It seems to me utterly impossible that man can receive any intellectual truth otherwise than through the immediate revelation of God."[32]

That claim about immediate revelation of "intellectual truth" might have made Peabody a little nervous. It sounded Quakerish, and she had recently finished that set of articles for the *Christian Register* on religion in America in which she shredded the Quaker belief in the inner light as opening a door to all kinds of subjective frenzies. Still, if spirit was God's presence in each person and if spirit is eternal, then perhaps communicating with the dead was a form of communicating with divinity. In any event, she continued her correspondence with Fisher, who wrote in 1854 that he and his family had been meeting with mediums, although they still had doubts about a literal afterlife.[33]

In 1858 the Fishers' son Charles William died, and Peabody took the opportunity to write an acknowledgment of their loss and a report on her own enthusiastic embrace of spiritualism. Fisher had written that he would be consoled only if he believed in "Modern Spiritualism," but he lacked the evidence. Elizabeth was more than happy to provide proof and reminded him that another dead Fisher son, Lindley, had communicated with his parents at a séance Peabody had attended with two mediums, the Leedoms. They had shared a harmony of thought and feeling, "and *that thought* was intensely *your son*."

Peabody also reminded him of her two spiritualist contacts with William Ellery Channing, who had died in 1842. At one contact, Channing was supposedly conversing with Peabody through a medium but abruptly cut off the conversation, saying, "I cannot say any thing more on this subject now, because this medium is inadequate. It is like pouring water into a vase; the water must take the shape of the vase; seek another medium." A year or so later, she reported to Fisher, she was talking with a "very spiritual minded" woman, who unexpectedly began talking of the way the soul continues to communicate with its heavenly companions, often during the state of dreamless sleep "(& hence sleep is so recreative)." Peabody, who realized that the woman was not speaking her own thoughts, and asked from whose mind she was speaking. "*'From Dr. Channing's.'* I said, 'From Dr. Channing's? Why should he speak to me?' 'I do not know,' said she, 'but as soon as you came in Dr. Channing seemed to say to me,—'I shall have something to say to this person'—& it is he who has answered your questions."[34]

Spiritualism and the causes of independent but impoverished women took Peabody's time and energy but could not provide any income. Responsible for her own maintenance and often giving money to her parents, Elizabeth frequently felt the pinch of her straitened circumstances. In January 1853 she estimated her debts at about $3,000. Wealthy friends helped with some of her burdens; Jonathan Phillips, for one, had been sending her small gifts since the late 1820s, totaling nearly $1,000.[35]

Now, in 1853, Peabody had an added burden in the care of her father. As she had often done before, she turned to teaching as a means of earning money, accepting an offer to teach school at the Raritan Bay Union at Eagleswood, New Jersey, where both she and Dr. Peabody could live. The school, headed by antislavery crusader Theodore Dwight Weld, emerged as the most important feature in this cooperative society that was founded by Marcus and Rebecca Spring, New York City philanthropists. Its teaching staff included Weld's wife Angelina Grimké Weld, who taught history, and her sister Sarah, who taught French, and Peabody herself. Moncure Conway described the school as "a pioneer institution in many ways, the first in which young women were found educating their limbs in the gymnasium, rowing in boats and making 'records' in swimming and high diving, under the tuition of Theodore Weld and his wife, one of the famous Grimke sisters."[36]

Judging from a letter Elizabeth wrote to Weld thirty years later, she did not have quite the proper appreciation of these abolitionist and feminist pioneers, never feeling *"very intimate"* with them. "I never read any thing they wrote—did not know they had printed any thing!—except 'Slavery as It Is.'" For their part, the sisters apparently avoided Peabody not out of ignorance but out of choice, or so it appears from Elizabeth's admission that she "always felt they did not take to me—& that my talk wearied them—."[37]

The death of his wife in 1853 sent Dr. Peabody on a downward spiral of ill health and low spirits. In August 1854 Elizabeth took him to New Hampshire to visit his family. The congestion in his lungs was nearly gone, she reported to Rawlins Pickman, but his energy was failing, and he was "desponding always, about others & himself." Elizabeth seemed much more interested in the visit to her uncle's homestead than was her father. "My Uncle is the model of a simplehearted religious New England farmer," she wrote. "He has united farming, miller's business, & carpentering in a rude [?] way & has brought up eight children & made a little something." His children, her cousins, had all prospered—the sons were carpenters or cattle ranchers, the daughter well educated and married to a missionary. In meeting these family members, Elizabeth Peabody glimpsed a world of happy and successful people, whose lives seemed so different from hers.[38]

Living at Eagleswood cost $25 a year, money that Elizabeth simply did have have. In September 1854, the Hawthornes sent two drafts for $25 each to their financial adviser William Ticknor, to be paid to Elizabeth. It is likely that these were for memberships, since Sophia wrote to her sister the following month, "I am very glad the drafts were so timely. . . . We [that is, Sophia and Mary] have always both said that whatever money we might earn from the sweat of our brows should go to Father, but that we should never feel authorized to *ask* our husbands for one penny for him or any of our relations."[39]

Neither Eagleswood nor trips to New Hampshire could do much for Dr. Peabody's health, which continued to fail through the fall and early winter of 1854. Sophia wrote from England to express her concern but also wondered whether perhaps her sister was exaggerating. "I allow for your always taking the darkest view of such things—always suggesting death when there is the remotest possibility of the event, & so my indomitable hope will admit light even now." But Elizabeth was right, and Dr. Peabody died January 1, 1855.[40]

Sophia must have felt guilty not only for questioning her sister's view of their father's condition but also for not being there in his final days. It would have been impossible to cross the Atlantic in midwinter, she wrote. In any event, Sophia went on, "if any thing could have softened the blow, it would have been the divine way in which my husband told me. . . . Mr. Hawthorne thinks father a very rare person & valued him more sincerely than any body else ever did. His sincerity, his childlike guilelessness, his good sense & rectitude—his singleness & unaffected piety—all & each of his qualities made him interesting & never tedious to my husband. I really do not believe any else ever listened to his stories & his conversation with love & interest excepting him." Elizabeth found that a little hard to take, writing in the margin that "Mr. Hawthorne does all this, but I cannot agree he was the *only* person who did."[41]

Hawthorne, meanwhile, wanted Elizabeth to keep the money he had sent for Dr. Peabody's Eagleswood expenses and use it for his funeral. In his last days, the old doctor had changed his mind about wanting to be buried next to his wife and chose instead the Eagleswood cemetery. Although this choice should have cost Elizabeth less money, not more, she apparently still needed funds for his expenses and asked the Hawthornes for more. Sophia asked, "Is it then possible that *all* his money & that also we sent him was spent so that you could not pay with it *all* his [expenses]?"[42]

Elizabeth's response to this outburst must have been intended to play on Sophia's sense of guilt for not being at her father's deathbed, for the next letter came not from Sophia but from Nathaniel, who fired off this blistering response: "I shall not let Sophia have your letter to her. . . . I sometimes feel as if I ought to indicate [to?] her (which would be so easily done) as to all those accusations of neglecting her father and family, which you both hint and express; and also to endeavor to enlighten you as to the relation between husband and wife, and show you that she fully comprehends it in its highest sense. But this conjugal relation is one which God never meant you to share, and which therefore He apparently did not give you the instinct to understand; so there my labor would be lost." As if all this guilt and innuendo about Dr. Peabody were not enough, then there was brother Nathaniel's situation. Hawthorne went on: "You *did* make the suggestion about my borrowing the money to set your brother up in life. What a memory! Perhaps you write in your sleep?" Sensing that this remark was perhaps too harsh and realizing that Elizabeth was, after all, going to be in his life for some years to come, he concluded in a softer tone:

> I did not mean to close all correspondence forever, but only on that particular subject. I hope, in whatever years we may have left, to exchange many letters, and see you many times; for there are few people whose society is so pleasant to me. I never in my life was angry with you; and if you will only allow me to think of you just as I please (or, rather, just as I cannot help) I really think we shall find great comfort in one another. Upon my honor, I consider myself the one person in the world who does justice to your character!!— an assertion at which you will probably laugh outright; especially as I not withdraw one word of my last letter, or any other I ever wrote you, all of which were considerately and conscientiously written.[43]

If Hawthorne hoped that this letter would quiet his own anxieties about having Elizabeth Peabody in his family and stave off more emotionally charged letters between the sisters, he was certainly wrong. For almost ten years, Elizabeth and Sophia exchanged strained, accusatory letters about politics, child-rearing, and family relations, with Nathaniel contributing several sharp responses of his own.

֍ SOPHIA MIGHT have had a pang of guilt about seeing neither her mother nor her father in their final hours, but at least in the case of Dr. Peabody, it would hardly have been possible for her to return. Whatever guilt inducement Elizabeth used in the letter that Hawthorne refused to pass on to his wife may have come not simply from Elizabeth's resentment at all this caretaking. It may also have reflected her deep sense of abandonment, having lost parents, brothers, and sisters to death or marriage.

Meanwhile, the practical issues kept bearing down. Rawlins Pickman had sent $15 to help with Dr. Peabody's expenses, but Elizabeth needed at least $200 for current bills. She hoped to earn $400 from teaching at Eagleswood, and also something from the sale of Bem's charts, but so far all she had there were orders, but no payment.[44]

Then, quite remarkably, her financial situation turned around, and with it, Peabody's sense of her own worth and regard. Sarah Clarke, her old student from the 1830s, wrote her in October 1855 with some unexpected news:

> Last year, some of your friends who love you & who think that you have spent your life & strength in working for others' benefit collected a sum of money & confided it to my brother William through me to invest for your use. This sum to which I added what you gave me and what Mr. Ogden had of yours is so placed as to yield one hundred dollars a year which will be paid you semiannually. The draft enclosed is the first half years' payment of fifty, less exchange one percent—& you will receive the same every six months. The principal, which in two years will amount to one thousand dollars, is yours to leave by will, but not yours to give away during your life. This is according to the wishes of those who gave this money. They do not wish you to know their names, but I can tell you that all of your friends who knew of the plan, and who were able to do so, gladly contributed. My brother William for his share undertook the management, & I, your humble servant, am trustee.[45]

Peabody's spirits lifted immediately. Other debts, money she owed to Marcus Spring and Samuel Gray Ward, were forgiven, although, as she confided to Rawlins Pickman, she simply had to spend some of her annuity for her brother Nat, who had become ill with a lung infection. She felt a new freedom, as care for family and anxiety about debts seemed at least momentarily lifted. "I must say I do enjoy *leisure* for study—All my life it has seemed to me that personally I wanted no other wealth than *leisure*—& now I have got it," she wrote in 1858.[46]

This new freedom prompted, or released, in Elizabeth Peabody a remarkable outpouring of writing—reminiscence, speculative history, philosophy. The categories of her writing in the last half of the 1850s are a bit hard to name, since her work seemed so uncategorizable, sometimes diffuse and slack. But writing was definitely one of her passions in those years, and even though her essays were not typically connected to specific causes, as in the 1830s and 1840s, they nonetheless revealed her mastery of contemporary scholarship and the range of her intellectual interests. While still at Eagleswood, she wrote Parke

Godwin to ask about the possibilities of a regular column in *Putnam's Magazine:*

> You know perhaps that I am now left with considerable freedom to do *what I please*, so death has given me a mournful immunity from all those cares for others, which have made it my duty and pleasure to postpone my own attractions to their interests. And now I wish to devote myself in some degree to my pen, for it seems to me that the harvest of half a century as well as of the present moment, ought to take some permanent form. . . . It seems to me I have *something to say* which may be valuable to others, and if I could be paid enough for my articles to keep me from *starving* I could feel at liberty to give myself up to saying it.[47]

Such a post never materialized, although her annuity and the forgiveness of her debts kept her from penury.

The essay that Peabody was working on in 1854 was "Primeval Man." Not published until 1881, this essay reflects Elizabeth's interests in ancient history, linguistics, and human moral development; and it constitutes, as one of her friends noted, "a theory which in one form or another constantly appears in her thought of the Spiritual Unity of all being—and of the perfection of promise in the beginning." Written before Darwin's *Origin of Species* and *Descent of Man*, as Peabody notes, the story she wishes to tell is not one of biological evolution but one of descent from primal greatness. Everywhere one looks in ancient history, she argues, one finds the ur-story of creation, fall, and redemption. Whereas Christian interpreters focus on the last two, she wants to add a word for the first, which suggests that humanity was created as one, and created morally free, in the image of God. Contrary to the notion of prehistoric barbarism, from which sprang the ancient civilizations of the Mediterranean, Peabody's claim is for prehistoric wisdom, recalled in the myths of Egypt, Greece, and Rome. "Joseph de Maistre's idea of savages being the degradation of the human race, not its germs, is far better authenticated by facts than the opposite opinion. . . . The whole trilogy [creation, fall, redemption] is perpetually reproduced, both in individuals and in History."[48]

"Primeval Man" reveals both Peabody's gifts and her limits. Her enormous erudition, her ability to range through ancient near Eastern religions and cultures and through classical civilizations, her grasp of contemporary archeological and linguistic scholarship—all these are immediately apparent. The essay develops more fully the insights offered in "Essay on the Earliest Ages," an appendix to *Manual of the Polish-American System of Chronology*. There Peabody explained the difficulty of representing pre-Egyptian cultures on Bem's charts but noted that these earliest human civilizations were not "savage tribes, but people with arts and ideas; not the germs of crude nations, but the polished fragments of a civilization higher in many characteristics than we have had since."[49] Just as apparent in "Primeval Man" is the maddeningly allusive quality of her writing, which amasses great bodies of material without really demonstrating their connection. To the modern reader, her scholarship is too deductive, based on conclusions already drawn, and too speculative, arguing a point for which conclusive evidence can never exist.

Four years after Peabody began work on "Primeval Man," Emerson wrote her that he would try to place the essay in the *Atlantic*. But the essay was rejected, and Emerson had to write to editor James Russell Lowell to get it back, since she wanted to read it to a history class that she was then conducting in Boston. "Primeval Man" appeared in *Journal of Speculative Philosophy* in 1881, and then in Peabody's 1886 collection of essays, *Last Evening with Allston and Other Papers*.[50]

Despite this rejection, she had several other writing projects in the works. In 1857 she published a reminiscence of Washington Allston in *Emerson's Magazine*. "Last Evening with Allston" is one of Peabody's most effective essays, combining an account of her last interview with the artist with a vivid description of his funeral. Peabody felt a particular kinship with Allston, in their shared desire to find transcendent significance in material reality. In one of the most florid sections of the essay, Peabody recounts the "long psychological biography of a young man whom I had known very intimately, who had lived—and nearly died—without any realizing sense of any relation between Jesus Christ and his own soul." This young man is likely her brother George. Hearing Elizabeth read "Paradise Lost" aloud, he understood the cosmic struggle Milton describes as a metaphor for the inner struggle between his "selfish propensities" and the filial sentiment of kinship with the divine.[51]

These two impulses—the psychologizing and the dualizing—are evident in other essays from this period. In 1858 she published "The Being of God" in the *Christian Examiner*, but she was so unhappy with how the editors rearranged and rewrote her work that she wrote a second essay "Egotheism, the Atheism of To-Day" as a clarification. Collecting her essays in 1886 for *Last Evening with Allston and Other Papers*, Peabody included her original version of "The Being of God" and renamed it "The Atheism of Yesterday," followed by "Egotheism, the Atheism of To-Day."

Like "Primeval Man," these essays demonstrate Peabody's interests in ancient history, her knowledge of classic and contemporary historians and philosophers, and her speculative and synthetic mind. Atheism is the mistaken worship of the material world, rather than of the immaterial God who created it. The created order is God's expression, but not God's identity. However, by transferring fuller knowledge of God into the invisible and internal realms, Peabody goes on in "Egotheism," we run the risk of the distinctive atheism of our time, which is self-worship. Egotheism "denies other self-consciousness to God than our own subjective consciousness;—not recognizing that there is, beyond our conception, inconceivable Power, Wisdom, and Love. . . ."

Egotheism could appear only in societies that recognize the human ability to reshape society. Abolishing slavery and polygamy, reforming the conditions of labor, appropriating more money for education—these constitute appropriate reforms. But Peabody points to much more far-reaching efforts to reconstruct society. This *"new organization"* proposed by radical socialists "contemplates quite new human relations, with a quite new morality, and quite new religion . . . including the so-called Free-Love in various specious forms, organizing free marriage, public possession of children, abolition of political law and family rights. . . ." Because "there are conventional marriages, tyrannical parents, and victimized children possible within our organization," social radicals like the Fourierists "call the time-honored morality immoral, the sacredness of all marriage laws impurity, the carefulness of all parental relations tyranny, and the devotion of all filial piety slavery." All this transfers moral and spiritual authority into the self, and equates the divine with the scope of the human imagination.[52]

Perhaps the lingering gentility of the Palmer and Peabody inheritance, or the social propriety of her Unitarian upbringing and its heavy influence of Channing, or perhaps her sense of the limits of what a

single woman dependent on employment offered by others—for whatever reasons, Elizabeth Peabody's social conservatism is most apparent
in these essays. A reader of Wordsworth and Coleridge, she had early
embraced the organic metaphor so favored by English and American
Romantics. But although the notion of society-as-organism may have a
plausible ring when applied to a small community, like a classroom or
Brook Farm, or may have some grandeur when applied to the vast
sweep of human history, it had a decidedly conservative cast to it when
applied to urban and industrial society or to the relations between the
genders. Antebellum labor leaders and social thinkers like Orestes
Brownson and Thomas Skidmore saw the organic metaphor as a dis-
traction from the very real class differences and power inequities that
marked modern society. An argument for "identity of interests" was
precisely what justified owners of the Lowell mills in cutting wages and
speeding up the looms. Social conflicts of all kinds—class, ethnic, racial,
and gendered—emerged in the 1840s and 1850s, making Peabody's
cautious organicism and her vision of a harmonious community ever
more untenable.

Nowhere do we see the limits of her organicism more than in her
attitude toward the prewar women's movement. From her mother, Peabody had inherited the notion that certain insights—the concern with
history was one—came distinctively under the purview of women. At a
time when female intellect was often disdained, any claim for female
expertise in the nondomestic realm was an advance for women, but
Peabody sought to combine intellectual achievement with existing assumptions about gender. In the 1870s, for example, Peabody would
argue that women were peculiarly fitted for kindergarten teaching because of their instinct for nurture. And, as the essay on "Egotheism"
made clear, she very much believed in the nuclear family and the marriage vows on which it is based as sacred, and angrily rejected those
who criticized such institutions. The family, she proposed in "The Philosophy of History in the Education of Republican Men and Women"
in *The Una* in February 1855, spared women the oppression of polygamy found in Asian cultures and in American Mormonism, and equally
spared men and women the egotheism of radical individualism. When
asked to sign a rights petition in 1837, she responded that she thought
women could do pretty much anything they wanted to do anyway
and that she would prefer to change the title of the movement from

Women's Rights to Women's Duties. Writing to Anna Barker Ward, probably in 1860, Peabody reflected her conventional view of women as nurturers and healers in commenting on Elizabeth Barrett Browning's long narrative poem *Aurora Leigh*, published in 1857. "Ah, is not *that Aurora!*—How rich—how deep—How *full of promise*. It is really a great sea of truth in which I trust many will be baptized & washed of ten thousand *crudities* about woman & love—bathe & be refreshed with the life of the resurrection!—I think it will prove a gospel of glad tidings to a multitude of women. . . ."[53]

Feminists, of which Peabody was definitely not one, saw the picture very differently. Over a broad range of issues—education, vocation, activism in reform and religion, property rights, suffrage—women struggled against patriarchal assumptions and amused condescension. One such outspoken advocate for women's rights was Peabody's friend from the West Street days, Caroline Healey Dall. One of the first female Unitarian ministers and a vigorous proponent for equality in education and in labor, Dall took on issues in public that Peabody thought best treated in private.

In February 1859 Peabody wrote Dall a long letter, chastizing her for her attacks on Horace Mann and then moving into a broader critique of Dall's behavior on the lecture platform.

I do not think that in all classical literature there is any thing so indelicate as your broad allusion to Madame Chevreuse's *menses* in your lecture upon her—when I heard *that* I felt that it was a special providence that I was not in company with any gentlemen. . . . I cannot disagree with others who say to me that you inflict more injury on the cause of woman by this bad taste than you can remedy by all your learning and talents—I heard you are going to write lectures upon *labour* & ăre going to make *painful statements*—I beg you will consider what I say—I do not think I am squeamish—but I would not go to hear your lectures with a gentleman by my side.—I do feel that the natural sphere of woman is above the slough of human nature. I would go to a Magdalene Refuge to *work in the reform of the inmates*—but I would not talk to men about prostitution. . . . I do not like conventions of women for Women's Rights—as you know—I did not when I first heard of them & would not sign the first call that was made—I like them still less in

practice—but the one held here over which you presided I thought
the best that I had known of.[54]

Dall commented in her journal that her allusion to Chevreuse had to do
with her blood-soaked saddle after a long ride rather than to menstrual
blood.[55] Still, the rocky relation between Dall and Peabody went far
beyond misunderstandings like this. Peabody encouraged the younger
woman's writing, including *"Woman's Right to Labor;" or, Low Wages and
Hard Work*, but shrank from Dall's outspoken public advocacy.[56]

There is a similar sense of Peabody's anxiety about propriety blinding
her to deeper issues about women's involvement in society in a letter to
her from one of the Blackwell sisters, either Elizabeth or Emily, among
the first American women in medicine. Peabody had apparently written
a critical comment on a mannerism that she thought possibly offensive.
Blackwell responded calmly: "Besides the fault you find, has been found
before, and I am entirely aware of the justice of the charge to some
extent. I have had all my life long to contend against a severity of
judgment toward individuals, which I feel to be unchristian. I am naturally interested in principles, not people. . . . I am very apt to regard the
mass of men, simply as manure out of which Man shall grow." As for
those who might be put off by Blackwell's refusal to receive strangers, "I
throw open my house and my feeling, most fully to any one who is
interested in the Cause—I would give any information about it. I would
have a world of patience for any amount of ignorance, opposition, or
prejudice in relation to the idea, and use my utmost endeavour, with all
gentleness to enlighten an enquirer, if the person be only in earnest, &
desirous of information, interested in the subject. But if instead of interest in the Cause, it is curiosity about my individuality, that is felt, I
should resent it as involuntarily and inevitably as gunpowder explodes
at a spark."[57]

With such articulate and passionate reformers in her circle of friends
and correspondents, it is not surprising that Peabody eventually began
attending women's rights meetings. In 1855 Sallie Holley attended a
Woman's Rights Convention in Boston and met Elizabeth there. "All
that is said of crushed bonnets, disorderly hair, poverty of dress, every
conceivable negligence of arrangement, is literally true," Holley recalled. "Yet, the childlike innocence in the face, the rare and exquisite
grace of expression that the thought comes clothed in from her lips,

make a mantle of decencies ample enough to cover crushed bonnet and tumble-down hair." In contrast, Holley described reformer Elizabeth Oakes Smith, who read a poem at the Convention's last session. Much to the dismay of the other women's rights advocates, Smith wore a thin, low-cut dress, rings, bracelets, "an immense pin on her bosom," and "her head rigged in the latest fashion." "'She is a self-intoxicated woman,' said Elizabeth Peabody to me as we left the hall. I laughed myself nearly into fits over it."[58] Peabody did not think this was so funny and wrote of Smith, either regarding this meeting or a later one, that she had made a "foolish theatrical display of herself—women do not seem to be able to divest themselves of a certain consciousness of their own personality—bodily or mental—and so make fools of themselves in public by thrusting *their own personality* before the audience."[59]

Sallie Holley's comment about "all that is said of crushed bonnets" suggests that Elizabeth Peabody had gained a reputation by the mid-1850s of absentmindedness and the embrace of sometimes dubious causes. Inevitably she became the subject of gossip and anecdote. Late in the decade, some stories were circulating in different versions. The most famous one involved Elizabeth and the tree: Harriet Hosmer recounted to her friend Cornelia Carr that Peabody walked into a tree at Lenox, "and upon being asked about it, said, 'Yes, I saw it, but I did not realize it.' Do you remember?" Sarah Forbes Hughes repeated her father John Murray Forbes's version of this story, which involved Elizabeth's being knocked over by a low-lying branch, with the same question and reply.[60]

This sense of obliviousness to the world around her makes its way into one of the most famous of stories about Elizabeth Peabody, at once endearing and grisly, this one told by Julian Hawthorne in *Hawthorne and His Circle*. One day while Julian and Una were in the nursery playing with blocks, Aunt Lizzie came in and sat down in "the big easy-chair."

> The cat was in the room, and she immediately came up to my aunt, and began to mew and to pluck at her dress with her claws. Such attentions were rare on pussy's part, and my aunt noticed them with pleasure, and caressed the animal, which still continued to devote its entire attention to her. But there was something odd in

the sound of her mewing and in the intent regard of her yellow eyes. "Can anything be the matter with pussy?" speculated my aunt. At that moment my father entered the room, and my aunt rose to greet him. Then the massacre was revealed, for she had been sitting upon the kittens. Their poor mother pounced upon them with a yowl, but it was too late. My dear aunt was a rather heavy woman, and she had been sitting there fifteen minutes. We all stood appalled in the presence of the great mystery.[61]

↭ DESPITE HER BURST of creative energy in middecade and involvement in many reforms, Elizabeth never avoided her responsibilities to her brother and sisters, although in the 1850s they must have wished that she had been a little less dutiful. Even before the deaths of their parents left Elizabeth without a secure family place, she was nosing about in the child-rearing practices of sister Mary and brother Nathaniel. Both wrote promptly to set her straight. Regarding her children's religious education, Mary wrote, "I have never tried to conceal any thing from you with regard to the children. I have simply left the subject untouched, since all you have ever said about it has been of the character I indicated in my last letter, and I am quite tired of being thought a mere waiter upon other people's ideas."[62]

Nat was much blunter in his dealings with Elizabeth, pointing out just how different his and his wife's practice was from the Hawthornes' child-rearing and from Elizabeth's theories. "I firmly believe that repression and restraint are necessary in the education of children. I believe that the neglect of this discipline is visible in the conduct of the boys and girls of the rising generation, one by no means rich in veneration for any earthly or divine law. . . . How Sophia's children will turn out is problematical. I fear that they will not be able to live in a world which has so much to shock fine sensibilities. I should not like to have my children see only the beautiful colors of the rainbow."[63]

It was exactly a "shock" to "fine sensibilities" that drove a wedge between Elizabeth and Sophia in the late 1850s, as Elizabeth relentlessly pursued a correspondence with the Hawthornes, then in England, about the interwoven issues of Una's moral education and the cause of antislavery. This correspondence exists only on Sophia's side; it is possible that she destroyed Elizabeth's letters to keep them from her eldest daughter's sight.

Elizabeth Peabody came late to the cause of antislavery. In the late 1880s she recalled that her "heart & judgment were always on the Antislavery side from my earliest infancy when my mother induced us children all to refuse to eat sugar because it was the fruit of slave labour." But she admitted to Theodore Dwight Weld that she did not go to the Grimké sisters' addresses in Concord in the mid-1830s because she was too busy with her school in Boston. Besides, her attitudes in that decade were hardly very advanced on the subject. In one of her "Cuba Journal" letters written in May 1834, she reported a conversation with Henry Ware, George Hillard, the Lees, and Charles Follen, the German émigré professor of languages and ardent abolitionist. "Mr Lee is terribly provoked at Dr. Follen. He asked Dr F if he should be willing to have Charley [his son] marry a negro—& he said *yes* if she was virtuous!!—!!—!!—Dr. Follen!!-!!" It seems clear that Peabody found this just as horrifying a thought as did most other members of the Unitarian elite, who closed ranks in forcing Charles and Eliza Follen out of Harvard College and Boston society.[64]

By the late 1850s, Elizabeth Peabody had embraced antislavery with all the energy of the recent convert. She had discovered the plight of Mattie Griffith, member of a slave-owning family who, like the Grimkés, had repudiated her background and fled north to write. Her *Autobiography of a Female Slave* had not sold well, and Griffith was nearly penniless, her only property back in the South in slaves whom she insisted on setting free. Peabody blamed some of Griffith's difficulties on Justus Starr Redfield, her publisher, but he insisted that he had done all he could for the book, calling it the best antislavery text after *Uncle Tom's Cabin*. Hoping to interest reform-minded women in subscribing money for Griffith's support, Peabody wrote a flurry of letters to such people as Frances Seward, wife of Republican politician William Henry Seward, and Eliza Follen. Follen's response was generous and warm, particularly in light of Elizabeth's mockery of her husband's idealism twenty years earlier. "Miss Griffith is I assure you the object of the deepest interest with us abolitionists & has been ever since we heard of her noble purpose. . . . You have dear Elizabeth rendered her a true service by writing this particular account of her trials, her temptations & her heroic determination. Fear not that we shall fail in our devotion one & all."[65]

Elizabeth's new devotion to antislavery and to Mattie Griffith spilled over into her letters to the Hawthornes. Nathaniel Hawthorne had never struck her as exactly passionate about reform, and she feared that the youngest daughter of the liberal Peabodys and *her* children would lose some of the family's crusading spirit. "All you tell me of Mattie Griffith is deeply interesting and what you say seems to show what is one of the profoundest miseries of this most miserable matter," Sophia wrote back. But she and her husband would absolutely refuse to expose their children to the horrors of slavery, and insisted that Elizabeth stop writing to the children, especially to Una, about such matters. "And you would display before her great, innocent eyes a naked slave girl on a block auction [sic]!!!/which I am sure is an exaggeration, for I have read of those auctions often and even the worst facts were never so bad as absolute nudity/."[66]

The Hawthornes had every intention of protecting their children from the moral confusion of both slavery and antislavery. "I do not call Providence your letters to her. I consider it Providence that she is here, away from all the excessive and morbid excitement of America. . . . 'Hot house culture,' is the very thing I *avoid*, and /to avoid it is/ the reason why I put my flower in cool mountain air that she may develop more slowly, instead of in the steam and heat of human misery, degredation, and crime as shown in slavery and abused human relations. . . . It is not necessary she should arrive at the idea of the beauty of holiness by means of knowing about Mattie Griffith. . . ."[67]

The conflict between the Hawthornes and Elizabeth Peabody went far beyond their efforts to shelter Una. Elizabeth was convinced, to judge by Sophia's responses, that the Hawthornes had turned proslavery during their stay in England. Sophia strenuously rejected this idea: "Not a person has spoken to me of slavery—my husband and I never discuss it nor speak of it, except when your letters of unaccountable accusation and solicitude about my morals arrive, and then we wonder what you can mean, as we both feel quite innocent, and hate the evil quite as much as you do."[68]

Still, if Sophia opposed slavery, she also opposed reformers who argued for civil disobedience in ending slavery. "When you get so far out of *my* idea of right—as to talk of it being proper to violate law sometimes because we can 'obey higher laws than we break'—this, dear Elizabeth, I used to hear in days past, and I consider it a very dangerous and demoralising doctrine, and I have always called it transcendental slang." Nathaniel's hostility to antislavery advocates was pointed and direct. He returned a manuscript pamphlet on abolition that Elizabeth had sent, saying that she might better publish it or else he would burn it. Two months later, Peabody sent the same pamphlet again. "Upon my word," Hawthorne fired back, "it is not very good; not worthy of being sent three times across the ocean; not so good as I supposed you would always write, on a subject in which your mind and heart were interested. However, since you make a point of it, I will give it to Sophia, and will tell her all about its rejection and return." As if this dig were not enough, Hawthorne reminded her that he was still in favor of legalized flogging aboard naval vessels. Sometimes a little cruelty is needed to prevent larger violence, a claim he knew would shock his warm-hearted sister-in-law.[69]

Much to Sophia's chagrin, Mary too thought that the Hawthornes had gone soft on the issue of antislavery, a cause the Manns ardently defended. Sophia had to see to her positions on that front as well: "I will venture my life upon it that you will find you have *inferred* such ideas, from a preconceived notion that both you and Elizabeth have taken that I have been corrupted by being in a democratic aura [that is, associated with the Democratic Party]. . . . It seems stereotyped into your mind that I have personal reasons for defending slavery, because you think Mr. Pierce defends it and other Administrative men, and that because Mr. Hawthorne has accepted a post from Government, he therefore subscribes to every one of its opinions, and modes of action, and that as he does, I do, of course, and so on."[70]

But all this quarreling about slavery was hushed in late 1858 and into 1859 as the Peabodys experienced the twin tragedies of Horace Mann's death in August 1859 and Una's nearly fatal struggle with malarial fever in fall and winter 1858, with a serious relapse the following spring. After a trip to the Roman Colosseum so much like the heroine's in Henry James's novella *Daisy Miller*, Una came down with a cold, which turned much more serious in the following weeks. Finally, in early spring she seemed better, although Sophia worried about her pallor and weakness. But Una collapsed again, with raging fevers and the infection settling into her lungs. After thirty days of nearly continuous care, Sophia sensed a change; the fever had broken. Writing to Elizabeth later that summer, Sophia recalled the tension and despair of those days:

I suffered her death a thousand times instead of once—because the phases of her state were so alarming—she so constantly seemed about to die . . . my husband expected every morning to find his hair turned to snow on his head. Alternations he could not bear of hope and fear and he sunk into fear alone—I not only had no time to give way to my natural expression of grief, but no place to go to, and no retreat. Una's chamber was between my chamber and the drawing room. Mr. Hawthorne was in my chamber—and I was hemmed in on both sides. Doubtless it was benign providence, for it was necessary that I should not yield one moment. In my fearful night watches, when I was always alone, I used sometimes to write to myself to keep my head steady. I wrote about Una in the past.[71]

In September 1853 Horace and Mary Mann and their children had moved to Yellow Springs, Ohio, where Horace became the first president of Antioch College. Organized in large part by the Christian Connexion denomination, Antioch embodied the dreams of many for moral and intellectual education in the American heartland. Its education was to be extended to both men and women, a goal that excited Mann's sister-in-law Elizabeth, ever the champion of female education.

But the first years of Antioch's life were troubled and divisive. While the College and its new president struggled to appoint a faculty and organize a curriculum, the Christian Connexion was insisting on a narrow denominational identity. What was worse, the College's financial officers were badly mismanaging, and the College continually faced financial collapse. Peabody did what she could, writing an impassioned letter to Park Godwin, the editor of the New York *Evening Post*, asking whether he would run a fund-raising appeal in his newspaper. "Now cannot you write a good strong article for the Evening Post on this subject? . . . And when will so much be accomplished for women, and for unsectarian religion again? Horace Mann is not to be picked up in every half-century. A million of dollars could not buy another such President. . . . Considering how likely it is that the larger number of the women educated at Antioch will be teachers, it is incalculable, the value of such an influence as Mr. Mann's, exerted on the classes."[72]

The issue of coeducation had caught Peabody's attention, although it also presented some dilemmas when men and women students worked and studied together. Her lingering anxiety about propriety caught her here, but in a letter to Caroline Dall, she put that consideration aside to write a ringing defense of Mann and Antioch. Dall had repeated some gossip about the school, and Peabody shot back,

> I think *nobody* is doing so much for woman's education and ad-
> vancement as he—and *so little to be regretted.* . . . I consider him one
> of the greatest Reformers of the day—on the woman question as
> well as on most others pertaining to our common humanity, & I
> think it wrong that any one should assert without absolute knowl-
> edge anything invidious about him as President of Antioch Col-
> lege—especially at its present crisis—for I do not believe that in
> another century there will be anything organized so important for
> woman's benefit as that college to whose success he is giving his
> *substance* & his *life.*[73]

Elizabeth was more right than she knew. By July 1859 Mann was absolutely exhausted from his crushing duties, worn out from ceaseless efforts at fund-raising and financial reorganization. He contracted the
typhoid fever that had already infected his sons, but his body was much
too weak to stave off the disease. With Mary at his side, Horace Mann
died in the early evening of August 2.

Whatever misunderstandings and injured feelings Mary and Elizabeth had inflicted in the days of their mutual attraction to Horace
Mann were now at least temporarily set aside. Indeed, on his deathbed
Horace told Mary to tell Elizabeth that "he loved her dearly and knew
she loved him. I was so glad he said it for with her generous nature it
will cancel all." Mary sent for her sister, and she came out to Ohio with
the Mann's eldest son Horace. To Rawlins Pickman Elizabeth wrote
that "Mary's face does not seem to be that of bereavement. She has not
come to pitying herself for her loss. She only agonizes over his sufferings that cut at last the work he was so earnest to do."[74]

Mary and her children planned to return to Concord, where the boys
could be trained for Harvard. Elizabeth helped her pack and return, and
by early September the Manns were settled into the Wayside, Sophia's
and Nathaniel's "blessed retreat," as Mary called it. "I have passed a few
weeks of the most busy occupation in getting ready to come away. It all
looks like a dream, and most of all that dread event which I can only at
time fully compass, & he may, wherever he may be, know what comforting I need—he only can give it. . . ."[75]

But Mary's grief was only temporarily masked by the intense activity of packing and moving back to Massachusetts. By October Elizabeth, who had come to live with the Manns in the Wayside, could write to Rawlins Pickman that Mary was suffering intensely. As Mary wrestled with her sorrow, she brooded on the past, a past where she, Elizabeth, Horace, and the memory of his first wife Charlotte interwove with complex and contradictory feelings. All that turmoil came back now. She had been rereading Horace's and Charlotte's early correspondence, she wrote Sophia, "& I love to dwell upon that picture of human felicity more than upon any thing else the world ever held for me. It was not unchequered, for their mutual anxiety for each other's frail health gave them deep heartaches, but that love & joy in each other were so exquisitely perfect, never I supposed dimmed for one moment of its short fruition. . . . Then I read his to me, & mine to him, & his correspondence with E, in those next years when we knew him in his inconsolable grief, & I see how completely my happiness sank under the effect of my sympathy for him."[76]

A month later Mary returned to these themes, the weaving together of joy and sorrow, the weaving together of all the people who had loved or admired Horace Mann. Never, it seemed, could she be alone with him, in life or in death. So we may only imagine what it cost Mary to write these lines to Sophia: "Ah, dear! there was so much sorrow blended with my love of him—the two never can be separated. I was the Consoler, rather than the bow of promise to him, you know—it was a holy office near such a being and he was consoled & happy & in the long eternity we three [Mann, Mary, and Charlotte] shall be one." And then Mary penned these remarkable lines, acknowledging at once Charlotte's prior claim on Horace and Elizabeth's failed claim: "Long before he had bathed himself in the radiance of unsullied purity in the bosom of his ideal love made manifest & real in Charlotte . . . he was my first love—the realization of my ideal—what a marvel this love is—Friendship, charming as that is, is nothing by its side—how fearful, terrible is its desecration!"[77]

8
"Apostles of the New Education"
ॐ

As the decade of disunion began, the Peabody sisters were coming home, not to Salem or Lancaster or Boston, but to Concord. There, in January, Mary Mann began a "journal of remembrance," recording her impressions of life with Horace Mann. She recalled their first meeting, the anxiety she felt at leaving him during her stay in Cuba, her confidence that she "retained my place in his affection and that I should always keep it, and find it fresh and green on my return." Grateful as she was for the sanctuary of the Wayside, Mary knew that the Hawthornes would soon return and reclaim the house. With the help of Concord schoolteacher and political activist Franklin Sanborn, Mary found and purchased a house at 7 Sudbury Road. There Mary sorted Horace's papers and worked on her biography of him, for which Elizabeth had found a publisher in Walker, Fuller. She was even able to organize and conduct a school for young children. That altogether happy experience is narrated in letters to Anna Lowell, published in 1863 as the first part of Elizabeth's and her *Moral Culture of Infancy and Kindergarten Guide*. [1]

Living in boardinghouses after the collapse of the Eagleswood community, Elizabeth Peabody was grateful for Mary's invitation to live with her, first at Wayside and then on Sudbury Road. Horace Mann had driven them apart, in a sense, in the 1830s, a situation that led to tense and accusatory letters flying between them, and now Horace Mann's death had brought them back together. Elizabeth's and Mary's old shared vocation and sisterly affection had survived the stresses of earlier decades, and now in the 1860s, they rediscovered their passion for early childhood education.

Shaken by Una's almost-fatal illness from which she had now just recovered, the Hawthornes also pondered a return home. For them, however, the return to Concord was a decidedly mixed prospect. Sophia longed for their own place; she envied her sisters the support that they could give each other in time of need. But Concord was also a center of antislavery activism, with Sanborn's membership in the "Secret Six" conspiracy to provide weapons to John Brown only the most sensational example of the town's sentiments. In this environment Hawthorne's Democratic politics and famous dislike of all reformers, especially antislavery advocates, would make him and his family suspect and disliked.[2]

Elizabeth worried much about the Hawthornes' reputation in Concord, much as she had worried about them in England and Europe. Hawthorne's steadfast support for his old schoolmate Franklin Pierce had enraged abolitionists, whose cause suffered major setbacks during his presidency, so much so that Lydia Maria Child thought his name should be pronounced to rhyme with "curse." In 1863 Hawthorne further alienated himself from reformers by dedicating *Our Old Home* to Pierce. Hawthorne, as usual, had little to say about politics, and Sophia, as usual, defended him passionately, even bitterly, to her sister, saying that she cared little about people's opinions:

> Is that plain? I do not care at all what any one thinks of his opinions, as I wrote you plainly from England. He can take care of himself very well. . . . I must say, for it is the truth, that if you and all the world *thought* my husband proslavery, I should be perfectly indifferent. My only interest would be whether he truly were so or not. No, Elizabeth—what I object to and can not allow with regard to my husband is to listen to any thing saucy /said/ about him, for (whatever you may or may not recollect)—you have been in the habit of saying caustic and disagreeable things in reference to him during my whole married life. It is unbecoming in me to give ear to any thing uttered in his disfavor, and it is still more unbecoming in you to utter any thing. . . . Whenever you think my husband opposed our views in any way, you have always sent a random shot at him through me—wounding me, if not him. This is wrong.[3]

The Peabodys' family quarrel over antislavery suddenly received a much larger and more ominous context in October 1859 with John Brown's failed raid at the federal arsenal at Harper's Ferry, Virginia. Concord's involvement in Brown's insurrection became apparent immediately, when captured letters named Sanborn as a weapons supplier. In April 1860 federal marshals from Boston tried to seize Sanborn in his house at Sudbury Road but were fought off by a crowd of Concordians. Sanborn's call for revolutionary resistance to the tyranny of slavery was given its best articulation not by Sanborn himself but by his fellow resident Henry Thoreau, whose address "A Plea for Captain John Brown" links Brown's execution in December 1859 to Christ's martyrdom.

In early March 1860, only two of Brown's raiders were still alive, Albert Hazlitt and Aaron Stevens. Stevens had been the organizer of the Free State Volunteers, who defended Kansas homesteaders from northern states against those who wanted to swing the state's referendum toward slaveholding status. Taken with the heroism of his behavior, Elizabeth Peabody apparently thought that she could "be instrumental in saving Stevens life," she wrote Sanborn. "I cannot explain for I am in a hurry going to Boston at 1 1/2 o clock—& *to Virginia* perhaps tonight." If Peabody's intervention did in fact take place, she must have seemed to Virginia's governor John Letcher the very epitome of New England reform: earnest, shabby, intense, a bit scattered, utterly serious in her application of moral idealism to the dirty, cruel business of statecraft and state security. Stevens was hanged on March 16.[4]

ɕ THE WAR that broke out a little more than a year later was never very far from Elizabeth Peabody's mind. Students from her Boston teaching days and children of her friends were enlisting, fighting, and dying. She would raise money for the care of the wounded through auctions of memorabilia. She would meet Abraham Lincoln twice and would witness the passage of the Thirteenth Amendment, which abolished slavery, from the gallery of the House of Representatives.

Ironically, in an era of unparalleled slaughter, Elizabeth Peabody's career as educator and public figure experienced a rebirth. After a decade-long diversion into fascinating but fruitless reforms and causes, she returned to her first and most beloved activity, the education of the young. Elizabeth's and Mary's schools in Maine, Brookline, and Boston, and Elizabeth's and Alcott's work at Temple School, all were committed to the nurturing of moral sensibility together with the training in history, languages, geography, and religion. Although adult education was important, the child's plasticity and openness marked the moment of greatest teachability.

Still, education of the young was a complex and often controversial activity, both on the private level, with frequent interference from anxious parents, and on the public, with continual concerns about funding, curricula, and sectarian conflict. Nationally the antebellum public-school movement revealed one face of liberal democratic reform, the training of young Americans for citizenship, and another face, that of fearful social control, zealous to clamp down on the seething masses and their democratic anarchy. The result was a confusing array of schools, philosophies, and agendas.

In such a situation, educators paid careful attention to developments in other countries, and particularly in Germany. German émigrés like Charles Follen brought with them new ideas about educational reform that seemed to flourish in their homeland, despite periodic waves of political repression. As early as 1836, Harriet Beecher Stowe's husband Calvin Stowe took note of German ideas in a speech entitled "The Prussian System of Public Instruction and Its Applicability to the United States." Four years later, educator Henry Barnard included a long essay on German primary education in his *Connecticut Common School Journal.* In 1854 Barnard mentioned something called a "kindergarten" in an essay in the *American Journal of Education.* Ednah Dow Cheney and Anna Parsons, an alumna of Peabody's very first school in Boston, reviewed a French manual on the kindergarten for the *Christian Examiner* in 1859. It would be just a matter of time, then, before Elizabeth Peabody would hear about Friedrich Froebel and his kindergarten.[5]

Born in 1782 in the German state of Schwartzburg-Rudolstadt, Froebel studied botany and forestry as a young man and then became interested in educational reform shortly after the turn of the nineteenth century. He worked with the Swiss reformer Heinrich Pestalozzi between 1807 and 1810. In the early 1830s, Froebel opened his own schools for the very young, emphasizing organized play and interaction with nature. As he worked with preschool children, Froebel began to formulate his characteristic "gifts and occupations" approach, which featured a set of physical activities geared to the child's mental and manual development. Although Froebel attracted the attention and support of such influential people as Baroness Berthe von Marenholtz-Bülow, his kindergarten was banned in Prussia in 1851 by the ministry of education, which confused Friedrich Froebel with his radical socialist nephew Karl. Crushed by this injustice, Froebel died in 1852. His followers, particularly his widow Luise and Berthe von Marenholz-Bulow, carried on his work, in other German states and cities, particularly Frankfurt and Dresden.[6]

Froebel's reform and Elizabeth Peabody's career intersected in 1859 when, at the home of some mutual friends in Boston, Peabody met Margarethe Schurz, wife of Wisconsin Republican politician Carl Schurz, and their daughter Agathe. Their hosts had four children whose father insisted on complete freedom until the children reached six, "at which age he proposed to put on the screws of discipline." Little Agathe "had the effect in the house of a calm coming upon the storm of young life," and Peabody observed to her mother, "'that child of yours is a miracle—so child-like and unconscious, and yet so wise and able, attracting and ruling the children, who seem nothing sort of enchanted.' 'No miracle, but only brought up in a kindergarten,' said Mrs. Schurz. 'A kindergarten! what is that?' 'A garden whose plants are human. Did you never hear of Froebel?' 'No, who is he?'" Margarethe Schurz explained who Froebel was, noting that she had heard his lectures on kindergartening while still in Germany. After emigrating to the United States, she set up a German-speaking kindergarten in Watertown, Wisconsin, in 1856, where Agathe was one of the first pupils.[7]

Elizabeth Peabody was captivated by this account and by the preface to Froebel's *The Education of Man*, which Margarethe Schurz had sent her. "Out of the perusal of this pamphlet [the separately published preface] (which was an abstract statement of Froebel's idea and aims concerning the earliest stage of education), together with this conversation, and glimpse of the perfect growth of a child, grew the first practical attempt at a kindergarten in Boston, in 1860," Peabody recalled in 1880.[8]

In 1860 Peabody opened the first English-speaking kindergarten in the United States, a private school at 15 Pinckney Street on Boston's Beacon Hill. A year later, by October 1861, she had relocated to 24 ½ Winter Street, which provided "a quiet, high, sunny room with seven windows to the east and south." Much as with Alcott's Temple School, Peabody canvassed her Boston friends for likely students. Not everyone found Froebel's principles persuasive. Lucretia Hale, for one, wrote that she did not think it so terrible to give children "*a little work*. There is such great capability in children to learn by rote, that I think it must have been given them for a good purpose, and that it is not amiss, to fill up their little heads with a good deal of matter which they only know the sound of but to which they attach ideas at their leisure." Still, enough were convinced by Peabody's prospectus that the kindergarten reopened in October 1861 with thirty pupils, two daily assistants, a third to teach French three days a week, and a fourth to guide gymnastics.[9]

In her April 1862 "Report and New Prospectus," Peabody outlined the day's activities at her kindergarten. Following a highly organized curriculum, the children moved through sessions of singing, academic study of arithmetic, reading and writing, supervised play, drawing, and periodic French and gymnastic lessons. "The idea of Kindergarten is organized play," she wrote in this report, and the emphasis must surely be on "organized." There seemed to be little unsupervised and no individual work unconnected with some group activity. Peabody reinforced this point in an essay for the *Atlantic* called "The Kindergarten: What Is It?" After rejecting several possible answers—not a nursery, nor a primary school—she identifies it as "children in society,—a commonwealth or republic of children,—whose laws are all part and parcel of the Higher Law alone. It may be contrasted, in every particular, with the old-fashioned school, which is an absolute monarchy."[10]

The key to the kindergarten's success is the kindergarten teacher, or kindergartner as she was called. With a dig at her more radically Romantic friends, Peabody claimed that children would not "inevitably develop into beauty and goodness. Human nature tends to revolve in a vicious circle, around the idiocyncrasy." A gardener of children was required, a teacher who would attend to their moral, physical, and intellectual growth and would draw out the moral potential that Peabody knew was there. Such a school "requires the experienced heart and mind of mature women, genial in temper, and sufficiently elevated in mind to understand what Jesus Christ meant when he said, 'He that receiveth a little child in my name receiveth me.'" Mary Mann, who often came out from Concord to help her sister, described the education of the very young this way: "The germ of everything is in the human soul; and this faith seems to me essential to a teacher. Education is not the creation, but only the bringing forth of these germs, and that alone is a true education which brings them forth in fair proportions. To make children learn something tangible, if I may so speak, and to keep them quiet, are the usual aims of a teacher, and success in these is the usual test of his value; but they seem to me not to be his highest merit."[11]

The work was *"all-absorbing"* and undoubtedly exhausting for a woman of nearly sixty years. But it also must have been energizing for Peabody to know that she was part of a renewed interest in early childhood education. Strangers, like John Williams of New Bedford, began writing for advice. Williams wrote that he had read about Peabody's leading role in the kindergarten movement in a recent issue of the *Christian Register* and told her that his granddaughter had begun a similar such experiment in their city. "Will your leisure and inclination permit you to communicate an outline or sketch of the system and the mode of its practical application for her benefit?"[12]

Pleased as Peabody must have been by this letter, she must have been even more gratified by Rebecca Moore's letter in April 1860, which clearly, perhaps even calculatingly, linked Transcendentalism with kindergartening. Moore had been host to Peabody's cause célèbre Mattie Griffith, who had come to England and the Continent to travel and promote her book. Sending Griffith's greeting, Moore went on to describe English Froebellian kindergartens in London and Manchester. From the original school founded in the early 1850s at 32 Tavistock Place in London, the system had spread out to include four kindergartens in Manchester. Moore wondered whether she might be allowed to head a kindergarten branch at the Eagleswood community: "I have so long & so closely sympathized with your great struggle in the U.S. cause & your still more profound struggles & achievements in the cause of mental liberation that I should not feel entirely unhomed in America. . . . Years ago I read your 'Record of a School' with much interest & I think met your name also in the pages of the 'Dial.' Mr. Alcott's works & efforts I have taken great interest in. Mr. Emerson was at my house two or three times during his stay in Manchester. . . ."[13]

℈ IT WAS PROBABLY just as well that Elizabeth was spending so much time in Boston and away from Concord, since relations with Sophia grew steadily more strained in the early 1860s. The issue, as was so often the case when it was not Hawthorne's politics, was the education of the children. To prepare for his eventual enrollment at Harvard, Julian was now enrolled in Franklin Sanborn's school, which was run on progressive principles including coeducation. Sophia was frankly skeptical, claiming in a letter to Elizabeth that even Julian spoke against this practice, saying "the boys are all the time speculating upon whom they shall fall in love with, and upon which one is in love with them instead of being earnest at their studies." Knowing full well how much Elizabeth agreed with Horace and Mary Mann's experiment in coeducation at Antioch, Sophia added that "Elizabeth Hoar entirely agrees with me on the point in question about young men and maidens being educated together at the most susceptible age. She told me in Rome that though she always wished to oblige you, that she would not sign a petition you sent to her for the incorporation of some Western college, because she knew it was intended to bring young men and girls together as at Antioch—and she thought such a plan very injudicious and foolish. To me it proved to be so by the results at Antioch." For this very reason, Sophia wrote, she would never enroll Una (Rose, also not enrolled, is not mentioned in this correspondence) at Sanborn's school, where "young men and maidens" were "being educated together at the electric age," although she did send her there for gymnastics on the advice of her "healer," a Mrs. Rollins of Cambridge, who "said it was important that she should use her feet and hands to make them warm by equalizing circulations—and also have a merry heart the while." This was the same Mrs. Rollins who used some form of electrical therapy to treat Una for the recurrence of her Roman fever, which was accompanied by alarming symptoms of mental breakdown.[14]

In 1863 with her children once more on her mind, Sophia organized some social gatherings "purely for the children's education in society and manners." Elizabeth was apparently "kept awake" by her sister's notions of who should be invited. Sophia wanted only interesting people invited, and so many of the Concord folk "are not edifying—but bores—and Una and Julian would not enjoy them or derive benefit from them." Among those not invited was their cousin Benjamin Mann.[15]

In contrast to these awkward and difficult exchanges, Elizabeth's relations with Mary's sons blossomed during and after the war years. "You are happiest among mothers with children of such *innocence* combined with such *thoughtful morale*," Elizabeth wrote Mary sometime in 1866.

"Your husband & yourself reappear to me in new combinations in these three boys—proving that your union was indeed one of those matches made in heaven. . . ." Young Horace, the eldest boy, seemed particularly self-possessed, modest, and intelligent to his proud aunt, who described a conversation between the boy and Emerson. Horace volunteered information about Ohio trees that must have been fascinating to his host, who had immersed himself in the particular lore of the trees in his region and in his orchard. Elizabeth reported that Emerson "said to me before I left, 'your nephew is a *very nice boy*' and the tone & emphasis were very satisfactory," even if the words were somewhat bland.[16]

Horace's father had never been convinced of Romantic idealism, the belief that "the Universe is the externisation of the soul," as Emerson put it in "The Poet." Aunt Elizabeth hoped that young Horace, who was interested in studying natural science under Louis Agassiz at Harvard, would follow Emerson's lead in seeing nature as the shell and symbol of spirit. "Mr. Emerson says the highest office which nature (studied scientifically) has—is to lead the mind into those spiritual facts which are of essential importance to its own growth," she wrote early in 1862. "Every phenomenon refers to some phenomenon back of it—or to some law which one wants to find is the *cause* of it."[17]

Sophia was working hard to keep her children away from the war and all unpleasantness, but Mary wanted her sons to keep up the Mann family's antislavery and reformist passions. To her middle son George, who was then in Washington, D.C., and had had the chance to shake hands with President Lincoln, Mary wrote a vivid description of a massive rally at Tremont Temple in Boston to celebrate the announcement of the Emancipation Proclamation. Elizabeth could not go "on account of her lameness," she wrote, but nearly everybody else was there, African-Americans and whites packed into the same hall where a year previous a meeting of the American Anti-Slavery Society had been mobbed. William Wells Brown spoke, a Scots clergyman named Father McClure read Scripture, and finally news came that the Proclamation had been signed, "at which three times three [cheers] were given— every one rising to their feet, ladies as well as men with a flying accompaniment of handkerchiefs, & the men swinging caps, hats, & arms & hurra-ing from their very *boots*." Frederick Douglass led the crowd in singing "Old Hundred," and the next morning, Mary concluded, "we wake to 'a new heaven & a new earth.'"[18]

Elizabeth, who had had her opportunity to be present at critical moments as well, made a point of sharing her impressions with Horace. She witnessed the final debate and vote in the House of Representatives on the Thirteenth Amendment, to abolish slavery, and described the scene to her nephew. "When the vote was declared it was found to be 7 above the majority of ⅔rds and then such a shout—while the floor on the right side of the house seemed to *blaze* with excitement—& the galleries wholly sympathized—On the *opposition* side the members threw themselves back and bore as quietly as they could. . . . But the eyes on the right side somehow showed out like stars—Some embraced—most shook hands—So we did in the gallery—Tears & smiles contended for mastery." How thrilling, Elizabeth observed, to participate in a nation "in whose public action it is possible for Christ to be manifested." Like other abolitionists, Peabody believed that "there are those who find the history of these United States a Revelation of God, which he who runs can read. . . . we have read our Bible in the American newspapers for the last seven years."[19]

Just as stirring were her two meetings with Abraham Lincoln, which she also described in a vivid letter to Horace. The Peabodys' family friend General Ethan Allen Hitchcock, one of Lincoln's military advisors, arranged for Elizabeth to meet him during one of Lincoln's public receptions, sandwiched in between the many others clamoring for the President's attention. "His face was very pale—his eyes very dark & bright—his countenance very mobile—& a certain fineness of fibre wholly took off the clownish effect of his g[au]nt figure, which was carelessly though cleanly drest—with black cravat & buff waistcoat." They spoke mostly of Horace's father, who had been in Congress with Lincoln and had shared an antislavery position, and Peabody told the President of the scene in the House when the Thirteenth Amendment was passed.

Shortly afterward Peabody had another occasion to see Lincoln, this at a more formal reception. Lincoln recognized her immediately and greeted her by name. They made small talk about flowers and music, but then their conversation turned to politics. Peabody wondered whether he had seen the recent speeches reprinted in *The Liberator,* and she gave Lincoln a copy of the newspaper. "'Here is Wendell Phillips speech on Reconstruction,'" she noted. "'This is not so respectful—He says he does not trust you on Reconstruction.' 'Oh that is no matter!' said he 'Give it to me. I like to read his sharp things!' . . . At last we had to move on to make room for the thickening crowd. . . . And so at last I went away—but I felt I should go again soon—I am astonished to see how I love him—trust him—feel as if he were a father."[20]

That meeting was in February 1865. Elizabeth Peabody spoke with all the confidence of a Washington insider when she told her nephew that "the War means of the Confederacy are exhausted—Lee has military ability—but he must succumb." But to families on the home front, the war seemed to drag endlessly on. Foster Haven, the little boy whom the Peabody sisters had cared for when his mother Lydia died back in 1836, who had grown up to become an army doctor, had fallen at the battle of Fredericksburg in December 1862. "He died at the same age as his mother," Elizabeth observed in a letter to Rawlins Pickman. Elizabeth had missed the funeral of her Aunt Pickman, Rawlins's mother, which was on the same day as Foster's in Worcester. And now Rawlins herself was "on the eve of the beatific vision. I trust that without suffering here you may enter it at last—& I do not believe that when you do, you will find yourself separated from those you love on earth."[21]

Other men from Peabody's circle were dying as well—Robert Gould Shaw, the brothers Edward and Paul Joseph Revere, grandsons of Revolutionary hero Paul Revere. Shaw, who came from a prominent Boston family, enlisted and fought with the Second Massachusetts at Winchester and Antietam, rising steadily in rank. After the Emancipation Proclamation, the first all-black unit was formed, the Fifty-Fourth Massachusetts, and Governor John Andrew, eager "to have for its officers . . . young men of military experience, of firm Antislavery principles, ambitious, [and] superior to a vulgar contempt for colour," offered its leadership to the twenty-five year old Shaw.[22] The story of their momentous engagement at Fort Wagner, South Carolina, in July 1863, is a familiar one, recently told in the film *Glory:* a night assault left half of the unit dead, including its colonel. Shaw was "buried in the ditch with his niggers," a Confederate officer observed with satisfaction. The Shaw family thought this burial an honor and refused to have him reburied in Massachusetts.

It was becoming customary to collect mementos of the war dead or autographs of famous people and to auction them off or publish them, the proceeds going to war widows or for the care of the wounded. Hearing that the Shaws were collecting some of their son's letters, Peabody apparently wrote to ask whether these were going to be publicly printed, and if not, to see whether something might be included in a volume being proposed by her friends Mrs. Fremont and Mrs. Quincy. Francis Shaw wrote back that his wife "is not preparing any for publication, nor has she any intention of doing so. She has been, indeed, collecting every thing that has been written about Rob & his fellow-martyrs of the 54th, for her own satisfaction, but that collection is too personal, not to say too egotistical, for publication."[23]

A note enclosed from Sarah Shaw drove home the point. "Will you say, to whoever proposes it, that it is my most *urgent request*, that neither that [a proposed article on the 54th by Lydia Child] or *any other* personal matter about Rob shd. be published." Two months later Sarah Shaw wrote again to defend her family's privacy. "[N]othing would tempt me to do a thing that I know would be perfectly obnoxious to the dear boy himself." She was indeed collecting his letters, but they were for her grandchildren and future descendants who might, if they wished, publish them, "but not while I live shall I give his private letters to be read & criticised by strangers."[24] Oddly, that is exactly what the Shaws did later in 1864. *Memorial of Robert Gould Shaw* and *Letters of Robert Gould Shaw* were privately printed in Cambridge that same year, handsomely bound in morocco.

The mother of the two Revere brothers likewise wrote Peabody to beg off participating in the proposed memorial volume. Her son Edward had been killed at Antietam in 1862, and his brother Paul Joseph was mortally wounded at Gettysburg on July 2, 1863, and died two days later. Their letters "could not be committed to even so dear a friend as Mrs. Quincy without infringing on the quick of my daughters, who have just attained the spirit of peace. So deep a sorrow as ours calls for all our faith & patience, & cannot be opened anew if it disturbs the sacredness of their treasures."[25]

In the Peabody family itself, the Mann and the Hawthorne boys were too young, or else, like Horace, off studying and traveling in the Pacific. Brother Nathaniel's son-in-law George How had become a Sergeant Major in the 47th Massachusetts Volunteer Militia. But the acid of the war had reached into the family nonetheless. Nathaniel Hawthorne was pursuing what his biographer Edwin Haviland Miller describes as a "duplicitous course" regarding the war, professing not to understand what the conflict was about but also glorying in the martial display of flags and drums and marching men. His "duplicity" was most evident in an essay published in the *Atlantic Monthly* in the spring of 1862, "Chiefly about War Matters by a Peaceable Man." The text satirizes the war effort and mocks "Uncle Abe," but the footnotes, which Hawthorne also provided, act as a kind of loyalist subtext, leaving readers confused and disgusted.[26]

To add to the confusion about Hawthorne's feelings was his insistence that his memoirs of the years in England, *Our Old Home*, be dedicated to Franklin Pierce. At the very moment, in July 1863, when the book was at the printer's, Pierce delivered himself of the opinion that the war was avoidable and the Emancipation Proclamation unconstitutional. Hawthorne's publisher, James Fields, urged the author to withdraw the dedication, but Hawthorne refused. To his sister-in-law Elizabeth, who had warned of the "momentous political consequences" of the dedication, Hawthorne wrote that it "can hurt nobody but my book and myself. . . . You do not in the least shake me by telling me that I shall be supposed to disapprove of the war, for I always thought that it should have been avoided. . . . The best thing possible, as far as I can see, would be to effect a separation of the Union, giving us the West bank of the Mississippi, and a boundary line affording as much Southern soil as we can hope to digest into freedom in another century." Still, Hawthorne was clearly tired of all this arguing; "the older I grow, the more I hate to write notes, and I trust I have here written nothing now that may make it necessary for me to write another."[27]

Later in her life, Elizabeth Peabody defended her brother-in-law as a naïf on issues of slavery and politics. "He had never been at the South," she wrote to Horatio Bridge in 1887. "He never saw a slave or fugitive slave. He looked at all antislavery literature as beneath the consideration of a reasonable man—It was perfectly true what he often said—that he knew nothing about contemporaneous history, that he could not understand history until it was at least a *hundred years old!*—" But even Hawthorne found it impossible to ignore the extent to which his friend Pierce had allied himself with the Southern cause. In that same summer of 1863 while Hawthorne was defending his choice of dedication, Union soldiers ransacked Jefferson Davis's house in Mississippi and found among his papers a letter from Franklin Pierce. This letter found its way to William Cullen Bryant, who published it in his *Evening Post* on September 19, the very day that *Our Old Home* appeared. In his 1860 letter, written before the outbreak of hostilities, Pierce "encouraged Davis to *secede* & trust that War would at once be transferred to the streets of the North where the Democrats would fight on the *Southern side*," Peabody recalled for Bridge. When the newspaper arrived at Mary's and Elizabeth's house in Concord, Sophia happened to be there and exclaimed that "it was 'a forgery *of course*' & she wondered Mr. Bryant could give it a place in his paper." Later that evening a request came from the Wayside for the paper, and after Hawthorne read it, he "never named Franklin Pierce to either Mary or me." Perhaps so, but Hawthorne and Pierce traveled together during the author's last journey; Pierce notified the family of Hawthorne's death; and Pierce sat prominently among the mourners at Hawthorne's funeral.

Pierce's letter to Davis appeared in print in time to embarrass Hawthorne, and years later Hawthorne's letter to Elizabeth Peabody from July 1863 also appeared in print, embarrassing his sister-in-law. In April 1887 Hawthorne's letter appeared in the *New York Tribune*, prompting Bridge to write Peabody about its origin. She certainly had not leaked it to the press, she protested. "But in regard to the publication of that letter," she wrote back in June, "never in my life was I [more] amazed as to see it in print. I never showed it to *any body but* to Ellery Channing who had asked me to write the letter that called it forth—& I should have sworn I did not give it into his hands that he might have taken a copy—for I did not want any body to see what he said about the want of any sincere Union sentiment in the North. . . . I mean to write to Ellery Channing & ask him if he *did* take a copy of that letter—to show to Fields perhaps—who had asked *him* to remonstrate with Hawthorne about printing the preface to 'The Old Home' & which he did not elect to do & so asked me."[28]

Given Hawthorne's intense loyalty toward his old college classmate, it was somehow fitting that Pierce, in the early morning hours of May 19, 1864, should discover Hawthorne's body in his room at Pemigewasset House in Plymouth, New Hampshire, where they had gone for a vacation into northern New England. Hawthorne's health and spirits had been deteriorating since his return from England, "shrunken in all his dimensions, and falter[ing] along with an uncertain, feeble step" in Oliver Wendell Holmes's words. Elizabeth Peabody thought that the "fear of paralysis . . . overshadowed him with what he conceived to be a living death of unutterable horror." Now, quietly and in his sleep, Sophia's "best beloved" had slipped away.[29]

Pierce sent a telegram to Elizabeth, and she and Mary planned to tell Una first. But the high-strung young woman intuited the worst from the looks on her aunts' faces, and her cry brought her mother running. "He dreaded illness & infirmity & old age more than death," Sophia said to her sisters, "& made himself miserable all the times with these dreads." Such an acknowledgment was good therapy for Sophia, who had spent an adult lifetime avoiding painful insights about her relationships with her husband and children. Still, she was unable to plan the funeral, putting this into the hands of Una and Judge Rockwood Hoar.[30]

On the afternoon of May 23, in Concord's First Church decorated with spring blossoms that Louisa May Alcott and other young people had picked, James Freeman Clarke, who had married Nathaniel and Sophia, led the congregation in a funeral service for Hawthorne. Afterwards, the body was taken to the new Sleepy Hollow cemetery, to be buried in a spot later to be named Authors' Ridge. Two days later Sophia Hawthorne sat down to describe the service—its flowers, its people—to her sister Elizabeth. The letter includes details that Elizabeth would surely have seen if she had been there, so Sophia's letter seems to suggest that her sister was, for some reason, absent from this great event. There seems to be no explanation for this possible absence.

In a kind of foreshadowing of her later efforts to regularize Hawthorne's reputation, Sophia went on in this puzzling letter to interpret her husband's relationship with Elizabeth. "I do not believe any one understood him better than you except myself /ourselves/. No one appreciated you—as he constantly said—so well as he. 'I am her best friend' he always said."[31] What Elizabeth made of that astonishing statement is not recorded, although in the 1880s she also sought to reinterpret her relationship with Hawthorne, writing a number of letters to various people, giving her versions of her first encounters with him in the 1830s, recasting their conflicts, and reframing Hawthorne's social and political attitudes as the naive opinions of a brilliant but unworldly artist.

❧ THE WAR HAD, in a sense, killed Nathaniel Hawthorne. It was also redrawing the social and demographic map of the South. Freed by their abandonment on farms and plantations or liberated by advancing Federal armies, African-Americans sought out places of relative safety.

One such dubious haven was Washington, D.C.,—dubious because its southernmost neighborhoods, adjoining the Potomac, were hotbeds of Confederate sympathy. Through precisely these neighborhoods came endless caravans of refugees, including hundreds of orphaned children.

In response to their need, Congress appropriated a Georgetown house and funds to open an "Orphans' Home for Coloured Children," employing Horace Mann's niece Maria Mann as teacher and Peabody's nieces Ellen and Mary as assistants. Despite Maria's efforts, which according to Peabody included "taking these poor little wretches who were found within our lines and in various forlorn places, uncared for and uncultivated as animals, [teaching] them to behave, sew, read, write, calculate, &c &c., and [nursing] them through small pox, measles, [and] camp fever," all without the help of a live-in matron, the neighbors were nonetheless outraged "that the Estate was assigned for the 'benefit of niggers,' altho its owner *is in* the Rebel Army." Shocked at this attack on a woman who was a Northerner, a reformer, an educator, and a relative, Peabody launched a letter-writing campaign to defend Maria's honor and save the school.[32]

Charged with stealing school property and fired in September 1864, Maria Mann had returned in February 1865 to find the school in chaos and disrepair. "Fifty children [were] sleeping in two or three rooms," there was mud everywhere, and the orphans' heads were swarming with lice, Elizabeth wrote her sister Mary from Washington on February 12. Charges and countercharges flew among northern reformers, Georgetown Common Council members, and neighbors. Among the abolitionists who criticized Maria Mann's management and blamed her for the children's condition was Lucy Colman, who wrote in her autobiography that "I will not say this woman was the worst woman who ever lived, because I have not seen all the bad women of my own time; but I have no hesitation in putting her at the head of all I have known, in selfish wickedness. A woman who will deliberately starve, and otherwise abuse, little children, who have no one to care for them, is a monstrosity that I do not wish to be acquainted with." Colman became matron of the orphanage and clashed immediately with the teacher, Maria Mann. After three months the worst abuses of nutrition and health had been cleaned up, according to Colman, and her health had utterly broken down, but not before she saw Maria removed from her post, whom Colman thought to be an alcoholic. "It was a hard fight, with great odds against me,—the prominent Antislavery men in Congress, and the Unitarian minister, the Rev. William Henry Channing, then resident of Washington." Only a few were on her side, including Jane Grey Swisshelm, a prominent feminist and abolitionist. Swisshelm's choice of sides prompted Anna Gibbons, one of Peabody's New York friends, to write that "the name of Swisshelm has ceased to be of consequence." The orphanage was still going as of 1866, when Emily Howland, a Virginia Quaker reformer much interested in black education in the District, wrote to Elizabeth that she would do what she could for Maria's school there. Perhaps the best solution would be to interest African-Americans in Washington in this cause. "What a blessing it is that low as they have been crushed they meet our efforts here with such zeal and enthusiasm, that whoso engages in teaching them without much interest, soon catches the enthusiasm and loves the work."[33]

The bitterness and losses of the war touched Peabody in other ways as well. Like millions of other Americans, she mourned the death of Abraham Lincoln, about whom Ethan Allen Hitchcock wrote "in deep distress," that "Mr. Lincoln has constantly been too careless about exposing himself. Many and many a time I have wished to speak to him about it; but it did not appear altogether proper." And Elizabeth began to have a sense of what Southerners had experienced during the war, as Peabody relatives broke through the wall of silence that had descended in 1861.[34]

The first to write was the Reverend Abner Leavenworth, who had married Elizabeth's cousin Elizabeth Manning Peabody, daughter of Uncle John Peabody. Writing from Petersburg, Virginia, where he had been a minister and principal of an academy for young women, Leavenworth reported that "thanks to a kind & ever-watchful Providence, our family have all been brought safely through the war—though with much hardship, suffering, sacrifice & loss of earthly goods." After news of individuals, he went on, "I have written thus much about the family as a sort of *challenge to you*, to give me a full account of your sisters & all their cedars & pomegranates from the eldest to the youngest" and to give an account of her own literary labors, her "Histories and Chronologies."

Peabody must have responded promptly, for on June 6 her unmarried cousin Mary Ann Peabody, another daughter of Uncle John, wrote to thank her for the note enclosed in the longer letter to Leavenworth.

Less grateful to Providence than her brother-in-law Abner, Mary Ann was bitter that "four years of intense suffering had borne with them not one word of love or remembrance from any of you." She was equally resentful that "unhappy feelings of prejudice exist in the north toward the South," if the newspapers are any indication. "With one result of the war, I mean the freedom of the slaves, the people of the South find no fault. They receive it, as the decision of the Almighty." But charges of deliberate cruelty toward Union prisoners were totally unfounded; the entire South was on short rations, she argued, and "this made scarcity for all." In contrast, Mary Ann mentioned reports of just such deliberate starvation of Southern prisoners "in retaliation," they were told, "for the short rations at Andersonville." This bold and unreconstructed letter seems to have spelled the end of Elizabeth's correspondence with her Southern cousins.[35]

⅏ THROUGHOUT HER ADULT LIFE, Elizabeth Peabody was always involved in several issues and causes simultaneously. The 1860s proved no exception. Family turmoil, the War, kindergartening—all shared space and time with intellectual concerns. Throughout the decade she engaged in vigorous letter-writing, and, by implication, intensive reading with prominent theologians and now-obscure theorists about religion, world history, and literary criticism. For Moses Coit Tyler, later an important historian of American Revolutionary writing, Peabody's reputation as an intellectual far overshadowed her unappealing physical appearance.

> I learned the other day some further facts about Miss Peabody [he wrote his wife in December 1862]. The latter has during her life, amid the activities of a very wide scholarship, given especial attention to two great branches, theology and history. She is a gifted linguist and has written considerably for the heavy quarterlies— like the *North American*. She was very intimate with Doctor Channing and imbibed profoundly his ideas upon theology and has studied deeply all systems of creed. She is said to be able in controversy. In history she is deeply versed and has for years had advanced classes of students in that department whose reading she has guided, and to whom she has expounded her philosophy. I think she is not free from the necessity of earning her own living,

which she has usually done by teaching, having been for years distinguished in Boston by her enterprise in adopting all the latest improvements in teaching. I think she is a remarkable woman, although a sight of her bulky form and pulpy face and watery eyes and a few minutes spent in hearing her talk about the kindergarten would not particularly impress a stranger. She seemed a little too fussy and kinky, but I doubt not, when at her ease and properly drawn out by stimulating questions, she would reveal both learning and original power.[36]

Sometime in the 1860s (possibly through Wilkinson, the English contributor to *Aesthetic Papers* who was James's best friend), Peabody met Henry James, theologian and philosopher, and father of a family of remarkable children. For a time they seem to have struck up a lively friendship. James left a copy of his major wartime work, *Substance and Shadow*, at Ticknor and Fields's Old Corner Bookshop in June 1863. Elizabeth must have written back immediately, praising the book, for on June 20 James thanked her effusively "for your cheering letter!" He was obsessed with reviews and notices of this book and was happy to report that his friend Parke Godwin, editor of the New York *Evening Post*, gave him a "generous notice." A month later he wondered whether Peabody knew what Emerson thought of the book, and went on about other reviews, including one forthcoming (but he didn't know when) in the *Christian Examiner*.[37]

In the midst of this letter exchange and James's concern about the reception of his book, two of James's son went off to battle. Wilkinson, called Wilkie, was an officer in Shaw's famous 54th Massachusetts and was shot in the foot at the debacle at Fort Wagner. While Wilkie still lay in a field hospital in South Carolina, Robert sailed for New Bern, North Carolina, with the 55th Massachusetts. Like Emerson and other once pacific Northern reformers, James saw the war as a great purifying crusade, making men out of boys and a sanctified nation out of conditions of sin. "[T]hough it cost me a heartbreak to part with one so young on a service so hard," he wrote Elizabeth, "I cannot but adore the great Providence which is thus lifting our young men out of indolence and vanity, into some free sympathy with His own deathless life. . . . [T]hough the flesh was weak I still had the courage, spiritually, to bid him put all his heart in his living or dying, that so whether he lived or died he might be fully adopted of that Divine spirit of liberty which is at last renewing all things in its own image."[38]

This persistent idealizing might have made James appealing to Elizabeth Peabody. Influenced, like many New England thinkers, by the work of Emmanuel Swedenborg, James saw the whole universe as awash in God. The Calvinist notion of sin as alienation and separation from God, James thought ludicrous; even if we feel apart from God, we are always in fact at one with the divine. Ultimately, James felt, our "fallen" institutions that serve only to convince us of our separateness from God will crumble, and humanity will live in perfected institutions, for, as the title of one of his books proposes, *Society The Redeemed Form of Man*.

Undoubtedly Peabody admired James's grand, cosmic thinking, the belief that social improvement would usher in God's kingdom. Not everybody felt that way, of course. Samuel Johnson, liberal clergyman and student of Asian religions, was distinctly unimpressed. He saw the book at Ticknor and Fields', "& was repelled by the wearisome & even endless track on which it beckoned; as well as by a sort of slow drag in the style & dismallness in the terminology, which was ominous of another Swedenborgian *Word*—dispensation," he wrote to Peabody. "I wish the man would publish a glossary, defining strictly the senses in which he uses words, & then adhere to it. It wld make it possible to follow his genius through the fogs." In any event, the connection with James seemed all but severed in 1865 when he took Caroline Dall's side in an obscure quarrel of hers with Peabody, one of the many that troubled that relation. James was so vociferous in his championing of Dall that he "not only offer[ed] sympathy but question[ed] Peabody's 'good-breeding' and personally reproach[ed] her," according to James's biographer Alfred Habegger.[39]

There were others, however, to offer compensatory intellectual stimulation. Unitarian minister and Biblical scholar David Wasson wrote Peabody a brilliant and insightful letter in March 1864, challenging the notion that she developed in "Primeval Man." There Peabody had argued that ancient civilizations of which we have record were degradations of earlier, more advanced cultures. At least with regard to Hebrew history, Wasson responded, this outcome was not so. The story of Abraham's willingness to sacrifice his son Isaac suggests that "the merit is here attributed frankly & solely to his willingness to offer up his son[.]" Religious sentiment advances, Wasson claimed, from rude efforts to dominate to "a kind of spiritual democracy in the soul. . . . It results indeed from the simplicity & intensity of Semitic genius that you get the steps of the progress of religion in a simple shape, mixed up indeed with ordinary human passions, but not set forth in the vast variety of coloring which is given by an ampler & abler imagination, nor comingled greatly with the logical necessities of the understanding. . . . I thank you for your many kind words, & prize the opportunity of comparing notes with you." Wasson had in effect called Peabody back to the historical scholarship she had practiced in her *Keys to History*, where the Biblical texts were contextualized with secular sources. Understandable as an outgrowth of her commitment of language as the key to human solidarity, "Primeval Man" nonetheless had violated Peabody's own sense of historical development and change over time.[40]

Distinctly less embedded in reliable scholarship was the work of Ethan Allen Hitchcock. Hitchcock, who was Lincoln's adviser on prison exchanges, had arranged for Elizabeth's meetings with the President in early 1865. As a relief from his exhausting official work, Hitchcock had developed an arcane interpretation of the poetry of Shakespeare, Spenser, and Dante, which featured their use of alchemical symbolism and their secret affiliation with radical pantheism. Anything that suggested nature as a kind of vast symbol system made Elizabeth Peabody just weak at the knees, and she enthusiastically championed Hitchcock's essays and books. Acting as Hitchcock's agent, she sent an essay of his to Charles Eliot Norton, new editor of the *North American Review*. Norton must have had some serious criticisms of this work, for in August 1864 Peabody wrote him to ask whether he would "mark what discrepancies you observe in that article. Perhaps, with omissions of some passages, it might still serve to introduce the sonnets under Gen. Hitchcocks idea." Norton was still unimpressed, even with revisions, and wrote this response to Peabody two months later: "On reading it carefully I came to the conclusion that, although it contained some very happy suggestions & interpretations, the theory advanced in the paper was fanciful & unsound. Unwilling, however to trust my own judgment I submitted the article to Mr. Lowell, who returns it to me today with an opinion confirmatory of my own."[41]

Despite Norton's and James Russell Lowell's dismissal, Hitchcock did manage to find outlets for his work, publishing both *Remarks on the Sonnets of Shakespeare* and *Spenser's Poem: Entitled Colin Clout Come Home Againe, Explained* in 1865. Ever the Hitchcock enthusiast like her sister Sophia, who found the General absolutely "diaphanous—a crystal medium of truth," Elizabeth wrote to Henry Wadsworth Longfellow in 1867, encouraging him to read Hitchcock's last work, *Notes on the Vita Nuova and Minor Poems*, published in 1866. "I think there is a great deal of most interesting suggestion in all *three* books and I think he adduces a great deal of good arguments for his general idea—I was very much struck with the book on the Alchemists—you know probably that he believes Alchemy was a symbolic language by which *philosophers* of the Spirit hid from profane Jupiters, working by strength & Force merely & Vulcan, the prophecies of Prometheus painfully uttered through the cycles of earthly life—." What Longfellow thought is not preserved, but Sam Ward, who was also urged to read Hitchcock, replied that he had "read one or two of his books with the same pleasure I should have in dreaming a pleasant intellectual dream of the past, but with the sensation of never getting my feet on the ground." For Peabody's benefit but probably not because he had any intention of following through, he added that he would "be encouraged by what you say to make further trial."[42]

Perhaps the strangest correspondence of the 1860s was Peabody's exchanges with William Batchelder Greene, the same man who back in the 1840s had found her so strange and New England Transcendentalism so atheistic. Only Greene's side of the correspondence seems to have survived, and only two letters at that, but they are very long and very bizarre. It is likely that they taxed even Elizabeth Peabody, who had enormous patience for the idées fixes. Greene was aware of Peabody's interest in the unity of humanity and in those theories that traded in large generalizations about human cultural origins. Greene had his own theories and spelled them out for her in November and December 1864. The current proliferation of races and nations stemmed originally from three peoples, the Atlanteans of the Mediterranean basin; the Caucaso-Arabians, or Shemites, of the Middle Eastern deserts; and the Indo-Germanians, or Arians, of northern and central Europe. Like Social Darwinists later in the century, Greene had all sorts of generalizations to make about these three "races" and their gifts and weaknesses. Much Christian history, for example, stemmed from the attempt on the part of Arians to impose their logic and order on the spiritual insights of Shemitic peoples, Greene thought.[43]

All this theorizing must have been fascinating to Peabody, who loved to think in these broad categories and was often impatient or uninterested in specific examples and local details. But what was really exercising her mind and interest in middecade was the kindergarten. In March 1866 she and Mary moved to a house on Follen Street in Cambridge, where she could be only a horse-car ride away from her kindergarten over the Charles River in Boston. Of course this proximity to Boston meant that Elizabeth was likely to venture out much more frequently, in all kinds of weather. In January 1867 she fell into an enormous snowdrift, from which she had to be rescued by three strangers. "I have not recovered from the terror caused by your being nearly buried in the snow!" Sophia exclaimed. "How on earth could you venture out in such a terrific storm, such as has not been for ten years? You are very daring. . . . Oh dear—Do promise never to do so again. Those three men must have been the three angels that went to see Abraham. May the Lord bless them!"[44]

The move was certainly better for Elizabeth's relationship with Sophia, which continued to be marked by conflict and misunderstanding. Sophia had grown even more protective of her children, particularly of Una, now in her twenties. Exercising the same concern for propriety that would mark her editing of Hawthorne's American notebooks for publication in the *Atlantic Monthly* beginning in January 1866, Sophia sought to shelter Una from all sorts of sexual and even physical references. Even the classics of English literature could not be exempt, she wrote Elizabeth in March 1865, who had sent Una a volume of early English poetry. "We who are old can take up such works as the early English poets and prosers and cull from them all that is profound and wise without being harmed by what is indelicate and bald and even shocking. . . . For Una's sake, I obliged myself to read much that I would not have wished to read for myself so as to guard her." These words recollect the old anxieties that Sophia and Mary had in the 1830s about Elizabeth's indecorousness, so much that Sophia hastily added, "the children all think you are 'splendid' (their word) and they have a sacred respect for you, and your influence will be great over them." Still, Sophia's position on proper behavior was clear: "I think children should never be told even physiological facts when they are so nasty—

there is no use in it, and they get perfectly disgusted with life, and cannot consider their bodies temples of God. It is too bad, isn't it? Oh for delicacy and tact—oh for gentleness! I do hate strongminded measures of every kind."⁴⁵

While Sophia's idea, at least with regard to her own children, was to postpone indefinitely the day when children would leave the parental nest, Elizabeth and Mary were working hard at an institution that functioned, in a sense, as a surrogate parent. In 1863 the first edition of their *Moral Culture of Infancy and Kindergarten Guide* was published. In many ways Peabody's approach to early childhood education recalled her work with Bronson Alcott thirty years earlier. The child possesses a "law of love," but "a wise and careful teacher" is required to "deal with them as God deals with the mature, presenting the claims of sympathy and truth whenever they presumptuously or unconsciously fall into selfishness." No blank slate or empty vessel, the child is nonetheless all potential, requiring guidance to bring out the divine self within. What is original about this early kindergarten is its emphasis on physical play, so different from the exclusively intellectual and moral education at Temple School. Here at the kindergarten one found organized "Romping, the ecstasy of the body." *Kindergarten Guide* is full of specifics about rooms, activities, materials, plays, games, and lessons.⁴⁶

Still, physical health was just one part of early education, Peabody understood, and so persuaded Mary "to give me her letters on the Moral Culture of Infancy, for an Appendix to my work, because moral culture is a twin object with physical culture in a Kindergarten; and the letters express the very spirit of Froebel, whose primary object was to give a moral and religious cast to the intelligence of healthy children." These letters were originally written to Anna Lowell, author of *Letters on the Theory of Teaching* (1841), while Mary was keeping school upstairs at West Street, but they could not be published then since they were full of specific references to real children. The passage of time had made that concern fade, and now Mary's letters could appear.

What is most striking about these letters is their strongly gendered nature. Mary expressed anger at the poverty and crudity of what passed for education in the 1820s and 1830s: "Benches without backs, long rote spelling-lessons, crowded and ill-ventilated rooms, tedious periods of idleness in which little darlings had to sit up straight and not speak or fidget. . . . Often when I am sitting in my pleasant school-room with these favored children of wealthy parents around me, my only thoughts recur to those crowded rooms, and the only remedy I see is, that school committees shall be formed of *women*. . . . What do *men* know about the needs of little children just out of nurseries?" The central figure, in Mary's letters as in Elizabeth's *Guide*, is the female teacher. For Mary this was her mother, who taught her not only history and religion but also natural science, "lessons in Astronomy and Chemistry," which "gave me such a realizing sense of the presence of God around me, whom I had already known as a Heavenly Father . . . that from that time I never lost the child's sense of nearness, or felt any of those fears of the supernatural which haunt the imagination of uninstructed childhood."[47]

᠍ GRADUALLY, however, Peabody felt that she had not fully grasped either Froebel's system or his theory. "What it had taken Froebel fifty years of suffering life and painful experimenting to work out of abstract first-principles, amid the confusions of a contradictory past, was not divined even by two experienced women, who had made child-culture their own life-work," Elizabeth recalled in 1882. "They [speaking of Mary and herself] did keep an infant-school, which was a very charming affair to the child and to most of the parents," and certainly did so for the sake of children rather than for "ambition or gain." People would write these pioneer teachers and ask for advice or give reports of other efforts, as did Sarah Baily of Davenport, Iowa, describing a German-speaking kindergarten there run on Froebellian principles, though with little equipment and poorly-trained teachers. "[Y]et the expected results did not appear. The children being taught to read, and plied with object-lessons of a really exhaustive kind, showed the precocity that Froebel deprecated as involving future intellectual weakness and disorder," while the children were being exercised physically "to the point of boisterousness. . . . Froebel's method was omitted, as is done in all so-called kindergartens conducted by those who have never mastered the art and science by means of a regular study of Froebel, in a personal training."[48]

Froebel's method could not be learned simply through books, Peabody concluded. She had to go to Europe and see the schools "kept by those whom Froebel had taught and trained" for herself. But this trip would be an enormous undertaking, and a myriad of questions immediately posed themselves: where would she go? for how long? with what funds? who would look after her during the journey? Surely not every-one thought this was a plausible idea. Peabody's Quaker friend Eliza-beth Pugh, for one, warned that "our friends write us from abroad that the prices of every thing have trebled in the last ten years, and urge any friend who wishes to visit Europe to bring a supply of every thing with them, even shoes. Then too dear Friend, you are like myself no longer young and I should much fear that your health would not stand so rapid a journey, and what would become of you if you were taken ill there[?]"[49]

Still, for one so often criticized for scattered and disorganized living, Peabody set herself to the task of raising money and setting an itinerary with speed and discipline. Money was of course the first consideration. She had her annuity that had been set up in the 1850s, plus $1,000 each from a nameless donor and from a Mr. Pickens. But these donations were meant to cover her ordinary expenses, not the extraordinary ones of a trip of many months in Europe. As she had done often in the past, Peabody turned to teaching as a source of income, offering a series of history classes and lectures on "Great Civilizations of Antiquity" in Concord, Boston, New York, and Philadelphia in 1866 and early 1867.[50]

Peabody's lectures and classes generated much interest and atten-dance, including Emerson's daughter Ellen, who attended a history class in Concord, and they netted her between $1,200 and $1,500. The Philadelphia series aroused some controversy, according to her friend Ann Dickson. Dickson reported that some auditors thought Peabody had contradicted orthodox theology: "I suppose that the discomfort of the amiable lady referred to arose from a habit of viewing the *fall* and *redemption* of man in the usual way." In any event, Dickson implied, Peabody's lectures were dense and thoughtful, reminding her of Henry James's *Substance and Shadow*. Peabody's old friend from her days in Waterville, Maine, Ann Sargent Gage, also wrote, possibly in response to something controversial that she had heard Elizabeth say during one of her lectures. To Gage, Peabody wrote to distinguish between the Church of Christ as a spiritual union of believers, and "Ecclesiastism," the human institution that so often results in spiritual bondage.[51]

The lectures and classes showed that Peabody had not lost her intel-lectual edge, bringing to bear as she did her vast knowledge of ancient civilizations and religious history. "I trust the hundred dollars will keep pouring in," Sophia wrote in early 1867. "I hope you will have the class in Concord, and when you have prowess and time come to my house." Sophia's letters from this period betray a certain inattention to Elizabeth's plans, which is understandable given her own financial insecurity and anxiety for her children. "If you decide to go to Europe, dear [which of course Elizabeth had long since decided], have made a peplum of nice waterproof cloth—a whole suit, and you will find your account in it, not only on deck, but in all promenades. Una and I have them, and they are the best contrivance yet invented for walking and wet weather, and for ship life, better than any thing. I do hope you will go. How I wish I had the money for you."[52]

Despite the success of these classes and lectures, which were even making the rounds in Philadelphia Quaker society in printed form, money was still a concern. Peabody had apparently approached another Friend, Susan Parrish, about the possibility of writing a series of articles for the *Friends Intelligencer* about her European travels, and of receiving some payment for them. "[I]t would indeed be very desirable to have in our paper thy fresh impressions of European scenes," Parrish replied, "interspersed, as I know they would be, with characteristic remarks and reflections, but I think our limited means would not admit of our offering thee a sufficient compensation. Indeed we know nothing of what is considered the *pecuniary* value of such contributions and would therefore prefer thou should fix the price per column." Despite the uncertainty about payment, Peabody did come to an agreement with the *Intelligencer* and wrote a series of columns for them.[53]

On the eve of her departure, some of Elizabeth's history students pooled their resources and bought her a new set of clothes, "a wardrobe most judiciously selected—which she received with the simplicity & delight of a child! For Miss Peabody loved dress," one of her old friends recalled, "paradoxical as that may seem. Thus went she forth—equipped as she was both in mind & externals—& that the latter did not fail her any more than did her heart & [word unclear] I can attest—for on one social occasion, I heard it said that Miss Peabody looked like a Duchess."[54] Peabody left on June 8, 1867, aboard the *Bellone*, bound for Brest, France.

⁓ FOR A WOMAN of sixty-three, Peabody kept up a remarkable pace of travel and sight-seeing, interspersed with some longer stays at some spots. For fifteen months she toured Chartres, Paris, several locales in Switzerland, Heidelberg, Antwerp, Hamburg, Dresden, Munich, Berlin, Ratisbon, Rome, and London. Her letters to the *Friends Intelligencer* and to individual correspondents reveal her appreciation of natural beauty, her fascination with religious practices and religious art, her interest in society and politics, and her boundless fascination with human variety. Most of all, the trip provided her an opportunity to visit kindergartens and to meet Baroness Berth von Marenholtz-Bülow, Froebel's patron and champion of his system of early childhood education.

Europe offered her much ammunition for her rather typical New England antipathy toward Catholicism. Chartres Cathedral was a contrast between a lovely statue of the praying Christ above the high altar and "this old droning service, and all its bowings and paraphernalia." In Ratisbon's St. Emmeran Church, she was repelled by the relics, "with jewels of great splendor in their sockets where eyes should be, and in the nostrils, on the mouth. . . . It seemed to me the worst possible taste,—a skeleton covered with jewels." But then religious art seemed nearly to overwhelm her with its beauty and symbolism. Rubens's *Descent from the Cross*, which she saw in Antwerp, was a miraculous combination of material creation and spiritual intensity, while Raphael's and Correggio's Madonnas in the Dresden galleries conveyed a sense of beauty, tenderness, and suffering.[55]

Like her comments thirty years earlier on Washington Allston, these perceptions betrayed Peabody's preference for a psychologizing and spiritualizing approach to art rather than an appreciation of formal elements of style. When it came to politics, she was on surer ground. By September 1867 she was in Dresden in Prussia, famous for its brutal military discipline to which all men were required to submit. "I passed by the drilling ground, and saw some of the exercises. They were terrible to witness," she wrote, so physically demanding that some young recruits committed suicide because they could not stand the drill. Dresden presented Peabody with the great contradiction felt by many American travelers. On the one hand, she revelled in the art and high sophistication of culture; on the other, "the government is felt at every turn. . . . For the first time in my life I have felt myself to be under a government that circumscribes my will. At home, I never thought of government but as the protector of my liberty," but in Europe she felt the state as power over the self. "Some persons told me that with all my love of art, when I came to Europe I should feel more reconciled to authority and less over-zealous for liberty, but it is not so. I see that the age of the fine arts has passed away, and there is no more creation, because authority, not liberty, is the spirit of the age."[56]

Conscious that her letters would be read by Americans interested in making a European tour themselves, Peabody included much advice about how much things cost, where to stay, and what kinds of transport to engage. She had herself been the recipient of just such good advice from Edward Whitney, who wrote her from Paris in August 1867 when she was in Switzerland and contemplating an excursion into Italy. Peabody's old Boston friend Caroline Sturgis also wrote from Heidelberg, apparently just on the eve of Peabody's arrival in that city, with details about places to stay and sites to see.[57]

All those suggestions indicate that Peabody was much concerned about economizing on her trip, which must have included traveling on overnight trains. In August 1867 as Peabody and her traveling companions arrived at Neuchâtel, Switzerland, they met Thomas Wentworth Higginson, who provided this priceless vignette of Peabody in Europe: "Mr [Higginson] saw once at Neuchatel, emerging from the railway train, a party of three ladies with the most villanous-looking courier he ever saw. One lady advanced toward him. She had a long and dusty black-silk skirt, a short black sack, with something like a short white night-gown emerging between, very tumbled; bonnet all smashed, having been slept in, spectacles on *chin*, and a great deal of dishevelled white hair. She was of great size and held her head inquiringly. It was Miss Elizabeth Peabody."[58]

By the late winter and spring of 1867–68, Peabody was in Italy, writing her nephew Horace from Rome. "I am very tired—Those three hours-*four* indeed—on the Corso were exhausting. The crowd was great & the noise; but it was a dismal Carnival. The Romans are too sad & none were there but a mixed low rabble—intent on stealing bouquets & bonbons & *selling* them. . . . I hear that in the Italian cities out of the Papal States—the carnival is more brilliant—especially in Venice & Milan . . . [but] Rome is very melancholy."[59]

Nonetheless, Peabody stayed in Rome for five months, largely through the hospitality of the actress Charlotte Cushman. Elizabeth had seen her perform in Boston in the previous decade and had received a season ticket from Cushman in 1860. In late 1867 she met Cushman

again, this time in the Eternal City, "and experienced the generous
friendship and hospitality which made those five months so rich in
opportunies of enjoyment. But even amid the glories of Rome there was
nothing that I studied with more interest and intensity than herself.
Such simplicity and directness and humility of heart was to me most
touching and wonderful in a person of such magnificent executive powers. You remember the conversations at those delightful breakfasts,"
Peabody wrote to Emma Stebbins, after Cushman's death in 1876, "to
which she invited me every morning? Never was my own mind in such
an intense state of activity. It seems to me that I came to my mental
majority that year, and all my own life and the world's life, as history
had taught it to me, was explained. Principles seemed to rise up over the
rich scenery of human life, like the white peaks of the Alps over the
Swiss valleys."[60]

While in Cushman's care, Peabody met Giuseppe Mazzini, the Italian revolutionary, and Robert and Elizabeth Browning. She also took
time to read Hawthorne's *The Marble Faun*, writing a review which that
be published in the *Atlantic Monthly* in September 1868 and collected in
her 1886 volume *Last Evening with Allston, and Other Papers*. She understood the intimate connection between Rome and Hawthorne's novel,
which offers "a picture of Rome, not only as it appears to the senses
and to the memory, but also to the spiritual apprehension which pene-
trates the outward show." Such a setting offers Hawthorne the opportunity to demonstrate the meaningless and hypocritical ritual practices
of the Roman Catholic Church, Peabody writes, in contrast to the simple, direct spirituality of the character Hilda. Sometime in the future,
Catholic tradition and Protestant individualism will join in a church
"whose *credo* is not abstract dogma, but the love of wisdom and the
wisdom of love."[61]

For all Cushman's generous hospitality, Peabody still had not quite
recovered her strength. Sometime in spring 1868, she wrote from Ge-
neva to an American friend then in Europe, again mentioning her exhaustion. This friend invited her to a quiet retreat at Brienz in Switzerland, which Peabody had visited in the first weeks of her trip.[62] In June
she traveled to Paris, and thence to London where she helped found the
English Froebel Society.

All this travel experience was by turns exciting, intellectually stimulating, and exhausting. But the center of the trip, Peabody's reason for

being in Europe, was the German kindergarten, particularly in Berlin, Dresden, and Hamburg, where she observed kindergartens and training institutes and met Froebel's disciples. What she saw was tremendously ironic: Germany, especially Prussia, seemed weighted down with tyranny and autocracy, yet Prussian compulsory free public education might eventually lead, she thought, to "the development of free institutions." In Berlin, she observed the kindergarten in action and was impressed by the array of equipment, Froebel's "gifts," available to the teachers. She met Matilde Kriege and her daughter Alma, both distinguished students in the Froebel institute, and encouraged them to go to the United States to begin the process of training kindergarten teachers in the approved Froebellian way. Surprisingly, the Krieges agreed immediately and left for Massachusetts months before Peabody did, carrying a letter of introduction to Elizabeth's sister Mary.[63]

Peabody also met the Baroness. Elizabeth's unnamed friend recalled, rather grandly, that "Madame Marenholtz had for years been awaiting the coming of the women from the New World—that she might transmit her message and so vitalizing the system of which she was the Apostle. . . . The meeting of those two women might almost be called historic—they joined hands and anointed each other as apostles of the New Education in which the old world and the new world could work unitedly for the education of *Mankind*."[64] In Dresden, Peabody met Louise Froebel, Friedrich's widow, and in Hamburg she encountered Emma Marwedel. Whereas the other Froebellians were content to develop their master's system for early childhood education, Marwedel wished to apply Froebel's insights to all levels of education and came to the United States to do so. Peabody, who recognized her visionary qualities, once said that Marwedel "inspired me with the courage to make the main object of the remainder of my life to extend the kindergarten over my own country."[65]

᠘ Upon her return to the United States, Elizabeth Peabody was prepared to plunge into her crusade for the kindergarten. However, even as she began to explain to her friends and students her new insights into early childhood education gained from her fifteen-month stay abroad, a family crisis demanded her attention.

In the volatile wartime and postwar financial situation, Sophia Hawthorne's income wavered precariously. Bank failures wiped out alarm-ingly large investments, her friend and financial manager George Hillard reported, and the family would have to economize drastically. Finally, in May 1868 Sophia wrote to James T. Fields to ask for an account of her husband's debts and royalties. After writing several times, Sophia finally received word that she would receive twelve cents per volume for Hawthorne's most recent publication, Sophia's heavily edited *Passages from the American Notebooks*. Anxious and fearful, Sophia blamed James and Annie Fields for betraying the friendship that she thought they had had with the Hawthornes and for profiting from the gentleman's agreements that Hawthorne always had with his publisher.

Responding to Julian's desire to study at the Dresden Realschule and hoping to find a place among the expatriated Americans already settled in that city, Sophia moved her family to Germany in October 1868. In her absence, others carried on the outraged widow's campaign.

Sophia's friend Mary Abigail Dodge, who wrote under the pen name Gail Hamilton, produced a volume called *The Battle of the Books*, in which she skewered Ticknor and Fields for their shady dealings both with her accounts and with Hawthorne's. Elizabeth also took up the cudgel. She wrote Fields several times, trying to make sense of the shifting royalty figures and verbal arrangements. She even threatened to have the Hawthorne rights transferred elsewhere, she reported to Moncure Conway: "Smith & Elder might make their bargain with Ticknor & Field or perhaps Putnam & Co to publish them [Hawthorne's books] in America. . . . I am not empowered to make any bargain with them—But Sophia has now for the first time taken me as her business advisor and wants to know what I think." What she thought was that somebody made a tremendous amount of money on the works of Nathaniel Hawthorne, and it was not her family. As she said to Conway, "could you believe that in the last 17 years during which *all* Hawthornes novels have been written,—he should have got *less* than 17000 dollars;—when Washington Irving's family have received for his . . . $150,000 dollars?" Eventually Peabody was persuaded that her own calculations were at least partially in error, but not before the relationship between Sophia and the Fieldses was irreparably broken.[66]

9

"A Little Child Shall Lead"

⁓

WHEN ELIZABETH PEABODY returned from Europe in the fall of 1868, she set about immediately to report on her new insights and to undo the damage of her premature kindergarten. One of her first stops was the New England Women's Club, which she addressed on December 21. Too many primary schools, including her own on Pinckney and Winter Streets, falsely treated play as "merely diversions," "intervening between short lessons on objects." Organized and supervised play, she now understood, was fundamental to all learning, as it familiarized the child with its own body and creativity. Supervised play was training in ethics, for it required children to play together harmoniously. Finally, she told the Women's Club, proper kindergartens required properly trained kindergartners, and recommended the training school opened earlier that year by Matilde and Alma Kriege at 127 Charles Street.[1]

Peabody's first efforts at kindergartening had brought her to the attention of other educators largely through word of mouth. Now the new gospel of Froebel had to be much more systematically disseminated. She began with a revision of her *Kindergarten Guide*, revising the preface to admit that she had not fully understood Froebel's message, and drastically altering the chapter on reading. She had devoted much space in the 1863 edition to criticizing English orthography for its inconsistencies and illogic; now she grasped that reading itself had no place in the kindergarten curriculum.

Then there followed in 1869 and early 1870 two essays that presented, as clearly as Peabody could, the central principles of Froebel's kindergarten. In 1869 she appended a "Plea for Froebel's Kindergarten as the First Grade of Primary Art Education," to a pamphlet by Cardinal Frederick Wiseman on "The Artist and Artisan Identified." Contemporary art had tended to emphasize the artist's genius over the imitation of nature and thus to separate the work of the artist from that of the craftsman, Peabody argued. But this artificial distinction could be overcome if we recall that all great art, like all good craft, begins in proper observation of nature. Froebel's kindergartens need to be understood as art schools, where children learn to blend the free play of their imaginations with the discipline of nature. Froebel's genius lay in his directive to use children's play as the principle means of education. Doing this requires not passivity on the part of the teacher but, instead, deep knowledge of the "constitution of human nature on the one hand, and the laws of the universe, in some degree, upon the other."[2]

The following year, Peabody articulated a third principle of Froebellian education. Together with the importance of organized play and the need for well-trained teachers, Froebel believed that kindergarten teachers were, in effect, surrogate mothers and that their maternal care toward their charges helped bridge the gap between nursery education and formal schooling. Peabody accepted the notion that women made the best kindergarten teachers, and in her 1870 essay "Kindergarten Culture" she extended that idea. Society was much concerned about "the woman question," she wrote in an essay appended to the "Annual Report for 1870 of the National Commissioner of Education," referring to the postwar debate about women's suffrage and women's legal status. "Teaching is the primal function of humanity, and women now feel it to be repugnant toil only because the true art has never before been discovered. When it becomes a fine art it will become for the teacher, like any other fine art, self-development and the highest enjoyment; for it is nothing short of taking part in the creativeness of *God*."[3]

Throughout the spring and summer of 1870, Elizabeth Peabody traveled widely to spread the word of Froebel's kindergarten. She gave her lecture, "Genuine Kindergartens versus Ignorant Attempts At It," to audiences in Chicago, Cleveland, and Watertown and Milwaukee, Wisconsin, wearing her nightdress under her frock and carrying her toothbrush in her handbag. In August 1870, now back at Follen Street in Cambridge, she wrote to William Torrey Harris, superintendent of

St. Louis's public schools, that she was sorry to have missed him on her midwestern tour, where she "met excellent conventions, and a glad reception of my doctrine of primary education," which she was calling "New Education."[4] Harris, founder of the *Journal of Speculative Philosophy* in 1867 and occupying his present post since 1868, was under no illusions that he had heard the last from Elizabeth Peabody. For ten years she bombarded him with letters about kindergartening, hoping to "make you a convert to my system." Eventually Harris did pay attention to the letters from "so voluminous a correspondent," as Peabody described herself, and permitted Susan Blow, a kindergartener trained in the school of Froebel's student Maria Kraus-Boelte, to open the first kindergarten attached to a public school in 1873.[5]

Unlike reform in pre–Civil War America, postbellum movements for social change were often highly organized, systematized, and national in their scope. The early childhood education movement was no exception. In the first months of 1871, Peabody was a resident expert in the office of the United States Commissioner of Education, John Eaton, who had asked her to come to Washington to consult with him "on the subject of: Froebel's kindergartening; whose great claims upon thinking people have begun to appear," so she wrote to fellow reformer Gerrit Smith.[6] In addition to this consultation, the Senate ordered the printing of 20,000 reprints of her 1870 report "Kindergarten Culture." A further piece of federal sponsorship was "The Kindergarten," an essay that the Bureau of Education published in July 1872.

It quickly became clear to Peabody that preschool education and kindergartening were two quite different entities. She had understood that concept back in 1863, when she distinguished between nursery schools and kindergartens in the first edition of her *Kindergarten Guide*. Now, with federal attention and the possibility of public school affiliation, the stakes were much higher. Nearly as promptly as Peabody announced her reconversion to Froebel's approach, other practitioners appeared on the field, advertising their "American" versions of this foreign creature, the kindergarten. One such person was Anna Coe, who opened a school—which Peabody labeled a "pseudokindergarten"—on Fifth Avenue in New York City.[7]

This business of the "Americanizing" of the kindergarten would be a persistent problem throughout the 1870s. In response to such competitors as Coe, who was teaching reading to her young students, Peabody wrote "When Should Children Be Taught to Read—Sham Kindergarten Culture." There can be no such thing as an "American" kindergarten, she argued. Froebel's system is based on universal and scientific principles that are unaffected by culture or geography. One of these is the principle of systematic development. True education begins not with learning to read but with the training of the senses. Such training does not delay true education but forms the basis and foundation of all that comes after. "I have taught several hundred children to read," she admitted, "and always suffered in doing it, when they were not as old as six or seven, because I sympathized with the painful effort of the brain."[8]

This belief in the universal truths underpinning the kindergarten movement drove Peabody to one more European trip. In September 1871 she was "escorted by a group of a hundred Boston admirers to the steamer in New York and sent directly to the American Embassy in London, where she made a long visit to her friend James Russell Lowell," Kate Douglas Wiggin reported. From there Peabody went to Italy to visit the Brownings and Mazzini. "I cannot recall the great personages who managed her return journeys, but they were conducted with great care for her comfort. I imagine she thought herself the guest of the various railways and steamships honored by her company. I know that whenever she had a ticket given her she mislaid or lost it, but no conductor ever disbelieved her or demanded that she leave the train."[9]

This trip, begun with such flair, wore the sixty-seven-year-old Peabody down. She caught cold in December but was still able to go to Rome in March as well as to see Baroness von Marenholtz-Bülow once more. But on returning to London, "I was so prostrated that my physician gave me no encouragement that I should be better there in time to enjoy the summer," she wrote to her friend Susan Cole, "& joined with my nephew George in persuading me to come home with him—The voyage cured me—though there was a little reaction again on getting upon land out of the ocean breezes which I so love."[10]

Another reason to cross the Atlantic was to see her nieces. In February 1871, while Elizabeth was working in the Commissioner's office in Washington, Sophia Hawthorne succumbed to her last illness. Sophia and her children had moved to Dresden in 1868, but the threat of the Franco-Prussian War in 1870 sent her fleeing to London. There she contracted pneumonia, a fatal blow to her already weakened respiration. Her death was long in coming and kept her struggling and gasping for breath through the long days of February. She begged for drugs to ease the pain and make her sleep, including chloroform, which the doctors said might kill her. They administered it at her insistence, but she awoke from the temporary respite to suffer some more. Finally, on February 26, she died. Six days later, Sophia was buried in a cemetery at Kensal Green.[11]

Sorrow over Sophia's death and continuing concern for her nieces and nephew were not the only links that bound Elizabeth Peabody to her family and to the past. Before she left for Europe, Peabody had learned that Bronson Alcott was planning to issue a new edition of *Record of a School*, in large part to cash in on the success of his daughter Louisa's novel *Little Men* with its Temple School–like Plumfield. She wrote him a detailed letter in July 1871, spelling out all the changes she hoped he would make, assuming that she still owned the copyright on the volume. That was in fact not the case, as the publisher Roberts Brothers made clear, and the revision went forward with only a revised preface. From London, Peabody wrote angrily to the publisher, "I did not know that when the author was *alive*—that it was considered *courteous* to publish his or her book without consultation—and it seems to me a *great injustice* and needing the protection of a new law—that this should be done."[12]

The real issue here, Peabody thought, was not so much any payments or royalties on the new volume but the possibility that readers might miss her new allegiance to Froebel's philosophy in this reminder of an older experiment. The students at Temple were always somewhat older than modern kindergarten pupils, she reminded Alcott, and then spoke to a larger audience in the preface to the third edition of *Record:* "I find myself, however, in the somewhat embarrassing position of seeming to affirm some crude ideas of my own, inevitably mingled with the narrative, and which in thirty-six years have given place to clearer ones. While my maturer age endorses the instinct which led me to set forth so lovingly this actual and most genuine outgrowth of Mr. Alcott's mind, and I believe with him—now as then—that education must be moral, intellectual, and spiritual as well as physical, from the very beginning of life, I have come to doubt the details of his method of procedure; and I think he will not disagree with me that Froebel's method of cultivating children . . . is a healthier and more effective way than self-inspection."[13]

The Alcotts viewed the situation very differently. The copyright had run out, Louisa reminded Mary Mann, and since "Miss P gave the book to father sometime ago he felt that he had a right to reprint." Alcott had always wanted his former assistant to benefit from the reprinting, which might be considerable given the connection to *Little Men*, and "he thought she would be satisfied & pleased." But instead, "Miss P's prefaces &c confuse the reader's mind, add nothing to the book, & seem to give the impression that the Recorder did not approve of what she recorded. She says she wishes to explain her own views, & retract certain observations of her own in the book. I think if she took out the observations & let the book stand simply as a Record of the school without implicating her in the least, it would be the best plan."[14]

It is unlikely that a reissue of *Record of a School* would have had much effect on the burgeoning kindergarten movement. In the years after her return from the second European trip, Peabody became the center of a growing national movement to spread Froebel's kindergarten. Two more educators trained in Froebel's institute came to the United States, Emma Marwedel in 1870 and Maria Boelte in 1872, both determined to organize training schools for future kindergartners. In the following year, Peabody helped found the *Kindergarten Messenger*, with herself as editor, intended to spread the news of the kindergarten and to distinguish between true Froebellians and those operating "pseudokindergartens." Kindergartens themselves appeared throughout the country: in Detroit and Lansing, Michigan, in 1871; a German-speaking one attached to a public school in Wisconsin in 1872; an English-speaking public school kindergarten in St. Louis in 1873; a kindergarten and training school operated by Emma Marwedel in Los Angeles in 1876; and a kindergarten and Public Kindergarten Society in San Francisco in 1878. Parallel to the movement to establish kindergartens as part of the public school system was an effort to found free kindergartens, particularly in poor neighborhoods, where no such public school kindergartens yet existed. Pauline Agassiz Shaw, who had been much influenced by Peabody's embrace of Froebellianism, devoted her share of her family's fortune to establishing charity kindergartens in Boston.[15]

MONCURE CONWAY once complained that "Miss Peabody's devotion to the kindergarten is one of the great literary tragedies. She could be the greatest woman of letters in America. She should spend her last years in writing her recollections of literary men and women.

She had a larger circle of friends than any other one person, and she should write of 'The Men and Women I Have Known.' It would be a literary history of her time, unsurpassed in interest. Instead, she is spending her energy and time in going about speaking for the kindergarten. It is a loss to literature."[16]

In a sense, Conway was right. Peabody wrote some vivid letters of reminiscence, gave some valuable interviews to her nephew Julian, and wrote her *Reminiscences of William Ellery Channing*. But her piles of manuscripts, journals, and letters, which could have been the sources of a fascinating retrospective, she left for others to sift through. In another sense, however, Conway had insufficient vision. The kindergarten was her greatest work, her *Nature, Walden*, "Song of Myself," *Woman in the Nineteenth Century*. Like those works, Peabody's version of the kindergarten was the self writ large, a summary and recapitulation of her life as she understood it. The movement reflected all the influences in her life and career: her mother's school and philosophy; the impact of Channing's affective Unitarianism; the Transcendentalist protest and the larger Romantic ideology; her devotion to history; and her emphasis on the self in the social order.

Peabody was always a great synthesizer and mediator, and nowhere is her power to blend often disparate influences clearer than in the kindergarten. The child comes into the kindergarten already possessing inestimable gifts and powers. Echoing Wordsworth, Emerson, Thoreau, and Alcott, she argued in scores of essays throughout the decade that the child possesses a "personal soul . . . pre-existent to the understanding of nature, and has a communion of sovereignty with the Author of nature." "It is of the last consequence that the kindergartner should take into her mind that this aesthetic soul [the child's intuitive grasp of beauty, harmony, and creativity] exists in children as a primary fact."[17] Her most successful and succinct essay on the kindergarten, "Origins and Growth of the Kindergarten," begins with the Coleridgean distinction between Reason and Understanding. Reason, or imagination as she calls it here, "is spontaneous—the self-activity of the mind. The understanding grows by sense and the intuitional perception of particulars and the laws of the material universe, and therefore proceeds by analysis. The development and conduct of the understanding is education."[18]

Together with this Romantic ideology, Peabody also expressed her view of early education in Christian rhetoric. Froebellian kindergartens effected "the *regeneration of humanity* by the second coming of the Christ-child," she wrote to Anna Ward, and echoed that view in "Origin and Growth": "Is not this method of developing the human being, perhaps the second coming of Christ, whose triumphs, the prophet says 'a little child shall lead'? Is the Christ-child anything but *childhood received* in the name of Christ?" The kindergarten teacher conceals her identity in absolute law, which ordains development through the senses toward intellectual and spiritual maturity.[19]

Into this already heady mix of idealist and Christian views (or rather, a Christian view much affected by idealist philosophy and study of comparative religions), Peabody blended a third influence, a developmental philosophy and the organic metaphor. Popular with eighteenth-century educational writers like John Locke, developmentalism stressed the organic changes that the child experiences over time, in the child's physical, moral, intellectual, and spiritual growth. Like other growing things and living organisms, the child needs to be nurtured in ways that are appropriate to the stage he or she occupies. The nurturer, the gardener in the child's garden, is an active shaper and molder of the lives entrusted to her, since, in Peabody's view, the child is all potential, and given to waywardness without proper care. "Children are generally fanciful," she wrote, "especially if left to themselves, but this lawless activity of mind may become a disease." Left "alone in the universe," all beings, including children, would become "depraved beings," she wrote to William Torrey Harris. "Children become causes of evil to themselves & others by the very nature that would make them causes of good if they were treated as living organisms instead of dead clay to be modelled by the will & according to the notions of others."[20]

Although the pieces may not logically fit together, Peabody's articulation of the kindergarten in mid-Victorian America was a triumph. For that small group of nostalgists still in the grip of Romantic idealism, Peabody presented the child as possessing a preexistent soul, imaginative power that needed only guidance. For moderate and conservative parents concerned about discipline, she insisted that kindergarten play be collective, organized, and supervised. She would not have dissented from the response of Mary Garland, the leading student of Matilde and Alma Kriege and an influential kindergartner in her own right, to the criticism that she seemed very severe in her classroom manner. "I intended to be severe . . . the situation demanded it; there must be law in that kindergarten before there can be freedom." The kindergarten could also be a way to address the heightened social problems caused by immigration and urban growth. For Peabody and other educators, the kindergarten functioned as an alternative home, somewhat in contradiction to Froebel's idea that the kindergarten was simply an extension of the nursery. In situations where the nursery was the street, kindergartens were safe havens, places of creativity and calm where "three years apprenticeship to evil could be changed to three years of blessed work made out of play."[21]

Finally, Peabody understood that the kindergarten, itself the product of systematic organization and advocacy, was the first site of socialization. It immersed children into the stream of society and history, without which they were, as she said, "depraved beings." Peabody had nearly always dissented from the radical individualism of some Transcendentalist thinkers. She had criticized Alcott for encouraging too much introspection among the Temple School students and had worried that Jones Very's radical self-emptying resembled Quaker anti-institutionalism. Always the practical intellectual, she had worked to embed reformist impulses within institutions like Temple, the West Street Bookshop, and Brook Farm. Emerson had understood her position very well when he listed her with Orestes Brownson, George Bancroft, and others who thought that "the vice of the age is to exaggerate individualism, & they adopt the word *l'humanitie* . . . and go for *'the race.'* Hence the Phalanx, Owenism, Simonism, the Communities."[22]

Now, in the last quarter of the nineteenth century, Peabody's concerns about the social implications of Romantic ideology found company in a new generation of reformers. Many postwar social theorists and reformers saw individualism and Romanticism as the chief obstacles to achieving a more systematized and harmonious society. An oppressive and tyrannical arrangement, romantic love was based on private passionate moments, thrilled to conflict and tumultuous reunions, and throve on fantasy. As a result, many women became the slaves of love and of masterful men. What was required was a new understanding of human relations, particularly affectionate ones, as fundamentally social and rational, that would be subject to scrutiny, debate, and even the advice of others. "Live in the open air" was the battle cry of Mary Putnam Jacobi, and she, Elizabeth Cady Stanton, and many other postwar feminists affected by Auguste Comte's positivism saw in rationality and social organization a new scientific basis for a reformed society.[23]

Some of this theory would have sounded plausible to Elizabeth Peabody, who had learned to equate revivalist religion with romantic passion and to reject both. Masterful men were few in her early life, but among them were the revival charlatan Dantworth and the putative home-wrecker Royall Tyler. Overbearing men, or else ineffectual ones like her father and Palmer grandfather, may have caused Peabody to flee heterosexual relations altogether, finding in men like Channing, Mann, and Hawthorne fantasy lovers rather than genuine partners. As for the new science, Peabody also tried to incorporate that as well, although clearly she was more comfortable with the older idealism. In an essay called "The Relations between the Kindergarten and the So-Called Positive Philosophy," she argued that although Froebel's outlook reflects his Christian beliefs, the kindergarten movement is equally amenable to a more scientific approach. Unlike, say, Alcott's method in the 1830s, the kindergarten acknowledges and works with the very material nature of the child, understanding the senses as foundational for human development and education.[24]

Still, by the end of the century, it was becoming clear that the Romantic organicism of Froebel and Peabody was a very different thing from the materialist organicism of younger reformers. To them, the child was an entirely physical entity, subject to testing and measurement, and to new insights from psychology and physiology. Unfolding the divine essence within each child seemed a quaint, slightly ridiculous idea to teachers like Patty Smith Hill, who taught the new scientific, secular approach in courses at Columbia Teachers College in the first years of the twentieth century.[25]

∿ As with the *Dial* of the 1840s, so with the *Kindergarten Messenger* of the 1870s: influence and prestige do not necessarily bring financial security. By 1875 the costs of publishing the *Messenger* had outstripped its subscription income. In the December issue, Peabody announced the merging of her journal with the *New England Journal of Education.* "I think the *Messenger's* special work of discriminating the kindergarten from the nursery life on the one side, and from the school life on the other, has been largely accomplished, and this important period of some three or four years has been vindicated as not time to be killed but to be most carefully employed to lay the foundations of intellect." Elizabeth had been promised her own column in the *Journal*: "I do not, therefore, consider the change as a death, but rather as an ascension into the dignity of the majestic 'we'; and I hope that the many mothers and young persons aspiring to be kindergartners who write to me now as an individual, will continue to do so, with the same confidentialness, for I shall still sacredly respect their confidence."[26]

The majesty of "we" soon descended, rather than ascended, into open partisan warfare. The 1876 Centennial Exposition in Philadelphia featured an exhibit of "The American Kindergarten," which was organized by Peabody's rival Anna Coe and advocated the teaching of reading and writing to preschoolers. Also advertising at the Exposition and claiming the name of kindergarten, Louisa Pollock advanced methods and techniques having nothing to do with Froebel's approach. The editor of the *Journal* recommended both Coe's and Pollock's exhibits, a move that outraged Peabody and her sister Mary. In December Mary wrote to Henry Barnard that "such a confusion of ideas as Miss Coe, for instance, introduces, just spoils the unity and simplicity and appropriateness of the kindergarten training, which is based on the soundest philosophical principles and is to be fought for tooth and nail until fairly understood and established."[27]

Despite the promise of independence in her column, Peabody was blocked from writing critical reviews of Coe and Pollock, and so she resigned in protest. Angry in turn at Peabody's championing of Froebel as the last word on kindergartening, the staff of the *Journal* wrote anonymous letters to the periodical, ridiculing Peabody for her persistent defense of Froebel and criticizing her for negativism toward Coe and Pollock. "I will resume my little monthly," she wrote in the first number of the *Kindergarten Messenger*'s new series, "whose original 'reason for being' was to describe and explain the moral and intellectual culture that should precede object teaching and book study." In 1878 Peabody joined with Wisconsin educator William Hailmann in forming the *Kindergarten Messenger and the New Education*, which became the journal of the new American Froebel Union, organized in 1877.[28]

This issue of an American kindergarten, which had arisen promptly in 1870 and now returned with force at the Centennial, was a difficult one. Peabody found herself in the position of advocating a system that seemed to admit of no change and no cultural variation. To someone like her who believed so strongly in universal law and cosmic truth, this position was perhaps not so difficult, but others found it more problematic. Harris, for one, "spoke of the adoption of the method into the American public schools—as *Americanizing it*—," and Peabody wrote promptly to quench that fire. "I hope before you drop the subject you will distinctly say that by *Americanizing* it *you* do not mean departing from Froebel's principle."[29]

Although Harris acknowledged that in his view, an American kindergarten could be nothing other than a Froebellian one, he always had his doubts about Peabody's single-minded advocacy. The newly formed American Froebel Union seemed a kind of self-appointed standards committee. "I think you will find our society a much more harmless thing than you fear," she responded. "In the first place it is a Publication Society, and its first act is to publish the memoirs of Froebel" and to create a standard library of "the canonical books as it were." As for her own role, she argued that she was simply distinguishing between those teachers who had received a Froebellian education and those who had not. "We do not mean to be an *impertinent* meddling body—but merely be what we are[:]*a light of intelligence* pointing out the *sources* of knowledge & skill in this preparation of children for school, to those who ask."[30]

Despite these controversies and Harris's continuing belief that kindergartens could best be understood as preparation for a life in the industrial workforce, the kindergarten along Froebel's model continued to spread, most spectacularly in St. Louis, which by 1879 had 53 classes, 131 paid teachers, and numerous unpaid assistants. The charity school movement, begun with Pauline Shaw's fortune, spread outward to New York City, Chicago, and San Francisco, and merged with the Progressivist concern for child welfare in urban and industrial environments. As long as this flood of kindergartens remained in the hands of such disciples as Susan Blow, Mary Garland, and Kate Douglas Wiggin, Elizabeth Peabody's life's work would remain secure.

ᔓ FROM THEIR HOUSE on Follen Street, Elizabeth Peabody and Mary Mann entertained a stream of visitors, many in quest of news or inspiration about kindergartening, but others involved in other reforms. In their backyard, their second cousin George Haven Putnam recalled, were pitched several tents that served as shelter for "Poles,

Hungarians, and South Americans. The sisters provided the lodging, while it was understood that the refugees would find their own board; but if they were absolutely destitute, they would receive a share of the modest meal of Boston beans or prunes and rice." Visiting her once after his marriage, Putnam found his relative entertaining a group of revolutionaries from Paraguay. Lizzie thought that George would make a perfect minister of education in the new government. He begged off, but "learned later, with some surprise, that this particular revolution had been a success, and that if I had gone to South America with my cousin's guests, I might have been minister of education for at least six months. This was at the time the average duration of the governments of Paraguay."[31]

Others came to visit: a Mr. Chaney was invited to "take a light lunch of hot cocoa & bread & butter at 1 o'clock" or to stay to "dine at 5." Horatio Bridge was given detailed instructions on how to take the streetcar to their house. At the Follen Street house, a group of friends gathered in May 1874 to help Elizabeth celebrate her seventieth birthday. Rebecca Weston recalled Peabody's flaxen hair's turning silver, but her manner as youthful as ever. Mary Mann was dressed, as usual, in severe and spotless perfection. A portrait of Sophia hung on the wall. "Miss Peabody always liked to express her indebtedness to Hawthorne for the help he gave her in her writing. He kept her from printing too much, she was wont to say. . . . There was always a feeling of comradeship between them, which began in youth." Peabody had a somewhat less sentimental view of the event, telling James Freeman Clarke that she felt "like the Egyptian corse at its own funeral."[32]

She should have had a less sentimental view of family as well, which was marked by anything but comradeship in these years. The tensions and conflicts of previous decades continued into the old age of the survivors, while the younger people experienced their own versions of the family romance. Care for her mother in her last illness caused Una Hawthorne another mental breakdown in 1871. Several more lapses followed, punctuated by another disastrous engagement, until Una died in September 1877 in Clewer, England, near Windsor.

Equally traumatized by her mother's death, Rose leaped into a hasty engagement and marriage with George Parsons Lathrop, an editor and a journalist. In 1876 Lathrop published the first critical account of Hawthorne's work based on family papers, *A Study of Hawthorne*. This work upset Julian Hawthorne, who saw it as an invasion of family privacy. In a bitter letter to the *New York Tribune* on July 8, 1876, Julian claimed that since 1872 he and Rose had been trying to get Lathrop to return papers that had come into his possession after his marriage to Rose. Lathrop had intruded himself "into prominence by attaching himself to a famous name" and had "composed and published [his book] in violations of a trust and in the face of repeated warning and opposition; and after all it conveys no just & truthful representation of its subject."

These charges of theft and misprision burst upon Rose and George through a letter from Ellery Channing as well as through the media. Received in September 1871, Channing's letter was written in a *"fit of insanity,"* according to Elizabeth, and set off profound emotional tremors in Rose. Five years later, the public controversy in the pages of the *Tribune* forced Rose, then pregnant, into "going over all the mental agonies that attended that fearful night when that *fatal letter* came by which she found her husband was so fearfully *misunderstood.—,"* Peabody wrote Ellen Conway. "And all the Sufferings they have had since—have come rushing back on her in her weakness!" Even though the baby, Francis, was born healthy, Rose was "raving mad at this present moment." When Peabody asked Lathrop whether the child would be named Hawthorne,

> he said no—neither he or Rose wanted to put the *curse* of that name on their child—while . . . all of the named (Julian Una & their aunt Elizabeth H) . . . did not retract their public accusation of *him*—*before the world*—He had begun his life worshipping Hawthorne in his books—he had . . . said he should grow up knowing himself as only . . . a Lathrop—& he & Rose would commence a new life entirely separate from the . . . blood of Hawthorne. And he said Rose felt this too—and that only in another world could that Ideal which he had worshipped & sacrificed to be *realized* & enjoyed.[33]

Julian himself eventually made use of family papers as well in his several memoirs of his parents, and even incorporated reminiscences of his aunt, who had so vigorously taken his sister's side in this family quarrel. Rose too wrote a family reminiscence, but not until she was divorced in 1895 from Lathrop, who had proved to be alcoholic and unreliable. Her book, *Memories of Hawthorne* (1897), contains vivid anecdotes drawn from her mother's papers. Reenacting the Protestant fascination with Catholic traditions of celibacy and service, Rose entered the Third Order of St. Dominic as Sister Mary Alphonsa in 1899 after Lathrop's death, and she devoted herself to the care of the poor who were dying of cancer. In New York City neighborhood clinics and then at Rosary Hill Home in Hawthorne, New York, Mother Alphonsa quietly and lovingly cared for the terminally ill, much as Hester Prynne did in her father's novel of half a century earlier. She died on July 9, 1926, her parents' wedding anniversary.[34]

Family conflict emerged even closer to home in the 1870s, indeed right at home. After a lifetime of intimacy and rivalry and ten years of shared housekeeping, it was not surprising that Elizabeth and Mary would be getting on each others' nerves. While vacationing in Northboro, Vermont, Elizabeth wrote a remarkable letter back to her sister, which speaks both of Peabody's idealizing cast of mind and of the conflicts that simmered between them.

I shall write those Reminiscences of Sophia's early life & development, with her letters to illustrate them without any view to publication—*because* they ought to have an immortality on earth . . . whatever may have been the "mistakes" she made about the education of her children—which *mistakes* by the way were only the inevitable shortcomings of the infinite. . . . If you think a true record requires that every mistake should be *recorded—I do not.* There is something false in finite facts. . . . I am going also to write my Reminiscences of Mother, in the same spirit—doing justice to her Ideal which she never lost—not in the darkest hour when she so determinatedly *denied facts* that contradicted that never abandoned Ideal—But there is nothing good & of good effect in me that I cannot trace up to *words of hers.* . . . In looking over the previous sheet, I feel as if it would give you an idea of my being self-intoxicated with this revival of the joy of the Ideal & about to become more insufferable than ever—But I assure you that it makes me more able to see all my own faults—& that I do not call evil good when I recognize the essential finiteness of all evil.[35]

It must have been extraordinarily hard to share a house with someone who lived so serenely on the ideal plane and who saw the denial of unpleasant facts as a spiritual advantage. Mary confided her unhappiness to her son George, who wrote back that he was "glad to be let more into your counsels about Aunt L[izzie]. I know perfectly well how she offends one's sense of justice,—and how impossible it is to make her see it." His aunt's serene otherworldliness was a form of "*violence*, for that it is," George thought, since it compelled everyone else to pick up the pieces. Perhaps Mary sometimes magnified, even aggravated, her trials, but in the end it would be best if the two sisters parted ways. "I am sorry she is to leave us while we [George, his mother, and his new wife Esther Lombard] form a household,—tho' of course it is practically the beginning of the general break-up . . . it will undoubtedly be a relief all around."[36]

Elizabeth's version of this breakup was that Mary "had been such an invalid these last years that she wants to give up housekeeping—& besides cannot afford to keep this expensive house in Cambridge." In any event, in early May 1878, Elizabeth moved in with her brother Nathaniel, who was then living in Concord. "Concord has immensely *improved*—the public library built & given by Mr Monroe occupies the Brooks house lot—& all the old houses are moved off and elegant edifices taken their place on both streets." Peabody added to this vigorous new public library by contributing her own private collection. Concord's annual report for 1878–79 describes her gift as consisting of 994 pieces, 839 volumes, and 155 pamphlets. Many of these originated with Peabody's circulating library and bookshop on West Street; others, writes Leslie Perrin Wilson, came from Horace Mann's collection, which Elizabeth apparently acquired after Mann's death.[37]

⟳ IN THE LAST YEARS of the 1870s, Elizabeth Peabody's vigorous pace of travel and speaking began to catch up with her. In 1877 she had a slight stroke. "I hope you have, or will have at my petition, Dr. Wesselhoeft's advice as to her diet and medicine," Rose wrote from New York City. "Her life is dear beyond words to me, and I naturally think of all the ways in which it can be hedged about. God give you both joyous, strong years to come." Peabody returned weakened and sick from a lecture tour in March and April, which took her to Florence, Massachusetts, to New York, and to Philadelphia, "engaged in the kindergarten propaganda during which time I gave 12 parlour lectures, and visited kindergartens new & old & other educational institutions." In

1879 Peabody developed cataracts and also experienced a serious fall. "I had a nurse & doctor *seven weeks*—it was a miraculous escape from instant death," she wrote her Wisconsin friend Aubertine Woodward. Her usual forgetfulness and unconcern about appearance grew more noticeable, more humorous, and often more troublesome in these years, prompting her sister and her friends to appoint young people to look after Elizabeth.[38]

One such young person was Lucy Wheelock, later an important educator and founder of Wheelock College. At nineteen she was delegated to take Peabody to New York City for a Froebel Union convention and to bring along a new, black silk dress for the public event. "Our first morning in New York I awoke to find myself alone in the room. Miss Peabody was gone. Where? I was filled with dismay. I was derelict to duty. Suppose she were run over in boarding a street-car?" No one in the house knew where she was, but then she came in safely, saying that she was concerned that the church building be opened in time for the meeting. She had gone early in the morning to the manse, awakened the household with her insistent ringing, and was reassured by Dr. Reginald Heber Newton that indeed the church would be available for use. The meeting was a great success, Wheelock recalled, but "Miss Peabody refused to wear the new silk gown unless she were invited out for tea or dinner. As no invitation was forthcoming, we returned to Boston with the gown none the worse for wear."[39]

10

"What a Reservoir Her Memory Is"

 ~

HAVING ALREADY ENDURED the deaths of parents, brothers, and a sister, Elizabeth Peabody now entered the decades when the losses of family, friends, and colleagues would multiply. Years earlier she quarreled with Abigail Alcott over opening and reading private mail, and more recently with Bronson and Louisa May over the reprinting of *Record of a School*. Now, with Abigail's death in November 1877, Peabody revisited those early days in a letter to Louisa: "I lived with your mother in perhaps the most intense period of her suffering experience of life—and feel as if I knew the heights & depths of her great heart as perhaps only you & Anna can do. For a few months we were separated by stress of feeling in most tragic circumstances—and she doubted my friendship—truth & honor. . . . But God gave me an opportunity to withdraw the veil & I have under her own hand her written expression of her conviction that I was *true to her* & her deepest worth *at that very time*." Praising Louisa for her fictional portrayals of her parents, Peabody closed elegiacally: "When we sit down together on the banks of the River of Life (or the fields of asphodel[)]—not before—we will talk of—what we cannot speak among the shadows & cross lights & confused echoes of time." Others too had crossed the river: "Miss Thoreau Mrs. Brooks old Mrs. Goodman—and Elizabeth Hoar," Charles Emerson's fiancée and an honorary member of the Emerson family.[1]

Still, it would have been unlike Peabody to retire altogether, despite her fragile health and family strains. In July and August 1879 she participated in the first session of the Concord School of Philosophy, Bronson Alcott's last educational experiment. Gathering the aging exponents of the idealist philosophy—Emerson, Peabody, William Torrey Harris—their last disciples like Frank Sanborn and David Wasson, and younger people eager to catch a glimpse of these lions, Alcott organized a series of lectures and discussions over six weeks beginning July 15. "I never felt so completely *at home* as I do in this School of Philosophy," she wrote Mary in August, "the spirit of which is to listen to & appreciate whatever may be said on the themes whose discussion 'makes the soul.'" Some of the presentations were mediocre, like John Albee's comments on Milton's *Paradise Lost*, but "all the lectures are superb & Mr. Alcott says better things than I ever heard him say before."[2]

Although not on the program for that first summer, Elizabeth Peabody was a vigorous participant in its programs. We catch a glimpse of her during that summer in the reminiscence of Kate Douglas Wiggin, a young kindergarten teacher whom Peabody had invited to visit her and attend the sessions of the School. "You must not go back to San Francisco [where she was to work in the famous Silver Street kindergarten] without seeing Concord. You are a hero-worshipper, and we have heroes of all sizes here just now at our great School of Philosophy," Peabody wrote, adding that the young woman should board with her at her brother Nat's house. "We are all old fogies in the house, and we want a fresh, young mind to help us with its happy intuitions." To the romantic and impressionable Kate, perhaps the most exciting part of the invitation was the promise that she would sleep in Charlotte Cushman's nightgown, left to Peabody in the actress's will.

After morning lectures, Kate walked with Alcott or Harris, visited Emerson's house and peered into his study, chatted with Lidian Emerson and daughter Ellen, increasingly her father's strong right arm. In the afternoons Kate "often strolled through Sleepy Hollow burying-ground in company with Mr. Emerson, Mr. Alcott, Mr. [William Ellery] Channing [poet and nephew of the clergyman], and Miss Elizabeth Peabody. . . . We wandered slowly among the graves of the illustrious dead, while each of the honored living related happy anecdotes of the comrades passed over and yonder. . . . The day was warm, and they had all bared their heads to the breeze. Mr. Channing had helped Miss Peabody to a seat, while Mr. Emerson and Mr. Alcott rested at the foot of a great, leafy tree.

"I shall never forget it: the sight of the four aged, benignant heads (three of them white with the snows of almost eighty winters) on which the mellow August sunshine poured its flood of light. There was no thought of time in the minds of these geniuses. They paused in their leisurely gait, sat down on a flat gravestone to discuss high themes, moved to another, always forgetting their hats or sticks or portfolios, which I gathered up in safety and retained until the proper moment when they might remember their next engagement."

But it was really the brilliant, educated woman who most captured Kate's imagination. "Every night that I spent in Concord was enriched by the conversation of that noble and venerable woman Elizabeth Peabody, the revered and eminent champion of childhood, who had been instrumental in inspiring a greater number of mothers and educators than any woman of her day. Her mind was a complete storehouse of fascinating and varied knowledge, and her memory endless." Brother Nat would often plead with his sister to go to bed, as she regaled Kate with story after story about the Brownings, Mazzini, Harriet Martineau, Margaret Fuller, William Ellery Channing, Emerson, and her famous brothers-in-law.[3]

As befitted an institution with Bronson Alcott as one of its founders, Concord School of Philosophy lived up to its educational promise. In an era when, as Bruce Kuklick notes, philosophy was becoming a professional academic discipline housed in universities, the Concord School offered a summer curriculum of courses, for a modest fee, to a diverse audience of adults, mostly women. Those courses were certainly rigorous: lecture series on Plato, Kant, Hegel, Schelling, the history of philosophy, Goethe, pantheism, Shakespeare, Homer, Milton, among other topics. Like the original Chautauqua and like the summer schools at Saint Cloud, New Jersey, and Farmington, Connecticut, inspired by the Concord School, Alcott's school offered challenging, sometimes inspirational, talks to audiences hungry for education in an era when university training was still limited to a handful.

But it was an education of a particular sort. This was, after all, the age of Darwin and Spencer, of industry, railroads, and captains of industry,

the age of realism and the worship of the fact. While not particularly
hostile to science, the lecturers at the Concord School were decidedly
idealist, theistic, and metaphysical in their approach, united in their
belief in the existence of eternal, invisible Truth of which earthly reality
was a shadow and symbol. To younger professional philosophers, and to
youthful journalists, the metaphysical tone of the School was retrogres-
sive and nostalgic, a weak reminder of an older approach now thoroughly discredited by advances in geology, chemistry, and evolutionary
biology. If the School is measured by its willingness to explore the
newest ideas in philosophy and art, then by that standard it was a noble
failure.[4]

Besides adult education and a rear-guard defense of metaphysics, the
Concord School had a third purpose. In its close connection to Alcott,
Emerson, and Peabody, the School served as a kind of historical retrospective of New England Transcendentalism. Although not a majority
of the presentations, the lectures on Emerson both in 1882 and in 1884
are among the best of those preserved. Collected and published as *The
Genius and Character of Emerson*, the 1884 session contained several
superb offerings, including Julia Ward Howe on Emerson as Bostonian, C. A. Bartol on Emerson's religion, and Peabody's "Emerson as
Preacher." Filled with sharply recalled anecdotes of her early encounters with Emerson, Peabody's talk restated her belief that Emerson was
a better believer than most professed Christians, despite his silence on
the subject. "I heard Mr. Emerson once say to Mr. Orestes A. Brownson, who was pressing on him the duty of explanation [of his religious
beliefs], 'I feel myself to be in the midst of a truth I do not comprehend,
but which comprehends me.'"[5]

Undoubtedly many attendees, like Kate Douglas, Julia Howe's
daughter Julia Anagnos, and Lilian Whiting came to hear just such
stories and see these giants of an earlier era of thought and reform.
Emerson attended the first three sessions before his death in April
1882, delivering an address on "Memory" at the first session, surely a
sad and bitter irony given his own vanished memory. Alcott was an
active participant in the first four sessions but was felled by a stroke in
October 1882. He returned to the School for visits in 1885 and 1886. At
one such visit, Elizabeth Peabody "rushed forward and threw her arms
around his neck in the exuberance of her welcome."[6]

Then there was Peabody herself. Too ill to attend in 1881, she gave a talk on "Childhood" in 1882, echoing the argument in Wordsworth's "Intimations Ode." "Childhood, she said, was the unfallen man as he first appears on the shores of matter, rushing into the darkness of an earth without form and void, and being individualized thereby, which individualization is the cause both of evil and good that are facts of human life." The following year she gave a lecture on Milton's "Paradise Lost," which prompted vigorous debate, according to Julia Anagnos. Allegorized as "Nestoria, the Old Woman Eloquent," in Anagnos's *Philosophiae Quaestor; or, Days in Concord,* Peabody "discussed Milton at the School, and a severe tournament followed her mild address. Milton was arraigned as the poet of Calvinism by a new-comer, who was, of course, rebuked by the philosophers on behalf of Milton, and by one of their number (who thought Milton shallow), on behalf of Calvin himself." In 1884 Peabody delivered her memorable remarks on Emerson as preacher.[7]

Nearly forty years after the close of the Concord School, Florence Whiting Brown said that it was a shame that "we young hearers remember more concerning the number of peppermints she [Elizabeth Peabody] could consume during a session than her words of wisdom." Peabody was already legendary for her causes, her prodigous education, her careless dress and love of ribbons and lace; and her friends at the School found ample evidence for her growing reputation as lovable, scattered, a bit dotty, and always brilliant. Lilian Whiting recalls her this way:

> Miss Elizabeth Peabody, who always sat faithfully through every half day of the four to six weeks' session . . . relapsed, at intervals, into apparent slumber, from which she would suddenly arouse herself with a movement that sent flying in various directions her bag, handkerchief, note-book, pencil, and all her various belongings which those of the younger and non-distinguished persons sitting near considered it an honor to scramble about and pick up for her. When it came to the discussion of the theme, however, it always turned out that Miss Peabody, half-blind, nearly deaf, and wholly asleep, had yet heard everything that was said to much better advantage than any one else in the audience.

Perhaps Elizabeth knew what was happening by osmosis, but more likely it is a tribute to her prior knowledge of the points of view that her fellow faculty would likely embrace.[8]

    IF ONE MAJOR PURPOSE of the Concord School was history and reminiscence, that was quite in keeping with Elizabeth Peabody's own writing projects during the 1880s. She never produced the grand memoir she was always promising, but she did leave, in several different forms, reminiscences of her own life and of influential people she had known. Like all memories, Peabody's are selective, and like all autobiography, her personal narratives reconstruct the past to serve present purposes.

In 1880 Peabody oversaw Roberts Brothers' publication of her *Reminiscences of William Ellery Channing*. Her injury in the preceding year had made completing the manuscript an excruciating task. "I cannot sit up & write but a few minutes at a time yet," she wrote Phillips Brooks. "My difficulty being a sprain—but it is a sprain in my neck which made it impossible to turn it a hairbreadth tho I can bend it forward. . . . Excuse my style it is hard to hold up my head." It is not surprising that she was dissatisfied with the result. "So little of that 'great range of thought' that I had record of in my journals and letters (returned to me by friends)—& in my memory—*did I attempt to put down*—(I had to fight with Roberts for the space I did fill)—and so much did I fear that the narrow window of individuality through which I must necessarily look would *curtail* /the view/—that you will believe me when I tell you that it was in a kind of agony of apprehension I left Boston—when it was just printed & not bound," she told James Freeman Clarke. Selecting from hundreds of manuscript pages, Peabody produced a valuable narrative of her first encounters with Channing and of his considerable influence on her intellectual development. Still, the narrative is sanitized, with the growing tension between the young teacher and the Channings over teaching and disciplining their children all but absent from the book. Even more, Peabody read her memories of Channing through her current preoccupation with the kindergarten. Channing's love of children, his and Peabody's shared devotion to moral and spiritual education as well as intellectual training—all these led to the exclamation of some Boston women whom Elizabeth quoted with delight when they heard of Froebel's insights: "But this is nothing new; more than fifty years ago Dr. Channing taught us to live with our children, and to look upon them as capable of the life of Christ, which is one with a life of love, from the beginning."[9]

Peabody similarly shaped her reminiscences of Emerson to suit her purposes. Always a liberal Christian, Peabody could not see that Emerson had abandoned any claim that the Christian revelation was unique or normative. In her 1838 review of *Nature*, she linked Emerson's call for self-redemption with an older theistic understanding. Forty years later she made the same connection. In an 1879 letter to James Eliot Cabot, who was collecting material for a life of Emerson, Peabody copied out her recollections of a week or two in July 1839 when she had visited the Emersons. Speaking of the relation between God and Jesus, Emerson was to have said, "the mission of the present time is to re-proclaim the Living God, and in order to do this, Christianity—and especially the person Jesus—must be set aside for the time—as if they were not." Peabody's gloss on this was that Emerson was a better Christian than his opponents, thinking that "the only way he can do full justice to it [Christianity] is to cease to mention it more & more. . . ." This is surely an odd interpretation of Emerson's effort to separate worship of the divinity that is in all things from the specific historical and cultural institution of Christianity, but is well in keeping with Peabody's integrative manner.[10]

Selective, sometimes distorted, Peabody's reminiscences in the 1880s are also richly detailed, sharp, opinionated, humorous, occasionally melancholy. Her memories of Nathaniel Hawthorne, in accounts given to her nephew Julian and in letters to Amelia Boelte, Thomas Wentworth Higginson, and Francis Henry Lee, form crucial parts of our knowledge of Hawthorne, as does her letter to William Andrews on Jones Very. Her portrait of her mother's upbringing and education, together with her own educational philosophy, published in 1882, are full of vivid detail, conveying the continuity that the daughter felt with the mother's outlook. Elizabeth clearly enjoyed telling stories about people she had known and causes she had championed. Indeed, she was not above telling others how to write *their* narratives. In a letter to Amelia Boelte explaining the relationship between Elizabeth and Nathaniel Hawthorne from her perspective, Peabody wrote this:

You might really do a service to the truth of facts if you were to say that at the time Hawthorne for the first time in his life made acquaintance with women in society, there was a story current that he was engaged to Elizabeth Peabody, who was the first lady-friend he became intimate with, and when six years after, he married her youngest sister Sophia it was conjectured that she had magnanimously given him up in her favour, but that you had learnt from Elizabeth herself that it was all a mistake. . . . I do not mean to dictate the *form* but only the important substance of what you shall say. If you had not the means as you say of propagating the mistake, it would be best I think not to even mention so delicate a matter.[11]

In what is surely one of the best accounts of Peabody's narrative powers, Jane Marsh Parker recalled a visit with Peabody in February 1885, just as *Century* magazine began serializing Henry James's novel *The Bostonians* with its thinly veiled portrait of her as Miss Birdseye. "She was then past eighty years old . . . a brisk, alert, cheery little woman . . . her snow-white, soft, silky ringlets curled back from her strong yet most delicate face." Peabody captivated the dinner guests with her stories and views. "Her intellectual vigor . . . surpasses everything, and what a reservoir her memory is, and how readily she turns on her stream from any one of its countless faucets. . . . Somebody led to the turning on of the Channing faucet just as we sat down at dinner last night. There was biography for you! Why didn't she put all those delicious memories into her Channing Reminiscences?"

The next morning Peabody was full of stories about Abraham Lincoln, Frederick Douglass, Wendell Phillips, William Lloyd Garrison, with Brook Farm begun just before lunch. "Such a pile of letters as she wrote while we were taking our naps—the rain shutting us all within doors." And then talk of Spiritualism, which prompted Peabody's memories of the Fox sisters and of communicating with Channing through a medium. The evening was given over to Peabody's parlor lecture on the Paiute Indians. Oblivious to the lateness of the hour and the protests of the waiting coachman, Elizabeth talked on when "at eleven o'clock, she brought her remarks to a close, without having shown the slightest annoyance or concern at what had disconcerted her hearers. In fact, an interesting appendix to the lecture was begun in the dressing room, and only the urgency of escorts had cut it short. The phenomenal little woman went down the stairs, assuring us that her cause was as good as won, for she was to have a special interview with the President the next day, and she was more than convinced. . . . The clattering of hoofs over the asphalt drowned her voice. . . . That was the last I saw of Miss Peabody."[12]

◇ JANE PARKER'S DESCRIPTION of Peabody as "brisk" and "alert" in 1885 suggests something of an improvement in Elizabeth's health by middecade, for despite her evident love of the Concord School of Philosophy and her completion of the Channing book, Peabody's health was poor in the early 1880s. She was slow in recovering from her fall in 1879, still feeling the pinched nerve and stiffness that she described to Phillips Brooks in 1880. "You said you wished I wouldn't think of my physique," she wrote Mary sometime early in the decade, "but it is impossible not to perceive what is so overpowering as this lethargy—It has been creeping upon me for months . . . a dim consciousness that the paralysis which I was threatened with in England & as Dr. Wilkinson said *just escaped* & which all our grandparents except Grandfather Palmer who was killed by accident—have past [?] *threatens* to say the least. Now I am perfectly willing to die though I see clearly there is important work for me to do for which all my past has educated me—but I am not willing to become a paralytic— to be perhaps for years neither dead nor alive & yet I have felt that this was a possibility." Her fear of paralysis was heightened by news of brother Nathaniel's state in the months before his death. Away from Concord in early summer 1881 and too ill to attend the School of Philosophy, she thanked Mary for news of their last remaining brother, sad as it was. "This darkness that *precedes death* is indeed the king of terrors—Heaven grant that he does not live *half dead* & I do not believe much that he will. . . . Don't you think it is really fortunate that I am *not there?* My money is of more value for them than my presence." Elizabeth was accurate in her prediction; Nat died June 23, 1881.[13]

For her part, Elizabeth explained to Mary, she had put herself in the hands of a kind of massage therapist, Mrs. Larned, who exercised Elizabeth's legs "which are in a dreadful state but she said the swelling could all be rubbed down—the capillary system restored to allow the congested vein [to be] unloaded." In fact, Peabody wrote her sister a short time later, Mrs. Larned "says I have great vitality & *no organic* disease but my heart—liver—stomach—kidneys &c are all right or only derivatively affected—She explains my heart affection as derivative contraction," perhaps meaning irregular rhythm. Elizabeth even preferred Mrs. Larned to Concord's Dr. Monroe: "I think she is more efficient than Dr. M in his old age can be—comparing her treatment with the two or three last one I had from him." Mrs. Larned thinks Elizabeth can "keep the enemy at bay by proper and steady exercise thereafter."

Perhaps Elizabeth's ill health and her own "more positively diseased" state prompted Mary Mann to suggest that she and Elizabeth again take up housekeeping. "I shall be very glad to live with you and take care of you when you have such *turns* as you just now tell of," Elizabeth wrote in the same letter that describes Mrs. Larned's rather modern therapies. "It seems as if providence ordered that we should live together & help one another—& I hope I may not annoy you in the future as I have in the past—I have made some spiritual progress actually in the last three years." Where might they live? Pinckney Street "is the highest part & most healthy"; there are South Boston and Roxbury, but Mary might rule out Jamaica Plain, Elizabeth thought.[14]

By May 1882 Elizabeth and Mary had found a flat at 54 Bowdoin Street in Boston. In her characteristically spacious and optimistic way, Peabody thought of their relationship as inspired by divine as well as consanguine impulses. Visiting in Lancaster, she wrote back to her sister:

> I thought of something you said to me one day about my singing in the Church—which I have thought of a hundred times since—with many other manifestations of your belief in me wh. I believe came to its culmination in Lancaster—when I very distinctly first defined to myself the beauty of your individuality & we married each other as it were. I felt it was a gracious tie in our lives—the realization of a spiritual communion—that has been somewhat shadowed since by our personal shortcomings—but which was part of the Eternal life—that shall in the end outflow all shadows and find the ocean of Heaven.

Less given to such grand claims, Mary Mann humorously described her sister and herself as "rather dilapidated old ladies, externally, but E. is one of those people who are immortally young in spirit, and circulates freely among her friends whenever she can get a helping arm, and continues to ply her pen assiduously. We rejoice greatly in the growth and prosperity of the kindergarten cause here."[15]

This move seemed to stabilize Elizabeth's health. Her annual income of a little over $700, dividends from the trusts set up for her, was sufficient for daily expenses, although she was trying to put some aside "for the possibly augmented expenses of my last sickness—when I should have to hire a nurse," she wrote Samuel Gray Ward in 1885. Around that time, Lilian Whiting, chronicler of "Boston Days," visited the sisters, climbing "the stairs to the rooms that the two ladies were occupying. The mixture of high thinking and plain living was striking." The simple rooms were decorated with a bust of Horace Mann, European engravings, "rare books and bits of *vertu*, and, with these, the meagre furnishing almost of tenement rooms. The two aged sisters—gentlewomen, whose manner would have graced any court—were living in utmost simplicity, but they lived and moved and had their being in the heavenly kingdom. They missed nothing that this world could have given them. They had bread to eat that the world knew not of."

> The guests drew their chairs before the fire. Miss Peabody was a large woman. Mrs. Mann was as tiny and delicate as a sparrow. The kerosene lamp flared and flickered, and finally went out, after the fashion of a lamp where the housekeepers are too much occupied with ethical problems to remember to fill it. The blustering March wind blew, the branches of trees against the windows, like ghostly finger taps, and the noble and high-souled women talked, and their friends listened and listened, even then half conscious that this was to be an historic hour.[16]

Peabody had begun the decade by publishing her memoir of Channing and looking forward to "writing two or three books," she told Mary, "my life of Christ—my experience as a teacher—the Science of Childhood & how to learn it." None of these appeared in book form, although "My Experience as a Teacher" forms one part of her long 1882 essay "Principles and Methods of Education." By middecade she had reached one last intellectual pinnacle. Her contributions to the Concord School of Philosophy and her many reminiscences of influential people had put her in a retrospective mood, which led to the collection of some of her best essays as *Last Evening with Allston, and Other Papers,* published by Daniel Lothrop in 1886. Writing to Lothrop's wife Harriet shortly after, Peabody wondered whether there could be a second volume, even proposing a parallel title, "Titian's Assumption and Other Essays by Elizabeth P. Peabody." It might make a good Christmas or New Year's gift, she thought, and could include such essays as "My Christmas at St. Peter's Church in Rome in 1867," "A Proposed Religious Service purely in music," and "The Origins and History in This Country of Froebel's Kindergarten." Although nothing came of this volume, Peabody did see into print a collection of educational papers called *Lectures in the Training Schools for Kindergartners,* published by D.C. Heath in 1888. This volume contains the memorable "A Psychological Observation," her gripping and novelistic account of the death of her former student Lydia Sears Haven and Peabody's "rescue" of Lydia's son Foster from a stunted and deprived upbringing.[17]

ﺯﻭ WHILE THESE PAPERS and volumes amply proved Theodore Parker's quip that Peabody was the Boswell of her age, reminiscence was far from her only work in her eighties. Much as the kindergarten seized her imagination and challenged her energies in the 1870s, so the cause of the Paiutes and their spokesperson Sarah Winnemucca became Peabody's cause in the 1880s. Daughter of Old Winnemucca, chief of the Paiutes of northern Nevada and southeastern Oregon, Sarah Winnemucca was an assertive, voluble, sensitive, and highly articulate spokesperson for her people. Early on she interacted with European culture and people, learning to speak and write English fluently, but always maintaining some deep and perfectly understandable reservations about white motives. Often drawn into conflict with American settlers and the military through the behavior of more warlike people like the Bannocks, the Paiutes were settled on Pyramid Lake Reservation and Malheur Reservation in the 1860s and 1870s. There Sarah and her people encountered honorable Indian agents like S. B. Parrish, who treated the Paiutes with dignity and respect, and vicious ones like W. V. Rinehart, who refused to pay Indians properly for their work or to protect their tribal lands against white squatter settlements.[18]

To counteract Rinehart's claims of Indian laziness and immorality, Sarah launched a speaking tour of San Francisco in 1879, speaking without notes to packed auditoriums, wearing a buckskin and fringed costume reminiscent more of Great Plains peoples than of her own intermountain tribe. But white listeners loved her "spontaneous flow of eloquence," accompanied by "gestures that were scarcely ever surpassed by any actress on the stage," according to one newspaper account. In January 1880 Sarah Winnemucca traveled to Washington, D.C. to plead her case with Secretary of the Interior Carl Schurz; however, she found that Rinehart had preceded her with an affidavit charging her with prostitution and drunkenness, describing her as "a notorious liar and malicious schemer." Although Winnemucca was able to meet with Schurz and even have a brief interview with President Rutherford Hayes, no fundamental changes improved the often desperate condition of the Paiutes, now reduced to farming and foraging on what barren land remained of the Malheur Reservation.[19]

In spring 1883 Sarah, with her new husband Lieutenant Lewis H. Hopkins, traveled east to conduct another lecture tour, hoping to raise money for supplies for the Paiutes. In Boston they met Elizabeth Peabody and Mary Mann, who would become mainstays of support and encouragement for nearly five years. Mary took on the task of editing Sarah's memoir, *Life Among the Piutes: Their Wrongs and Claims*, which moved and impressed even such a confirmed New England liberal as herself. "I was always considered fanatical about Indians," she wrote Eleanor Lewis in April 1883, "but I have a wholly new conception of them now, and we civilized people may well stand abashed before their purity of life & their truthfulness." Elizabeth was equally impressed by the book, calling it an "artless narrative." *Life Among the Piutes* made clear the radical stance that Winnemucca was taking in resisting calls for the assimilation of indigenous peoples into the cultural mainstream. Peabody understood the point as well: "It would be a poor exchange for them to make—to be citizens at the expense of their religion & morality which has [sic] vital relation with their tribal relation—to scatter the Indians among our population—instead of keeping them together— would be like scattering the members of a private family," she wrote Harriet Lothrop.[20]

For her part Elizabeth Peabody took on multiple duties in advocating for Sarah Winnemucca and the Paiutes: she organized and accompanied lecture tours for Sarah, canvassed her friends for moral and financial support, and bombarded politicians with advice and pleas. "[S]he has spoken in my hearing in Providence Hartford New York Newburgh Poughkeepsie Dorset in Vermont Salem Cambridge Boston again and in Philadelphia—& already more than 3000 names to her petitions which three of our Representatives are about to present," she wrote to Edwin Munroe Bacon, editor of the *Boston Daily Advertiser* in 1883. Peabody explained to Congressman Newton Booth that her support for Winnemucca had something to do with the fact that one of Peabody's great uncles had married an "Indian princess," although no other family record supports such a claim. More likely, Sarah Winnemucca touched Peabody's instinctive sympathy for victims of injustice, especially if those victims were women, combined with Peabody's attraction for Sarah's project of educating the Paiutes.[21]

Through 1884 Elizabeth and Mary continued to champion Sarah's cause, raising money and gaining influential supporters like John Greenleaf Whittier and Lidian Emerson. Elizabeth was particularly interested in an effort on behalf of the Paiutes by Massachusetts Senator Henry Dawes to resettle them on a new reservation near Fort McDermit, Oregon. She and Sarah had already met with Dawes, who had given her his most enthusiastic support. But the Fort McDermit idea also aroused Sarah's enemies, like the editors of *The Council Fire and Arbitrator*, a journal supportive of Indian agents. These men have "endeavoured to misrepresent and fabricate monstrous lies about the tribe which are pronounced fabrications and demonstrated to be absurdly false by citizens of Nevada who have been written to" and who testify to the honor and decency of the Paiutes, she wrote to Congressman John Long. Whereas the machinations of the "Indian ring" seem apparent, Winnemucca's cause was also hurt on her own side by the reckless behavior of her husband.[22]

Unfortunately for Sarah and her supporters, Congress refused to establish this new reservation. Perhaps even worse, Sarah had to admit that the money Peabody had so assiduously raised was nearly gone, gambled away by her husband Lewis Hopkins while Winnemucca was busy with lecturing. Worst of all, some of this money had come from Peabody herself. Kate Douglas Wiggin tells the story in her autobiography:

> Before her eightieth birthday I raised among kindergartners a thank offering of a thousand dollars for a birthday present, sending

it to Jamaica Plain where she passed the last years of her life in very simple fashion. It chanced that Sarah Winnemucca, a benevolent and highly cultured Indian Princess, had been lecturing in New York and Boston in an attempt to raise funds to give to the tribe to which she belonged farming utensils of all kinds with which to educate and support themselves by intelligent labor.

In due course dear Miss Peabody wrote thanking me and all her beloved young teacher-friends for the birthday gift.

"It came at such a welcome time," she said, "for I was able to send the good Princess Winnemucca eight hundred dollars out of your generous thousand, to carry on her noble and self-sacrificing work."[23]

In early 1885 Sarah's brother Natchez Overton was able to obtain some land near Lovelock, Nevada, and hoped to employ some of his fellow Paiutes there and on nearby farms. Peabody sprang into action once more, canvassing her friends for aid. "E. has been absent since the middle of March," Mary wrote of her eighty-one-year-old sister, "but she has had much satisfaction in what she has been able to achieve for her beloved Indians (for her love for Sarah diffuses itself over the whole race) and Ben [Benjamin Pickman Mann, Mary's son] sends me word that he has been able to send a huge gift of seeds to Sarah from the Agricultural Bureau. Betty has sent three tents, a wagon & plow, and now I think they can go to work and till & plant, & even before the new administration [that of Democratic President-elect Grover Cleveland] has shaken itself down & got to work in all departments, there is some hope that effectual measures will be taken to relieve that unfortunate tribe."[24]

Elizabeth seized the opportunity of a change in administration to petition for support at the very highest level. She wrote to Cleveland's sister Rose Elizabeth, who was mistress of the White House from Cleveland's inauguration until his marriage in June 1886. "Miss Peabody, an old lady of 80 years, sister in law to the late Horace Mann,— craves a private interview with Miss Cleveland. She has received from the Princess Winnemucca of the Piute tribe, a letter addressed to President Cleveland which she wishes Miss P to *deliver* & which certainly does require a little explanation." Peabody was particularly concerned to tell the President about the *"maladministration of the Indian office,"* which had become in her view "the greatest element of evil—the Indians being *men* who are virtually deaf & dumb & cannot speak for themselves as the other interests can." Despite Rose Elizabeth Cleveland's skepticism that advocacy can do much good—"I cling desperately to the belief that the thing that ought to happen is the thing that will happen in the long run"—Peabody was able to have a brief interview with Grover Cleveland, probably in late 1885 or early 1886, who agreed with the strategy of private land ownership, or severalty, that many political liberals were then advocating.[25]

Peabody and her friends were able eventually to send goods, equipment, and cash, valuing $1,000, while Sarah Winnemucca turned her attention increasingly to educating the tribe's children. Throughout the summer of 1885, she trained about twenty-five youngsters in physical exercise, English language, and Christian teachings. Most distinctive was Sarah's emphasis on bilingual education, which Peabody felt "would rend the veil that has been hanging between the two races from the beginning; a veil as impenetrable as that dividing the castes of Eastern India from each other!" By December a permanent structure had been completed for what Sarah was now calling "The Peabody Indian School." Still, despite support by New England kindergartners like Alice Chapin and Elizabeth Powell Bond, and Peabody's continued support and fund-raising, the Indian School was on shaky ground. No governmental agency recognized its existence, and no organized private charity sponsored it. Indeed, Sarah had already rejected an offer to send the children to an industrial-arts boarding school in Grand Junction, Colorado.[26]

Elizabeth threw herself into a final flurry of work in support of the Indian School. She ended a letter to Harriet Lothrop this way, so very indicative of the energy that the nearly blind elderly woman was expending in defense of the cause: "Yours truly in *desperate haste* for I am full of Indian work & Sarah Winnemucca's *School*—which is answering my highest hopes—Have you seen my articles about her in the Transcript including the letter of those seven visitors to her School which was published March 23rd [?] I went to Lawrence last week & spoke two hours to a full vestry & got $50 dollars for her. I suppose you have heard of the late attempts to break her reputation but she will triumph over all 'the contradiction of sinners' with her thoroughly acted out faith in her Spirit Father." She also set to work writing *The Piutes*, a summary of Sarah Winnemucca's career and of the various injustices done to the Paiutes. She was particularly eager to describe Sarah's peda-

gogical method with its multicultural emphasis and to criticize calls
to send Indian children to distant boarding schools. Indeed, some Indian parents wanted Sarah to set up her own boardinghouses near the
school, "which their parents are pressing on her to take, having been
frightened because the despotic agents of Pyramid Lake Reservation
had forced 10 or 12 children to go, against shrieking protests of their
mothers, to a Colorado Industrial School to learn of teachers who do
not know Indian languages which disheartens & demoralizes the children, besides breaking the parents hearts," she added in her own handwriting to a copy of the tract now at Yale University.[27]

Despite all this effort, Elizabeth Peabody had exhausted the goodwill of her supporters and had also exhausted herself in advocating for
Sarah's school. "I am curious to see how far E. has been battered in the
strife," Mary Mann observed to Eleanor Lewis. "She declares she is
well, but she is apt to believe what she wishes to, & I shall not know till
I get her into her own bed, which I made up yesterday, & feel as if we
were going to have a wedding." Meanwhile, the report from Washington was not encouraging. In 1887 Congress passed the Dawes Severalty
Act, supported by many progressive thinkers and reformers, which dis-
tributed communal reservation land to heads of households, selling the
remaining land to white settlers and business interests. Although they
were generally supportive of this bill, introduced by Sarah's supporter
Senator Henry Dawes, Peabody and Winnemucca vigorously opposed
the educational portion of the bill, which called for boarding school
education for Indian children. Support for bilingual education dwin-
dled during the next several years, and Peabody, once Winnemucca's
most faithful supporter, turned toward reminiscence and memoir in the
last few years of her life. Winnemucca herself returned to Nevada,
where she died under mysterious circumstances on October 17, 1891.
She was forty-seven years old.[28]

 ᕲᑀᗡ In 1886 Elizabeth and Mary moved from Cheshire Street,
where they had lived briefly after leaving Bowdoin Street, to rooms at
298 Lamartine Street in Jamaica Plain, the neighborhood that Elizabeth was sure Mary would disdain. But they seemed quite happy there;
their flat, with a large parlor and two sunny rooms above, was in a "large
square detached house" opposite a garden, greenhouse, and florist, and
just down the street from the horsecar station. Mary suffered from
"alarming feebleness," so much so that "it seemed as if a removal to a

still more *lively* residence were impending—first, for her—then, for me—so that we surrendered ourselves successively into the hands of a physician who has put me again into the way of recovery." Mary seemed recovered enough to write to Eleanor Lewis in November 1886 in her usual crisp and funny way: "I am going to send you Elizabeth's Report of Sarah Winnemucca's School for Indian Children, which we think the correct pattern for all Indian schools. She still rules the ascendant with E. and scarcely less with me though there is not so much of the fanatic in me as in E. We live with two most amiable people lately married—one of the right sort of marriages which is saying a good deal in these days."[29]

Elizabeth also used the metaphor of marriage to describe the relationship of the sisters, recalling that when sixty years earlier in Lancaster, she understood the "beauty of [your] individuality . . . we married each other as it were." Like other long relationships, this one had its inevitable complement of affection, companionship, injury, and duplicity, and it ended on February 11, 1887, when Mary died. She had suffered several weeks of pain from swollen limbs and wished to be released from life. Still, four days before she died, she "wrote a long letter with flying pen" in response to a woman's assertion that there was more reason to doubt immortality than to believe it, especially since most people were already dead in a spiritual sense. "She added that the only striking exception *she knew*(!) was *Mary & me*—& our youthful ardor engaged in works of love, *not transient* in their *nature!*"[30]

Mary's funeral was on Monday, February 14, in Boston, with services at the same hour at Antioch College. The many outpourings of sympathy helped Mary's sons George and Ben, and in March, when Elizabeth wrote all these details, she could still say that she did not feel separated, "rather *nearer* than ever—feeling she could understand just what I thought & felt better than my words could tell it." But by the end of the year, as Mary's birthday of November 16 approached, Peabody felt "indescribable loneliness & desolation." Her absence was felt not only in the empty rooms but also in the "innumerable little charities" Elizabeth now had to ask friends to do, she wrote Eva Channing.[31]

⁓ UNLIKE MARY MANN, who was more reserved in her expression and private in her behavior, Elizabeth Peabody in her seventies and eighties had become a public figure: her appearance, causes, and eccentricities were known to friends and strangers alike. In a new age of "instant" journalism, with high-speed presses pouring out millions of copies of newspapers and magazines, reporters loved the "human interest" story, and readers soaked up the amusing anecdote. In such an atmosphere, stories of Miss Peabody, the eccentric old reformer, were irresistible: Miss Peabody falling into a snowbank, and when rescued, asking her helpers whether they knew about Sarah Winnemucca; Miss Peabody at the Concord School; Miss Peabody sitting "serenely and meditatively in her [streetcar] seat, her hoop skirt flying up before her, disclosing a black-and-red petticoat and white stockings . . . perfectly unconscious of any disarray in her appearance"; Miss Peabody, "The Grandmother of Boston."[32]

For some, in those last decades, Elizabeth Peabody was an honored figure, someone about whom they could smile in love and respect. The younger women whom she had recruited into the kindergarten movement and who were so visible at her funeral in 1894, were among these admirers. Survivors of an earlier age of "plain living and high thinking," Elizabeth and Mary seemed to people like Lilian Whiting to be more deeply in touch with essential truth than were the millions who chose to live on the material surface of life. Self-sacrificial, scattered and disorganized, perpetually optimistic, Peabody was a symbol of dying to self and living for others. For a new generation of reformers coming of age at the turn of the century, who like Jane Addams felt sickened at the gap between the comfort of their lives and the poverty around them, Peabody was among the models whom they emulated.

But Elizabeth Peabody as the heroic and self-forgetful reformer was not the only version of the Peabody myth circulating in the 1880s. For many writers, artists, and intellectuals, philosophical idealism that was unwilling to take account of scientific insight and literary idealism that was unable to look squarely at the facts of modern urban life were equally despised enemies. Although they might treat Elizabeth Peabody in person with respect, she nevertheless stood for a vague, sentimental, dreamy optimism and a large speculative vision untroubled by facts, relics of an antebellum past that refused to fade away.

Some of these traits are evident in the portrait of the reformer that was pieced together, in part, from the life of Elizabeth Peabody and presented in Henry James's 1886 novel *The Bostonians*. The James family already had had some encounters with Peabody. Henry James the elder had corresponded with her during the Civil War years until a quarrel about Caroline Dall severed that connection. Another Jamesian connection came from an anecdote told by Edward Emerson, who was present at the James's dinner table when William told of the enthusiasm with which Peabody [disguised in the anecdote as "Jane Smith"] "beset" him about the lectures of William Rimmer. Henry Senior burst out in response, "the man's a fraud! It's impossible he should be anything else if Jane Smith believes in him! Wh-wh-why! Jane Smith—she's one of the most d-d-dissolute old creatures that walks the earth!" The James family "shouted with joy," Emerson recalled, "though knowing well the saintly, if too optimistic character of the old lady, at the Jamesian felicity of the adjective. For they saw, in memory, the gray hair falling down under the bonnet askew, the spectacles slipping down with resulting upturned radiant face, the nondescript garments and general dissolving effect, symbolizing the loose reasoning and the charity falling all abroad—yes, in a sense a dissolute personality."[33]

When chapters of *The Bostonians* began to appear in serial fashion in *Century Magazine* in February 1885, Henry James found himself roundly criticized for his portrait of the aged reformer Miss Birdseye, whose characteristics, though not physical size, seemed remarkably like those of Elizabeth Peabody. James's aunt Kate Walsh, family friend James Russell Lowell, and brother William all protested the satire. James rejected the criticism. He had not seen Elizabeth Peabody for twenty years, never had but the most casual observation of her, and in fact did not know whether she was alive or dead. "I absolutely had no shadow of such an intention," he wrote William. "Miss Birdseye was evolved entirely from my moral consciousness, like every other person I have ever drawn, and originated in my desire to make a figure who should embody in a sympathetic, pathetic, picturesque, and at the same time grotesque way, the humanity and ci-devant transcendental tendencies." James felt that the Miss Birdseye figure was an honorable figure in his portrayal. "She is treated with respect throughout, and every virtue of heroism and disinterestedness is attributed to her. She is represented as the embodiment of pure, and purest philanthropy." He was concerned only that *she* might feel maligned by the treatment.[34]

James constructed his characters from observation, recollection, and his own imagination. Miss Birdseye is no exception, although he clearly borrowed more than he admitted from the real-life Miss Peabody. In her forever-wandering spectacles and perennial optimism, his portrait of her as the vague, anachronistic do-gooder captured precisely the traits that many found in Elizabeth Peabody. "She had a sad, soft, pale face, which . . . looked as if it had been soaked, blurred, and made vague by exposure to some slow dissolvent. . . . The waves of sympathy, of enthusiasm, had wrought upon them in the same way in which the waves of time finally modify the surface of old marble busts, gradually washing away their sharpness, their details." She was a "confused, en-tangled, inconsequent, discursive old woman, whose charity began at home and ended nowhere, whose credulity kept pace with it, and who knew less about her fellow-creatures, if possible, after fifty years of humanitary zeal, than on the day she had gone into the field to testify against the iniquity of most arrangements." James altered some of the details in his portrait, but there was enough to give credence to his family's concern about the parallel. Indeed, this opening presentation of Miss Birdseye is sharp, even hostile, satire. Anyone who found herself in this character might well feel ill-used.[35]

But this is not James's final word on Miss Birdseye. Midway through the novel, James contrasts the self-sacrificing life of this old reformer with that of one of the more central characters, Olive Chancellor, who seems more in love with the idea of causes than with their reality. Olive loved to return to her comfortable Beacon Street apartment, filled with flowers and European journals, and bitterly compared her life of ease with that of Miss Birdseye. "[I]t struck Miss Chancellor . . . that this frumpy little missionary was the last link in a tradition, and that when she should be called away the heroic age of New England life—the age of plain living and high thinking, of pure ideals and earnest effort, of moral passion and noble experiment—would effectually be closed." Here, at least to Olive Chancellor, Miss Birdseye is far from inconse-quential but rather embodies "the unquenched flame of . . . transcen-dentalism."

Toward the end of the novel, James returns once more to Miss Bird-seye. The main characters are on Cape Cod: Olive Chancellor, Verena Tarrant, Basil Ransom, and Miss Birdseye. Olive and Basil are engaged in a bitter rivalry for the affection and attention of the young Verena, whom Olive wants to recruit into the women's rights crusade and whom Basil wants to marry. The characters gather around the dying Miss Birdseye. Seeing Ransom, she thinks that he has been persuaded to join the reform ranks, although the other women know that he is in fact the enemy of reform. James sidesteps the temptation to satirize Miss Bird-seye once again, for her obliviousness to the truth. Instead, he gives us a delicate and tender portrait of a dying heroine. "'You mustn't think there's no progress because you don't see it all right off; that's what I wanted to say. It isn't till you have gone a long way that you can feel what's been done,'" Miss Birdseye said to the party. "'That's what I see when I look back from here; I see that the community wasn't half waked up when I was young.'

"'It is you that have waked it up more than anyone else, and it's for that we honor you, Miss Birdseye,' Verena cried, with a sudden violence of emotion. . . . You are our heroine, you are our saint, and there has never been anyone like you.'"[36]

Miss Birdseye died in the pages of James's novel, but Miss Peabody lived on, into the late 1880s and early 1890s. She had outlived her family and many of her colleagues. Emerson had died in 1882, Mary Mann in 1887, Bronson and Louisa May Alcott in 1888. "I have never felt so much that life was giving way as now—and am just going by advice of an old physician of mine to begin a course of vitalized phosphates—in order to foreclose what seems an impending 'nervous prostration,'" Peabody wrote to Harriet Lothrop sometime in the late 1880s. At age eighty-three, she was quite deaf and blind, but happy that causes like the kindergarten and Sarah Winnemucca's school had been so well established (although shortly after the expression of that happiness, the Peabody School collapsed). In 1888 she moved to the Gordon, a residential hotel in Jamaica Plain, from which she dictated a letter to the secretary of the New England Women's Club on October 16— "The Woman's Club was formed when I was in Europe in 1867–68. When I came home I found they had made me an Honorary Member of it: sometimes I was made the Vice-President; sometimes Director of its Art and Literature meetings. If you wish this as an autograph from me, or your history, you are welcome to it"—and signed it herself.[37]

Peabody's last intellectual act was editing her sister Mary's manuscript novel *Juanita*, which was based on Mary's experiences in Cuba more than fifty years earlier. Just before and just after moving from Lamartine Street, she wrote Harriet Lothrop, whose husband published the novel in 1887, several letters full of editorial business and reminiscence. "My sister was in Cuba in 1833, when slavery with all its existing [exciting?] contrasts first burst upon a New Englander—for it was before the Abolitionist Excitement began here, & Cuba was then in a treaty with England to *forbid* slavery *importation*—But as the cholera had just decimated the plantations—there was a great *smuggling* of slaves into Cuba by a conspiracy of the great slaveholders." Mary's and Sophia's host in Cuba, himself a New Englander, had received several smuggled slaves. But the real moral dilemma lay in the way that the "wives were tortured in various ways by the inevitable play of all [the] contradictory social principles," that is, by the sexual relations between their husbands and the slaves. All this recollection was part of the "historical truth of the book," as well as of its "romance."[38]

   In her very last years, Elizabeth Peabody was content to stay at the Gordon and receive the occasional visitor. Her eyesight had failed, and she found herself living increasingly in the remembered past. She told Harriet Lothrop that "there seems to be but one thing left for me to do on earth since the plans for my life work have come to this [final?] issue—but to record for others' encouragement the history of how the Lord seems to have helped me by involving in my activity the action of so many noble workers & thinkers—with whom He has generously brought me into relation—& to this work I seem to be shut up by the failure of all my powers to do any thing else!" In 1890 she wrote to her old friend Samuel Gray Ward, who was sorrowing that his wife Anna was so unwell, inquiring about his health and spirits. "I wish we could have some talk together—for you seem less inclined than ever to write—In the world to come we shall understand one another without words which at best only *point* to what we want to say—this *yearning* is not so healthy a state as *tranquillity* which I only occasionally feel but perhaps you feel it all the time.—I am content to *muse* His praise— while the fire burns." George and Benjamin Mann cared for their aunt's finances. George wrote to his brother in 1889 proposing that Ben take over the management of Aunt Lizzie's publications. "There is not much money in them, and I presume not much can be made out of them, but I suppose you will keep them alive; where that can be done, as that is her wish." The brothers also shared news of their last remaining Peabody aunt with those who inquired, like Mary Beedy, principal of a girls' high school in Chicago, who wrote to George in 1892, thanking him for news of Peabody and praising her as "the mother of kindergartens in America."[39]

Elizabeth Peabody died at the Gordon on January 3, 1894. Her funeral was held on Saturday, January 6, in Boston's Church of the Disciples. On the platform behind the casket sat Ednah Dow Cheney, Julia
Ward Howe, Franklin Sanborn, and the church's minister Charles
Ames. After Scripture and a rendition of "Lead Kindly Light" sung by a
choir of kindergarten teachers, Cheney eulogized her friend as a brilliant and loving teacher and a ceaseless advocate of the oppressed, in
other countries and in this one. "When she walked down the street arm
in arm with a colored man the whole town was aflame with indignation
while she was calm, dignified, and unimpassioned," Cheney recalled of
Peabody's late but unequivocal embrace of racial equality. Sanborn described her as "an eager and sympathetic spirit to whom age seemed
foreign and activity the only mode of life." In an era that had forgotten
the passionate idealism of an earlier time, "she forgot not the shrine of
her youth and hope: the garden never ceased to bloom for her, however
sterile and deserted others might deem it; the fountains still flowed
from its concealed perennial source, and where its waters went they fed
the roots of undying flowers." From Boston her body was taken to
Concord, where it was buried in Sleepy Hollow Cemetery, near the
graves of Emerson, Thoreau, and Alcott.[40]

Elizabeth Peabody's friends and admirers took the occasion of her
death to remember and praise her. Her old friend Sarah Clarke recalled
that "while most mortals instinctively take care of number one, she
alone totally neglected that important numeral, and spent all her life, all
her strength, her marvellous enthusiasm, her generous fiery ardor in
the cause of others. She was no longer herself Elizabeth Peabody, she
was a company of exiled Poles, of destitute Germans, banished French-
men, expatriated Italians or Hungarians, all of whom must be helped,
must be put on their feet, must be made known to those able and
willing to help them."[41] Kindergarten teacher Mary Garland wrote that

> every noble cause had her ready sympathy, her helping hand,—the
> slave in America, the Hungarian struggling against oppression in
> Europe, the Indian suffering injustice at the hands of the race
> which had disinherited him, the young children everywhere who
> waited to be educated for the service and blessing the world,—each
> class in turn had a champion in Miss Peabody.

No capriciousness led her to drop one thing to take up something else; her interests were abiding, and each enthusiasm helped every other, for all had a common source, the "enthusiasm of humanity," the love of God. . . . She literally gave herself to the cause, for she received, if anything, the most meagre compensation for what she did; if her travelling expenses were paid she was more than satisfied, thinking nothing of her own great personal sacrifices; and as she saw the gradual triumph of the better way, and others making easier conquests, she rejoiced simply and fervently.[42]

Epilogue:
The Elizabeth Peabody House

ॐ

ON JANUARY 10, 1894, Elizabeth Peabody's will was filed at Suffolk County Probate Court, naming her nephew Benjamin Pickman Mann as executor. But Benjamin refused this task, and on March 23 the Court assigned his brother George Combe Mann the duty of fulfilling their aunt's final wishes. Ironically, the unwilling nephew received the bulk of Peabody's meager estate: her copyrights, her bookcase containing portraits of herself and of her father painted by Chester Harding "in gratitude, as he said, for my education of his children," thirty-one shares of stock in Calumet and Hecla Mining Company, and $500 held in trust by Sarah Clarke and Samuel Gray Ward. The books, clothing, and furniture in her apartment were valued at $100, and her outstanding debts at $461.[1]

In the decades around the turn of the twentieth century, Progressive reformers opened settlement houses in many American cities. These houses acted as social centers, where immigrants would find social services and where middle-class reformers lived and interacted with those whose lives they hoped to affect. In the months following her death, Elizabeth Peabody's friends in the kindergarten movement collaborated on a project to organize and open a settlement house, "a living monument," in her honor. "A house has been secured at 156 Chambers Street [in Boston], in a neighborhood where there is especial need of such work," the "Prospectus for the Elizabeth Peabody House" noted. "A Kindergarten will be opened for the children who are unable to gain admission to the public schools, owing to their crowded conditions. There will be a group of kindergartners and normal students in residence, whose purpose it will be to obey literally the injunction of Froebel, 'Come, let us live with our children.'"

In the spring of 1896, with the particular labor of Rebecca Weston and some anonymous donors, "the Elizabeth Peabody House was formally opened, taking its place as the first kindergarten settlement." On the copy of the "Second Annual Report" of the Peabody House, its address at Chambers Street is crossed off and "86 Poplar St." is written in its place.[2]

In 1978 the Elizabeth Peabody House moved to Somerville. Now a hundred years old, the House is located in an old church building on Broadway in that working-class, richly multicultural town, home to people of African-American, Caribbean, Russian, and middle eastern cultures, and many others as well. A Haitian congregation meets in the House on Sunday, and theater groups, daycare groups, and after-school programs crowd the space. Children play in the brightly lit basement daycare area, its walls filled with colorful drawings and announcements. On the main floor, next to the stage and above the battered piano, there hangs a faded portrait of Elizabeth Peabody, by Daniel Creighton, looking out over the fruit of her work.[3]

Notes
Index

Notes

Abbreviations

AAS   American Antiquarian Society
ABA   Amos Bronson Alcott
Antioch   Robert Straker Collection, Antiochiana, Olive
                   Kettering Library, Antioch College
CE   *Centenary Edition of the Works of Nathaniel Hawthorne*,
                   ed. William Charvat et. al. (Columbus: Ohio State
                   University Press, 1962—).
ELetters   *Letters of Ralph Waldo Emerson*, ed. Ralph Rusk and
                   Eleanor Tilton. (New York: Columbia University
                   Press, 1939).
EP   Elizabeth Palmer Peabody (mother)
EPP   Elizabeth Palmer Peabody (daughter)
FLetters   *Letters of Margaret Fuller*, ed. Robert Hudspeth
                   (Ithaca: Cornell University Press, 1983—).
HM   Horace Mann
Houghton   Houghton Library, Harvard University
JMN   *Journals and Miscellaneous Notebooks of Ralph Waldo
                   Emerson*, ed. William Gilman et. al. (Cambridge,
                   Mass.: Belknap Press of Harvard University Press,
                   1960–1982).
Letters   *Letters of Elizabeth Palmer Peabody: American
                   Renaissance Woman*, ed. Bruce A. Ronda. (Middletown,
                   Conn.: Wesleyan University Press, 1984).
MF   Margaret Fuller
MHS   Massachusetts Historical Society
MME   Mary Moody Emerson

347

MMEL	*Selected Letters of Mary Moody Emerson*, ed. Nancy Craig Simmons. (Athens: University of Georgia Press, 1993).
MPM	Mary Peabody Mann
ms	manuscript
MTP	Mary Tyler Peabody
NCP	Nathaniel Cranch Peabody
NH	Nathaniel Hawthorne
NHHW	Julian Hawthorne, *Nathaniel Hawthorne and His Wife*, 2 vols. (Boston: Osgood, 1884).
NP	Nathaniel Peabody (father)
npnd	no place, no date
NYPL-Berg	Henry W. and Albert A. Berg Collection, the New York Public Library, Astor, Lenox, and Tilden Foundations
NYPL-Bryant-Godwin	Bryant-Godwin Papers, Manuscripts and Archives Division, the New York Public Library, Astor, Lenox, and Tilden Foundations
NYPL-Duyckinck	Duyckinck Family Papers, Manuscripts and Archives Division, the New York Public Library, Astor, Lenox, and Tilden Foundations
ps	postscript
Radcliffe	Schlesinger Library of the History of Women, Radcliffe College of Harvard University
RWE	Ralph Waldo Emerson
SAP	Sophia Amelia Peabody
SPH	Sophia Peabody Hawthorne
SSC	Sophia Smith Collection, Smith College Library, Smith College
ts	typescript
ts copy	typescript made by other than author
//	material contained within slashes written above or below line
[]	uncertain place or date

Preface

1. Louise Hall Tharp, *The Peabody Sisters of Salem* (Boston: Little, Brown, 1950); Ruth M. Baylor, *Elizabeth Peabody, Kindergarten Pioneer* (Philadelphia: University of Pennsylvania Press, 1965); John B. Wilson, "Elizabeth Peabody and Other Transcendentalists on History and Historians," *Historian*, 30 (1967), 72–86; John B. Wilson, "A Transcendentalist Minority Report," *New England Quarterly*, 29 (1956), 147–158. A review of Peabody scholarship and sources up to the early 1980s is Margaret Neussendorfer, "Elizabeth Palmer Peabody," in *The Transcendentalists: A Review of Research and Criticism*, ed. Joel Myerson (New York: Modern Language Association, 1984), pp. 233–241. Unpublished sources on Peabody include Mary S. Adams, "Two Women Transcendentalists: Margaret Fuller and Elizabeth Palmer Peabody," M.A. thesis, University of Houston, 1968; Queenie M. Bilbo, "Elizabeth Palmer Peabody, Transcendentalist," Ph.D. thesis, New York University, 1932;

Hersha Sue Fisher, "The Education of Elizabeth Peabody," Ed.D. thesis, Harvard University, 1980; Doris L. McCart, "Elizabeth Peabody: A Biographical Study," M.A. thesis, University of Chicago, 1918; Josephine E. Roberts, "A New England Family: Elizabeth Palmer Peabody, 1804–1894, Mary Tyler Peabody (Mrs. Horace Mann), 1806–1887, Sophia Amelia Peabody (Mrs. Nathaniel Hawthorne), 1809–1871," Ph.D. thesis, Case Western Reserve University, 1937; Robert J. Saunders, "The Contributions of Horace Mann, Mary Peabody Mann, and Elizabeth Peabody to Art Education in the United States," Ph.D. thesis, Pennsylvania State University, 1961; and Catherine C. Tinhof, "Elizabeth Palmer Peabody: Female Intellectual in the Transcendental Circle," M.A. thesis, Washington State University, 1989.

2. *The Transcendentalists*, ed. Perry Miller (Cambridge, Mass.: Harvard University Press, 1950).

3. Anne Rose, *Transcendentalism as a Social Movement, 1830–1850* (New Haven: Yale University Press, 1981).

Introduction

1. Theodore Parker, quoted in Franklin B. Sanborn, *Recollections of Seventy Years* (Boston: Badger, 1909), p. 548.

2. *ELetters*, vol. 1, pp. 449–450, fn 70.

3. Louise Hall Tharp, *The Peabody Sisters of Salem* (Boston: Little, Brown, 1950); Ruth Baylor, *Elizabeth Peabody, Kindergarten Pioneer* (Philadelphia: University of Pennsylvania Press, 1965).

4. Julian Hawthorne, *The Memoirs of Julian Hawthorne*, ed. Edith G. Hawthorne (New York: Macmillan, 1938), p. 44.

5. See, for example, *Reader-Response Criticism: from Formalism to Post-Structuralism*, ed. Jane Tompkins (Baltimore: Johns Hopkins University Press, 1980); and Roland Barthes, *Images, music, text*, trans. Stephen Heath (New York: Hill and Wang, 1977).

6. Thomas Groome, *Christian Religious Education: Sharing Our Story and Vision* (San Francisco: HarperCollins, 1980), p. 154. For other treatments of *praxis*, see Richard J. Bernstein, *Praxis and Action: Contemporary Philosophies of Human Activity* (Philadelphia: University of Pennsylvania Press, 1971); Paulo Freire, *Pedagogy of the Oppressed* (New York: Seabury, 1970); Jurgen Habermas, *Theory and Practice* (Boston: Beacon, 1973); Martin Jay, *The Dialectical Imagination* (Boston: Little, Brown, 1973); Nicholas Lobkowicz, *Theory and Practice: History of a Concept from Aristotle to Marx* (Notre Dame, Ind.: University of Notre Dame Press, 1967).

7. "Introduction," *An American Reformation: A Documentary History of Unitarian Christianity*, eds. Sydney Ahlstrom and Jonathan Carey (Middletown, Conn.: Wesleyan University Press, 1985), p. 18. For some of the voluminous literature on the liberal challenge to orthodoxy, see notes for chap. 2 in this volume.

8. Elizabeth Palmer Peabody, *Reminiscences of William Ellery Channing* (Boston: Roberts, 1880), pp. 58–59.

9. Sherman Paul, *Emerson's Angle of Vision: Man and Nature in American Experience* (Cambridge, Mass.: Harvard University Press, 1952), p. 60.

10. Catherine Albanese, *Corresponding Motion: Transcendental Religion and the New America* (Philadelphia: Temple University Press, 1977), p. 3.

11. EPP, "Mrs. Elizabeth Peabody," *American Journal of Education*, 32 (1882), 740.

12. EPP, "Method of Spiritual Culture," in *Record of a School*, second edition (Boston: Russell, Shattuck, 1836), p. 252.

13. EPP, "Principles and Methods of Education," *American Journal of Education*, 32 (1882), 722.

14. Charles Capper, *Margaret Fuller: An American Romantic Life: The Private Years* (New York: Oxford University Press, 1992), p. 317; Nina Baym, "The Ann Sisters: Elizabeth Peabody's Millennial Historicism," *American Literary History* 3 (Spring 1991), 27.

15. Octavius Brooks Frothingham, *Transcendentalism in New England* [1876] (Philadelphia: University of Pennsylvania Press, 1972); Arthur Ladu, "Channing and Transcendentalism," *American Literature*, 11 (1939), 129–137; Conrad Wright, "The Rediscovery of Channing," in *The Liberal Christians: Essays on American Unitarian History* (Boston: Beacon, 1970), 22–40; Rose, *Transcendentalism as a Social Movement, 1830–1850*.

16. William R. Hutchison, *The Transcendentalist Ministers: Church Reform in the New England Renaissance* [1959] (Boston: Beacon, 1965); David Robinson, *Apostle of Culture: Emerson as Preacher and Lecturer* (Philadelphia: University of Pennsylvania Press, 1982); Robinson, "The Legacy of Channing: Culture as a Religious Category in New England Thought," *Harvard Theological Review* 74 (1981), 221–239.

17. RWE to EPP, 12 October 1840, *ELetters*, vol. 2, p. 345.

18. SPH to EP, 29 September–10 October 1850, NYPL-Berg.

19. See T. Walter Herbert, *Dearest Beloved: The Hawthornes and the Making of the Middle-Class Family* (Berkeley and Los Angeles: University of California Press, 1993), pp. 37–43.

20. EPP to Caroline Healey Dall, 21 February 1859, *Letters*, p. 297; EPP to Ellen Conway, 28 June 1880, *Letters*, p. 402.

21. Moncure Conway, quoted in Lucy Wheelock, "Miss Peabody As I Knew Her," in *Kindergarten and Child Culture Papers: Pioneers of the Kindergarten Movement in America* (New York: Century, 1924), pp. 33–34.

22. EPP to Horatio Bridge, 4 June 1887, *Letters*, pp. 445–446.

Prologue

1. EPP to MTP, 30 August [1834], "Cuba Journal," NYPL-Berg.

2. *NHHW*, vol. 1, p. 45.

3. NCP, "Palmer Family Genealogy," ts copy, Ruth M. Baylor Collection of Mss. Notes, MHS. The whereabouts of the originals is unknown.

4. "Obituary," *Kindergarten News*, 4 (February 1894), 45.

1. "A Rightly Educated Woman"

1. "Biographical Sketch of General Joseph Palmer," *The New Englander*, 9 (January 1845), 1–2.

2. Mary Beth Norton, *Liberty's Daughters: The Revolutionary Experience of American Women, 1750–1800* (Boston: Little, Brown, 1980), p. 38.

3. Mary Palmer Tyler, *Grandmother Tyler's Book: The Recollections of Mary Palmer Tyler, 1775–1866* (New York: Putnam's, 1925), pp. 23–25.

4. See T. Walter Herbert, *Dearest Beloved: The Hawthornes and the Making of the Middle-Class Family* (Berkeley and Los Angeles: University of California Press, 1993), pp. 39–40, for a discussion of this episode.

5. Tyler, p. 18.

6. Tyler, p. 29.

7. Tyler, pp. 32–36; "Biographical Sketch," 18–19.

8. Norton, pp. 157, 167.

9. Tyler, p. 47.

10. EPP, "Mrs. Elizabeth Palmer Peabody," *American Journal of Education*, 32 (1882), 739.

11. "Biographical Sketch," 20, 22, 23.

12. Tyler, pp. 84, 88.

13. Tyler, p. 98.

14. Tyler, p. 74.

15. Tyler, p. 98.

16. For information on Tyler, see Thomas Tanselle, *Royall Tyler* (Cambridge, Mass.: Harvard University Press, 1967); for letters on Tyler's relationship with Nabby Adams, see *The Book of Abigail and John: Selected Letters of the Adams Family 1762–1784*, ed. Lyman Butterfield (Cambridge, Mass.: Harvard University Press, 1975), pp. 338–340.

17. NCP, "Elizabeth Palmer," ts copy, Ruth M. Baylor Collection of Mss. Notes, MHS. The whereabouts of the originals is unknown.

18. Mrs. Elizabeth Palmer Peabody [EP], "Seduction," *Christian Examiner* (November 1833), 163.

19. NCP, "Palmer Family Genealogy," ts copy, Baylor Collection, MHS.

20. Anon. [EP], ms, Peabody II Papers, MHS.

21. Tanselle, pp. 7–8.

22. Tyler, pp. 141–143.

23. Tyler, pp. 142–143.

24. Sarah Loring Bailey, "Young Ladies at Andover," *Boston Daily Advertiser*, 30 January 1879.

25. Tyler, p. 177.

26. Bailey, "Young Ladies."

27. Bailey, "Young Ladies."

28. Tyler, pp. 205.

29. NCP, "Elizabeth Palmer," Baylor Collection, MHS.

30. EPP, "Mrs. Elizabeth Palmer Peabody," *Boston Daily Advertiser*, 10 February 1879.

31. Tyler, p. 204.

32. Norton, pp. 171, 172.

33. Norton, p. 225.

34. Ruth Bloch, "The Gendered Meaning of Virtue in Revolutionary America," *Signs* 13 (Autumn 1987), 41.

35. William Lyman, quoted in Bloch, 45–46.

36. Bloch, 54.

37. Linda Kerber, *Women of the Republic: Intellect and Ideology in Revolutionary America* (Chapel Hill: University of North Carolina Press, 1980), p. 199.

38. Bernard Bailyn, "Education as a Discipline: Some Historical Notes," in *The Discipline of Education*, eds. John Walton and James Keuthe (Madison: University of Wisconsin Press, 1963), p. 138.

39. Benjamin Rush, quoted in Kerber, pp. 227–228. See also Jill Ker Conway, "Perspectives on the History of Women's Education in the United States," *History of Education Quarterly* 14 (Spring 1974), 1–12; Ann Gordon, "The Young Ladies Academies of Philadelphia," in *Women of America: A History*, ed. Carol Ruth Berkin and Mary Beth Norton (Boston: Houghton, Mifflin, 1979); Joseph F. Kett, *The Pursuit of Knowledge Under Difficulties: From Self-Improvement to Adult Education in America, 1750–1990* (Stanford: Stanford University Press, 1994), pp. 32–41; Harriet Webster Marr, *The Old New England Academies* (New York: Comet Press, 1959), pp. 98–99; Robert Middlekauff, *Ancients and Axioms: Secondary Education in Eighteenth Century New England* (New Haven: Yale University Press, 1963), p. 130.

40. Megan Marshall, "Two Early Poems by Mrs. Elizabeth Peabody," *Proceedings of the Massachusetts Historical Society*, 100 (1988), 40–59.

41. NCP, "Elizabeth Palmer," Baylor Collection, MHS.

42. NCP, annotations to EP to Mary Cranch, in "Elizabeth Palmer," Baylor Collection, MHS.

43. EP to George C. Peabody, 30 October 1836, ts copy, Antioch.

44. EPP, "Mrs. Elizabeth Palmer Peabody."

45. NCP, "Elizabeth Palmer," Baylor Collection, MHS.

46. EPP, "Mrs. Elizabeth Palmer Peabody."

47. NCP, "Elizabeth Palmer, " Baylor Collection, MHS.

48. Sarah Loring Bailey, "Mrs. Elizabeth Palmer Peabody," *Boston Daily Advertiser*, 10 February 1879.

49. Bailey, "Mrs. Elizabeth Palmer Peabody."

50. NCP, "Elizabeth Palmer," Baylor Collection, MHS.

51. EP to Mary Cranch [?], npnd, in Bailey, "Mrs. Elizabeth Palmer Peabody."

52. Selim Peabody, *Peabody Genealogy* (Boston: Charles Pope, 1909); Charles M. Endicott, *A Genealogy of the Peabody Family* (Boston: David Clapp, 1867); Edwin P. Hoyt, *The Peabody Influence* (New York: Dodd, Mead, 1968).

53. Bailey, "Mrs. Elizabeth Palmer Peabody."

54. NCP, "Elizabeth Palmer," Baylor Collection, MHS.

55. EP to Mary Cranch, npnd, in Bailey, "Mrs. Elizabeth Palmer Peabody."

56. EP to "my friend" [Nathaniel Peabody], [17] February 1800, Peabody II Papers, MHS.

57. EP to Nathaniel Peabody [NP], 1 March 1800, Peabody II Papers, MHS.

58. EP to "my friend" [NP], 16 March 1800, Peabody II Papers, MHS.

59. Sarah Loring Bailey, *Historical Sketches of Andover* (Boston: Houghton Mifflin, 1880), pp. 543, 552.

60. Bailey, "Young Ladies at Andover."

61. Bailey, "Young Ladies at Andover."

62. EP to NP, 16 February 1802, Peabody II Papers, MHS.

63. EPP, "Mrs. Elizabeth Palmer Peabody," *American Journal of Education*, 740.

64. NCP, "Elizabeth Palmer," Baylor Collection, MHS.

65. Bernard Farber, *Guardians of Virtue: Salem Families in 1800* (New York:

Basic Books, 1972), pp. 160–168; Alfred F. Rosa, *Salem, Transcendentalism, and Hawthorne* (Rutherford, N.J.: Fairleigh Dickinson University Press, 1980), pp. 22–23; *Maritime Salem in the Age of Sail* (Washington: National Park Service, 1987), pp. 126–135.

66. NCP, "Elizabeth Palmer," Baylor Collection, MHS.

67. EPP, *Lectures in the Training School for Kindergartners* (Boston: D.C. Heath, 1886), pp. 102–103.

68. Farber, pp. 168–169.

69. NCP, "Elizabeth Palmer," Baylor Collection, MHS.

70. EPP, "Mrs. Elizabeth Palmer Peabody," in *American Journal of Education*, 742.

71. Farber, pp. 38–39; Frank Preston Stearns, *The Life and Genius of Nathaniel Hawthorne* (Philadelphia: Lippincott, 1906), p. 117; EPP, "Mrs. Elizabeth Palmer Peabody," in *American Journal of Education*, 742; NCP, "Elizabeth Palmer," Baylor Collection, MHS.

72. EPP to Francis Henry Lee, [1885], *Letters*, p. 419; Mary Peabody Mann, "Reminiscences," ts copy, Antioch.

73. *NHHW*, vol. 1, p. 47.

74. *NHHW*, vol. 1, pp. 47–50.

75. EPP to Sophia Amelia Peabody [SAP], 23 June 1822, NYPL-Berg.

76. EPP to Julian Hawthorne, in Norman Holmes Pearson, "Elizabeth Peabody on Hawthorne," *Essex Institute Historical Collections*, 94 (1958), 270.

77. Pearson, "EPP on Hawthorne," 270; *NHHW*, vol. 1, pp. 60–61; EP to Mary Tyler Peabody [MTP], 8 January 1828, Antioch.

78. Catherine Palmer Putnam to EPP, 12 December 1850, Antioch.

79. EPP, *Reminiscences of William Ellery Channing* (Boston: Roberts, 1880), p. 30.

80. EPP, *Lectures*, pp. 70–72.

81. EPP, *Reminiscences*, p. 14; "Preceptress of a Young Ladies Academy in Salem" [EP], *Sabbath Lessons; or, An Abstract of Sacred History; to which is annexed, A Geographical Sketch of the Principal Places Mentioned in Sacred History*, second edition (Salem: Joshua Cushing, 1813), np.

82. EPP, *Reminiscences*, pp. 113–114.

83. EPP, *Reminiscences*, pp. 34–35.

84. EPP, *Reminiscences*, pp. 37–38.

85. EP to EPP, 25 April 1819, Antioch.

86. EPP, "Principles and Methods of Education," *American Journal of Education*, 32 (1882), 722–730; NHHW, vol. 1, p. 61.

87. EPP, *Reminiscences*, pp. 39–40.

88. NCP, "Elizabeth Palmer, " Baylor Collection, MHS.

2. *"Mind Has No Sex"*

1. See Andrew R. L. Cayton, "The Fragmentation of a 'Great Family': The Panic of 1819 and the Rise of the Middling Interest in Boston, 1818–1822," *Journal of the Early Republic*, 2 (Summer 1982), 143–167; Mary Kupiec Cayton, *Emerson's Emergence: Self and Society in the Transformation of New England, 1800–1845* (Chapel Hill: University of North Carolina Press, 1989), pp. 17–32; Robert McCaughey,

"From Town to City: Boston in the 1820s," *Political Science Quarterly*, 88 (June 1973), 191–213.

2. EPP to Maria Chase, [May 1821], *Letters*, pp. 55–56.

3. EPP to Maria Chase, 20 May 1822, Sophia Smith Collection, Smith College, Northampton, Massachusetts (SSC).

4. Anna Q. T. Parsons, "Reminiscences of Miss Peabody," *Kindergarten Review*, 14 (1904), 539.

5. EPP to SAP, December 1825, SSC.

6. EPP to SAP, 23 June 1822, August 1822, NYPL-Berg.

7. EPP to SAP, 15 May 1824, NYPL-Berg; 12 July, ny, NYPL-Berg.

8. EPP to SAP, 23 June 1822, NYPL-Berg.

9. EPP to SAP, 23 June 1822, NYPL-Berg; EPP to Maria Chase, 18 January 1822, SSC.

10. EPP, "Emerson as Preacher," in *The Genius and Character of Emerson*, eds. Franklin B. Sanborn and William Torrey Harris (Boston: Osgood, 1884), p. 150.

11. Elizabeth Hunt Palmer to Mary Palmer Tyler, March 1823, Royall Tyler Collection, Gift of Helen Tyler Brown, Vermont Historical Society; EPP to EP, May 1822, *Letters*, p. 58; EPP to Maria Chase, 12 June 1822, SSC; EPP to Maria Chase, 3 September 1824, SSC.

12. NP to EPP, 26 April 1823, ts copy, Antioch.

13. Laurel Thatcher Ulrich, *A Midwife's Tale: The Life of Martha Ballard, Based on Her Diary, 1785–1812* (New York: Random House/Vintage, 1991), pp. 13–14.

14. Emma Huntington Nason, *Old Hallowell on the Kennebec* (Augusta, Me.: privately printed, 1909), p. 87.

15. EPP to EP, [September 1823], *Letters*, p. 65; EPP to Maria Chase, 23 January [1824], *Letters*, p. 66.

16. EPP to SAP, 15 February 1824, NYPL-Berg.

17. EPP to Maria Chase, 4 October 1823, SSC; EPP to SAP, 24 December 1823, NYPL-Berg.

18. EPP to SAP, 15 May 1824, NYPL-Berg; Delia Gardiner to Miss Buckminster, [1824?], Antioch.

19. Nason, pp. 269–270.

20. EPP to SAP, 24 December 1823, NYPL-Berg.

21. EPP to Maria Chase, 4 October 1823, SSC; 31 May 1824, SSC.

22. EPP to MTP, April 1834, NYPL-Berg, "Cuba Journal"; NCP to EPP, 13 April 1838, ts copy, Antioch.

23. Ulrich, pp. 105–106.

24. EPP, *Reminiscences of William Ellery Channing* (Boston: Roberts, 1880), pp. 45–46.

25. EPP, *Reminiscences*, p. 58.

26. EPP, *Reminiscences*, p. 59.

27. Peter Cartwright quoted in Ann Douglas, *The Feminization of American Culture* (New York: Knopf, 1977), pp. 41–42.

28. EPP to SAP, 31 March 1823, *Letters*, p. 59; EPP, *Reminiscences*, p. 40.

29. For the growth of liberal religion in the colonies and new nation, see Sydney Ahlstrom, *A Religion History of the American People* (New Haven: Yale University Press, 1972), ch. 22; Joseph Haroutunian, *Piety versus Moralism: The Passing*

of the New England Theology (1932) (Hamden, Conn.: Archon Press, 1964); Daniel Walker Howe, *The Unitarian Conscience* (Cambridge, Mass.: Harvard University Press, 1970); and Conrad Wright, *The Beginnings of Unitarianism in America* (1955) (Hamden, Conn.: Archon Press, 1976).

30. On Channing, see Howe, *Unitarian Conscience*, passim; Arthur W. Brown, *Always Young for Liberty: A Biography of William Ellery Channing* (Syracuse: Syracuse University Press, 1956); Andrew Delbanco, *William Ellery Channing: An Essay on the Liberal Spirit in America* (Cambridge, Mass.: Harvard University Press, 1981). For a useful discussion of Channing's influence on EPP, see Susan H. Irons, "Channing's Influence on Peabody: Self-Culture and the Dangers of Egoism," *Studies in the American Renaissance*, 1992, 121–135.

31. EPP to Maria Chase, April 1820, *Letters*, pp. 52–53; EPP to EP, [26] May 1822, *Letters* p. 57.

32. Channing, "Discourse on the Ordination of John Emery Abbot," 1815, quoted in Howe, *Unitarian Conscience*, p. 153.

33. EPP, *Reminiscences*, p. 81.

34. MTP to Rawlins Pickman, 2 December 1827, Horace Mann II Papers, MHS.

35. EPP to Maria Chase, 14 June 1821, SSC.

36. EPP to Maria Chase, 24 January [1824], *Letters*, p. 67.

37. EPP to Maria Chase, 18 March 1824, SSC.

38. EPP, *Reminiscences*, p. 78; EPP to HM, 2 March 1835, *Letters*, p. 141.

39. EPP, *Reminiscences*, pp. 71–72.

40. MTP to Maria Chase, December 1825, SSC; 8 March 1826, SSC.

41. See Daniel Walker Howe, *Making the American Self: Jonathan Edwards to Abraham Lincoln* (Cambridge, Mass.: Harvard University Press, 1997), pp. 130–133; Channing, "Likeness to God," in *An American Reformation: A Documentary History of Unitarian Christianity*, eds. Sydney Ahlstrom and Jonathan Carey (Middletown, Conn.: Wesleyan University Press, 1985), p. 141.

42. Olivia Coolidge, note to Delia Gardiner to Miss Buckminster, [1824?], ts copy, Antioch: "It is notable that R. H. Gardiner finally got rid of Elizabeth on the ground that the children did not make sufficient progress."

The account of the dedication of the Bunker Hill monument and Elizabeth's and Mary's subsequent encounter with Lafayette is found in EPP to Maria Chase, 3 September 1824 [really 1825], SSC, which has also been printed in *Essex Institute Historical Collections*, 85 (October 1949), 360–368. The monument was dedicated on 17 June 1825, the fiftieth anniversary of the Battle of Bunker Hill. See Irving Bartlett, *Daniel Webster* (New York: Norton, 1978), p. 109.

43. EPP, *Reminiscences*, pp. 8–9.

44. EPP, *Reminiscences*, p. 151.

45. EPP to SAP, 23 August 1825, NYPL-Berg.

46. EPP, *Reminiscences*, p. 113; MTP to Rawlins Pickman, 27 January 1825, Horace Mann II Papers, MHS.

47. MTP to Rawlins Pickman, [1 June] 1826, Horace Mann II Papers, MHS.

48. EPP, "Principles and Methods of Education," *American Journal of Education*, 32 (1882), 724–725.

49. Cayton, *Emerson's Emergence*, p. 46.

50. EPP to EP, June 1826, *Letters*, p. 72.

51. EPP to Nathan Appleton, [1827?], *Letters*, pp. 78–82; MTP to Rawlins Pickman, 27 January 1825, Horace Mann II Papers, MHS; MTP to Maria Chase, [October 1827?], SSC.

52. MTP to Rawlins Pickman, 1 May 1827, Horace Mann II Papers, MHS.

53. MTP to Maria Chase, 10 November 1826, SSC.

54. MTP to Maria Chase, 10 November 1826, SSC; SAP to Maria Chase, 8 October 1827, SSC; SAP to Maria Chase, 9 January 1828, SSC.

55. "William Russell," *Dictionary of American Biography*, vol. 8, pp. 249–250; Frederick Dahlstrand, *Amos Bronson Alcott: An Intellectual Biography* (Rutherford, N.J.: Fairleigh Dickinson University Press, 1982), pp. 53–57.

56. EPP, "Account of a Visit to an Elementary School," *American Journal of Education*, 4 (1829), 74–76; ABA, "Journal for 1829," *59M-308 (3), by permission of Houghton Library, Harvard University.

57. MTP to Rawlins Pickman, 3 October 1827, Horace Mann II Papers, MHS.

58. EPP to Nathan Appleton, [1827?], *Letters*, pp. 78–82.

59. EPP to Orestes Brownson, [1840], *Letters*, p. 248.

60. EPP, *Reminiscences*, p. 127.

61. See Jerry Wayne Brown, *The Rise of Biblical Criticism in America, 1800–1810: The New England Scholars* (Middletown, Conn.: Wesleyan University Press, 1969); William Hutchison, *The Transcendental Ministers* (New Haven: Yale University Press, 1959).

62. See Hans Frei, *The Eclipse of Biblical Narrative: A Study in Eighteenth and Nineteenth Century Hermeneutics* (New Haven: Yale University Press, 1974).

63. EPP, "Spirit of Hebrew Scriptures: Creation," *Christian Examiner*, 16 (May 1834), 175.

64. Sophia Pickman to Mary Palmer Tyler, ps to Elizabeth Hunt Palmer to Mary Palmer Tyler, 29 June 1822, Royall Tyler Papers, Gift of Helen Tyler Brown, Vermont Historical Society; Elizabeth Hunt Palmer to Mary Palmer Tyler, March 1823, Royall Tyler Papers, Gift of Helen Tyler Brown, Vermont Historical Society.

65. MTP to Maria Chase, [June 1825], SSC.

66. EPP to Dorothea Dix, July 1827, *Letters*, p. 75.

67. EPP to Sarah Sullivan, [November 1827], *Letters*, p. 76.

68. EPP, *Reminiscences*, p. 313.

69. EPP to Elizabeth Davis Bliss, 8 July [1830], *Letters*, pp. 94–95.

70. Norman Holmes Pearson, "Elizabeth Peabody on Hawthorne," *Essex Institute Historical Collections*, 94 (1958), 274. See also *Chronicles of Old Salem: A History in Miniature*, ed. Diane Robotti (New York: Bonanza Books, 1948); Edmund Pearson, *Murder at Smutty Nose, and Other Murders* (Garden City: Doubleday, 1927); and Joseph Barlow Felt, *Annals of Salem*, 2 vols. (Boston: Munroe, 1845–1849), vol. 2, pp. 465–467. I also found helpful a file of broadsides and clippings on the White murders at the Peabody Essex Museum, Salem, Massachusetts.

71. EPP, *Reminiscences*, pp. 316–317.

72. James L. Campbell, *Edward Bulwer-Lytton* (Boston: Twayne, 1986), pp. 26–31; EPP, *Reminiscences*, p. 320.

73. EPP, *Reminiscences*, pp. 316–318.

74. EPP to Sarah Sullivan, 18 March 1831, *Letters*, p. 100.

75. EPP, *Reminiscences*, pp. 303–304, 322.

76. MTP to Maria Chase, 8 March 1826, SSC; EPP to Maria Chase, 16 March 1826, SSC.

77. EPP to Sarah Sullivan, 17 May 1830, *Letters*, p. 92.

78. EPP to Elizabeth Davis Bliss, [4 March 1835], *Letters*, p. 148.

3. *"You Think I Have No Judgment"*

1. Sklar, "Founding of Mt. Holyoke College," in *Women of America: A History* (Boston: Houghton, Mifflin, 1979), pp. 179–180; Richard Bernard and Maris Vinovskis, "The Female Schoolteacher in Antebellum Massachusetts," *Journal of Social History* 10 (March 1977), 333–337.

2. Michael Katz, *The Irony of Early School Reform* (Boston: Beacon, 1968); Bruce A. Ronda, "Genesis and Genealogy: Bronson Alcott's Changing Views of the Child," *New England Historical and Genealogical Register* (October 1981), 259–273. See also Daniel Walker Howe, *Making the American Self: From Jonathan Edwards to Abraham Lincoln* (Cambridge, Mass.: Harvard University Press, 1997), pp. 158–160.

3. MTP to Mary Tyler, January 1824, Royall Tyler Collection, Gift of Helen Tyler Brown, Vermont Historical Society; Marilyn Butler, *Maria Edgeworth: A Literary Biography* (Oxford: Clarendon Press, 1972), pp. 33, 58, 64–65, 171–172.

4. EPP to Sarah Sullivan, September 1826, ts copy, Antioch.

5. Joseph Neef, in Will S. Monroe, *History of the Pestalozzian Movement in the United States* (Syracuse: C. W. Bardeen, 1907), p. 83; MTP to Maria Chase, 17 January 1830, SSC.

6. (Boston: Carter and Hendee, 1830), p. 6; EPP to Elizabeth Davis Bliss, 8 July [1830], Library of Congress. In September, Peabody wrote to Sarah Sullivan: "The sale of Degerando goes on nicely. Have you read Mr. Ripley's review of it? It was quite an offset to the Massachusetts Journal!" (September 1830, Antioch). In his review in the *Christian Examiner* (9 [September 1830]), Ripley praised the "taste and ability of the translator," whose work "bears marks of a faithful study of the original, a sufficient knowledge of the author's language, a ready perception of his style of thought and illustration, and a deep sympathy with the beauty and elevated spirit of his philosophy" (100, 106).

7. EPP, *Reminiscences*, pp. 113, 246–247, 261, 266.

8. EPP, *Reminiscences*, pp. 266–267; EPP to Dorothea Dix, 24 January 1828, *Letters*, p. 82.

9. MTP to Lydia Sears Haven, 26 May 1832, ts copy, Antioch.

10. *First Steps to the Study of History: Being Part First of a Key to History* (Boston: Hilliard, Gray, 1832).

11. EPP, *First Steps*, pp. 9–12; EPP to SAP, nd, NYPL-Berg.

12. Of the major U.S. cities in 1832, only Boston and Charleston escaped the worst of the cholera epidemic of that year, although there were some deaths and much anxiety. See Charles Rosenberg, *The Cholera Years: The United States in 1832, 1849, and 1866* (Chicago: University of Chicago Press, 1962); MTP to EPP, [June 1832], Horace Mann Papers, MHS.

13. MTP to EPP, 11 July 1832, Horace Mann Papers, MHS; MTP to EPP, [June 1832], Horace Mann Papers, MHS.

14. Jacob Abbot, "Preface," EPP, Introduction, to *Key to History: Part Two: The Hebrews* (Boston: Marsh, Capen, and Lyon, 1833), pp. 1–2.

15. EPP to SAP, [ca. 1833], NYPL-Berg.

16. EPP to Sarah Hale, [April 1833], *Letters*, pp. 105–106; EPP to SAP, npnd [1833], NYPL-Berg.

17. EPP to Maria Chase, [April 1833], *Letters*, p. 107.

18. EPP to Sarah Hale, [15 May 1833?], *Letters*, pp. 109–110. Boston Athenaeum Circulation Records, volume 1, 1827–1834 (last page of unpaginated volume), contains this note: "Miss Peabody. Per Special Vote of the Trustees for 6 months, renewed to 31 December 1833." This record expands on the note in *The Athenaeum Centenary* (Boston: The Athenaeum, 1907), that EPP was allowed to visit and read in the library (p. 84).

19. EPP to SAP, npnd [1833], NYPL-Berg.

20. Salem *Gazette*, 10 September 1830.

21. EP to EPP and MTP, 2 October [1827], Antioch.

22. EP to EPP and MTP, npnd [1827], Antioch.

23. Pearson, "Elizabeth Peabody on Hawthorne," 271; NCP to MTP and EPP, 1 June 1827, Antioch; EP to MTP [1827?], Antioch.

24. EP to EPP, npnd [1832–1833], ts copy, Antioch; EPP to MTP, 2–5 June 1834, "Cuba Journal," NYPL-Berg.

25. EPP to SAP, nd [1833], NYPL-Berg.

26. NCP to SAP and MTP, 8 February 1835, ts copy, Antioch.

27. EP to SAP and MTP, 9 June 1834, "Cuba Journal," NYPL-Berg.

28. NCP to George Peabody, 27 April 1836, ts copy, Antioch; EP to George Peabody [1836], ts copy, Antioch.

29. EPP to George Peabody, October 1836, ts copy, Antioch; EP to George Peabody, [November] 1836, ts copy, Antioch.

30. MTP to SAP, 17 February 1833, NYPL-Berg; Caroline Healey Dall, "Studies Toward the Life of a 'Business Woman,' Being Conversations with Mrs. R.P. Clarke," ms. Radcliffe.

31. MTP to SAP, npnd [1833], ts copy, Antioch.

32. EPP to SAP (two letters), npnd [1833], NYPL-Berg.

33. MTP to SAP, npnd [1833], ts copy, Antioch.

34. Horace Mann to EPP, npnd [1833], Horace Mann Papers, MHS.

35. Claire Badaracco, "'The Cuba Journal' of Sophia Peabody Hawthorne, volume one, edited from the manuscript, with an introduction," Ph.D. dissertation (Rutgers University), 1978, xliv.

36. Dorcas Cleveland to SAP, 1830, in Badaracco, lxv.

37. EPP to MTP, 21 December 1833, "Cuba Journal," *Letters*, pp. 120–121.

38. EPP to MTP, 12 February 1834, "Cuba Journal," *Letters*, pp. 126–129.

39. EPP to Horace Mann, npnd [1834], *Letters*, pp. 135–137.

40. EPP to MTP, 22 March 1834, "Cuba Journal," ts copy, Antioch.

41. EPP to MTP, 10–13 April 1834, "Cuba Journal," *Letters*, pp. 130–131.

42. Jonathan Messerli, *Horace Mann: A Biography* (New York: Knopf, 1972), pp. 173–175.

43. EPP to Horace Mann, 2 March 1835, *Letters*, pp. 139–147.

44. EPP to MTP, 13–17 May 1834, "Cuba Journal," NYPL-Berg.

45. EPP to MTP, 15 [July 1834?], "Cuba Journal," NYPL-Berg.

46. EPP to MTP, 8–10 August 1834, "Cuba Journal," NYPL-Berg.

47. EPP to MTP, 20 September–6 October 1834, "Cuba Journal," NYPL-Berg.

4. *"The Only Practical Transcendentalist There Is"*

1. EPP to MTP, 8 February 1834, "Cuba Journal," *Letters*, p. 123; 7 February 1834, 24–25 February 1834, "Cuba Journal," NYPL-Berg.

2. EPP to MTP, 3 June 1834, "Cuba Journal," NYPL-Berg.

3. Information in this and the next three paragraphs is drawn from Frederick Dahlstrand, *Amos Bronson Alcott: An Intellectual Biography* (Rutherford, N.J.: Fairleigh Dickinson University Press, 1982), pp. 53–105.

4. ABA, *Observations on the Principles and Methods of Infant Instruction* (Boston: Carter and Hendee, 1830), pp. 24, 26–27; *The Journals of Bronson Alcott*, ed. Odell Shepard (Boston: Little, Brown, 1938), p. 32.

5. EPP to MTP, 14 July 1834, "Cuba Journal," NYPL-Berg.

6. EPP to MTP, [21?] July 1834, "Cuba Journal," NYPL-Berg.

7. EPP to MTP, 17–22 July 1834, "Cuba Journal," NYPL-Berg.

8. EPP, *Record of a School* (Boston: Roberts, 1835), p. 13; EPP to MTP, 14–19 September 1834, "Cuba Journal," NYPL-Berg.

9. EPP, *Record*, p. 15; EPP to MTP, 22 September 1834, "Cuba Journal," NYPL-Berg.

10. EPP to MTP, 16 December 1834, "Cuba Journal," NYPL-Berg; ABA, "Life, Speculative and Actual, 1835," 21, *59M-308 (8), by permission of Houghton Library, Harvard University.

11. EPP, *Record*, p. 217.

12. EPP, *Record*, pp. 31, 263–264.

13. EPP, *Record*, pp. 276–277; EPP, "Explanatory Preface," *Record of a School*, second edition (Boston: Russell, Shattuck, 1836), p. 12.

14. EPP to MTP, 6 January 1835, "Cuba Journal," NYPL-Berg; 14 September 1834, "Cuba Journal," NYPL-Berg.

15. Eliza Lee Cabot Follen, *Works of Charles Follen, With a Memoir of His Life*, 2 vols. (Boston: Hilliard, Gray, 1842), vol. 1, pp. 343–347, 358–360.

16. EPP to Elizabeth Davis Bliss, nd, *Letters*, pp. 50–52.

17. MTP to HM, 30 May 1835, ts copy, Antioch; MTP to Rawlins Pickman [July 1835], Horace Mann II Papers, MHS.

18. EPP, *Reminiscences of William Ellery Channing* (Boston: Roberts, 1880), p. 144; EPP to Orestes Brownson, [1840], *Letters*, p. 248.

19. HM to EPP, npnd, [September 1834], ts copy, Antioch.

20. Guillaume Oegger, *The True Messiah; or The Old and New Testaments, Examined According to the Principles of the Language of Nature*, trans. Elizabeth Palmer Peabody (Boston: Elizabeth P. Peabody, 1842); *JMN*, vol. 5, pp. 60–61; Robert Richardson, *Emerson: The Mind on Fire* (Berkeley and Los Angeles: University of California Press, 1995), p. 199.

21. *ELetters*, vol. 1, pp. 450–451.

22. EPP to HM, 2 March 1835, *Letters*, p. 139; ABA, "Life, Speculative and Actual, 1835," 110; *ELetters*, vol. 7, p. 243.

23. *JMN*, vol. 5, p. 63; *ELetters*, vol. 7, p. 245, addendum to vol. 1, pp. 449–451.

24. EPP to MTP, 25 February 1835, "Cuba Journal," NYPL-Berg; Sarah Clarke to James Freeman Clarke, 28 February 1835, in Ellen Emerson, *The Life of Lidian Jackson Emerson*, ed. Delores Bird Carpenter (East Lansing: Michigan State University Press, 1992), p. 49.

25. EPP to Elizabeth Davis Bliss, [4 March 1835], *Letters*, pp. 147–148.

26. *The Selected Letters of Lidian Jackson Emerson*, ed. Delores Bird Carpenter (Columbia: University of Missouri Press, 1987), pp. 29–30.

27. EPP to Nahum Capen, 9–10 September 1835, Elizabeth Palmer Peabody Papers, Phillips Library, Peabody Essex Museum, Salem, Massachusetts; EPP to William Wordsworth, 7 September 1835, in Margaret Neussendorfer, "Elizabeth Palmer Peabody to William Wordsworth: eight letters, 1825–1845," *Studies in the American Renaissance*, 1984, 193–194.

28. EPP to ABA, 8 October 1835, in Franklin B. Sanborn and William Torrey Harris, *Amos Bronson Alcott*, 2 vols. (Boston: Roberts, 1893), vol. 1, pp. 189–190.

29. MTP to Rawlins Pickman, 8 October 1835, Horace Mann II Papers, MHS.

30. EPP, "Method of Spiritual Culture," in *Record of a School*, second edition, pp. 252, 260–261, 263.

31. Alcott, "1836 Journal," ed. Joel Myerson, *Studies in the American Renaissance* (1978), 27.

32. Alcott, "1836 Journal," 18–19, 54.

33. EPP, "Journal," 11–15 April 1836, NYPL-Berg.

34. EPP to MTP, [April 1836], *Letters*, pp. 159–160; SAP to Mrs. William Russell, 26 July 1836, in ABA, "Memoir 1878," Houghton bMS *59M-306 (23), by permission of Houghton Library, Harvard University.

35. EPP, "Method of Spiritual Culture," p. 256.

36. Dahlstrand, pp. 135–139.

37. EPP to Elizabeth Davis Bliss, 23 December 1836, *Letters*, p. 190; Perry Miller, ed. *The Transcendentalists* (Cambridge, Mass.: Harvard University Press, 1950), p. 106.

38. ABA, *Conversations with Children on the Gospels*, 2 vols. (Boston: James Munroe, 1836–1837) [EPP] "Recorder's Preface," vol. 1, p. iv.

39. ABA, "1836 Journal," 64.

40. EPP to ABA, 7 August 1836, *Letters*, pp. 180–181.

41. *Boston Daily Advertiser*, 21 March 1837; Buckingham, quoted in Dahlstrand, p. 141; Harriet Martineau, *Society in America*, 2 vols.(New York: Saunders and Otley, 1837), vol. 1, pp. 277–278.

42. [EPP], "Mr. Alcott's Book and School," *Christian Register and Boston Observer* 16 (29 April 1837), 65.

43. EPP, ps to MTP to Lydia Sears Haven, 23 October 1832, NYPL-Berg.

44. EPP to MTP, 14 March 1834, "Cuba Journal," NYPL-Berg.

45. EPP, "A Psychological Observation," in *Lectures in the Training Schools for*

Kindergartners (Boston: D.C. Heath, 1888), pp. 109, 111; EPP to MTP, 9 August [1834], "Cuba Journal," NYPL-Berg.

46. MTP to Rawlins Pickman, [July 1835], Horace Mann II Papers, MHS.

47. "Observation," pp. 110–113; EPP to SAP, npnd, NYPL-Berg.

48. "Observation," p. 125; EPP to SAP, npnd, NYPL-Berg; "Observation," pp. 140–142

49. EPP to HM, npnd, ts copy, Antioch.

50. EP to George Peabody, 24 April 1836, ts copy, Antioch; see also NCP to George Peabody, 27 April 1836, ts copy, Antioch.

51. Eliza Guild to MTP, 15 May 1836, Horace Mann II Papers, MHS; SAP to George Peabody, 15 May 1836, NYPL-Berg; Sarah Clarke to MTP, 4 May [1836], bMS Am 1569.8 (138), by permission of Houghton Library, Harvard University.

52. *ELetters*, vol. 2, pp. 18–19.

53. EPP to MTP, 15 May 1836, *Letters*, p. 167.

54. MTP to Rawlins Pickman, ts copy, Antioch.

55. EPP to MTP, week of 16 May 1836, *Letters*, pp. 169–176.

56. MTP to EPP nd [after 1843], NYPL-Berg.

57. Lidian Emerson to EPP, nd, bMS Am 1280.226, by permission of Houghton Library, Harvard University.

58. EPP to John Sullivan Dwight, [1836], *Letters*, pp. 187–189.

59. HM to EPP, [6 September 1836], Horace Mann Papers, MHS; MTP to HM, 4 August 1836, Horace Mann Papers, MHS.

60. "Prospectus," for *The Family School*, 1 (September 1836), np.

61. RWE to EPP, 13 September 1836, *ELetters*, vol. 7, pp. 264–265; ABA to SAP, 23 August 1836, *Letters of A. Bronson Alcott*, ed. Richard Herrnstadt (Ames: Iowa State University Press, 1969), p. 29.

62. EP to George Peabody, 30 October 1836, ts copy, Antioch; EPP to Elizabeth Davis Bliss, 23 December 1836, *Letters*, p. 190.

5. *"One's Inward Instinct Is One's Best Guide"*

1. EP to MTP, 7 September 1834, "Cuba Journal," NYPL-Berg.

2. NH to John O'Sullivan, 19 May 1839, *CE*, vol. 15, p. 313; *ELetters*, vol. 1, pp. 449–450, fn 70; SAP to EPP, 8 August 1838, ts copy, Antioch.

3. EPP to HM, 4 September 1836, ts copy, Antioch.

4. *ELetters*, vol. 2. p. 110; EPP to MTP, 23 November 1836, *Letters*, pp. 183–187.

5. EPP to HM, 16 December 1836, ts copy, Antioch.

6. HM to EPP, 8 January 1838, ts copy, Antioch; MTP to Rawlins Pickman, 14 December 1836, Horace Mann II Papers, MHS; SAP to EPP, ms copy, 27 April 1838, Library of Congress.

7. Sally Gardiner to MTP, 2 February [1837?] ts copy, Antioch.

8. EPP to George Peabody, October 1836, ts copy, Antioch.

9. EPP to HM, [1836], ts copy, Antioch; RWE to EPP, 15 November 1836, *ELetters*, vol. 2, p. 46.

10. EPP, "Nature: a Prose Poem," *United States Magazine and Democratic Review* 1 (February 1838), 327; Susan H. Irons, "Channing's Influence on Peabody:

Self-Culture and the Danger of Egoism," *Studies in the American Renaissance*, 1992, 129; David Robinson, *Apostle of Culture: Emerson as Preacher and Lecturer* (Philadelphia: University of Pennsylvania Press, 1982), pp. 56–57.

11. MTP to Rawlins Pickman, 14 December 1836, Horace Mann II Papers, MHS.

12. 3 [December] 1836 *JMN*, vol. 5, p. 262; EPP to George Peabody, 18 June 1836, ts copy, Antioch.

13. EPP to William P. Andrews, 12 November 1880, *Letters*, p. 405.

14. RWE to EPP, 5 April 1838, *ELetters*, vol. 2, p. 124.

15. EPP to William P. Andrews, 12 November 1880, *Letters*, p. 406.

16. EPP to RWE, 24 September 1838, *Letters*, pp. 208–210.

17. RWE to MF, 28–29 September 1838, *ELetters*, vol. 2, pp. 164–165.

18. MTP to EPP, npnd, ts copy, Antioch.

19. EPP to RWE, 20 October 1838, *Letters*, pp. 215–217.

20. EPP to RWE, 3 December 1838, *Letters*, pp. 218–221.

21. Edwin Gittleman, *Jones Very, The Effective Years, 1833–1840* (New York: Columbia University Press, 1967).

22. Daniel Walker Howe, *Making the American Self: From Jonathan Edwards to Abraham Lincoln* (Cambridge, Mass.: Harvard University Press, 1997), pp. 189–211.

23. See Taylor Stoehr, *Nay-Saying in Concord: Emerson, Alcott, and Thoreau* (Hamden, Conn.: Archon Books, 1979).

24. EPP to SAP, 31 July 1838, *Letters*, p. 206.

25. "Notebook of Margaret Fuller Ossoli," *JMN*, vol. 11, pp. 60, 99.

26. RWE to EPP, 15 November 1836, *ELetters*, vol. 2, p. 46.

27. Charles Capper, *Margaret Fuller: An American Romantic Life: The Private Years* (New York: Oxford University Press, 1992), p. 189; MF to EPP, 26 May 1837, *FLetters*, vol. 1, p. 275.

28. MF to Frederic Henry Hedge, 12 July 1837; Hedge to MF, 2 August 1837, *FLetters*, vol. 1, pp. 292–293.

29. MF to EPP, 26 December 1844, *FLetters*, vol. 3, pp. 253–254; Channing, quoted in Capper, p. 318.

30. MF, quoted in Barbara Welter, "Mystical Feminist," in Welter, *Dimity Convictions: The American Woman in the Nineteenth Century* (Athens: Ohio University Press, 1976), p. 174.

31. HM to EPP, 8 January 1838, ts copy, Antioch; EPP to HM, 11 January 1838, ts copy, Antioch.

32. EPP to MTP, 10 June [1834], "Cuba Journal," NYPL-Berg; 16–20 June [1834], "Cuba Journal," NYPL-Berg.

33. EPP to MTP, 2–5 June 1834; [7–10 July 1834], "Cuba Journal," NYPL-Berg; EPP to Amelia Boelte [May–June 1886], *Letters*, pp. 428–429.

34. EPP to HM, 1 December [1839], ts copy, Antioch; SAP to EPP, 24 April [1838], 14 May 1838, ms copy, Bancroft Library, University of California at Berkeley.

35. EPP to HM, 3 March 1838, *Letters*, p. 198; SAP to EPP, 26 May 1838, ms copy, Bancroft; EPP to HM, 1 December [1839], ts copy, Antioch.

36. EPP to George Peabody, 10 July 1837, 14 June 1837, 22 June 1837, ts copy, Antioch; NCP to EPP, 17 August 1837, ts copy, Antioch.

37. EPP to MTP, 21 April [1838], Horace Mann II Papers, MHS; EPP to SAP, 31 July 1838, *Letters*, p. 207; NCP to EPP, 13 April 1838, ts copy, Antioch.

38. EPP to Francis Henry Lee [1885], *Letters*, pp. 418–419.

39. Pearson, "EPP on Hawthorne," 263.

40. EPP to Francis Henry Lee [1885], *Letters*, p. 420.

41. Pearson, "EPP on Hawthorne," 264–266. The essay in question was "Claims of the Beautiful Arts," *United States Magazine and Democratic Review* 3 (November 1838), 253–268.

42. Edwin Havilland Miller, *Salem Is My Dwelling Place: A Life of Nathaniel Hawthorne* (Iowa City: University of Iowa Press, 1991), p. 88.

43. EPP to HM, 3 March 1838, *Letters*, pp. 199–200; HM to EPP, 10 March 1838, Horace Mann Papers, MHS.

44. [EPP], "Review of *Twice-Told Tales*," *The New-Yorker* 5 (24 March 1838), 1–2; EPP to Elizabeth Hawthorne, [1838], *Letters*, p. 223.

45. The documents on which Julian Hawthorne based his account of his father and Mary Silsbee are reproduced in Pearson, "Hawthorne's Duel," *Essex Institute Historical Collections* 94 (1958), 229–242.

46. NH to Horatio Bridge, 8 February 1838, *CE*, vol. 15, p. 262.

47. Pearson, "Hawthorne's Duel," 232, 233 fn 4.

48. EPP to Elizabeth Hawthorne, 24–25 September 1838, NYPL-Berg; NH to Henry Wadsworth Longfellow, 21 March 1838, *CE*, vol. 15, p. 267; SAP to EPP, 27 April 1838, in NHHW, vol. 1, p. 185; SAP to EPP, 23 July 1838, NYPL-Berg.

49. NH to John O'Sullivan, 19 April 1838, *CE*, vol. 15: p. 272.

50. NH to John O'Sullivan, 13 May 1838, *CE* vol. 15, p. 313.

51. Pearson, "Hawthorne's Duel," 238.

52. Caroline Dall to Thomas Niles, quoted in James Mellow, *Nathaniel Hawthorne in His Times* (Boston: Houghton Mifflin, 1980), p. 146; EPP to Amelia Boelte, 30 June 1886, *Letters*, pp. 431–432.

53. *Letters*, p. 432.

54. EPP to Elizabeth Hawthorne [19 October 1838?], *Letters*, pp. 213–214; EPP to Elizabeth Bliss, 6 November 1838, *Letters*, pp. 217–218; NH to George Bancroft, 11 January 1839, *CE*, vol. 15, p. 283.

55. Pearson, "EPP on Hawthorne," 271–274; SAP to Maria Chase, 9 January 1828, SSC; EP to MTP, 8 January 1828, ts copy, Antioch.

56. EPP to SAP, npnd, NYPL-Berg.

57. EPP to Maria Chase, 20 May 1822, SSC; SAP to Maria Chase, 15 December 1829, SSC.

58. Washington Allston, *Papers on Art and Poems, with Monaldi*, ed. Nathalia Wright (Gainesville, Fla.: Scholars' Facsimiles and Reprints, 1967), x; Wassily Kandinsky, *Concerning the Spiritual in Art*, trans. Michael Sadleir [1947] (New York: George Wittenborn, 1955), pp. 74–75.

59. 10 November 1838, *JMN*, vol. 7, p. 144.

60. EPP, "Allston the Painter," *American Monthly Magazine* 1 (May 1836), 439, 442, 443.

61. ABA, "1836 Journal" 56; EPP to SAP, npnd, NYPL-Berg.

62. Elizabeth Garrity Ellis, "The 'Intellectual and Moral Made Visible': The 1839 Washington Allston Exhibition and Unitarian Taste in Boston," *Prospects*, 10 (1985), 39–75. See also David Bjelajac, "The Boston Elite: Resistance to Washing-

ton Allston's *Elijah in the Desert*," in *American Iconology*, ed. David C. Miller (New Haven: Yale University Press, 1993), pp. 39–57.

63. Philo Kosmos [EPP], *Remarks on Allston's Paintings* (Boston: William D. Ticknor, 1839), pp. 5, 10–11, 14.

64. EPP to RWE, 24 September 1838, *Letters*, p. 213.

6. *"A Transcendental Exchange"*

1. See Joseph Kett, *The Pursuit of Knowledge Under Difficult Circumstances: From Self Improvement to Adult Education in America, 1750–1990* (Stanford: Stanford University Press, 1994), pp. 42–44; David H. Hall, "The Uses of Literacy in New England, 1600–1850, in *Printing and Society in Early America*, eds. William Joyce, David Hall, Richard Brown (Worcester, Mass.: American Antiquarian Society, 1983), p. 38; William Gilmore, *Reading Becomes a Necessity of Life: Material and Culture Life in Rural New England, 1780–1835* (Knoxville: University of Tennessee Press, 1989), pp. 1–9.

2. NCP to EPP, 29 July 1850, Antioch.

3. John Tebbel, *A History of Book Publishing in the United States* (New York: Bowker, 1972), pp. 386–443; Madeleine Stern, *Imprints on History: Book Publishers and American Frontiers* (Bloomington: Indiana University Press, 1956), pp. 45–50.

4. RWE to EPP, 1 December 1842, *ELetters*, vol. 3, pp. 101–102.

5. Anna McAllister, *In Winter We Flourish: Life and Letters of Sarah Worthington King Peter* (New York: Longman's, 1939), p. 117; George Willis Cooke, *An Historical and Biographical Introduction to Accompany the "Dial"*, 2 vols. [1902] (New York: Russell and Russell, 1961), vol. 1., p. 148; Edward Everett Hale, *A New England Boyhood* (Boston: Little, Brown, 1900), p. 248; Madeleine Stern, "Elizabeth Peabody's Foreign Library," *American Transcendental Quarterly* 20, supplement (1973), 5–12; *Autobiography, Diary, and Correspondence of James Freeman Clarke*, ed. Edward Everett Hale (Boston: Houghton Mifflin, 1891), p. 143.

6. RWE to MF, December 1840, *ELetters*, vol. 2, p. 363; George Bradford, quoted in *Memorial History of Boston*, ed. Justin Winsor (Boston: Osgood, 1881–1882), vol. 4, p. 329, fn 1; Clarke, p. 144; Thomas Wentworth Higginson, *Cheerful Yesterdays* [1895] (New York: Arno, 1968), p. 86.

7. EPP to Samuel Gray Ward, 13 September 1841, dated in another hand, AAS.

8. Anne C. Rose, *New England Transcendentalism as a Social Movement* (New Haven: Yale University Press, 1981), pp. 93–103.

9. *Memoir of Margaret Fuller Ossoli*, ed. Ralph Waldo Emerson et. al., 2 vols. (Boston: Phillips, Sampson, 1852), vol. 1, pp. 324, 328, 331, 332; Elizabeth Hoar to RWE, 27 March [1841], quoted in Joel Myerson, "Mrs. Dall Edits Miss Fuller: The Story of *Margaret and Her Friends*," *Papers of the Bibliographical Society of America*, 72 (1978), 191.

10. EPP, "Journal of Margaret Fuller's Conversation," nd, Elizabeth Palmer Peabody Papers, AAS.

11. *Memoir*, vol. 1, pp. 336–337.

12. EPP, "Journal," AAS.

13. *Memoir*, vol. 1, pp. 339, 343.

14. Myerson, "Story," 192.

15. *Memoir*, vol. 1, pp. 340, 347–348.

16. Caroline Dall, in Joel Myerson, "Caroline Dall's Reminiscences of Margaret Fuller," *Harvard Library Bulletin*, 22 (1974), 419.

17. Dall, in Myerson, "Reminiscences," 423.

18. *Selected Letters of Lydia Maria Child, 1817–1880*, ed. Milton Melzer and Patricia Holland (Amherst: University of Massachusetts Press, 1982), p. 243.

19. *Memoir*, vol. 1, p. 351.

20. Orestes Brownson, "The Laboring Classes," in *The Transcendentalists*, ed. Perry Miller (Cambridge, Mass.: Harvard University Press, 1950), p. 439; Rose, pp. 111–114.

21. RWE to EPP, 8 September 1840, *ELetters*, vol. 2, p. 330.

22. 26 November 1842, *JMN*, vol. 8, p. 249.

23. EPP to John Sullivan Dwight, 20 September 1840, *Letters*, p. 245.

24. 17 October 1840, *JMN*, vol. 7, pp. 407–408; MF to William Henry Channing, 25 and 28 October 1840, *FLetters*, vol. 2, p. 174.

25. EPP to John Sullivan Dwight, 26 April 1841, *Letters*, pp. 249–251; for recent studies of the origins and development of Brook Farm, see Carl J. Guarneri, *The Utopian Alternative: Fourierism in Nineteenth-Century America* (Ithaca: Cornell University Press, 1991); and Richard Francis, *Transcendental Utopias: Individual and Community at Brook Farm, Fruitlands, and Walden* (Ithaca: Cornell University Press, 1997).

26. EPP to John Sullivan Dwight, 24 June 1841, *Letters*, p. 259.

27. EPP, "A Glimpse of Christ's Idea of Society," *Dial*, 2 (October 1841), 217.

28. EPP, "Plan of the West Roxbury Community," *Dial*, 2 (January 1842), 370.

29. EPP, "Fourierism," *Dial*, 4 (April 1844), 473–483; on Fourier and Brook Farm, see Rose, pp. 140–161; Zoltan Haraszti, *The Idyll of Brook Farm as Revealed by Unpublished Letters in the Boston Public Library* (Boston: Trustees of the Public Library, 1937); Lindsay Swift, *Brook Farm: Its Members, Scholars, and Visitors* (New York: Macmillan, 1900); and Guarneri, pp. 44–59.

30. EPP, "Fourierism," 476–479.

31. Christina Zwarg, *Feminist Conversations: Fuller, Emerson, and the Play of Reading* (Ithaca: Cornell University Press, 1995), p. 38.

32. EPP to John Sullivan Dwight, [20 May 1840], 18 June 1840, [10 June 1841], 24 June 1841, *Letters*, pp. 240–260.

33. EPP, "Principles and Methods of Education; My Experience as a Teacher," *American Journal of Education*, 32 (1882), 736–737.

34. Joel Myerson, *The New England Transcendentalists and the "Dial"* (Rutherford, N.J.: Fairleigh Dickinson University Press, 1980), pp. 19–31.

35. Joel Myerson, "A Calendar of Transcendental Club Meetings," *American Literature*, 44 (May 1972), 197–207; EPP to John Sullivan Dwight, 20 September 1840, *Letters*, pp. 245–246.

36. EPP to Orestes Brownson, ca. 1840, *Letters*, p. 248.

37. RWE to EPP, 12 October 1840, *ELetters*, vol. 2, p. 345; RWE to MF, 20 October 1840, *ELetters*, vol. 2, p. 350.

38. RWE to MF, *ELetters*, vol. 5, p. 262.

39. "Catalogue of the American and Foreign Circulating Library, kept by E. P. Peabody," ms, Houghton.

40. NH to EPP, 23 June 1841, *CE*, vol. 15, p. 547.

41. *The Confessions of St. Augustine*, ed. Elizabeth Palmer Peabody (Boston: E. P. Peabody, 1842). Higginson's copy is signed and dated "January 1844." His notes in the volume indicate that he bought the book on January 8 and read it thoroughly in March; EPP, *The Polish-American System of Chronology, Reproduced, with Some Modifications, from General Bem's Franco-Polish Method* (Boston: 13 West Street [E. P. Peabody], 1850).

42. RWE to EPP, 23 February 1842, *ELetters*, vol. 3, p. 15.

43. RWE to MF, 9 April 1842, *ELetters*, vol. 3, p. 58; MF to RWE, 18 April 1842, *FLetters*, vol. 3, p. 60.

44. RWE to MF, 1 March 1843, *ELetters*, vol. 3, p. 157; Myerson, *New England Transcendentalists*, pp. 71, 74, 88–90.

45. Lidian Jackson Emerson to EPP, 8 January 1837, bMS Am 1280.226, by permission of Houghton Library, Harvard University; Lidian Jackson Emerson to EPP, ca. 1837, bMS Am 1280.226, by permission of Houghton Library, Harvard University.

46. RWE to EPP, 28 January 1842, *ELetters*, vol. 3, p. 8.

47. NH to SPH, 27 June 1848; *CE*, vol. 16, p.228.

48. Julian Hawthorne, *Nathaniel Hawthorne and His Circle* (New York: Harper and Brothers, 1903), p. 7.

49. EPP to Rawlins Pickman, 1 May 1843, *Letters*, p. 262.

50. 26 June 1842, *JMN*, vol. 8, p. 181.

51. See William Batchelder Greene, *Transcendentalism* [1849], ed. Martin K. Doudna (Delmar, N.Y.: Scholars' Facsimiles and Reprints, 1981); Mary Moody Emerson to Ruth Emerson et. al. 17 November [1841], *MMEL*, p. 438.

52. EPP to Orestes Brownson [1842], University of Notre Dame Archives, Orestes A. Brownson Papers, Undated Correspondence, "P," CBRO I-3-d; William Batchelder Greene to Orestes Brownson, 24 August 1842, University of Notre Dame Archives, Orestes A. Brownson Papers, CBRO I-3-f.

53. EPP, "Spirit of Hebrew Poetry," *Christian Examiner*, 60 (May 1834), 175; Philip Gura, "Elizabeth Peabody and the Philosophy of Language," *ESQ*, 23 (1977), 155; see also Gura, *The Wisdom of Words: Language, Theology, and Literature in the New England Renaissance* (Middletown, Conn.: Wesleyan University Press, 1981), especially chap. 4.

54. EPP, *Reminiscences*, pp. 185–186; in 1857 Peabody edited and published a collection of Hazard's writings, called *Essays on Language and Other Papers*.

55. This summary draws on Gura, *Wisdom of Words*, and "Peabody and the Philosophy of Language."

56. Mary Lowell Putnam to James Russell Lowell, in Sculley Bradley, "Lowell, Emerson, and *The Pioneer*," *American Literature*, 19 (November 1947), 237.

57. Diane Brown Jones, "Elizabeth Palmer Peabody's Transcendental Manifesto," *Studies in the American Renaissance*, 1992, 197.

58. EPP, "A Vision," *The Pioneer*, 1 (March 1843), 97–100.

59. EPP to MME, ca. 1845–1846, *Letters*, p. 264.

60. EPP to MME, ca. 1845–1846, *Letters*, p. 266.

61. EPP to MME, 7 October 1845, Elizabeth Palmer Peabody Papers, AAS.

62. EPP to MME, ca. 1845–1846, *Letters*, p. 266.

63. Franklin Benjamin Sanborn, "Concord Notebook," in *Transcendental Epi-*

logue, ed. Kenneth Cameron, 3 vols., (Hartford: Transcendental Books, 1965), vol. 3, pp. 40–42.

64. MME to Charles Emerson, 29 September 1832, *MMEL*, p. 323; MME to Ann Sargent Gage, 30 March 1833, *MMEL*, p. 337. Mary Emerson's distinctive spelling has been preserved by the editor of her letters and is reproduced here.

65. MME to RWE, 4 May [1837], *MMEL*, p. 380; MME to Elizabeth Hoar, 17 December [1837], *MMEL*, p. 385.

66. MME to Elizabeth Hoar and Samuel Ripley, 28 January 1843, *MMEL*, p. 449; MME to Lidian Emerson and Ruth Haskins Emerson, 30 October 1844, *MMEL*, p. 464.

67. MME to Elizabeth Hoar and Samuel Ripley, 28 January 1843, *MMEL*, p. 449; *Christian Examiner*, 24 (6 September 1845); *Christian Examiner*, 24 (29 November 1845).

68. *Christian Examiner*, 24 (29 November 1845); MME to Elizabeth Hoar, 11 January 1846, *MMEL*, pp. 479–480.

69. EPP to MME, 7 October 1845, Elizabeth Palmer Peabody Papers, AAS.

70. MME to EPP, 12 December 1845, *MMEL*, pp. 477–479.

71. MME to Elizabeth Hoar, ca. 1846, *MMEL*, pp. 490–491.

72. EPP to Frances Gage, 26 August 1846 (?), Gage Family Additional Papers, AAS.

73. EPP to Ann Sargent Gage, ca. 1846, Gage Family Additional Papers, AAS.

74. MME to Elizabeth Hoar, two letters, ca. 1846, *MMEL*, pp. 490–492; MME to Ann Sargent Gage, 31 March [1854], *MMEL*, p. 565; and 29 December 1857, *MMEL*, p. 587.

75. EPP to Ann Sargent Gage, ca. 1846, Gage Family Additional Papers, AAS.

76. EPP to Ann Sargent Gage, ca. 1846, AAS.

77. RWE to Lidian Jackson Emerson, 9 October 1846, *ELetters*, vol. 3, p. 354; EP to EPP, 24 June 1847, Antioch; EP to EPP, 5 July 1847, Antioch.

78. EPP, "Mary Moody Emerson," *Boston Evening Transcript*, 14 May 1863. My thanks to Robert Richardson for bringing this obituary to my attention.

79. EPP to Ann Sargent Gage, 15 February 1849, Gage Family Additional Papers, AAS.

80. EPP to Charles Nagy, 1849, ts copy, unsigned, Antioch.

81. EP to EPP, [1849], ts copy, Antioch.

82. EPP, "My Experience as a Teacher," 732–733.

83. Julian Hawthorne, *Hawthorne and His Circle*, pp. 1–2.

84. EPP to Charles Folsom, November [1849] and 27 November [1849], *Letters*, pp. 293–294. In *Letters* I date these letters as 1858, but that is evidently an error. See also *The Athenaeum Centenary* (Boston: the Athenaeum, 1907), p. 84.

85. Joseph Jones, "Introduction," *Aesthetic Papers* [1849] (Gainesville, Fl.: Scholars' Facsimiles and Reprints, 1957), p. v.

86. Elizabeth Peabody, "Prospectus," *Aesthetic Papers*, p. iv.

87. *NHHW*, vol. 1, pp. 330–332.

88. Henry David Thoreau to EPP, 5 April 1849, The Historical Society of Pennsylvania.

89. EPP to Ann Sargent Gage, 15 February 1849, Gage Family Additional Papers, AAS.

90. EPP, "The Word 'Aesthetic,'" *Aesthetic Papers*, pp. 1–4.

91. Zoltan Haraszti, "Letters of T. W. Parsons," *More Books. The Bulletin of the Boston Public Library*, 13 (October 1938), 358.

92. EPP, "The Dorian Measure," *Aesthetic Papers*, pp. 109–110.

93. John Wilson to EPP, 20 February 1849, ts copy, Antioch.

7. *"Inconceivable Power, Wisdom, and Love"*

1. EPP, "My Experience as a Teacher," *American Journal of Education* 32 (1882), 735; MPM to HM, 20 July 1856, ts copy, Antioch.

2. EPP to Samuel Gray Ward and Anna Hazard Barker Ward, 13 September 1850, bMS Am 1465, by permission of Houghton Library, Harvard University.

3. "A New Method of Teaching History," Philadelphia *Evening Post*, ca. 1850s, ts copy, Antioch; EP to EPP, August 1852, ts copy, Antioch.

4. EPP, "Bem's Charts—A Letter to Mr. Woolworth, of the State Normal School, Albany, New York," reprinted in *The New York Teacher* from *The Free Presbyterian*, 4 (4 April 1855), 90.

5. EPP to Rawlins Pickman, 8 July 1852, Horace Mann II Papers, MHS.

6. EPP, "My Experience," 742.

7. EP to EPP, February 1852, and 28 March 1852, ts copy, Antioch; Sophia was also concerned about her sister's whereabouts in a letter of 24 October 1850, NYPL-Berg.

8. These letters have been collected and annotated in Pauline Greason, "Letters of Elizabeth Palmer Peabody and Others Concerning a Problem at 13 West Street," *Essex Institute Historical Collections*, 12 (1985), 21–43.

9. EP and NP to EPP, 16 February 1851 and 2 April 1852, ts copy, Antioch; EP to EPP, 4 January 1852, ts copy, Antioch.

10. EP to EPP, nd, ts copy, Antioch; Boston City Directories, 1847–1855.

11. EP to EPP, 8 February 1852, ts copy, Antioch.

12. EPP to Mr. Phillips, 28 December 1855, Boston Public Library; Eliza Clapp to EPP, 16 March 1856, ts copy, Antioch.

13. EPP, *Chronological History of the United States, Arranged with Plates on Bem's Principles* (New York: Sheldon Blakeman, 1850), p. 5

14. NP to EPP, 16 February 1851, ts copy, Antioch, EP to EPP, 4 January 1852, ts copy, Antioch

15. SPH to EPP, 3 April 1851, NYPL-Berg.

16. NH to EPP, 3 April 1851, *CE*, vol. 16, p. 414.

17. 4 November 1851, ts copy, Antioch.

18. EPP to SPH, 6 April [1852], NYPL-Berg; 11–12 January 1853, *NHHW*, vol. 1, pp. 485–487.

19. EPP to Samuel Gray Ward, 30 January [1853], bMS Am 1465, by permission of Houghton Library, Harvard University.

20. EPP to Samuel Gray Ward and Anna Hazard Barker Ward, 13 September 1850, bMS Am 1465, by permission of Houghton Library, Harvard University.

21. *JMN* [1851], vol. 11, p. 431.

22. George Haven Putnam, *Memories of a Publisher, 1865–1915* (New York: G. P. Putnam's Sons, 1915), p. 32; EPP to Samuel Gridley Howe, 20 April 1856, *Letters*, pp. 280–281; Catherine Sedgwick to EPP, 31 December 1853, ts copy, Anti-

och; MPM to NP, 19 February 1854, ts copy, Antioch; EPP, "Memorial of Madame Susanne Kossuth Meszlenyi," privately printed December 1856, reprinted in *Last Evening with Allston, and Other Papers* (Boston: Lothrop, 1886), pp. 282, 287; Margaret Neussendorfer, personal correspondence, 28 July 1980.

23. *Crimes of the House of Austria*, ed. Elizabeth Peabody (New York: Putnam's, 1852); EPP to E. A. Duyckinck, 13 October 1852, NYPL-Duyckinck Papers.

24. Biographical information on Delia Bacon is drawn from Vivian Hopkins, *Prodigal Puritan: A Life of Delia Bacon* (Cambridge, Mass.: Harvard University Press, 1959).

25. Hopkins, p. 145; Eliza Rotch Farrar, *Recollections of Seventy Years* (Boston: Ticknor and Fields, 1866), pp. 321–323; EPP to Leonard Bacon, 23 October 1860, *Letters*, p. 300.

26. SPH to EPP, 13 February 1857, 22 April 1857, NYPL-Berg.

27. Leonard Bacon to EPP, 11 February 1860, Bacon Family Papers, Manuscripts and Archives, Yale University Library.

28. Putnam, *Memories*, p. 32.

29. Of the many treatments of mesmerism and spiritualism, I have found helpful Sydney Ahlstrom, *A Religious History of the American People* (New Haven: Yale University Press, 1972), pp. 488–490; Ann Braude, *Radical Spirits: Spiritualism and Women's Rights in Nineteenth-Century America* (Boston: Beacon, 1989); and R. Laurence Moore, *In Search of White Crows: Spiritualism, Parapsychology, and American Culture* (New York: Oxford University Press, 1977).

30. EP to EPP, 12 January 1851, ts copy, Antioch.

31. SPH to EPP, 3 February 1851, NYPL-Berg; EPP to SPH, 23 March 1851, NYPL-Berg.

32. William Logan Fisher to EPP, 5 March 1851, ts copy, Antioch.

33. William Logan Fisher to EPP, 15 March 1854, ts copy, Antioch.

34. EPP to William Logan Fisher, 4 July [1858], *Letters*, pp. 286–290.

35. EPP to Samuel Gray Ward, 30 January [1853], bMS Am 1465, by permission of Houghton Library, Harvard University.

36. Moncure Conway, quoted in Maud Honeyman Greene, "Raritan Bay Union, Eagleswood, New Jersey," *Proceedings of the New Jersey Historical Society*, 68 (January 1950), 11.

37. EPP to Theodore Dwight Weld, 11 November 1886, Autograph File, by permission of Houghton Library, Harvard University.

38. EPP to Rawlins Pickman, 28 August [1854], Horace Mann II Papers, MHS.

39. *CE*, vol. 16, p. 259; SPH to EPP, 31 October 1854, NYPL-Berg.

40. SPH to EPP, 14 November 1854, NYPL-Berg.

41. SPH to EPP, 25–26 January 1855, NYPL-Berg.

42. SPH to EPP, 8 February 1855, NYPL-Berg.

43. 20 April 1855, *CE*, vol. 16, p. 330.

44. EPP to Rawlins Pickman, 2 September 1855, Horace Mann II Papers, MHS.

45. Sarah Clarke to EPP, 22 October 1855, ts copy, Antioch.

46. EPP to Rawlins Pickman [1858], Horace Mann II Papers, MHS.

47. EPP to Parke Godwin, 20 April 1854, NYPL-Bryant-Godwin.

48. "JMH," "Impressions and Recollections of Miss Elizabeth Peabody, 1894,"

Boston Public Library; "Primeval Man," in *Last Evening with Allston*, p. 172. Peabody's claims for ancient and advanced civilizations preceding those of Egypt, Greece, and Rome anticipate some of the controversial arguments recently put forward by Martin Bernal in *Black Athena: The Afroasiatic Roots of Classical Civilization* (New Brunswick: Rutgers University Press, 1987) that classical civilizations built on, but also suppressed, the art and myth of earlier African cultures.

49. EPP, "Essay on the Earliest Ages," in *Manual of the Polish-American System of Chronology* (Boston: 13 West Street [Elizabeth P. Peabody], 1850), p. 114.

50. RWE to EPP, 23 October [1858], ts copy, Antioch; RWE to James Russell Lowell, 27 February [1859], *ELetters*, vol. 5, pp. 134–135.

51. EPP, "Last Evening with Allston" (1857), reprinted in *Last Evening with Allston, and Other Papers*, p. 10.

52. EPP, "Egotheism, the Atheism of Today" (1858), reprinted in *Last Evening with Allston, and Other Papers*, pp. 245, 250.

53. EPP, "The Philosophy of History in the Education of Republican Men and Women," *Una*, 3 (February 1855), 29; EPP to Anna Barker Ward, 26 December [1860?], bMS Am 1465, by permission of Houghton Library, Harvard University. This letter, with its references to Elizabeth Barrett Browning's *Aurora Leigh*, is clearly headed "1850." But that must be in error, since Browning did not publish her poem until 1857.

54. EPP to Caroline Healey Dall, 21 February 1859, in *Letters*, pp. 297–298.

55. Dall, ms. journals, 25 February 1859, quoted in Helen R. Deese, "A New England Women's Network: Elizabeth Palmer Peabody, Caroline Healey Dall, and Delia S. Bacon," *Legacy*, 8 (Fall 1991), 80.

56. EPP to Caroline Healey Dall, 4 January 1860, *Letters*, p. 313.

57. E. Blackwell to EPP, 12 September 1856, ts copy, Antioch.

58. Sallie Holley to ?, 24 September 1855, in *A Life for Liberty: The Letters of Sallie Holley*, ed. John White Chadwick (New York: Putnam's, 1899), pp. 148–150.

59. EPP to Caroline Healey Dall, 21 Feburary 1859, *Letters*, p. 298.

60. Harriet Hosmer to Cornelia Carr, in *Harriet Hosmer, Letters and Memories*, ed. Cornelia Carr (New York: Moffat, Yard, 1912), p. 32; John Murray Forbes, *Letters and Recollections of John Murray Forbes*, 2 vols. (Boston: Houghton, Mifflin, 1899), vol. 1, pp. 20–21.

61. Julian Hawthorne, *Hawthorne and His Circle*, pp. 17–18.

62. MPM to EPP, July 1850, ts copy, Antioch.

63. NCP to EPP, 29 July 1850, ts copy, Antioch.

64. EPP to Theodore Dwight Weld, 11 November 1886, ts copy, Antioch; EPP to MTP, 16 May [1834], "Cuba Journal," NYPL-Berg.

65. EPP to Frances Adeline Seward, 22 May 1857, *Letters*, pp. 282–286; EPP to Justus Starr Redfield, 6 June 1857, ts copy, Antioch; Eliza Lee Follen to EPP, 13 May [1857], ts copy, Antioch.

66. SPH to EPP, ca. 1857, NYPL-Berg.

67. SPH to EPP, ca. 1857, NYPL-Berg.

68. SPH to EPP, ca. 1857, NYPL-Berg

69. SPH to EPP, ca. 1857, NYPL-Berg; NH to EPP, 13 August 1857, *CE*, vol. 18, pp. 89–91; NH to EPP, 6 October 1857, *CE*, vol. 18, pp. 115–117.

70. SPH to MPM, September 1857, ts copy, Antioch.

71. SPH to EPP, 21 March 1859, NYPL-Berg; SPH to EPP, 3 July 1859, NYPL-Berg.

72. EPP to Parke Godwin, [Spring 1858], NYPL-Bryant-Godwin.

73. EPP to Caroline Dall, 21 February 1859, *Letters*, pp. 296–297.

74. MPM to SPH, 4 August 1859, ts copy, Antioch; EPP to Rawlins Pickman, 10 August 1859, ts copy, Antioch.

75. MPM to SPH, 6 September 1859, ts copy, Antioch.

76. EPP to Rawlins Pickman [October 1859], Horace Mann II Papers, MHS; MPM to SPH, 18 October 1859, ts copy, Antioch.

77. MPM to SPH, 27 November 1859, ts copy, Antioch.

8. *"Apostles of the New Education"*

1. MPM, "Journal of Remembrance," MHS; *Moral Culture of Infancy and Kindergarten Guide* (Boston: T.O.H.P. Burnham, 1863).

2. SPH to EPP, 27 February 1860, NYPL-Berg.

3. SPH to EPP, [1861], NYPL-Berg.

4. EPP to Franklin Benjamin Sanborn, March 1860, *Letters*, p. 315.

5. On this early interest in German early childhood education, see Ruth M. Baylor, *Elizabeth Palmer Peabody, Kindergarten Pioneer* (Philadelphia: University of Pennsylvania Press, 1965), p. 30.

6. For Froebel, see Robert B. Downs, *Friedrich Froebel* (Boston: Twayne, 1978), pp. 40–46. On Froebel's "gifts" and their relationship with modernist art, see Norman Brosterman, *Inventing Kindergarten* (New York: Harry N. Abrams, 1997).

7. EPP, "Origins and Growth of the Kindergarten," *Education*, 2 (May–June 1882), 522–523.

8. EPP, "Origins," 523.

9. EPP, "Report and New Prospectus of Kindergarten," April 1862 [pamphlet; privately printed], Baylor Collection, MHS; Lucretia Hale to EPP, 27 September 1861, ts copy, Antioch.

10. EPP, "The Kindergarten—What Is It?" reprinted in *Moral Culture of Infancy*, p. 14.

11. EPP, "Report," 5; *Moral Culture of Infancy*, p. 113.

12. John Williams to EPP, 9 December 1861, ts copy, Antioch.

13. Rebecca Moore to EPP, 2 April 1860, ts copy, Antioch.

14. SPH to EPP, [1861], NYPL-Berg.

15. SPH to EPP, [1863], NYPL-Berg.

16. Robert Richardson, *Emerson: The Mind on Fire* (Berkeley: University of California Press, 1995), pp. 433–435; EPP to MPM, [1866], ts copy, Antioch.

17. EPP to Horace Mann, Jr., 1 January 1862, *Letters*, pp. 320–321.

18. MPM to George Combe Mann, 1 January 1863, ts copy, Antioch.

19. EPP to Horace Mann, Jr., 25 February 1865, *Letters*, pp. 325–326; EPP, "Letter to the Editor," *The Radical*, 2 (1866–1867), 746–747. I am grateful to Margaret Neussendorfer for providing this source.

20. EPP to Horace Mann, Jr., [February 1865], *Letters*, pp. 326–331.

21. EPP to Rawlins Pickman, [January 1863], ts copy, Antioch.

22. John Andrew, quoted in announcement for sale of first printing of *Memo-*

rial of Robert Gould Shaw and *Letters of Robert Gould Shaw*, in "The Month at Good-speed's," 26 (June 1955), 208–211, ts copy, Antioch.

23. Francis Gould Shaw to EPP, 16 February 1864, ts copy, Antioch.

24. Sarah Shaw to EPP, 10 April 1864, ts copy, Antioch.

25. M. Revere to EPP, 19 February 1864, ts copy, Antioch.

26. Edwin Havilland Miller, *Salem Is My Dwelling Place: A Life of Nathaniel Hawthorne* (Iowa City: University of Iowa Press, 1991), p. 471.

27. NH to EPP, 20 July 1863; *CE*, vol. 18, pp. 589–592.

28. EPP to Horatio Bridge, 4 June 1887, *Letters*, pp. 444–446.

29. Miller, p. 516; EPP to Elizabeth Curson Hoxie, npnd, *Letters*, p. 455.

30. SPH to EPP and MPM, quoted in Miller, p. 518.

31. SPH to EPP, 25 May 1864, NYPL-Berg.

32. EPP to William Cullen Bryant, October 1864, NYPL-Bryant-Godwin.

33. EPP to MPM, 12 February 1865, ts copy, Antioch; Anna Gibbons to EPP, 5 March 1865, ts copy, Antioch; EPP to Emily Howland, 9 March 1865, *Letters*, pp. 332–333; Emily Howland to EPP, 9 July 1866, ts copy, Antioch.

34. Ethan Allen Hitchcock to EPP, 15 April 1865, Horace Mann III Papers, MHS.

35. Abner Johnson Leavenworth to EPP, 6 March 1866, ts copy, Antioch; Mary Ann Peabody to EPP, 6 June 1866, ts copy, Antioch.

36. 14 December 1862, in Jessica Tyler Austin, *Moses Coit Tyler* (Garden City: Doubleday Page, 1911), pp. 15–16.

37. Henry James, Sr., to EPP, 10 June [1863], 20 June [1863], 22 July [1863], Horace Mann III Papers, MHS.

38. Henry James, Sr., to EPP, 22 July [1863], Horace Mann III Papers, MHS.

39. Samuel Johnson to EPP, 14 October 1864, ts copy, Antioch; Alfred Habegger, *The Father: A Life of Henry James Sr.* (New York: Farrar, Straus, and Giroux, 1994), p. 456.

40. David Wasson to EPP, 16 March 1864, ts copy, Antioch.

41. EPP to Charles Eliot Norton, 30 August 1864, *Letters*, p. 323; Charles Eliot Norton to EPP, 13 October 1864, ts copy, Antioch.

42. Miller, 479; EPP to Henry Wadsworth Longfellow, 20 January 1867, *Letters*, p. 340; Samuel Gray Ward to EPP, 28 February 1867, Horace Mann III Papers, MHS.

43. William Batchelder Greene to EPP, 30 November 1864, 21 December 1864, Antioch.

44. SPH to EPP, 20 January 1867, NYPL-Berg.

45. SPH to EPP, 5 March 1865, March 1866, NYPL-Berg.

46. *Moral Culture of Infancy and Kindergarten Guide*, p. 14.

47. *Moral Culture of Infancy and Kindergarten Guide*, pp. 106, 110–111. Mary's (and Elizabeth's) understanding of women's peculiar suitability for the work of education is reminiscent of the work of Catharine Beecher, for whom see Kathryn Kish Sklar, *Catharine Beecher: A Study in American Domesticity* (New Haven: Yale University Press, 1973).

48. Sarah Baily to EPP, 17 September 1865, ts copy, Antioch; EPP, "Origins," pp. 523–524.

49. Elizabeth Pugh to EPP, 25 February 1867, ts copy, Antioch.

50. EPP to Samuel Foster Haven, [1865], *Letters*, pp. 338–339.

51. Ellen Emerson to RWE, 9 November 1865, *ELetters*, vol. 5, p. 434; "Impressions and Recollections of Miss Elizabeth Peabody, 1894," Boston Public Library; Ann Dickson to EPP, 27 October 1866, ts copy, Antioch; EPP to Ann Sargent Gage, [1866 or 1867], Gage Family Additional Papers, AAS.

52. SPH to EPP, 3 March 1867, 11 February 1867, NYPL-Berg.

53. Henrietta Wright to EPP, 2 February 1867, ts copy, Antioch; Susan Parrish to EPP, 1 March 1867, ts copy, Antioch.

54. "Impressions and Recollections," Boston Public Library.

55. EPP, "European Correspondence," *Friends Intelligencer*, 24 (10 August 1867), 361; "European Correspondence," *Friends Intelligencer*, 24 (18 January 1868), 731; "European Correspondence," *Friends Intelligencer*, 24 (19 October 1867), 523; "European Correspondence," *Friends Intelligencer*, 24 (28 December 1867), 682. Peabody's fascination with Catholicism dates back at least to 1830. In that year she wrote to Sarah Sullivan, "There are two things which I am sometimes inclined to envy the Catholic Church—*one* is their belief in *Mary Sweet Mother* as mediatrix—& the other—& especially—their Confessional. Oh *to have a right* to tell one's sins—& wicked states of mind—to some holy old man—experienced—& whose duty it is to consider the state & to counsel us—without feeling one's self chargeable with egotism—or intrusion—seems to me the most blessed thing!" (EPP to Sarah Sullivan, 6 July 1830, ts copy, Antioch).

56. "European Correspondence," *Friends Intelligencer*, 24 (21 December 1867), 669–670.

57. Edward Whitney to EPP, 10 August 1867, ts copy, Antioch; Caroline Sturgis to EPP, 27 August 1867, ts copy, Antioch.

58. *Letters and Journals of Thomas Wentworth Higginson, 1846–1906*, ed. Mary Thatcher Higginson (Boston: Houghton Mifflin, 1921), pp. 240–241.

59. EPP to Horace Mann, Jr., 25 February 1868, ts copy, Antioch.

60. *Charlotte Cushman: Her Letters and Memories of Her Life*, ed. Emma Stebbins (Boston: Houghton Mifflin, 1878), pp. 139–140.

61. "Hawthorne's *Marble Faun*," (1868), reprinted in *Last Evening with Allston, and Other Papers* (Boston: Lothrop, 1886), p. 330.

62. "Impressions and Recollections," Boston Public Library.

63. "European Correspondence," *Friends Intelligencer*, 24 (21 December 1867), 669.

64. "Impressions and Recollections," Boston Public Library.

65. Emma Marwedel, quoted in Baylor, p. 133.

66. EPP to Moncure Conway, [1868], *Letters*, pp. 344–345. This account of Sophia Hawthorne's dispute with her husband's publisher is based on Randall Stewart, "Mrs. Hawthorne's Quarrel with James T. Fields," *More Books: The Bulletin of the Boston Public Library*, 21 (1946), pp. 254–263.

9. *"A Little Child Shall Lead"*

1. "Record Book of the Weekly Social Meetings of the New England Women's Club, Monday, December 21, 1868," Radcliffe.

2. "A Plea for Froebel's Kindergarten as the First Grade of Primary Education," appendix to Frederick Cardinal Wiseman, *The Identification of the Artisan and the Artist* (Boston: Lee and Shepard, 1869), p. 46.

3. "Kindergarten Culture," in *Annual Report for 1870 of the National Commissioner of Education*, pp. 7–8.

4. EPP to William Torrey Harris, 25 August [1870], *Letters*, p. 360.

5. The story of Harris's gradual conversion to kindergartening and the heroic work done by Susan Blow in St. Louis is told in several sources, including Elizabeth Dale Ross, *The Kindergarten Crusade: The Establishment of Preschool Education in the United States* (Athens, Ohio: Ohio University Press, 1976), pp. 12–16.

6. EPP to Gerrit Smith, 8 February 1871, *Letters*, p. 353.

7. EPP to Anna Barker Ward, [1871], *Letters* p. 364.

8. "When Should Children Be Taught to Read? Sham Kindergarten Culture," *Herald of Health and Journal of Physical Culture*, ns 17 (August 1871), np.

9. Kate Douglas Wiggin, *My Garden of Memory* (Boston: Houghton Mifflin, 1923), p. 157.

10. EPP to Susan Cole, 10 July [1872], *Letters*, pp. 369–370.

11. Una Hawthorne to NCP, 19 March 1871, Peabody II Papers, MHS.

12. EPP to Mr. Roberts, 28 September [1871], *59M-312 (132), by permission of Houghton Library, Harvard University.

13. *Record of Mr. Alcott's School*, 3rd ed. revised (Boston: Roberts, 1874), p. 4.

14. Louisa May Alcott to MPM, [August] [1873], Horace Mann III Papers, MHS.

15. The story of the spread of kindergartens is told in Ross, *The Kindergarten Crusade*, and in Ruth M. Baylor, *Elizabeth Palmer Peabody: Kindergarten Pioneer* (Philadelphia: University of Pennsylvania Press, 1965), pp. 40–65.

16. Moncure Conway, in Lucy Wheelock, "Miss Peabody as I Knew Her," in *Kindergarten and Child Culture Papers: Pioneers of the Kindergarten in America* (New York: Century, 1924) pp. 33–34.

17. "Command of Language to be Gained in Kindergarten," *Kindergarten Messenger*, 7 (November 1873), 7–11; "Glimpses of Psychology," *Kindergarten Messenger* 2 (January 1874), 1–6.

18. "Origins and Growth of the Kindergarten," *Education* 2 (May–June 1882), 507.

19. EPP to Anna Barker Ward, [1871], *Letters*, p. 364; "Origins and Growth," p. 518.

20. "Command of Language," 7–11; EPP to William Torrey Harris, 25 August [1870], *Letters*, p. 362.

21. Margaret Stannard, "Mary J. Garland," in *Kindergarten and Child Culture Papers*, p. 111; EPP, "When Should Children Be Taught to Read? Sham Kindergarten Culture," np.

22. 26 November 1842, *JMN*, vol. 8, p. 249.

23. On postwar hostility to individualism and Romanticism, see William Leach, *True Love and Perfect Union* (New York: Basic Books, 1980).

24. EPP, "The Relations between the Kindergarten and the So-Called Positive Philosophy," *Kindergarten Messenger*, 7 (August 1873), 3–5.

25. Ross, pp. 67–80.

26. *Kindergarten Messenger*, 3 (December 1875), 265–268.

27. MPM to Henry Barnard, December 1876, ts copy, Antioch.

28. *Kindergarten Messenger*, ns 1 (January-February 1877), 1; Ross, pp. 9–10;

EPP to William Torrey Harris, 10 January [1877], William Torrey Harris Papers, Missouri Historical Society, St. Louis.

29. EPP to William Torrey Harris, 19 January 1877, *Letters*, p. 357.

30. EPP to William Torrey Harris, 6 February [1877] and 19 April [1877], William Torrey Harris Papers, Missouri Historical Society, St. Louis.

31. George Haven Putnam, *Memories of a Publisher, 1865–1915* (New York: G.P. Putnam's Sons, 1915), pp. 32–33.

32. EPP to Mr. Chaney, npnd, Antioch; EPP to Horatio Bridge, 15 October [1872], *Letters*, pp. 370–371; Rebecca Weston, "A Birthday Visit," *Kindergarten News*, 4 (February 1894), 42; EPP to James Freeman Clarke, 14 April 1880, Houghton.

33. EPP to Ellen D. Conway, 21 November 1876, *Letters*, pp. 378–381; for more information on the conflicts among the Hawthorne siblings and their spouses, see Maurice Bassan, *Hawthorne's Son: The Life and Literary Career of Julian Hawthorne* (Columbus: Ohio State University Press, 1970).

34. Information on Rose Hawthorne comes from James Mellow, *Nathaniel Hawthorne in His Times* (Boston: Houghton Mifflin, 1980), pp. 586–587.

35. EPP to MPM, 19 August [1877], ts copy, Antioch.

36. George C. Mann to MPM, 12 January 1878, 15 January 1878, ts copy, Antioch.

37. EPP to Ellen D. Conway, 27 April [1878], *Letters*, p. 384; Leslie Perrin Wilson, "Introduction to a Bibliography of Books Presented to the Concord Free Public Library by Elizabeth Palmer Peabody," unpublished ms, 1982, pp. 1–4.

38. Rose Hawthorne Lathrop to MPM, 14 April [1877], ts copy, Antioch; EPP to Ellen D. Conway, 27 April [1878], *Letters*, p. 383; EPP to Aubertine Woodward, 23 December 1879, *Letters*, p. 390–391.

39. Wheelock, "Miss Peabody as I Knew Her," pp. 28–30.

10. *"What a Reservoir Her Memory Is"*

1. EPP to Louisa May Alcott, [December] 1877, *Letters*, pp. 382–383; EPP to Ellen D. Conway, 27 April [1878], *Letters*, p. 384.

2. EPP to MPM, August 1879, *Letters*, pp. 388–389.

3. Kate Douglas Wiggin, *My Garden of Memory* (Boston: Houghton, Mifflin, 1923), pp. 146–150.

4. Bruce Kuklick, *The Rise of American Philosophy* (New Haven: Yale University Press), pp. 57–59.

5. EPP, "Emerson as Preacher," in *The Genius and Character of Emerson*, eds. Franklin Sanborn and William Torrey Harris (Boston: Osgood, 1885), p. 163.

6. Florence Whiting Brown, "Alcott and the Concord School of Philosophy," in *Concord Harvest, The Later Transcendentalists*, ed. Kenneth Cameron, 2 vols. (Hartford: Transcendental Books, 1970), vol. 2, p. 399.

7. EPP, "Childhood," in *Concord Lectures in Philosophy*, ed. Raymond Bridgman (Cambridge, Mass.: Moses King, 1883), p. 122; Julia Anagnos, *Philosophiae Quaestor; or, Days in Concord*, quoted in Cameron, ed., *Concord Harvest*, vol. 2, p. 406.

8. Florence Whiting Brown, in *Concord Harvest*, vol. 2, p. 399; Lilian Whiting, *Boston Days* (Boston: Little, Brown, 1902), pp. 169–170.

9. EPP to Phillips Brooks, [1879–1880], Elizabeth Palmer Peabody Papers, Phillips Library, Essex Peabody Museum, Salem, Massachusetts; EPP to James Freeman Clarke, 14 April [1880], bMS Am 1565 (1029), by permission of Houghton Library, Harvard University; EPP, *Reminiscences of Dr. William Ellery Channing* (Boston: Roberts, 1880), p. 92.

10. EPP to James Eliot Cabot, 30 June 1879, *Letters*, pp. 386–387.

11. EPP to Amelia Boelte, 30 June 1886, *Letters*, pp. 433–434.

12. Jane Marsh Parker, "Elizabeth Peabody: A Reminiscence," *The Outlook*, 49 (February 1894), 214–215.

13. EPP to MPM, [June 1881], ts copy, Antioch.

14. EPP to MPM, [1881], ts copy, Antioch; EPP to MPM, [May 1881], ts copy, Antioch.

15. EPP to MPM, 14 August 1882, ts copy, Antioch; MPM to Ellen D. Conway, 7 January 1883, ts copy, Antioch.

16. EPP to Samuel Gray Ward, 28 April 1885, bMS Am 1465, by permission of Houghton Library, Harvard University; Whiting, pp. 444–445.

17. EPP to MPM, [May 1881], ts copy, Antioch; EPP to Harriet Lothrop, 5 October [1886], Radcliffe; EPP, *Lectures in the Training Schools for Kindergartners* (Boston: D.C. Heath, 1888).

18. These paragraphs on Sarah Winnemucca are based on Gae Whitney Canfield, *Sarah Winnemucca of the Northern Paiutes* (Norman: University of Oklahoma Press, 1983).

19. *San Francisco Chronicle*, November 1879, quoted in Canfield, p. 164; W. V. Rinehart, quoted in Canfield, p. 173.

20. MPM to Eleanor Lewis, 25 April 1883, ts copy, Antioch; EPP to Harriet Lothrop, 17 August [ny], Radcliffe.

21. EPP to Edwin Munroe Bacon [1883], *Letters*, p. 415; see also MPM to Eleanor Lewis, 17 November 1883, ts copy, Antioch, on Sarah's and Elizabeth's tours; EPP to Newton Booth, [1883], ts copy, Antioch.

22. EPP to Edwin Munroe Bacon [1883], *Letters*, pp. 414–415; EPP to John Long, [March] 1884, ts copy, Antioch.

23. Wiggin, p. 158.

24. MPM to Eleanor Lewis, 25 May 1885, ts copy, Antioch.

25. EPP to Rose Elizabeth Cleveland [1885], *Letters*, p. 422; Rose Elizabeth Cleveland to EPP, 18 November 1885, ts copy, Antioch.

26. EPP to Rose Elizabeth Cleveland, 22 December [1885], (microfilm edition, item #1090, roll 4); Allyn Kellogg Ford Collection of Historical Manuscripts, Minnesota Historical Society; Canfield, p. 249.

27. EPP to Harriet Lothrop, 7 June [1885], Radcliffe; EPP, *The Piutes: Second Report of the Model School of Sarah Winnemucca, 1886–1887* (Cambridge, Mass.: John Wilson, 1887).

28. MPM to Eleanor Lewis, 25 May 1885, ts copy, Antioch; see also MPM to Harriet Lothrop, [1886], Radcliffe; Canfield, pp. 258–259.

29. MPM to Eleanor Lewis, November 1886, ts copy, Antioch; EPP to Theodore Dwight Weld, 11 November 1886, Autograph File, by permission of Houghton Library, Harvard University; EPP to Anna Cabot Lowell, 26 December 1886, *Letters*, p. 438.

30. EPP to MPM [June 1881], ts copy, Antioch; EPP to Eleanor Lewis, 27 March [1887], *Letters*, p. 441.

31. EPP to Eva Channing, [1887], Radcliffe.

32. Thomas Wentworth Higginson, *Cheerful Yesterdays* (Boston: Houghton, Mifflin, 1898), p. 87; Whiting, p. 182; Maria S. Porter, "Elizabeth Palmer Peabody," *The Bostonian*, 3 (January 1896), 340.

33. Mark DeWolfe Howe, *The Later Years of the Saturday Club, 1870–1920* (Boston: Houghton Mifflin, 1927), pp. 156–157.

34. *Henry James Letters*, ed. Leon Edel (Cambridge, Mass.: Belknap Press of Harvard University Press, 1980), vol. 3, pp. 68–70; see also Edel, *Henry James: 1882–1895, The Middle Years* (Philadelphia: Lippincott, 1962), pp. 142–143.

35. Henry James, *The Bostonians* (New York: Library of America, 1985), pp. 824–826, 1169–1170.

36. My reading of the death of Miss Birdseye differs from that of Jean Fagan Yellin, who, in *Women and Sisters: The Antislavery Feminists in American Culture* (New Haven: Yale University Press, 1989), argues that James's portrait of Miss Birdseye is vicious to the very end and slanders not only the elderly reformer but also the entire alliance of women's rights and antislavery advocates. Indeed, Yellin notes, James went out of his way to diminish women's activism by making Miss Birdseye the surviving reformer, since the real-life Miss Peabody was only marginally involved in women's reform issues and in antislavery (p. 166). Although James reduces much antebellum reform to caricature and nervous tics, he repents his version of Elizabeth Peabody near the novel's end by showing the genuine affection and admiration she prompted in her young followers.

37. EPP to Harriet Lothrop, 5 October, ny, Radcliffe; EPP to Ednah Dow Cheney [May 1887], *Letters*, pp. 443–444; EPP to Miss Sprague, 16 October 1889, Radcliffe.

38. EPP to Harriet Lothrop, two letters, [1887–1888], Radcliffe.

39. EPP to Harriet Lothrop, [after 1887], Radcliffe; EPP to Samuel Gray Ward, 19–20 June [1890], *Letters*, p. 452; George Mann to Benjamin Mann, 28 October 1889, ts copy, Antioch; Mary Beedy to George Mann, 8 March 1892, ts copy, Antioch.

40. Ednah Dow Cheney, "Funeral Service," *Kindergarten News* (Springfield, Mass.), 4 (February 1894), 60.

41. Sarah Clarke, "This Comes Saluting the Friends of Elizabeth Peabody," ms, Boston Public Library.

42. Mary Garland, "Elizabeth Palmer Peabody, May 16, 1804–January 3, 1894," *Report of the Committee on Necrology of the Massachusetts Teachers' Association*, 1894, ts copy, Antioch.

Epilogue

1. Ruth M. Baylor Collection, MHS.

2. "Prospectus for the Elizabeth Peabody House"; "Second Annual Report of the Elizabeth Peabody House," copies at Antioch.

3. These observations are based on a visit to the Elizabeth Peabody House in October 1996.

Index